The Enthusiastic Heart

Living with the awareness of God's empowering presence in our hearts

Don L. Fischer

PASTORAL REFLECTIONS INSTITUTE,

DALLAS, TEXAS

Pastoral Reflections Institute
P.O. Box 181313
Dallas, TX 75218

PastoralReflectionsInstitute.com

Printed in the United States of America
ISBN: 978-0-9678535-5-0

This book contains the homilies from the beginning of Advent 2012 through Christ the King in 2013. Cycle C.

Cover image of the Sacred Heart comes from a stained glass window in the original Sacred Heart Church of Rowlett, Texas, dedicated in July, 1900.

Photo by Don Fischer

In preparation for his retirement in 2010, Msgr. Don formed the Pastoral Reflections Institute, and on November 22, 2009, tax exempt status was granted by the Department of the Treasury, and the Institute became a nonprofit corporation, exempt under section 501(c)(3).

This enabled the Institute to raise tax-exempt contributions to continue his ministry. In the beginning, the primary need was to fund his Sunday radio program on WRR fm, but has grown to include operating a website that brings his Sunday homilies to anyone in the world; publishing in book format the radio homilies; writing and publishing a book on spirituality, due to be released in the fall of 2014; plus "days of reflection," weekend workshops, parish missions, and pilgrimages to sacred places, particularly those in Italy. There are also plans for an annual spiritual lecture series, inviting outstanding spiritual leaders to speak in Dallas.

Like many retirees, Msgr. Don's plate is full. Your contributions enable him to continue his work of reaching those who long for his message of awakening hearts to the indwelling power of God.

The Enthusiastic Heart

It is very curious that so many people have said to me lately that they are "spiritual but not religious." It strikes me that they are making a distinction between being identified with a particular religion versus being personally engaged in a spiritual path that brings them peace, a peace they did not find in church. Often the incentive to find our own path is a rejection of what is unhealthy in religion, and let's face it, there is a lot that's unhealthy. Separating oneself from religion because of the unhealthy parts can, however, result in an unintended loss of the wisdom upon which it is based. The truth is that wisdom is the essential ingredient in forming our personal spiritual path. And by "personal," I do not mean that it is something we tailor to fit our own needs but rather *personal* in the sense that we *own* it; it is not something we do but is who we are.

How do we move beyond doctrine and morals and find a path built on wisdom? As a Catholic seminarian I was told not to form a personal path but rather I was *given* a path. After I finished my training, I felt confident that I knew the path. It was the Church; believe what it teaches, participate in what it offers, and do what it tells you to do. Being a good Catholic meant you were on the right path. It was simple, direct, logical, and safe. It seemed to me my future as a priest would be connecting people with the Church. Yet after three years in the ministry I began to wonder where was the joy, excitement, and enthusiasm I hoped to find in me and in those I served? Where were the miracles? Something was missing. So it became obvious to me that I had to find out *what* was missing.

That is the best description I can give you of my life's quest. Now almost 50 years into the mission and with copious amounts of asking, seeking, and knocking, it became clear that what was missing was *intimacy*. I was keeping God at a distance. I kept busy and kept my focus on my *performance*. This kept me unaware of what God really wanted and blind to what he was offering. Something needed to be awakened, ignited, and to my surprise it was not my mind but my *heart*. The recent medical discoveries about the heart's ability to think, feel, and remember intrigued me. But its ability to resonate a measurable electromagnetic field extending 12 feet from our chest blew me away. Is this what was missing?

Did I need science to awaken in me a way of believing in what religion has been trying to put me in touch with? So with an awakened heart I began to look again at the message of the gospels. I wanted to see what was the core (heart) message. I found myself drawn to what all major religions have in common and I found the following:

All religions believe in a God who shares with us his wisdom, which enables us to become enlightened, to become more aware of what is true and real, to put aside our illusions. They all call us to greater awareness.

All religions believe in our capacity to connect with God. They believe that this is God's greatest longing and our most important task. They all challenge us to allow God to enter into us.

And all religions require us to love one another, forgive and support one another. They all recognize this as our primary role in the world and that it can only be accomplished through the flow of God's presence in us.

They are all about awareness, connection, and presence; and the order is important.

The path begins when our hearts are awakened and we begin to see what is real. We wake up and see God as he is and ourselves as we are. We see his goodness, his beauty, and all that he has created, and we want to be a part of it. We fall in love with him.

But he loves us first, which means we can never merit his love or lose it. And because his love is not just an affectionate feeling, but rather a passionate longing to enter into us and dwell in us, our task is to *allow* him to enter "under our roof." He will never force his way in. Our minds resist such intimacy, but our hearts long for it.

When he enters, without judgment, he opens for us the joyful and sometimes embarrassing experience of unmerited love. This compassionate presence takes root in our hearts, our spiritual center, and overflows and resonates into the world. This experience of being a vessel of God's loving, healing presence becomes our "daily bread." It gives us a sense of value and a peaceful joy, far greater than what the things of the world offer. We feel alive, there is excitement, enthusiasm, and there are miracles!

Welcome, and a few notes!

Welcome to this new book! It is my hope and prayer that you will find it nurturing and transforming.

We're working on a collection of topical essays based on the homilies, but for this book, we've kept the chronological order. There is an annotated list of them, with one line per homily, following the Table of Contents. Following that is a list of some key spiritual needs and the homilies that focus on that need. For example, feeling unworthy; feeling distant from God, etc. Feel free to browse these lists and read any homily that catches your eye. We're always open to any suggestions in this area!

A couple of notes about usage. The Vatican some time ago decided to allow modern rules of capitalization, such as no longer capitalizing the pronouns (he and him) for God and Christ. Also the term Holy Spirit is now *beginning* to be written as holy Spirit. In essence, capitalization is reserved for the words *Father, Son,* and *Spirit,* the three persons of the trinity. Even the word *gospel* is left as is, unless it is part of a title, such as the *Gospel According to John* or if it refers to the New Testament as a whole.

Otherwise, capitalization is only used to reduce ambiguity. For example, the word *church* may become *Church,* to avoid confusion with a particular building of worship. And the word *law* may become *Law* to refer to the religious laws of the Old Testament, to avoid confusion with political law. *Scripture* is sometimes capitalized, sometimes not, depending on the context. The aim here is clarity.

For non-Catholic readers, the term *Ordinary Time* means time "outside the seasons of Advent, Lent, and Easter." The term means *Ordinal* Time, not time that isn't special!

The core message of the Gospel is that if we will allow the Spirit of God to enter into us and allow it to transform us, we can become instruments of that same grace for others. We'll find that the resonance of the Spirit will reach though our hearts to the hearts of others, allowing *them* to be nurtured and transformed, even as we were. The Good News is all about shifting our attention from the mind to include the heart, which cares so much about all of our brothers and sisters, about God and our world, about connection, nurturance, and transformation. Learning to live in this kingdom is what our adventure, our journey is all about.

I have been so uplifted by the message of Christ and hope that this may continue for us all!

If you live in the Dallas-Fort Worth area, you know we do a Sunday morning radio program on WRR 101.1 FM at 10 am.

You can also follow me on Twitter, @msgrdonfischer. I tweet reflections from my Sunday homilies as the Spirit moves me. And, if you'll go to our website, *PastoralReflectionsInstitute.com,* you'll see a "Share" button that enables you to share these homilies with the people you feel would be blessed and gifted by them. The programs, both audio and text, are free to download at any time.

I'd also like to ask you to be partners with me in this ministry, which needs your support. You can use your credit or debit card to make a one-time donation, or a recurring donation. And it's also possible, if you would like, to sponsor a program. Then that program can be dedicated to someone you'd like to honor. So again, I'd like to thank you for your continued support. Without it, the time that we spend together would not be possible. So again, thank you, and may God bless you.

Acknowledgments

A very special thanks to Melissa Fairley, Julie Condy, and Stuart Dean for their valuable help.

Contents

A Key Theme for Each Homily

Some liberties were taken by abbreviating, as needed, to keep each theme on a single line. For instance, "Ordinary Time" often becomes "OT." Page numbers are at the line's end.

Spiritual Needs, and Homilies that Help with Them

Having trouble seeing any unity or harmony in the world? p.144 (Ascension 201); p. 156 (Trinity Sunday 2013)

Having trouble with excessive anxiety, anger, or shame? p. 13 (3rd Advent 2012)

I'm not sure the world is a good place or even a safe one. p. 156 (Trinity Sunday 2013)

Wanting better spiritual direction or guidance? p. 207 (16th ord 2013)

Who could love me unconditionally? p. 31 (Epiphany 2013); p.62 (5th ord 2013)

Why am I suffering? What does it mean? p. 182 (12th ord 2013)

Wishing you could see the light in the darkness? p.31 (Epiphany 2013)

Wondering how best to pray? p. 126 (4th Easter 2013)

Wondering how to "give back" to others, to the world? p. 207 (16th ord 2013)

FIRST SUNDAY OF ADVENT

Jeremiah 33:14-16; 1Thessalonians 3:12–4:2; Luke 21:25-28, 34-36

Grant your faithful, we pray, almighty God, the resolve to run forth to meet your Christ with righteous deeds at his coming so that, gathered at his right hand, they may be worthy to possess the heavenly kingdom, through our Lord Jesus Christ, your Son, who lives and reigns with you in the unity of the holy Spirit, one God for ever and ever. Amen.

We begin our church year with this wonderful season called *Advent.* The word means *Coming.* If I could use an image of the call of this season, it is for us to come to God, to come to the truth, to come to our true self, and to allow God to come to us. It's an image of a *connection* that is essential if we're going to do whatever this new church year encourages us to do. And you know that every year as we go through a cycle of readings, we're invited to grow in our understanding of the *core* issues: *Who is God? Who am I? What am I here for?*

This is "the work." And unless the scriptures, the preaching, the rituals of the communities you belong to, unless they lead you into a place of new insight, into a place of change, they're really not doing the work they're called to do. We're always called to grow, to change, to become more. Not "better" in the sense that we say we didn't do any bad things last year, and this year we started to do some bad things, so this year is bad. No. A good or bad year isn't so much in what is happening to us as external things that are going on, but what is happening to us on the inside. Because the kingdom of God is always a kind of "inside job."

The *kingdom* is what we're drawn to. The kingdom is a place of awareness, a place of seeing, a place of knowing. And that's my longing, that's my desire, to be there, to draw you there with me, to have you draw me with you—all that incredible, communal thing that we are as a people of God. But on this first Sunday, there are some beautiful images in the readings that I want to draw from, and I want to open your hearts, I hope, to a way of seeing this season so that you can enter into it, and there's always something unique and special about doing things *in community*. So this call that goes forth on Advent to come closer to God, to self, to your neighbors, is something that we're going to do *together*, and when we do it together, there's great power, there's great energy, there's great grace as we, together, work on this *challenge*, the challenge of the season: to come to the truth, to come to the kingdom.

Now the first reading is something I sense and feel scripture is filled with, Old Testament, New Testament. It seems to always be inviting us into a place that has not yet been experienced. Something is being prepared for us, something is coming, something good is around the corner. And I don't know what image comes to your mind, but what I'd like you to imagine is this image I've been using of growth and development and change—*that's* the thing that's coming. What's coming is a greater awareness, a greater consciousness of the things that really matter. It's a process. And the process has some unique parts that I think we need to be aware of so that we're not confused by having the wrong expectations of how we grow and how we move.

I don't know if you're like me, but so often I think, Well, I'm a human being and I have a will and I have a mind and I can understand things and I can make things happen. So I use my will and my mind to "force" things to be what I believe God wants them to be, in terms of the situations I'm in, in terms of who I am. And it becomes a kind of self-created kingdom that I'm making—"for God," you know? And when we do that work, the unfortunate thing about it is that when we're using simply our mind and our will, especially if our will is very strong, we're going to find ourselves slipping into something that is *absolutely natural* to our will, and *that* is a form of *narcissism*. We basically, when we're working out of our own will, we're working out of a part of us that is very concerned about self-preservation, about how we're doing, if we're comfortable; and that's what it's *supposed* to do; that's what it's made to do. There's nothing wrong with the will that is somewhat self-oriented because that's why the will has been given to us, to make sure that we take care of ourselves, protect ourselves. It's in all the species that God has created; it keeps us alive, keeps us from going extinct.

But there's another thing, it seems to me, when we talk about the spiritual life and what it is we're called to become; there's something else that we're asked to deal with, and it's not simply our will, not simply our mind, but it's this mysterious thing called our *heart*. There it is again: the heart. Both the second reading and the gospel mention the heart. Paul, in the second reading, tells us we should do everything we can to *strengthen* our hearts. What's interesting about that: When I say, "OK, Don, strengthen your heart," what am I going to do, what am I going to make happen to make my heart stronger? So right again, I'm in my *will*. And then when I listen to Jesus in the gospel passage, and he talks about the heart, he doesn't say to *strengthen* your hearts. He just says, *Be careful that your heart isn't asleep. Be careful that your heart is not drowsy.* And it gets drowsy because, I think, of all the anxieties, all the worries. You know, the more you're anxious and the more you're worried about whether or not you're going to make it, the more your self-preserving will kicks in and the more it runs your whole life. So anxiety and fear and shame and anger—those are the things that basically put the heart asleep; they make the heart "drowsy." And then what happens is, you're in a state of a kind of "drunkenness." That's the other thing Jesus says: *Beware of carousing and drunkenness.* That always sounds like, "OK, all you party animals, you're in trouble." [chuckles] But it's much more than that. Or it's not really that at all, in a way. It's about anybody who goes into a situation where their will is not able to create the peace they want, and they still find nothing but worry and anxiety. So what do they do? You just have to have a break somewhere, so you go unconscious, whether you use alcohol or watching TV or compulsively doing work, whatever. It doesn't matter. It's just something you do that keeps you from recognizing the fact that the will and your mind are not able to create the community and the kingdom that you want.

And it's so frustrating because if you think that's all that you have to work with, then you're in deep, deep trouble. [chuckles] We have something *more* to work with. We have this organ called the heart, and it has this capacity we've only recently discovered: to think, to remember. It's very much like our brains; it has the same kind of neuron cells that the brain has. So how are we to deal with this? What are we to take from this new discovery of the heart as an organ of thinking and feeling and understanding? Well, you go back to the ancients, and you find that *all* the ancient religions and most ancient cultures believed the heart was always seen as the center of the human being. In Egypt, when you were embalmed, put into a pyramid if you were rich [chuckles], and they placed everything there because they believed in the world on the other side, and you needed all your parts. Well, they threw the brain out, but they made sure they embalmed the heart and placed it in the center of the chest in the mummy because that was who the person was. The heart. And what do we know about the heart? Well, we know that it does three things, that it has a *wonderful* capacity for connection; that it thrives with and loves the work of nurturing; and that it wants nothing more than transformation, growth. Transformation and growth.

So here's what I think we are learning from this first set of readings, from the first Sunday in Advent; it's this: When Jesus is talking in the gospel about a cataclysmic event in our lives, somehow we'll come to a point where everything seems to be destroyed. There'll be signs everywhere—in the sun and the moon and the stars. There'll be great anxiety and people will be perplexed, and there'll be the roaring of the sea and the waves and people will die of fright. All these images! You know, we almost always take those to mean there's going to be some kind of end of the world, and we're all going to go through this traumatic, incredible physical tragedy of the earth, and we're going to end up terrified, and then as the whole world is about to implode, we see one like the Son of Man coming on a cloud to save us. Well, if that were literal, it would be something where you could watch the weather channel to make sure your life is OK. But the truth is, it's not referring to cataclysmic, terrible events. What it's going to be about is the world that the mind and the ego have created, have created together, is likely to be something that isn't real, that isn't really true. And when you're living in anything that isn't true, when you're living in anything that's a lie, what life is going to do for you, what grace is going to do for you, what God is going to do for you, is expose those lies. And when those lies are all you have to live on, and when your whole world is constructed around something that isn't real, and reality comes, you might as well be in a world that is completely falling apart.

So the issue is, how can we learn to live in the world of reality, the world of truth, when we're so prone by our will and our ego to live in a world that is illusionary? Well, the task is first and foremost to realize that's our dilemma. That's one of the big problems. Once you realize that's a problem, once you know that's something you're prone to do, and you realize that's a *natural* thing to do, there's nothing wrong or unusual about it, or selfish about it. It's just the way our minds are put together. And yet we know we're made for something more than that! And so we go to a place called "the heart," which is this consciousness we have to *be* connected, to be engaged in life fully, and to be nurtured by it and to want to nurture it. The world that God created, it gives praise to God simply be being what it was meant to be. In fact, I'd say that's a good description of how we should imagine what God wants of those things that he's created. All he wants them to be is what he *made* them to be. You need to be who you were made to be, not the person you created. And so when we see that that is the call, then we can sense that when we connect with things as they really are—Nature in particular, then we're recognizing the beauty and the value of what it looks like when it's close to something that is absolutely authentic. A tree is a tree. It doesn't want to be anything else. So to be in the presence of that which is real is a very good exercise for you and for me, to be able to recognize the kind of quality that the creation that God has made carries in terms of being *nurturing*. When you are yourself, in the presence of others, you are nurturing them. Absolutely. And when they are truly themselves, whatever they truly are will nurture you. And that leads to all the wonderful transformation that we have in this kingdom.

So Advent begins with a very simple reminder: We're on a journey. The journey is not to be what *we* think we're supposed to be, in terms of perfection. It is simply a call to be who God has made us to be. The temptation, if we fall into it, is to be involved in creating a world that is more than it was ever intended to be, in terms of—well, I say "more," but it's actually *less* than it was intended to be. It's more like what *we* think it should be, and that's where the problem comes. So what do we want? We want one like the Son of Man—an image of humanity. "Son of Man" is a human being. It's Christ, who is the fullness of humanity. When the fullness of humanity comes to our consciousness and we see that, when we recognize that, and we know we're called to that, the heart's awakened. And somehow the ego is disarmed.

Father, our journey is always to come to the truth, to come to the place that you've created for us. Free us from the imprisoned places we've often created for ourselves so that we can experience the true freedom of being your sons and daughters, filled with an awareness of your love for us and your desire for nothing more than for us to become all that you've called us to be. Bless us on this journey, draw us closer to you that we may truly abide with you and you in us. Amen.

Jeremiah 33: 14-16

14The days are surely coming, says the LORD, when I will fulfill the promise I made to
the house of Israel and the house of Judah.
15In those days and at that time I will cause a righteous Branch to spring up for David;
and he shall execute justice and righteousness in the land.
16In those days Judah will be saved and Jerusalem will live in safety. And this is the
name by which it will be called: "The LORD is our righteousness."

1Thessalonians 3:12 – 4:2

12And may the Lord make you increase and abound in love for one another and for all,
just as we abound in love for you.
13And may he so strengthen your hearts in holiness that you may be blameless before
our God and Father at the coming of our Lord Jesus with all his saints.

1Finally, brothers and sisters, we ask and urge you in the Lord Jesus that, as you learned
from us how you ought to live and to please God (as, in fact, you are doing), you should
do so more and more.
2For you know what instructions we gave you through the Lord Jesus.

Luke 21: 25-28, 34-36

25"There will be signs in the sun, the moon, and the stars, and on the earth distress
among nations confused by the roaring of the sea and the waves.
26People will faint from fear and foreboding of what is coming upon the world, for the
powers of the heavens will be shaken.
27Then they will see 'the Son of Man coming in a cloud' with power and great glory.
28Now when these things begin to take place, stand up and raise your heads, because
your redemption is drawing near."

34"Be on guard so that your hearts are not weighed down with dissipation and drunkenness and the worries of this life, and that day does not catch you unexpectedly,
35like a trap. For it will come upon all who live on the face of the whole earth.
36Be alert at all times, praying that you may have the strength to escape all these things
that will take place, and to stand before the Son of Man."

SECOND SUNDAY OF ADVENT

Baruch 5; Philippians 1:1, 4-6, 8-11; Luke 3:1-6

Almighty and merciful God, may no earthly undertaking hinder those who set out in haste to meet your Son, for they are learning of heavenly wisdom. Gain us admittance to his company who lives and reigns with you in the unity of the holy Spirit, one God for ever and ever. Amen.

There's a strong image in the readings today about making a journey, going from one place to another. The first reading is filled, like it was last Sunday, filled with the image of a promise. God promises something. He promises to you and to me, no matter where we are in our own journey, no matter how close we are to being ourselves or how far we are from the integrity that God longs for us to experience, he calls us, he draws us to a place. *Jerusalem* is the image, in the first reading, of that place. Jerusalem is a very fascinating image in the Old Testament. It's the image of the kingdom of God, the community we're all called to live in.

And we wander away from that so often. We're led astray by our enemies, our distractions, and God is constantly calling us back to the kingdom, calling us back to the place of integrity, calling us to the place of peace. He wants so much for us to be there. And his promise is, if we respond to that call, if we respond to him and invite him, allow him, to come into us, and if we accept the invitation to return, he will take us there. That's the promise. It's always our choice. Timing is not our choice; how it works is not our choice; but whether or not we go—that's our choice. That's what the season of Advent is asking us to check on: What *is* our choice? What is our fundamental desire as we live this life that God has called us to live?

John the Baptist is a voice; he's the voice calling us back. But more than calling us back, he's saying something about the process of *getting* back. He's saying something very powerful when he says,

"I've come to announce something," and I don't know exactly what to call this thing that he's announcing, because it could be many things, but the thing I'd like to think about with you this morning is that it could be a kind of *awareness,* a kind of level of consciousness, a calling you to recognize something. And the level of consciousness that you need to be in has to do with letting go of old ways of seeing, old ways of being, and maybe we can just say that one of the things that we need to do to get past the things that are "unfortunate" in our past is simply to experience forgiveness. We are forgiven for where we've been, and we're called to be somewhere new. And the process of getting there is very clearly described in both the gospel and in the first reading: There's something about entering a level of consciousness, a level of awareness, where the journey is no longer filled with deep, dark gorges, or no longer encountering on the journey do we see gigantic mountains that are too high to scale, or winding roads or confusing places or forks in the road where we don't know which way to go.

Somehow as we grow in awareness, as we grow in consciousness, we can begin to see what Paul talks about in the second reading when his love for his people kind of overflows out of his heart and he says to the people around him, *I just love you and I just want you to see, to know—knowledge and perception—and to somehow see and know what's really valuable.* What's *really* valuable. I think that's a good description of our levels of consciousness that we know are part of our human nature as we grow from the lowest forms of consciousness, where we're motivated by nothing but fear and shame and anger, and we move into a place of communion and union and to places of ecstasy which take us out of a kind of narrow view of our world that looks at it as drudgery and sees it only as things that have to be done and taken care of, and as soon as we get those done, there's more to be done.

Ecstasy takes us out of that place of drudgery because it shows us that there's something much more than just that ordinary aspect of life. We're on a journey, moving ever closer to a place called Jerusalem, to a place of wholeness, to a place of integrity where there's a kind of inner, wonderful sense of peace, a sense that all things are as they must be. And we wander, you know? We wander around, trying to find that place, and it seems that the readings today are inviting us to look more carefully at how we get to the place called Jerusalem. And what St. John the Baptist is trying to show us, what he's saying is that something is happening, something is coming, and he's talking about the Messiah, and he's talking about how the effect of the Messiah in the world is going to be an amazing increase in consciousness and awareness. We're going to see so much more because no longer are we going to be called simply to conform our lives to rules and regulations, but we now have the gift of God inside of us that doesn't simply enable us to conform our wills to something, but to transform our hearts into *being* something that is amazingly satisfying to the person whose heart is awakened and amazingly challenging and helpful to the people *around* that kind of person. Awakened hearts, hearts that resonate an amazing capacity to connect, to nurture, and to transform.

But how do we imagine this transformation? How do we imagine it changing? I want to share this thought with you. It seems like—I don't know what you might imagine as you're walking along the winding, twisting road where you don't have a GPS [chuckles] to get you to the place you want to go, and you're not sure. I just want to call that place where we're not sure, a kind of place of doubt. And we're just scared of making a mistake. What if we go the wrong way? What if there's no way back? So one of the things, it seems to me, that an awakened heart is capable of doing is trusting enormously in the plan of God to get us to this place, so if we make a mistake, if we go in the wrong direction, we believe that this God who is so merciful and forgiving and loving is going to make sure that we find a way back to the main road.

So I can see that a winding, confusing path might diminish one's enthusiasm to get to the place. Or it might even do something like leading a person to say, "It's useless. I'm too lost. I'm never going to find my way." And that's kind of a tragic place to be as a human being, saying, "I am who I am. I'm not going to get better. I don't know how to get better. I'm caught in my addictions. I can't get out of them. Why even try?" So the Messiah is going to fill you with this gift called *trust*. The dark, dark canyons, the valleys that are so dark. I don't know exactly how to say that, but it strikes me that it's a kind of place of darkness and depression, and it's not that it's too hard to do. It's just that you don't know *what* to do, in terms of a kind of depression that goes into darkness. And always when we go into that place—sometimes it's a very important place to go—but to imagine that this gift from the Messiah is going to make the twisting, confusing roads straight and it's going to fill these dark valleys.

So it's interesting to imagine: What is it that will get us out of those dark valleys? If it's trust that keeps us finding the way, then it seems to me it's also this thing called *hope*. Hope is that virtue that isn't just a wish: "I hope it happens. I hope it happens." Hope is that virtue that *knows* it's going to happen, knows it's going to happen. We have hope that this way that we're on, to get back to the place we call the kingdom, it *is* going to take us there, no matter what the obstacles are, no matter how dark it gets. There's a way in which the darkness can be a falling down, but then it can become a kind of lifting up, if we're conscious that even if we go down, it's a process that's important so that we can come up! And that's realizing that no matter how bad or confusing or hard life becomes, there's something we know will happen eventually, and that is that we'll get to the destination, to the place we're called to be.

And then there are those high, high, almost insurmountable mountains, the place where we say I just can't do it, I just can't do it. It's too hard. It's too difficult. And there's probably something inside of us that's much like my body. In the morning, when I wake up, and now that I'm retired I don't *have* to get up, and that's not a good thing. "I could still lie here for another hour, maybe two, if I want to." When your body isn't told it has to do something, it sometimes just lies there and says, "I don't want to get up, I don't want to get up, I don't want to get up. I don't want to make the climb, I don't want to make the climb. I don't want to struggle. I don't want to struggle." It's a kind of laziness, I guess, and what is interesting to me, and I find this fascinating: I don't know if you know anyone who's a mountain climber. I find it a strange passion—to me, at least. I have no passion to climb a mountain. But when I think about the things I really care about, I think about my passion: I like to renovate a church; I like to make something better. When I'm filled with that kind of passion, there isn't any job that seems too big or too high.

So it seems to me that one of the gifts that God gives us in terms of the gift of Christ's presence in the world that we're getting ready to celebrate in this great feast of the Incarnation—it's interesting to feel, he's saying, *I not only want to increase your trust and your hope, I want to increase your passion, I want to give you an enormous passion.* And that goes back to what Paul says in the second reading, *What I really want for you guys is to see and know what's really valuable, what's really valuable, what really means something to you.* Value is an interesting thing, because it means, What is it, that when you're involved in it, and when you do it, you feel so right, so good, so connected with that which is real? Getting up and getting started in the day is a very different thing from sort of wallowing there in the warm bed, you know? Somehow, you know this isn't the place I'm supposed to be, the place I need to be. I really feel better, I'm more engaged, I'm more alive, I'm more awake, I'm more alert when I'm up and doing things. How you feel when you've got that coffee in you and you've brushed your teeth, and your shoes are on. *Let's climb; let's climb.* So the *passion* is an amazing gift that God longs to give us.

So when we see gifts that we need, and we ask for them, what we're really doing is saying to God, "You knew that I need these; you want to give them more than I want them. So when I ask for them, what I'm really doing is giving you permission. I'm giving you permission to fill me with things that I believe I need to be able to find Jerusalem." Now, why is that so important? Well, because human nature being what it is, whatever we really, really want is what we're going to get. Whatever we desire is what happens. *Intention* is a very, very powerful thing. We find studies all over the place now that say what people intend: *I intend to keep living; I intend to die; I intend to succeed; I intend to lose.* Whatever we have as our fundamental sense of things, our intention, is very, very powerful. If I intend that I'm going to get lost, or if I intend that it's going to be so dark and depressing that I'm not going to be able to hope in anything, or I intend that I'm not going to make it—those are dangerous, dangerous dispositions. And it makes total sense to me that human nature being what it is, you know what we believe about ourselves is ending up to be who we are.

How important it is to see ourselves as the God who created us sees us, and the best clue we have to how he sees us is the person that we're getting ready to celebrate his birth, Jesus. And the thing that I find fascinating about *his* life is how *open* he was to people, how *forgiving* he was to people, how *understanding* he was to people. More than his teaching, you just look at his life and the way he lived it. It was ordinary for such a long time, and then he did his extraordinary work, and then that work seemed to be shocking and dismaying to so many people who were living in their heads, and it seemed like Jesus lived out of his *heart*. He just liked people, and he liked the things that made up the earth. He enjoyed his life, and embraced it, and always wanted people to be freed of every single limitation that kept them from entering fully into life. So he opened their eyes, their ears; their tongue he loosed, made their limbs strong. He just wanted us to enter into life. And what I'm saying is that John the Baptist came to announce that: a time of trust, a time of hope, a time of great passion to be who God has called us to be.

Father, a season like Advent calls us to a greater sense of anticipation, anticipating the greatest gift that you have given to the world—your wisdom, your heart, in the form of your Son. And bless us with a great openness to his sacred heart that burns with love for each of us. Help us to have hearts that are warmed and ignited by that fire of his heart as we continue our journey toward the place of wholeness and peace, and we ask this in Jesus' name. Amen.

Baruch 5

1 Take off the garment of your sorrow and affliction, O Jerusalem, and put on forever
the beauty of the glory from God.
2 Put on the robe of the righteousness that comes from God; put on your head the diadem of the glory of the Everlasting;
3 for God will show your splendor everywhere under heaven.
4 For God will give you evermore the name, "Righteous Peace, Godly Glory."
5 Arise, O Jerusalem, stand upon the height; look toward the east, and see your children
gathered from west and east at the word of the Holy One, rejoicing that God has remembered them.
6 For they went out from you on foot, led away by their enemies; but God will bring
them back to you, carried in glory, as on a royal throne.
7 For God has ordered that every high mountain and the everlasting hills be made low

and the valleys filled up, to make level ground, so that Israel may walk safely in the glory of God.
8 The woods and every fragrant tree have shaded Israel at God's command.
9 For God will lead Israel with joy, in the light of his glory, with the mercy and righteousness that come from him.

Philippians 1: 1, 4-6, 8-11
1Paul and Timothy, servants of Christ Jesus, To all the saints in Christ Jesus who are in Philippi, with the bishops and deacons:

4 [I am] constantly praying with joy in every one of my prayers for all of you,
5because of your sharing in the gospel from the first day until now.
6I am confident of this, that the one who began a good work among you will bring it to completion by the day of Jesus Christ.

8For God is my witness, how I long for all of you with the compassion of Christ Jesus.
9And this is my prayer, that your love may overflow more and more with knowledge and full insight
10to help you to determine what is best, so that in the day of Christ you may be pure and blameless,
11having produced the harvest of righteousness that comes through Jesus Christ for the glory and praise of God.

Luke 3: 1-6
1In the fifteenth year of the reign of Emperor Tiberius, when Pontius Pilate was governor of Judea, and Herod was ruler of Galilee, and his brother Philip ruler of the region of Ituraea and Trachonitis, and Lysanias ruler of Abilene,
2during the high priesthood of Annas and Caiaphas, the word of God came to John son of Zechariah in the wilderness.
3He went into all the region around the Jordan, proclaiming a baptism of repentance for the forgiveness of sins,
4as it is written in the book of the words of the prophet Isaiah, "The voice of one crying out in the wilderness: 'Prepare the way of the Lord, make his paths straight.
5 Every valley shall be filled, and every mountain and hill shall be made low, and the crooked shall be made straight, and the rough ways made smooth;
6 and all flesh shall see the salvation of God.'"

THIRD SUNDAY OF ADVENT

Zephaniah 3:14-18; Philippians 4:4-7; Luke 3:10-18

O God, who sees how your people faithfully await the feast of the Lord's nativity, enable us, we pray, to attain the joys of so great a salvation and to celebrate them always with solemn worship and glad rejoicing—through our Lord Jesus Christ, your Son, who lives and reigns with you in the unity of the holy Spirit, one God, for ever and ever. Amen.

This third Sunday of Advent is always considered to be one that focuses on the theme of joy. It's interesting that the source of joy that we're invited to look more carefully into is the whole notion that we have a *savior.* Someone has come into the world to make a difference in your life, my life. Particularly, the difference is to overcome what it is that *sin* created in us. Original sin. It's a very mysterious, strange thing. In some ways, you can look at it and say that it was a tragedy that happened, that wasn't really supposed to happen. Human beings had free will; Adam and Eve had free will; they chose to live autonomously from God, and it messed everything up, and now we're in this "terrible place." That's one way of looking at it, perhaps. The other way of looking at it is that this story of original sin is something that *had* to happen, in a sense. That the whole notion of human beings being given free will is that we had to go through an experience of learning *how* to choose, *what* to choose, to find wisdom, to grow in our understanding—not because we were made that way but because we *chose* that way. It seems that God has placed us on this earth so that we can have the freedom to say, "Yes, I want you to be the source of everything in my life," or "No, I can handle things without you." The difference between the two is often the difference between a life of drudgery and a life of joy.

So let's look more carefully at the readings and see if we can discern from them the essence of where this thing we call *joy* comes from, how it works in us. There's a statement in the first reading that's a promise that God will somehow, in this world, come to the place where he refuses to use judgment against us. He will overlook our faults and not hold us accountable. He will not judge us as worthy or unworthy. He will make a statement to you and to me that we are loved as we are, no matter what we do or what choices we make. We are loved. And the description of love in this first reading is awesome! I don't know if you've ever thought of it this way—I certainly have not—but it's like the image in this prophecy is that when God sees us as we are and he wants us to know that he sees us this way, he is so pleased with what he's created that he's *singing* to us, like he's *dancing* and *singing* over the fact that we are who we are. I just never thought about God dancing, and singing my name. But that's the image of what it's like to be in a relationship with God, who loves without judgment.

Now to say that God doesn't judge flies in the face of so many things we hear in scripture where God *does* judge. So what's the difference between this image of God who doesn't judge or hold anything against us and the God who *does* judge? Well, judgment is tricky because if judgment leads to condemnation, if judgment is the kind of thing where we decide that something that *should* have been is not that way and therefore something or someone has to be punished, to make justice—that made me see that *that's* the kind of judgment that God invites us to imagine he has let go of. When it comes to discerning what's right and wrong—these things as positive, these things as negative, by their very nature—that's a judgment that is simply nothing other than living in the truth, and God always lives in the truth. So how do we make a distinction between the judgment of that which is objectively healthy or unhealthy, real or unreal—how do we stay with that and not at the same time think about anytime we have participated in something that isn't the way it should be, that *we* are somehow found unworthy or need to be condemned?

When I was young, I had this image of good and bad, and it was kind of simple. I probably got it from movies and stories, nursery rhymes. But there was always the wicked witch and there were the good people and there were the bad criminals. To me, the bad guys were just bad—all the way through. They were just evil. But then I began to learn that anyone who does anything that's wrong also carries within them this mysterious thing called *innocence*, called *goodness*, and it is never extinguished completely, though it can be overridden by choices that we make, where we actually do things that are wrong. But somehow I believe now very clearly that whenever we do these things, there's something in us that produces negativity because we're acting against our nature, acting against our nature. Our nature is to be "in union with." That's the whole key to what it means to be human, to be fully human. We're called to be spiritual beings; we're *created* as spiritual beings. What *is* a spiritual being? One of the ways I'd like to imagine a spiritual being is that we have the capacity within us to engage in a thing called *transcendence,* and transcendence is when we go beyond our human nature. Jesus walking this earth—as a fully human, fully spiritual being; filled with divinity but totally, totally human—was able to transcend the limitations of time, space, cause, effect. He was able to do things that we simply call *miracles*—opening eyes that couldn't see, opening ears that couldn't hear, enabling legs that couldn't hold a body up to be able to stand up, pick up something, and walk away with it. And then to think about transcendence that not only do we go beyond those things, but think about the *wound* in human nature that we inherited through original sin—our weakness through being self-centered, selfish, egocentric, narcissistic. We can transcend that. A spiritual being can transcend the limitations of their human nature and enter into a place we call *the kingdom*. And when we do that, when we're entering into this better place, then we find this mysterious thing called joy. Joy. The words that I like to use that help me understand the kind of joy that God is speaking of in the scriptures is a kind of inner core, calm, peaceful place where everything is all right and everything is as it should be and everything seems like it's connected and it's all good. What a nice feeling! I've had it off and on throughout my life, more of it recently as I have time to sit quietly and reflect. But what a gift God has promised you and me through his coming into the world, a gift that is this core, inner place of calm. And as we get closer to the feast of Incarnation, the desire of the Church, the desire of our hearts, is that we see this gift more clearly, and we recognize it for what it is, and we drink of it and we take it in. And when we do, we see a change that happens to us, and that's what I'd like to talk about. What do we expect to be different in a life that has this joy, this core, inner peaceful place? What's different in that kind of life and the life that does not have it? What's it like to live in the world without the conviction that we've been given this incredible gift? Well, remember that the original sin was that Adam and Eve were tempted to eat of one of the trees in the middle of the garden, the tree of the knowledge of good and evil. One way I'd like you to think about that is that they were tempted to be the determiners of what is good and what is bad, so they could say, "This is the way life should be. It's the way I decide it should be. Whether that's the way it is, it doesn't matter. I say this is what it should be." That's *determining* what should be. What is good for me, what is not good for me—without openness to something more *real,* without surrendering, submitting. *Suffering* is the word we use in scripture to mean "accepting things as they are," so that once we are living in a world that *is* real, we have such a better chance of finding the peace that God has called us to.

And there are *signs* that we're living in a world that is not real, when you're living in a world where you say God is supposed to be taking care of us and he's supposed to make sure that all negative things don't happen, (and of course we're the ones who determine the negativity).

But also even to say that the world that God has promised me is a world without negativity, without disappointment, without pain—sometimes we do that without even realizing it—we find ourselves often caught in a situation. You often hear it expressed this way: Some horrible thing happens and people turn around and say, "Where was God? Why didn't God take care of this? Why would he allow such a horrible thing to happen to innocent people? I can't trust in this God. I can't believe in a God who would allow such innocent, beautiful, young or old people to be tortured or destroyed."

So we lose a sense of trusting in this God, and when you lose a sense of trust in God, what is the most logical thing you're going to feel all the time? On some low-grade sort of level, it's fear; and so many people live in fear. It's because they have an expectation, they have a vision, they have an idea of God, and God doesn't seem to fulfill it. They're comfortable in their judgment that this is the way that God should be, and they're not budging; they're not questioning. And they seem to then believe, in some mysterious way, that "God is not concerned about the fear that I feel because I think the world is too dangerous and no one is really in charge of it, other than crazy egos, you know?" And then there are people who look at others and say, "Well, what God should do is make people better, he should be improving people; and people aren't doing what they're supposed to do. I just don't feel I can *trust* people any more. So what *is* this thing that God talks about that is goodness in people? I don't see the goodness in them. All I see is that they don't know what to do and they make stupid mistakes and I judge them for that." Which is interesting. It's really a projection of the fact that we don't think *we're* doing very well, so we project it onto everyone else. But in either case, then you live in this constant state, a state of simple anger. "You know, I'm just angry because nobody's doing it right; I'm angry at politicians and clergy, people who make decisions and they're stupid decisions—Not the way *I* think they should be made." So we live in anger. And then there's also *this* kind of expectation: "God is supposed to fix *me*, and I'm not supposed to have my faults and weaknesses. I'm supposed to be better. If he's there in my life, then he should make me strong enough to not fail, and whenever I fail I feel horrible and so God doesn't seem to be doing much for me. So why should I be so happy about him when he allows me to wallow in my shortcomings?" And then this kind of person lives all the time in *shame*.

So shame, fear, and anger. There they are again, and they're always the things that say you're not in the kingdom. This is not where God wants you to be—excessive levels of those things—that's not God's will. So you have to say, "Alright, then, God, if I am a spiritual being, and you are my savior and redeemer, then help me get past that." And the first thing he'll say is, *You don't have to change anything around you. Just change the way you SEE. Be illuminated, so you can connect with me and connect with yourself and connect with other people, connect with the world.* Well, it's *not* the way you think it should be. But what a gift, to be able to connect, to feel one with things, when they're not perfect!

In the gospel passage, we see this invitation on the part of John the Baptist, and what he's trying to create in us is an anticipation of this incredible thing that's going to come, and it's going to change everything, and we have to look toward this light, and what you have to see in that light is that which transforms shame, fear, and anger into this mysterious thing called *joy*. We need to expect it, long for it. And how does it happen? Well, what happens when you are out of this fear, shame, and anger, your *heart* begins to awaken, and all of a sudden you become less self-centered, less selfish. You become more concerned about the needs of others. That's our natural state, our natural goodness. So people are coming to be baptized by John and asking, "What are we supposed to do?" Look at what he says: *Stop being greedy, stop wanting more than you should have, and give to other people.* And they kind of wonder, OK, we'll do that. But the core message of John the Baptist is, *I can't get you to do this by willing it; I've got to get you to do it by being baptized.* And the baptism is an awareness of a gift that has been given to you, given to me, and when we believe that gift is there, it is like fire, it is filled with spirit, it purifies those things called shame, fear, and anger out of our system, and fills us with the spirit of love, the spirit of union, the spirit of connection. That's the promise of the great feast of Christmas, to say, "At one time into the world came this gift that now constantly comes into my heart, into me, and it gives me the ability to move into this awesome place." So there *is* joy, in recognizing what the fullness of what the Incarnation invites us into: a place of truly regaining our spiritual nature, and when that spiritual nature transcends all the limitations of our self-centeredness, we can find, finally, the place of inner peace.

Father, your gift, the gift of your presence that dwells within our hearts, is the key to finding this incredible promised place of peace. Bless us with this gift as we open our hearts to the longing that is there to find this awesome gift. Let us see the effectiveness of this gift as we find ourselves drawn more and more into unity with the world that you've given us, unity with each other, and unity with ourselves; and we ask this in Jesus' name. Amen.

Zephaniah 3: 14-18

14 Sing aloud, O daughter Zion; shout, O Israel! Rejoice and exult with all your heart, O daughter Jerusalem!
15 The LORD has taken away the judgments against you, he has turned away your ene-

mies. The king of Israel, the LORD, is in your midst; you shall fear disaster no more.
16 On that day it shall be said to Jerusalem: Do not fear, O Zion; do not let your hands
grow weak.
17 The LORD, your God, is in your midst, a warrior who gives victory; he will rejoice
over you with gladness, he will renew you in his love; he will exult over you with loud
singing
18 as on a day of festival.

Philippians 4: 4-7
4Rejoice in the Lord always; again I will say, Rejoice.
5Let your gentleness be known to everyone. The Lord is near.
6Do not worry about anything, but in everything by prayer and supplication with
thanksgiving let your requests be made known to God.
7And the peace of God, which surpasses all understanding, will guard your hearts and
your minds in Christ Jesus.

Luke 3: 10-18
10And the crowds asked him [John the Baptist], "What then should we do?"
11In reply he said to them, "Whoever has two coats must share with anyone who has
none; and whoever has food must do likewise."
12Even tax collectors came to be baptized, and they asked him, "Teacher, what should
we do?"
13He said to them, "Collect no more than the amount prescribed for you."
14Soldiers also asked him, "And we, what should we do?" He said to them, "Do not ex-
tort money from anyone by threats or false accusation, and be satisfied with your wages."
15As the people were filled with expectation, and all were questioning in their hearts
concerning John, whether he might be the Messiah,
16John answered all of them by saying, "I baptize you with water; but one who is more
powerful than I is coming; I am not worthy to untie the thong of his sandals. He will
baptize you with the Holy Spirit and fire.
17His winnowing fork is in his hand, to clear his threshing floor and to gather the wheat
into his granary; but the chaff he will burn with unquenchable fire."
18So, with many other exhortations, he proclaimed the good news to the people.

FOURTH SUNDAY OF ADVENT

Micah 5:1-4; Hebrews 10:5-10; Luke 1:39-45

Pour forth, we beseech you, O Lord, your grace into our hearts, that we, to whom the Incarnation of Christ, your Son, was made known by the message of an angel, may by his passion and cross be brought to the glory of his resurrection, who lives and reigns with you in the unity of the holy Spirit, one God, for ever and ever. Amen.

This is the last Sunday we have before the great feast of Christmas. And Christmas often falls not on a Sunday but during the week, so this is my Christmas homily for you! And what I'm feeling, what I'm longing to do, the passion inside of me is how do I awaken in myself, in you, an awareness of the extraordinary gift of what we call the Incarnation?

When I was a child, I went to bed on Christmas Eve with such anticipation of the next day, and I knew always, always knew there would be a gift, multiple gifts for me. It was more exciting than birthdays, maybe because *everybody* got gifts and maybe because we got *more* gifts than we got on our birthday. But the thing that's interesting to me is that the anticipation of the day was not the hope that *maybe* I would get a gift, but the realization that the gift is there, and all I have to do is go downstairs, open the gifts, and I *have* them.

There's a gift, called *Incarnation,* that came into the world at a particular time, at the exact right time, and it radically changed everything. It was the fulfillment of a promise that God would somehow enter into us and do something for us that could not be seen as anything but an enormous gift—never deserved, never earned—something that made *such* a difference in our life, gave us so much pleasure, so much joy. But even deeper than pleasure and joy is the promise, as we see in that first reading, that this figure who had been promised from the very, very beginning, would come, and he would bring something, not by so much telling us how to get it, but he would *be* it.

So we see, in that first reading, that this shepherd, this awesome presence of divinity, would come inside of us, and *he is peace*. He is peace. So *peace* is coming into us. Peace is that mysterious thing that is different from the world going the way we want it to go. Peace is that extraordinary capacity the human being has to *see through* whatever we're going through that might be painful or difficult, to see through it and to somehow see something—well, I don't even want to name it, because it's more mysterious than that. On the other side so often of the difficulties and the painful things in our life, there's something more. And to say that all pain just creates something better is just too oversimplified. But it *is* true that this image of the Incarnation is the thing that can bring us something that is not able to be received in any other way.

So let's look at it. What *is* the Incarnation? What is it about? Well, in that reading from Hebrews, it's so amazing because it's so packed with wisdom that when you read it quickly, you don't always *feel* that wisdom, but let's look at it more carefully and more slowly and find out what is really being said. And what is being said is that there came a time in the way in which God wanted to work with his people . . . God called Abraham and said, *I want to take you to a new place, a place called the kingdom, a place of peace.* The Old Testament is filled with images of taking people out of slavery into freedom. That has always been the theme. God is always, always concerned about this mysterious gift that he gave us, called free will, how it can often enslave us, instead of freeing us. And the enslavement of what we might call our human nature, our freedom, is that we often—daily—because we basically are on one level very narcissistic, very self-centered, we can create a world that we like and we want to live in it, and that's the world that we want to *be*. Whether it is the way the world is, or not, doesn't seem to matter to our ego. We will create something and say, "There! That's what I want. *That's* going to make me happy. That's going to be my source of peace. And I will do anything to keep that world together that I have created." It's a very, very natural, human thing. It should not be anything that we're feeling bad about. It's just the way it is.

So into this place where we have this strong, strong sense of the way we think the world should be, that we've created, we've been in that world; and yet we always hear this other world that is being described by a God who created us. In the beginning as we struggled with the world as we want it to be and the world as it truly is, we had this Father who came on the scene—a beautiful, powerful, providing father—who called together a family that we call the Israelite people, and he wanted so much to take care of them, he wanted them to know they were his special people, he loved them, and he would take care of them by conquering their enemies, making sure that they had everything that they needed. And he wanted to do nothing other than lead them into a place I might call *the truth*.

So he gave them some laws, some rules, just like a father gives a child rules and laws to live by before the child understands *why* he has to do these things.

And the way the father often has to control the child is to tell them if you *do* these things, because perhaps you can't see the ramifications of what might happen to you if you *did* do them, I have to punish you. I have to make you sense and feel the danger you're in when you're breaking my law. So all through the Old Testament, when people don't perform well, he's angry and he's often upset, like a father might be with his son or daughter who won't choose what's best for them. And he simply says you've *got* to do this or something terrible is going to happen to you.

So he's working primarily out of the issue of fear. It's a great motivator to get us to do the things that are difficult for us to do. And so often that's as far as we go with God and the Church, and that's it. So as we outgrow that need for a disciplinarian, we sometimes find ourselves outgrowing what we think is religion. But nothing could be further from the truth than that religion is simply God the lawgiver telling us what to do and if we don't, we're going to be punished; because when the time was right, when human beings had evolved enough to understand the fullness of God and who he really is, he did the most unbelievable thing. He decided he would become one of us. Still remaining God, he enters into the fullness of humanity and he walks this earth with us. God becomes then not just Father but also brother. It's interesting how we have our parents and they're very influential, and they form us. But really in a sense, they form us so we can make other relationships; we find relationships in our family, our brothers and sisters, we find relationship through friendship, someone to love, someone to commit ourselves to. In a way, parents have a very difficult job of creating us and then letting go of us.

What I'd like you to think about is that the father who disciplines us through rules and laws, we have to *let go* of that if we're going to develop. And what we enter into then is a relationship with God where he's not our disciplinarian but our brother. And he does two things—mysterious things. He looks into us deeply and sees all the good that is within us. Yet he also knows we have this ego, this narcissistic side that can create such agony in us and other people—people doing *horrible* things, destroying innocence, destroying goodness. When the self-will is out of control, we call it self-will run riot, and it can do the most painful things.

So if we're not going to have the Father any longer telling us what to do, not listening to that voice, then we're going to need a brother who's going to *show* us what to do. He's going to do it by first doing what he's going to ask us to do. He *models* for us in a way that the Father couldn't. And so fully human being, this brother, Jesus, reveals to us his passion, his passion, his longing, his desire, his heart burning with love for people around him, and he wants so badly for them to be free of that which enslaves them, free of that which destroys their capacity to love. He wants to free them from the illusions they're caught in. And whenever this brother enters into our life, different from the Father who has a law and a rule, this brother *mirrors* what is going on inside of us, and when the ego sees itself for what it really is, sometimes, oh man! That doesn't make the ego very happy—especially if it sees things that it should let go of, but can't; when it sees things that are painful, really painful, but refuses to deal with that cause of pain, or doesn't know *how* to deal with that pain, that cause of pain, and when it sees the pain that it can't understand, or surrender to, it rages. And we know that anger inside of us so well. So this brother shows us first that he has this incredible passion to free us, and that passion is so intense, so powerful, that he will do anything, *anything*. We know what real passion is like. It is this force, this drive that is inside of us, that is bigger than us, and it longs for the truth. It longs for something. When the passion is directed towards goodness, it longs for the truth. And then it gives us the capacity to do whatever is necessary to achieve our passion. The passion that Jesus longed for more than anything else was to save the world, bring it into a place of peace. I don't know what he had in his mind as a young man, but he must have thought, *I have lots of years to do this. I'm going to take my time. I'm going to do the best I can.* He was just getting started. Three years into it, his disciples weren't ready to be on their own. The church that he was trying to mirror the truth to was screaming and ranting and raging at him, and he found himself in this horrible place, where instead of being able to feel the excitement of the beginning of his ministry, he had to face the truth in the Garden of Gethsemane that this ministry was about to be over, and instead of accomplishing it the way he *thought* he would, he had to fail. He had to let go of it all. He had to accept that. Now think about that—the very thing he longed for the most, he had to say, *I can't get it. I can't have it. And what God is asking me to do, I can't believe. You're asking me to drink this cup. I can't. I can't.* And he finally did, and that's when he realized something his Father had always been saying, *You know what? People have been doing what I told them to do. People have been sacrificing things that I told them to sacrifice, they give me what they have, but I can't reach their hearts. I can't get into them. I'm bored with their sacrifices. What I want is not what they own. I want them to give themselves to me, trusting in me, giving <u>themselves</u> over to me. Everything I can do for them!* The extraordinary wisdom of the twelve-step program is based in this whole notion of "I am powerless." Jesus had to say, *I can't give this up, I can't go through this, but I know you're my Father and you're there and you can give something to me and you can enable me to do it, and I'll surrender to that. I'll <u>surrender</u> to that. I allow it to happen.*

That's the key. Jesus, our brother, God-brother, comes into our life and shows us that this is part of what it takes to find the truth, to be yourself. He asks you to *please, please look at what I'm doing, watch what happens to me in terms of the work I wanted to do.* It exploded when he died and then he says to you and me, *I'm asking you to look into this, to understand it, to grasp it, to allow it to touch your hearts; and then I want you to allow me to come into you, and for me to help you do it. You can't do it on your own. You are powerless. I couldn't do it without my Father. You can't do it without the same God in you, and I am in that God, that God is in me. I'm your brother and I've shown you what it is, and I want you to do it. I'll do it with you. I'll go through it with you. I'll sit there with you through the whole thing. I'll weep when it's sad, and I will give you strength when you can feel the need to rise above the pain that you're in, to surrender to it. I'll do all that with you. That's my gift to you.*

We call it the Spirit, the holy Spirit, God's presence, living presence, our brother's presence inside of us, our sister's presence inside of us. I love the image of the two women in the story of the gospel: Elizabeth, Mary, something new being born inside of them. One, a person who had a miraculous birth in the sense that she was so old that she was well past the time of being able to have a child. She's pregnant with this voice that's finally ready to proclaim—*It's not me; it's about something coming after me. It's not my ego that's going to save the world; it's someone who's coming who I'm not worthy to even loose his sandals. And I'm so excited that he's here, and I'm ready to announce him.* John is an incredible figure! And when he sees this Christ coming, he feels this Incarnation moving into his life, into the world, he *leaps* for joy. I mean, it's a wonderful image. He's so excited. He's the child that jumps out of bed in the morning and says, "I want my presents, I want my presents. I want to open it, I want to feel it, I want to be what this God wants me to be." And that's someone who trusts and believes, who gives himself over to a plan that is so much bigger than they are, and they find this mysterious thing that the Messiah is. He is peace.

Father, your gift, the gift of your presence, the gift of you in me and me in you; the gift of this unity that draws me, draws all of us to this place of understanding, the place of wisdom, the place of being able to see truly where you long for us to be; the place of union with you that creates a capacity for us to endure ALL things; a place that brings unbelievable peace, and we ask this through Christ our Lord. Amen.

Micah 5: 1-4

1 Now you are walled around with a wall; siege is laid against us; with a rod they strike
the ruler of Israel upon the cheek.
2 But you, O Bethlehem of Ephrathah, who are one of the little clans of Judah, from you
shall come forth for me one who is to rule in Israel, whose origin is from of old, from
ancient days.
3 Therefore he shall give them up until the time when she who is in labor has brought
forth; then the rest of his kindred shall return to the people of Israel.

4 And he shall stand and feed his flock in the strength of the LORD, in the majesty of the
name of the LORD his God. And they shall live secure, for now he shall be great to the
ends of the earth;
5 and he shall be the one of peace.

Hebrews 10: 5-10

5Consequently, when Christ came into the world, he said, "Sacrifices and offerings you
have not desired, but a body you have prepared for me;
6 in burnt offerings and sin offerings you have taken no pleasure.
7 Then I said, 'See, God, I have come to do your will, O God' (in the scroll of the book it
is written of me)."
8When he said above, "You have neither desired nor taken pleasure in sacrifices and offerings and burnt offerings and sin offerings" (these are offered according to the law),
9then he added, "See, I have come to do your will." He abolishes the first in order to establish the second.
10And it is by God's will that we have been sanctified through the offering of the body
of Jesus Christ once for all.

Luke 1: 39-45

39In those days Mary set out and went with haste to a Judean town in the hill country,
40where she entered the house of Zechariah and greeted Elizabeth.
41When Elizabeth heard Mary's greeting, the child leaped in her womb. And Elizabeth
was filled with the Holy Spirit
42and exclaimed with a loud cry, "Blessed are you among women, and blessed is the
fruit of your womb.
43And why has this happened to me, that the mother of my Lord comes to me?
44For as soon as I heard the sound of your greeting, the child in my womb leaped for
joy.
45And blessed is she who believed that there would be a fulfillment of what was spoken
to her by the Lord."

THE HOLY FAMILY

Sirach 3:2-6, 12-14; Colossians 3:12-21; Luke 2:41-52

O God, pleased to give us the shining example of the Holy Family, graciously grant that we may imitate them in practicing the virtues of family life in the bonds of charity, and so in the joy of your house, delight one day in eternal rewards, through our Lord Jesus Christ, your Son, who lives and reigns with you in the unity of the holy Spirit, one God, for ever and ever. Amen.

In our liturgical year, we always follow the feast of Christmas with the feast of the Holy Family. And there are some obvious connections. Jesus was born into the world as one like us, and he grew up in a family. And somehow what we're encouraged to do, as you listen to the opening prayer, is we're invited to learn something from the experience that Jesus had as he grew in age and wisdom, living in a family. Now I smile when I think about learning from the example of the Holy Family, Mary, Joseph, and Jesus, when you figure good Joseph was such a humble man; and Mary never committed a sin—she was born without sin; and Jesus was God. So I don't think that's exactly a normal family. But the *dynamic* in a family is always the same, always the same. There are roles that people take on.

In a way, when you listen to the first reading, and it's an interesting book, the book of Sirach, which is also called the book of Ecclesiastes. The book of Sirach is not in the Hebrew canon, and it's not in many of the Christian bibles that are not Catholic. And one of the things that is interesting about this book is that it was written about 200 years before the coming of Christ, and it was written by a man by the name of ben Sira. One of the things that so touched him was the Law that was given by God, the Law of the Old Testament, and he saw in it so much wisdom, and what he longed to do was to write a book that tried to draw out of the Law the wisdom that is there. It's a fascinating book to read because it's so clearly a practical application of how we should live. Some of it's humorous to me, some of it disturbing. For example: Never go to a feast of someone who is wealthier than you and say, "Wow! What a feast!" Another one is, if your host is looking at something on the table, and he wants it, don't grab it first. Another one that's interesting: Be ashamed of yourself if you ever put your elbows on the table. And then the disturbing things. One passage about being a parent: A good father beats his son. And: A father who plays with his son is creating a great problem for him and for his son. So all of this strikes me as, there's a way in which the Law, when you see it presented purely as law, often seems to fly in the face of our *emotional* life, what we *feel* inside.

So I'd like to begin by looking at the image we have in the first reading, and it's clear that it's saying to us, "You know, we should honor the *roles* that people have. We should honor our parents, and by honoring them, what we're doing is showing respect for the role that they have and allowing that role to take its course and always being filled with great reverence and respect for it. In the same way that a child, in this system where the parent is called to be the one who nurtures and cares for the children, the children's response is to appreciate what is being offered and then in turn honor and respect the parents when *they* are in need.

That all makes perfect sense, but how it works out, how it unfolds is so complex. We know there are healthy parents, and parents that are not able to be the kind of healthy mentors to their children that ultimately I would like to think that they would really want to be, and we have children who are not receptive to the healthiest of parenting, and it's all very complex. That's why I love the *second* reading, from St. Paul, which is filled with the one single thing that is absolutely essential if you are going to live in a family, to live in a system where people have authority over other people, where there are responsibilities that need to be carried out by both sides, those who give and those who receive. And one of the things it says so clearly, if you're going to live in this system, and be somehow not damaged by it if it's not what it should be, then you have to be filled with all kinds of—let me list them: compassion, kindness, humility, gentleness, patience, love, gratitude. Isn't that interesting? All those dispositions to me are the dispositions that make the difference between a reaction to the Law—we can be held up against the Law, or the Law can be imposed upon us, and if there isn't compassion, if there isn't kindness, if there isn't patience, if we're not able to put up with the grievances we have against one another, if there's no forgiveness, then it strikes me that the wisdom of the Law cannot take us very far, cannot help us develop as individuals who are called, ultimately, to live our own destiny.

The fascinating thing in the system that God has created for us is that we come into the world with a task, with a destiny, with something we're called to become. There is no law that can make us into what we are intended to be by God. We have to learn how to *find* our destiny; we have to learn how to listen attentively with our hearts to the things that are deep inside of us. How do we find the place where we know we are doing what we're called to do? How do parents know enough about their children to guide them into that place? It's a great, great mystery. So if this is our call, to become who we are, then it seems we're going to be coming flat up against a lot of tension and pressure when it comes to somehow living under the Law—let's say, even living under the law of our parents. "Law" might be too strong a word. Let's just call it "what they would like, what they wish, what they hope for." I guess parents come in all flavors, and there are those who could care less maybe about what happens to their children. Once they're raised, they're on their own, and the parents go off and live their life. There are others who call their children every single day, want to know exactly what they're doing. But most are in between those extremes. So how do we deal with this whole issue of having respect and honor for those who have real authority over us; at the same time how do we follow what *we're* called to do?

I find it fascinating that the liturgy of the Word for this feast of the Holy Family is not the same stories we listened to last week when we celebrated the end of Advent and the beginning of Christmas—and all these beautiful stories about Jesus and everyone coming and loving the baby and honoring the baby and the joy you find in a family with a new baby. It's always exciting, filled with potential. But the story we're asked to look at as a description of the Holy Family and to look into that experience that Jesus had with his family to find an example of how we should live in *our* family—it's a story that's pretty horrendous when you look at it. Here's Jesus at twelve. Now twelve here is a lot older than *our* twelves. So many people getting married, girls getting married at thirteen and fourteen. So a twelve-year-old then might be more like a seventeen-year-old in our own time; anyway, certainly a teenager. Now imagine this. Let's put it in a contemporary setting. You take your adolescent child to a place, let's say you go to Washington for some reason, and let's say there's a tour group. Somebody's taking care of the children, and so you expect that the tour guide is going to be watching your son, your daughter, and you go out to the airport and you get on the plane. You look around and your child is not there, and you go, "Whoa! Wait a minute! Where is my child?" And the tour guide says, "I thought he was with the other director." All of a sudden, you get this panic. Now think about this. They go looking in a city for their son for three days and two sleepless nights, wondering what happened to him. "Was he abducted? What could keep him away from us? What could allow him to separate himself from us?" And the thing that's so fascinating about this story: They finally find him, and the reaction of Jesus is not unlike the reaction of any adolescent. It's like, "What's the deal? I was doing what I knew I had to do. This is just where I have to be. This is my destiny. This is my Father's house. Didn't you know that's where I would be?" Maybe he was even saying, "Didn't you know to look here first?"

In either case, you have this strange tension between a child and his parents, and so we're invited in the opening prayer of this liturgy to somehow pray for some kind of example that we find in this set of readings, in this feast. It strikes me that the lesson from the Holy Family is the lesson that I think is probably, in relationship to parents and children, the *core* issue in family: How do parents let go of their children, allow them to fulfill their destiny? How does a child *find* his destiny when it isn't necessarily what his parents want? Interesting! Think of all the shades of differences when it comes to the tension between children and parents—between *any* authority: between the Church and you, between the Law and you and your work and your destiny.

It seems to me that the mystery of the Incarnation *continues* to draw us into this place where we're invited to imagine that there's a spirit given to us, placed in our hearts. In the book of Ecclesiastes there's a wonderful line that says, "You've been given a heart so you can think." When you think with your heart, it seems like you're not working out of the Law but out of this intuition, this thing deep inside of us. And ultimately, parents are there to involve their children in a process that awakens their heart to their destiny and supports that destiny. What a challenge for parents! And yet it's also such a challenge for young people to realize that the parents are perhaps not going to be able to do that as smoothly and as easily as they wish, and they have to learn patience and understanding and forgiveness. On both sides, those things are required.

So the thing we learn from this great feast of the Holy Family is mostly that we are called in a relationship where we have mentors and those who are being mentored. We have all that interaction between members of a community where we haven't chosen these people—they've been given to us. In the process of working through that whole thing, what is necessary is that we have these qualities of the heart, qualities of patience and understanding and forgiveness. That's the challenge: to live in *that* disposition as we work with those who are our teachers and work to learn what, ultimately, our *ultimate* Father is calling us to.

Father, there are often great tensions in our families. We long for freedom from the tension that robs us of an appreciation of who we are and what we're seeking from one another in a family system. So bless us with the patience, the love, the compassion, the understanding that is necessary for us to be able to grow and become ALL that you've called us to be, and we ask this in Jesus' name. Amen.

Feast of the Holy Family

Sirach 3: 2-6, 12-14

2 For the Lord honors a father above his children, and he confirms a mother's right over her children.
3 Those who honor their father atone for sins,
4 and those who respect their mother are like those who lay up treasure.
5 Those who honor their father will have joy in their own children, and when they pray they will be heard.
6 Those who respect their father will have long life, and those who honor their mother obey the Lord;

12 My child, help your father in his old age, and do not grieve him as long as he lives;
13 even if his mind fails, be patient with him; because you have all your faculties do not despise him.
14 For kindness to a father will not be forgotten, and will be credited to you against your sins;

Colossians 3: 12-21

12 As God's chosen ones, holy and beloved, clothe yourselves with compassion, kindness, humility, meekness, and patience.
13 Bear with one another and, if anyone has a complaint against another, forgive each other; just as the Lord[£] has forgiven you, so you also must forgive.
14 Above all, clothe yourselves with love, which binds everything together in perfect harmony.
15 And let the peace of Christ rule in your hearts, to which indeed you were called in the one body. And be thankful.
16 Let the word of Christ dwell in you richly; teach and admonish one another in all wisdom; and with gratitude in your hearts sing psalms, hymns, and spiritual songs to God.
17 And whatever you do, in word or deed, do everything in the name of the Lord Jesus, giving thanks to God the Father through him.
18 Wives, be subject to your husbands, as is fitting in the Lord.
19 Husbands, love your wives and never treat them harshly.
20 Children, obey your parents in everything, for this is your acceptable duty in the Lord.
21 Fathers, do not provoke your children, or they may lose heart.

Luke 2: 41-52

41 Now every year his parents went to Jerusalem for the festival of the Passover.
42 And when he was twelve years old, they went up as usual for the festival.

43 When the festival was ended and they started to return, the boy Jesus stayed behind in
Jerusalem, but his parents did not know it.
44 Assuming that he was in the group of travelers, they went a day's journey. Then they
started to look for him among their relatives and friends.
45 When they did not find him, they returned to Jerusalem to search for him.
46 After three days they found him in the temple, sitting among the teachers, listening to
them and asking them questions.
47 And all who heard him were amazed at his understanding and his answers.
48 When his parents saw him they were astonished; and his mother said to him, "Child,
why have you treated us like this? Look, your father and I have been searching for you
in great anxiety."
49 He said to them, "Why were you searching for me? Did you not know that I must be
in my Father's house?"
50 But they did not understand what he said to them.
51 Then he went down with them and came to Nazareth, and was obedient to them. His
mother treasured all these things in her heart.
52 And Jesus increased in wisdom and in years, and in divine and human favor.

FEAST OF THE EPIPHANY

Isaiah 60:1-6; Ephesians 3:2-3, 5-6; Matthew 2:1-12

O God, who on this day revealed your only begotten Son to the nations by the guidance of a star, grant in your mercy that we who know you already by faith may be brought to behold the beauty of your sublime glory, through our Lord Jesus Christ, your Son, who lives and reigns with you in the unity of the holy Spirit, one God for ever and ever. Amen.

The theme of this feast of the Epiphany is always the same: the work that we share together, of seeking a greater understanding, a greater knowledge of our God. We also find this feast at the same time of the year, right after the great feast of the Incarnation, so it has something to do with the fact that we believe so deeply that the Incarnation, God becoming one of us, is the most beautiful, the most amazing way of discovering the fullness of who God is. I love one of the phrases that Jesus used at the end of his life when he was with his disciples at the Last Supper. He said, *You do believe in God. Now I'm asking you to believe in me.* It can be a problem for us to make the distinction between God the Father and then Jesus. And often we see God the Father as strict and kind of distant; and Jesus as a brother who's close to us and who understands us. Yet we have to be so careful not to separate the two, not to imagine that Jesus is different from God. But this amazing process of God revealing himself is so clearly done in stages. He begins by simply saying, *I LOVE you, my Israelite people. You are my favorites. I will take care of you; I'll fight your battles for you; I'll call you into a place of freedom; I'll take care of you. I'll be your God. Just do what I ask, and you'll find life.*

But that system was somehow very much dependent on what we had to do in order to find life, what we were called to follow in terms of the rules and laws. That was important. It had its role, but we in a sense outgrew it as we needed to sense more the intimacy that God ultimately really wants to have with us. He wants to be so much more than our teacher. He wants to marry us; he wants to enter into our life; he wants to be intimately connected to everything that we're doing. It's always hard for us to make that transition, from this awesome, great God who is so much more than we are and then to imagine him as someone like us and then someone who wants to dwell within us, in terms of the Third Person of the Trinity, the Spirit, living in you and in me. That movement from outside to inside is part of what Jesus was trying to say when he said, *You believe in God being out there; now believe that God is coming into you.*

One of the ways in which we're asked to reflect on this feast of the Epiphany, as to getting to know this God, somehow it seems that we're invited to look into darkness because we keep hearing these words, that the understanding and the wisdom that we long to have of who God is comes when we focus on a light *in* the darkness.

And so it's interesting to me that so often the way we understand fully both who God is and our need for God is when we look deeply into our human existence and realize that we're not enough, that somehow there are things that overwhelm us and overpower us, and when they do, there are things like anger and fear and shame that somehow darken our life. The core issue that it seems to me we need to be reflecting on when we think about God in our life, God becoming more intimate and more personal in our life, is that he has a goal, and what he wants to do is enlighten us, and when he enlightens us, we then see so much more, and what we see is something that is often hidden in the darkness. And what it is, to me, is the way in which *love* works. His love for us, our love for ourselves, and our love for each other. Think about it. All through the Old Testament, there's an image that we have, that many times he's disappointed with his people and he often punishes them, and the punishment always takes the form of allowing them to experience the darkness that they chose, and once they taste enough of that, they may realize that that choice was really the wrong one, and then they work to do better at choosing life; but it seems like over and over again in the Old Testament, we find that human beings just can't seem to do it. Instead of success, they're often filled with a sense of shame or their own imperfection, maybe even their "unattractiveness," if that's a word that God has for them. And it seems like in the person of Jesus, what we have is a manifestation of the Father's love for us *as we are*. So one of the things that it seems the first reading, for example, is talking about is something that is going to happen, some light is going to come into the world, that when we see it, we'll *become* that light. We will see the radiance of something, and that radiance takes root in us, and we become radiant. And this may sound oversimplified, but one of the things that God in the person of Jesus is so powerfully capable of doing, and it's all about this key way of loving called forgiveness, mercy. God's favor, God's grace in the Old Testament was often given to those who did what was right. Then in the New Testament,

God's grace turns to *mercy*. Grace is God's love, God's favor; mercy is God's love, God's favor given to one who doesn't deserve it. So when we sense this love of God for us as we are, in spite of our weaknesses, something shifts inside of us when we believe that, when we actually believe that there is something about us that is so good and attractive that God is drawn to it with an intense, intense longing to connect and to perfect and to enrich it, to enlighten it. It gives us a sense of enormous importance when you think about it. And when a person senses that kind of gift of affirmation coming from a God who created us, who knows everything, who knows every weakness that we have, but still he looks deeply into us and sees past the darkness of our imperfection and sees the light that's core to us, and loves it into brightness, what do we do with that? We don't just sit there and bask in the light of our own beauty, in the eyes of God, but what happens—and I think our human nature is wired this way—what happens when we sense that beauty and we feel the kind of patience and the kind of trust and the kind of *hope* that it brings to us, we just want to give that to somebody else. That's the most amazing thing about it. We become carriers of this incredible desire of God to be connected to the same work that he does in awakening people. It's our longing to love, our longing for the world to be more than it is, a longing to fix the problems that are there, a longing to bring goodness to people. It's the most beautiful part about being, in the words of the second reading, co-partners with God. And in the Old Testament it was considered that a certain group of people were uniquely blessed with this affirmation of God's love, and they would in turn be his partners in the world. And then Paul comes along and says the unthinkable. He says, *I've been told this, and no one else has really been told this before. It's been told to us not by me but by Christ, who's speaking through me now. What this whole thing is about is somehow that God's love is for everyone. The dreaded Samaritans are loved by God; the dreaded lepers, the misfits, the whole group that don't belong to the inner group*. They're called Gentiles. *All* of them have been invited into this extraordinary process of God, seeing through their darkness, seeing the light in them, enlightening it, and then enabling them with that light in them to be co-partners in doing the same thing for the people around us. It's in a way so simple and so beautiful. Don't you think it's fascinating that the story of the Epiphany is all about a group of people—they're called Zoroastrians—and you would think that the people seeking knowledge of this Messiah would have been the leaders of the Temple, the religious leaders, but instead it was this sort of mystic that dealt in magic and all kinds of things. And yet they had an imagination that was able to look and see signs. I think that's so amazing. In order to find this love that God has for you, and to be enlightened to be able to love others the way he loves you, it has something to do with reading signs. And they're always following a light that's in the darkness back to that image. I don't know if you do this, but there's a way to listen to people who are talking to you, listen to stories that you're hearing, listen to your dreams, listen to the news. And somehow, if you're listening for wisdom, listening for something that is there for you, to ponder, to wonder about, to draw you through the darkness into light, you're going to *find* it. So the Zoroastrians are a fascinating model for us as we seek to see and to know our God. It's not that we have necessarily to be into astrology, though astrology is a fascinating, fascinating thing, but it's all about being engaged in something that has an expectation that there is a message, that there is a meaning that I'm looking for. Well, think about it. If you and I have a relationship with God where he is the one who longs to enlighten us, wouldn't you think that he would use any way possible to do that, and wouldn't you think that you should be open and receptive to the many ways in which he speaks? It doesn't mean you're just going to hear what God is all about on Sunday, or listening to a radio program, or whatever. The liturgy, these reflections that I share with you, they're like the ways in which we're awakened to a process going on all the time—to see light in darkness, to see something, to see insights. They're hidden within things that are sometimes very difficult to think about. Or maybe they're not. Maybe they're in things that are joyous and wonderful. But there's something about being in the world with an expectation of a God who loves you, is wanting you to understand more fully who you are, who he is, and how this whole thing works. What more would he want you to do than to say, "Teach me, show me, reveal yourself to me." I have to speak from my own experience. Being retired, I have so much more time to think and to reflect, to ponder and to wonder. I sort of feel bad that I was so busy in the past that I didn't give myself much of a chance to think and reflect, but the more you do, the richer it all becomes. It seems to carry a certain—I don't know—I call it "excitement." *Enthusiasm* is a great word because it literally means to be infused with *Theos*, God. But you begin to feel God everywhere, and that everything is somehow connected, and it's all there to help you and me understand this most basic, the simplest of things, that we have a God who is deeply, deeply in love with the beauty he created in us and that he longs for it to be awakened so we can feel a sense of fullness, and out of that fullness, we have a sense of wanting to do exactly what he does, for the people around *us*. It's *natural*. It's comfortable, in a sense—not easy. The comfort is that when we're doing it, we feel good. "This is it. This is what we're supposed to be doing." Think of the things that distract us. Think of all the places and times where we are caught up in something that isn't so essential. We just need to make time for the things that *are* essential. We need to make time to take a journey, to follow some kind of intuition that light is there, and we long for it to be awakened.

Feast of the Epiphany

Father, the gift of your presence in our world has awakened in us an understanding of your longing for the transformation that we carry as a potential within us to become so much like you. So bless us with this grace, this power that enables us to be co-partners with you as we draw others out of darkness into the amazing light of your love, and we ask this through Christ our Lord. Amen.

Isaiah 60: 1-6

Arise, shine; for your light has come, and the glory of the Lord has risen upon you. 2For
darkness shall cover the earth, and thick darkness the peoples; but the Lord will arise
upon you, and his glory will appear over you. 3Nations shall come to your light, and
kings to the brightness of your dawn. 4Lift up your eyes and look around; they all gather together, they come to you; your sons shall come from far away, and your daughters
shall be carried on their nurses' arms. 5Then you shall see and be radiant; your heart
shall thrill and rejoice, because the abundance of the sea shall be brought to you, the
wealth of the nations shall come to you. 6A multitude of camels shall cover you, the
young camels of Midian and Ephah; all those from Sheba shall come. They shall bring
gold and frankincense, and shall proclaim the praise of the Lord.

Ephesians 3: 2-3, 5-6

2for surely you have already heard of the commission of God's grace that was given me
for you, 3and how the mystery was made known to me by revelation, as I wrote above
in a few words

5In former generations this mystery was not made known to humankind, as it has now
been revealed to his holy apostles and prophets by the Spirit: 6that is, the Gentiles have
become fellow heirs, members of the same body, and sharers in the promise in Christ
Jesus through the gospel.

Matthew 2: 1-12

In the time of King Herod, after Jesus was born in Bethlehem of Judea, wise men from
the East came to Jerusalem, 2asking, "Where is the child who has been born king of the
Jews? For we observed his star at its rising, and have come to pay him homage." 3When
King Herod heard this, he was frightened, and all Jerusalem with him; 4and calling together all the chief priests and scribes of the people, he inquired of them where the
Messiah was to be born. 5They told him, "In Bethlehem of Judea; for so it has been written by the prophet: 6'And you, Bethlehem, in the land of Judah, are by no means least

among the rulers of Judah; for from you shall come a ruler who is to shepherd my people Israel.'" [7]Then Herod secretly called for the wise men and learned from them the exact time when the star had appeared. [8]Then he sent them to Bethlehem, saying, "Go and
search diligently for the child; and when you have found him, bring me word so that I
may also go and pay him homage."
[9]When they had heard the king, they set out; and there, ahead of them, went the star
that they had seen at its rising, until it stopped over the place where the child
was. [10]When they saw that the star had stopped, they were overwhelmed with joy. [11]On
entering the house, they saw the child with Mary his mother; and they knelt down and
paid him homage. Then, opening their treasure chests, they offered him gifts of gold,
frankincense, and myrrh. [12]And having been warned in a dream not to return to Herod,
they left for their own country by another road.

THE BAPTISM OF THE LORD

Isaiah 42:1-4, 6-7; Acts 10:34-38; Luke 3:15-16, 21-22

O God, whose only begotten Son has appeared in our very flesh, grant we pray that we may be inwardly transformed through him whom we recognize as outwardly like ourselves, who lives and reigns with you in the unity of the holy Spirit, one God for ever and ever. Amen.

Today we end this special time when we've been focusing so much on the Incarnation, the season of Christmas, and we'll now move into Ordinary Time, but in this last feast of that time when we focus on the coming of the Christ into our world, we celebrate his baptism, the beginning of his ministry. So I want to talk about baptism and what it symbolizes and what it means. But in order to do that, I think we have to look at a broader picture of what religion is trying to accomplish. What religion is seeking, in a true sense, what all of it is about, what *every* religion is about if it's truthful, if it's healthy—has one fundamental goal: to bring us to a place of transcendence, to grow, to become, to be freed of everything that encumbers us and keeps us in darkness and blindness, to enter into the fullness of who God has created us to be.

It's very interesting to me that religion can become *toxic* in some ways when it ends up not inviting us to grow and to change but somehow to limit us, imprison us, and hold us down. It can be the kind of thing that when we desire to grow and become who we are, there are norms that the Church has for how we should behave and what we should do that seem to impede our progress and keep us from *being* ourselves. That's maybe why we see many people in the world today saying, "I'm not religious; I'm not drawn to religion, but I'm deeply spiritual." That's like saying, "I don't believe that the institution that I call the Church has helped me to grow spiritually, to become more of who I really am, and to be going beyond my own human limitations and enter into this *incredible* place that God has called us to where we become not only fully alive, but we become sources of life to our brothers and sisters.

So when we look at baptism as the entrance into this world of religion, what we sense in it is two things. Baptism seems to emphasize a new beginning, a crossing over. The image of the baptism of John is that it was mostly about *the past,* about getting the forgiveness of sins. We can see often, when we look at the forgiveness of Jesus, the forgiveness that he's revealed to us that's in the Father's heart, we can say, "Well, it's wonderful that we don't have to dwell excessively in the past; we can let go of the past because we are forgiven of what has happened in the past." But if that's all that forgiveness offers, it just seems like it stops then with the present. And the reason we're forgiven, the reason why forgiveness is such a key part of the teaching of Jesus is because what God *wants* us to do is to be pouring our lives and our attention into the present moment, into *the now.* And what he wants us to sense and feel is that the challenge he's given to everyone is to open our eyes to see the world that God has created, as it is; to see him, our God, as he is; and to see ourselves as we really are. So the *real* work of religion is to begin within us a spiritual journey wherein we continue to evolve and grow and develop and become all that God has called us to be. It's an exciting, exciting, wonderful journey.

And as we go through that journey, it seems it's very important at times to have people around us who are experiencing the same thing. So we thrive in community. And religion, of its nature, is a binding together, a calling together of a community—not just the people who are in the same building, sitting together, but a group of people who are experiencing, together, this incredible work of transformation that happens when we open ourselves to the Spirit, and we share the enthusiasm of that, the stories of that. And that can become extraordinarily valuable. And often, religion offers *ritual* or some kind of experience that we go through together that enhances our excitement and our capacity to go *in* the direction of fullness.

Yet what Jesus was so upset about with the institution of religion at the time he walked this earth, he kept saying, *What you all do is you put burdens on people that are too heavy to carry. You also do something else: You place upon them your human traditions and you say that those are God's laws.* Isn't that interesting! "Your human traditions are God's laws." If we truly are an evolving species—and I truly believe we are—it is definitely easy to see that throughout history so many people have said things about the generation that is presently living, and the older members of that generation will often say something like, "What's happened to these people? They just don't have the same integrity, the same qualities we have. They seem to be losing everything that we had in the past." Maybe that's the normal process of what it means to be engaged in a species that continually evolves and changes. I'm not saying that the *core* changes; the Ten Commandments don't change, you know. But how we interpret those, how we live those, how people use them as guides, often involves things that are not necessarily the way things used to be done. Does that mean that the new way in which we're engaged in living out the truth of the Gospel means that it's wrong, because it's different than it used to be? That doesn't make sense!

So we see in this action of the baptism of Jesus a symbol of what happens to us when we enter into this thing we call the spiritual world. *The Spirit enters into us.* Now just look at that, how different that is. We had a Law in the Old Testament outside of us, guiding us. Now in the New Testament, we have the Spirit *inside* of us, guiding us from the inside. The Law couldn't transform us; that's its limitation. The Spirit, the image of fire in the Spirit, is the image of transformation. The fire of the Spirit can *change* us and make us into different kinds of people in the sense of more awake, more alert, less caged in darkness—those are the images I think are so powerful.

When I think about the way I used to imagine religion as a young Catholic boy, it was always that I had to do the rules and laws, and if I followed them, I would be rewarded. It was so simple! And then, as I matured and grew and began to understand the message of Jesus, I recognized that when he came into the world, his greatest problem, his greatest conflict was that he ended up going against the traditions of his religion, and he was *destroyed* by that religion. Well, let me put it this way: They *thought* they could destroy him. And when he gave into that, when he didn't decide to fight that or try to destroy that—so often people want to destroy those things that didn't produce life in them—no, he wanted to *transform* those things. So by giving in to what they were, without becoming what they were asking him to be—enslaved in the Law—he broke free. That's the journey. That's what every single one of us is supposed to do.

Does that mean religion is an enemy? Of course not! It's an enormously valuable thing. When people say, "I'm not religious, but I'm spiritual," it's like saying, "I like eating. That's my spiritual life. I like feeding on the gifts of the Spirit. But I don't like food." Religion is supposed to be the food that enhances our awareness of the gift of the Spirit in us, encourages us and holds us accountable with each other so we can move and grow in a direction that brings life to all of us. We flourish in community; we're better in community. So it's not a case of an either-or situation. It's a case of both of these things work when they are healthy and when they are all that God intended them to be.

So on this feast of the baptism of Jesus, we are looking at him—divine as well as human—pocketing, in a sense, setting aside his divinity so he could show us what we as human beings need to do in order to live the life that he's called us to live. And he says, *You have to surrender to this gift that is going to be given to you; you have to be anointed.* You have to become like the Christ. (The word "Christ" means "the anointed one.") So we go through a ritual that reminds us that you and I are given the most extraordinary gift, this inner voice, this extraordinary power that if we say "yes" to it, it will do the things it was always promised to do: open our eyes, free us from imprisonment, get us out of darkness. The imprisonment, the darkness, the blindness—they show up in our doing bad things. But the key is not to stop doing those bad things as much as it is to be enlightened, to be freed, and to be set on this extraordinary journey. Can you feel how important forgiveness is that frees us from the past so that we can continue to work in these present moments you and I have so that we're always in the process of growing and changing?

Transformation, as I said at the beginning of the program, is "the work" of healthy religion; it's the fruits of a spiritual life. That means going beyond our limitations. Now when we see what Jesus is able to do, what we sense that he did, and what his baptism seemed to enable him to do so clearly is that he began a ministry where—what was he doing?—he was opening the eyes of the blind, the ears of those who couldn't hear, the mouths of those who couldn't speak; he was giving the ability to walk and move around. All those images that we see of this spiritual giant, Christ, in the world—*this* is what I'm talking about as transformation. We're transformed into being *like* him. Now I don't know whether you think of yourself like that. One of the things that's a negative in most religions is it tends to focus on our getting our act together so we can get into heaven. But "getting your act together" is one thing; but once it's together, using it to accomplish what our destiny is here is *another* thing. And *that's* the part that gets me so excited about the spiritual life, and why I long for a healthy religious community that will nurture me, encourage me, sustain me, awaken in me things that I tend to lose, because to be a spiritual person in the world today is to be the most effective, the most powerful person that could ever exist because your *task*, your opportunity, is to be able to move among the people that you care about and you love and to be an agent where you can help them to become all that they need to be, and they in turn, once they can become the fullness of who they are, they have the same challenge and the same opportunity of being able to be that transforming power to the people around them.

You look at the world today and you listen to people complain and gripe, and they say politics are all screwed up, and the Church is all screwed up, and the banking industry is all screwed up. Everything is all messed up, and we've got to change these institutions. How do you *change* institutions, you know? How do you go about that, I mean? OK. You've got to find the right leader. We evaluate everybody that might be a new leader in some division of the government, so we know that they're the ones who are going to help change the institution, but is it really the institutions that we have to change so that those institutions will serve us and create in us the ability to live healthy, fruitful, and peaceful lives? I don't think so! No, the key is that we, individuals, will change, and when *we* change, and when we change those around us, the *world* will change. Joseph Chilton Pierce, who's an amazing, amazing educator and teacher and a wonderful mind, he always says the way we're going to change the world is when we train children to enter into this world with enormous confidence in their goodness and their value, and recognizing then that they have this goodness and value and it's both for themselves and for the world around them and they begin to use it and they begin to transform the people around them and they transform other people; and it all begins with that core issue of *becoming* what God wants us to be.

That's what baptism is designed to do, because the *becoming* is the commingling of Spirit and flesh, of our humanity and the divinity that has been given to us to transform our limitations into the same exact extraordinary ministry that we see in this person Jesus. That's what we're called to be. That's what we're called to do. It's not rocket science; it's not that difficult to sense what this whole thing's about. But you can feel and I can feel that when institutions, particularly religious institutions that are not as healthy as they should be, are somehow robbing us of our freedom to make the choices that the Spirit is leading us into, when it judges us unnecessarily about the choices we make, and instead of being a determiner of what's right and wrong, they're really telling us, "Well, this is comfortable for me," or "This is uncomfortable for me; I don't like you doing that; I'd rather you do it this way." No institution should have the power to override the guidance of the Spirit that lives inside of us. So it's through our baptism, through this extraordinary gift of the God who lives within us. And remember, in our tradition, Roman Catholicism, we believe that you don't have to be literally baptized in a church ceremony to have the Spirit. We believe that for anyone who really seeks the good, the baptism of desire is enough for the Spirit to fill you. Or if you have a heart that is geared toward taking care of others above yourself, where you give your life for others, it's called the baptism of blood. It's so important that no religion should claim that it has the only way to find a connection with Spirit. It is our inheritance from God that he wants us to have it. And we will have it, and it will make the ride, the journey toward a place of fullness—it will make it happen.

Father, you've chosen each of us from the very beginning to be instruments that carry your Spirit into the world, to co-partner with you in creating a world of fullness and life and goodness for ourselves and those that we love. We thank you for this great gift, this great privilege. And open our eyes to see it more clearly, to enthusiastically respond to the transforming grace that brings us and those we love into fullness, and we ask this in Jesus' name. Amen.

Isaiah 42: 1-4, 6-7
Here is my servant, whom I uphold, my chosen, in whom my soul delights; I have put
my spirit upon him; he will bring forth justice to the nations. 2He will not cry or lift up
his voice, or make it heard in the street; 3a bruised reed he will not break, and a dimly
burning wick he will not quench; he will faithfully bring forth justice. 4He will not grow
faint or be crushed until he has established justice in the earth; and the coastlands wait
for his teaching.

6I am the LORD, I have called you in righteousness, I have taken you by the hand and
kept you; I have given you as a covenant to the people, a light to the nations, 7to open
the eyes that are blind, to bring out the prisoners from the dungeon, from the prison
those who sit in darkness.

Acts 10: 34-38
34Then Peter began to speak to them: "I truly understand that God shows no partiali-
ty, 35but in every nation anyone who fears him and does what is right is acceptable to
him. 36You know the message he sent to the people of Israel, preaching peace by Jesus
Christ—he is Lord of all. 37That message spread throughout Judea, beginning in Galilee
after the baptism that John announced: 38how God anointed Jesus of Nazareth with the
Holy Spirit and with power; how he went about doing good and healing all who were
oppressed by the devil, for God was with him.

Luke 3: 15-16, 21-22
15As the people were filled with expectation, and all were questioning in their hearts
concerning John, whether he might be the Messiah, 16John answered all of them by saying, "I baptize you with water; but one who is more powerful than I is coming; I am not
worthy to untie the thong of his sandals. He will baptize you with the Holy Spirit and
fire.

21Now when all the people were baptized, and when Jesus also had been baptized and
was praying, the heaven was opened, 22and the Holy Spirit descended upon him in bodily form like a dove. And a voice came from heaven, "You are my Son, the Beloved;
with you I am well pleased."

SECOND SUNDAY IN ORDINARY TIME

Isaiah 62:1-5; 1Corinthians 12:4-11; John 2:1-11

Almighty, ever-living God, who governs all things both in heaven and on earth, mercifully hear the pleading of your people and bestow your peace on our times, through our Lord Jesus Christ, your Son, who lives and reigns with you in the unity of the holy Spirit, one God, for ever and ever. Amen.

This is the second Sunday in Ordinary Time, and it means that we are going to once again, through different scriptures than we've used for the last two years, be focusing on the ministry of this amazing, this *amazing* figure that has come into the world. Our challenge is to believe in him, and as a believer, we are then able to see him as he truly is and able to understand what he's truly doing for us. We are receptive. We're open. I love the line in the miracle story of the water turned to wine at the wedding in Cana—that the disciples who were present at this event—they *began* to believe in him. Isn't that interesting? You would think that belief is either you believe or you don't, but there must be—and I believe there is—a process wherein we *grow* in our capacity to believe because it takes grace, copious amounts of God's loving power being poured into us for us to make the transition from lower states of consciousness to higher states of consciousness where we can actually open our hearts and minds to the awesome *power* of this God. And as I said earlier, to *receive* what he offers.

Let's go to the first reading because it's very important. It's from the prophet Isaiah, and it's about the promised Messiah and what he's going to accomplish and what he's going to do. When you listen to this, you realize that these words were spoken to a people who must have felt at times that they were not loved or cared for. They were judged often; their land was considered to be desolate, empty. And there's a promise in this prophecy that there will come a change in their lives where the God who created them will create for them an awareness, where they live, of the relationship that they have with this God where they are *enormously* blessed, and what they're blessed with in a way is surprising: They're going to be blessed with *intimacy* with a power that is greater than all other powers. So let's say they were people living in fear of judgment from the God who created them; and *that* could be truly, clearly seen in the Old Testament where we see human beings failing over and over again to keep the Law and God having to punish them, to show them that this was a bad choice. It wasn't that he *wanted* to punish them, but what do you do with a child who can't fully yet understand that they shouldn't do certain things, and when they break the rules, you have to show them that "this is unacceptable, and I have to give you some kind of motivation to follow this rule." And sometimes the motivation is punishment of some sort. So these people who were used to that relationship with their higher power, they all of a sudden are told that there will come a time that this God they often fear as a judgmental God is going to be a God who *ceases* to judge and longs to *connect*, to connect with us as we are and to love us in a way where the only example the scripture could use that could carry the weight of what the scripture is trying to say is that God has the kind of love for us that moves a person to make a commitment to someone that is life-long. Marriage is an amazing, amazing, powerful thing. It is a super-powerful commitment not to leave the other. And it's not just a commitment to be present to each other, to live in the same house, but it's the commitment to *be there* for each other, to be a source of life for each other, to forgive each other, to challenge each other to grow. That's the relationship that the God who's created us wants to have with us. And why, why does he want this relationship?

Well, the second reading gives us a good indication because the second reading is talking about the kingdom that God has come to establish. Jesus is the one who establishes it, and it's a kingdom of forgiveness, it's a kingdom of connection, and it's a kingdom where someone makes a commitment to you and says, "I will be there as a source of life for you no matter who you are or what you do. No action on your part can keep me from loving you." That's the kind of commitment that the New Testament describes, that God longs to make with you and me. And the reason he needs that commitment to be believed in and to be received is because his plan is that he wants to use each and every one of us to be sources of salvation for the world. So he calls each of us to have certain gifts. And the Spirit is God's presence living in you and me, so if God says. *I want to marry you*, it means, *I want to live with you*. And the way he lives *with* you and with me is in the form of the Spirit. So he's inside of us in this form, and the presence of the Spirit enables us to go beyond human limitations, to *transcend* human limitations and to be an instrument of knowledge and of wisdom, of prophecy, healing—all those things. So you can see that the plan of God in this world for us is that it's necessary for him to be connected to us so that he can use us for all that he longs for us to be.

And yet, there's a problem. It's always been the problem with our relationship with God. It's that thing he gave us that you feel sometimes in the Old Testament he almost regrets that he did it—though he really doesn't—but it's *free will.* He's given us the ability to make our own decisions and to choose to do things that are not good for us, not good for the people we love, that we might perceive are not good for our relationship with God. So that's *sin* I'm talking about, alright? Sin is the problem. Now the Old Testament is filled with the issue of sin, and it seems that as we went through those 3,000 years of God working with his Israelite people that sin never seems able to be conquered. So Jesus had to come, God had to come into the world to *conquer* sin. How did he do it? Well, if conquering sin was getting rid of it, he didn't. No, this is the way he conquered it: by not allowing it to ever be for him any kind of obstacle between his love for you and me. Let me say it again: God conquered sin (and the result of sin is the division between ourselves and God—separation) and God dissolved the *power* of sin by not allowing it to separate his love from us. So our challenge is to believe in forgiveness. And the strangest thing in my experience of being a priest is how many times I have felt people not really being able to receive forgiveness from God.

There's an amazing story in the scriptures. It's not the story from this particular Sunday. But remember the story of the rich man who owed his master so much money and he went and pleaded with his master, "Please, please, please, forgive me," and the master let him off the hook? Then he goes out and finds a friend of his who owes him a fraction of what he owed, and he chokes him and says, "You have to pay back everything" and throws him into prison. And then the master in that story goes and finds that cruel man and throws *him* into a dungeon. Now is that about God, who is all about forgiveness, who forgives a man once but when he fails a second time, he doesn't forgive him? No, it's about the importance of *receiving* forgiveness. That man did not sense or feel that he had received a gift when he was forgiven. It didn't change him.

But to be aware of the love of God, the intensity of that love, and to know that it forgives every single thing we've ever done wrong, or anything that anyone has ever done to us, when we know there's the potential within us to be free of all that negativity—until that really sinks in, until we know that that's how much we've been loved, we won't fall in love with God like we're supposed to. It's like God has given us the one gift that frees us from every single thing in our life that causes pain, shame, causes fear, causes anger, causes stress. Forgiveness is the heart of the healing power of the love of God. So this gospel passage is all about that being inaugurated in the world, and I want you to see with me a connection between two things: The story today is the first miracle Jesus performed, the story in the gospel today, and then the story of the last time that Jesus was at a dinner banquet with his disciples. At Cana, he changed water into wine. At the last supper, he took that wine and turned it into blood. So hang onto that image and let me get back to it. There are a couple of things about this story that are fascinating. Number one: It wasn't Jesus' time to do this. It wasn't on his schedule, and there's something about that I've learned to love, because Mary comes up and brings up a point that doesn't seem at first to be important—I mean, it's not a world event—these people are having a party and they run out of wine, and Jesus says, "Well, why should I worry about it?" And she just sort of dismisses that and gets his mind to be thinking, and I don't know what he was actually thinking, but somehow without it being planned, without him *having* to do it, he didn't say, "Alright, if you tell me I have to," he just *did* it. So know that this gift of forgiveness is something that just *is*. Never should we be praying and begging God to forgive us. I mean, that sounds wrong, but he wants to, he longs to—his deepest longing is to stay connected with you and me, and the only way he can do that is to forgive, OK? So he does it without having to.

Then there's this image of abundance. I was trying to figure it out. Six water jars, each holding twenty or thirty gallons, all turned into wine. Maybe a thousand bottles of wine. Five thousand glasses. That's a lot of wine for a party! So he creates it. And he does it as a miracle. It's not anything that's logically done. He just does it by willing it. *This water is now wine.* The water in those jars was used for purification. Every time a good Israelite would get ready to be close to God, he would know himself and his sins, and he would go through a ritual, and he would say, "I want, I want, I need to be purified." They would wash, with ceremonial washing, before they did anything that was sacred. And so what we sense here is Jesus, using the ceremonial waters that purify, and giving them such greater power. You know, John has been trying to explain to people what his baptism in water was, the washing away of sins, washing away of impurity in a ritual done over and over again. To me, it's almost like Jesus is saying, "No, I'm using something way beyond water," and John called it fire and spirit. Well, take a couple of glasses of water and a couple of glasses of wine, and you'll know what fire and spirit feels like! It just sort of shifts everything and changes everything in you.

So it's an interesting image that in this miracle what Jesus is saying is, *There's a new form of forgiveness coming into the world that is so potent it's actually intoxicating—in the good sense—in that it changes our whole demeanor and we find ourselves in a whole new place.* What an incredible thing, to be inviting people into a new relationship with God, where our sins are not the issue. Does that mean we don't want to change? No, no, of course it doesn't! It means not that sin doesn't matter; *of course* it matters! To choose sin is to create pain for yourself and for other people. He doesn't want that. But with every fiber of his body he wants you to be *free* of that. And so what he says is, *I've got to be connected with you in your struggle with sin. I've got to do that, and the only way I know to do that is to redeem you, is to change you, so eventually I'm going to do more than make water into wine; I'm going to do more than give you a stronger dose of what it means to be forgiven; I'm going to actually do something with my blood, with my very body, and I'm going to change everything. I'm going to change YOU, in terms of your potential for love, to draw you away from sin.* Isn't it interesting? We think *punishment* is going to draw us away from sin. Sometimes we're so longing for freedom from the shame that sin creates that we go into such deep depressions. This is what God knows about our nature, and he knows that we need, more than anything else, to have a core sense of our value. And here's a God who said, *I am going to do the most amazing, transformative thing. I can change water into wine; I can change wine into my blood; my blood can be poured out for you, so you don't have to owe me anything for what you do. No punishment required; just change; just believe.* I will just begin to believe that nothing, no weakness, no fault, no history of bad behavior can keep me from the love, from the transforming grace of my God.

Father, your gift of grace, your gift of mercy, the love you pour into our hearts when we are unworthy, is your greatest gift. Give us freedom from all that might demand that we earn something from you. Help us to grow in our awareness that everything that you want to give us is your gift. And we ask this through Christ our Lord. Amen.

Isaiah 62: 1-5

For Zion's sake I will not keep silent,
  and for Jerusalem's sake I will not rest,
until her vindication shines out like the dawn,
  and her salvation like a burning torch.
2 The nations shall see your vindication,
  and all the kings your glory;
and you shall be called by a new name
  that the mouth of the Lord will give.
3 You shall be a crown of beauty in the hand of the Lord,
  and a royal diadem in the hand of your God.
4 You shall no more be termed Forsaken,
  and your land shall no more be termed Desolate;
but you shall be called My Delight Is in Her,
  and your land Married;
for the Lord delights in you,

and your land shall be married.
5 For as a young man marries a young woman,
so shall your builder marry you,
and as the bridegroom rejoices over the bride,
so shall your God rejoice over you.

1Corinthians 12: 4-11

4 Now there are varieties of gifts, but the same Spirit; 5and there are varieties of services,
but the same Lord; 6and there are varieties of activities, but it is the same God who acti-
vates all of them in everyone.7To each is given the manifestation of the Spirit for the
common good.8To one is given through the Spirit the utterance of wisdom, and to another the utterance of knowledge according to the same Spirit, 9to another faith by the
same Spirit, to another gifts of healing by the one Spirit, 10to another the working of
miracles, to another prophecy, to another the discernment of spirits, to another various
kinds of tongues, to another the interpretation of tongues. 11All these are activated by
one and the same Spirit, who allots to each one individually just as the Spirit chooses.

John 2: 1-11

On the third day there was a wedding in Cana of Galilee, and the mother of Jesus was
there. 2Jesus and his disciples had also been invited to the wedding. 3When the wine
gave out, the mother of Jesus said to him, 'They have no wine.' 4And Jesus said to her,
'Woman, what concern is that to you and to me? My hour has not yet come.' 5His mother said to the servants, 'Do whatever he tells you.' 6Now standing there were six stone
water-jars for the Jewish rites of purification, each holding twenty or thirty gallons. 7Jesus said to them, 'Fill the jars with water.' And they filled them up to the
brim. 8He said to them, 'Now draw some out, and take it to the chief steward.' So they
took it.9When the steward tasted the water that had become wine, and did not know
where it came from (though the servants who had drawn the water knew), the steward
called the bridegroom 10and said to him, 'Everyone serves the good wine first, and then
the inferior wine after the guests have become drunk. But you have kept the good wine
until now.' 11Jesus did this, the first of his signs, in Cana of Galilee, and revealed his glory; and his disciples believed in him.

THIRD SUNDAY IN ORDINARY TIME

Nehemiah 8:2-4a, 5-6, 8-10; 1Corinthians 12:12-30; Luke 1:1-4; 4:14-21

Almighty, ever-living God, direct our actions according to your good pleasure, that in the name of your beloved Son, we may abound in good works, through our Lord Jesus Christ, your Son, who lives and reigns with you in the unity of the holy Spirit, one God, for ever and ever. Amen.

When I was growing up as a young Catholic in Chicago, Saint Louis, Philadelphia, Cincinnati, I never heard stories from the Old Testament very often at Mass. Sunday Mass, back then, before the Vatican Council, always had readings from the New Testament. There were exceptions, but almost every Sunday had just an epistle and a gospel. So the priests at the time I was young—before the Vatican Council, which happened in, say 1963, fifty years ago—didn't have the richness of being able to compare the Old Testament with the New Testament as much as I do. And I find it fascinating, because I think we're ready now to look more carefully at the way God works in the Old Testament compared with the way he works with us now.

Let's look at this powerful passage from the Old Testament, from the book of Nehemiah, and grasp one of the struggles that human beings had as they worked with the way that God was working with them. The setting is that the Israelite people have been in exile for some time, away from Jerusalem. They are now back. They have just finished building their temple. And it's a kind of new beginning for them, so as they're getting ready to enter into their new city and worship in their new temple, the priests call them all together outside of their temple and say, "We're about to have a new beginning, and it's important that you understand the wisdom that God has presented to us in the Law, and we want you to hear the Law again and make sure that when you come into this new place, you'll be living according to the way God has called you to live."

So they gather everybody—men, women, and children old enough to understand—outside the temple, and the priests stand on a platform, and they begin to proclaim the Law and to explain exactly what it means. What's *interesting* to me is that they begin with praising God for giving this wisdom and then instead of standing and facing those who are proclaiming it, they prostrate themselves and put their head to the ground. Now I know that's an image of adoration to God, but it's also an interesting image to me that their face and their eyes are looking right into the earth. And I think of human beings coming from the earth and our humanity is described often by our being part of this earth that we come from. It's the *human* part of us; we're of the earth, but we're also human beings of the heavens. We're this strange combination of heaven and earth, of divinity and humanity. But their focus seems to be, in this disposition of their heads down facing the ground, that they are so aware of where they come from and who they are.

What happens is that as they listen to what God is calling them to do, they begin to weep. Now imagine the image: All these people with their head down in front of their new place of worship, weeping because either what they're hearing is really hard to do and they weep over the fact that it's going to be difficult; or more likely, it seems they're weeping over the fact that they know themselves, their humanity, so well that they know that this is not going to work! [chuckles] And we're not going to be able to do this all the time. And remember, forgiveness was not yet revealed as to what it would be in the New Testament.

So the priests say, "No, you have to rejoice in this; you have to be glad you're being told what to do. So go party! Because rejoicing has to be what we're all about." Well, I think it's interesting that there may not have been that much to rejoice about in terms of listening to what God wants you to do. It's like when you and I, especially if we're addicted to something, we're caught in something, and someone says, "You just have to stop that. Just don't do it anymore," and you know how hard that's going to be, and you probably aren't going to be able to do it. Those words are not necessarily words you want to go and rejoice over.

So we have *that* image in the Old Testament. And then there are two images in these New Testament readings. The first one I think is really interesting. Let's just imagine that these people who in the Old Testament are struggling with this challenge to live according to the Law, they're very aware that they're on their own and they've got to do this. They have to figure out *how* to do it. Let's just say that mostly in those days they felt pretty much like it was up to them to perform for God, and they focused on themselves. They had to be the ones to make this happen.

I know there was community. I *know* that, but I'm not sure it was what is described by St. Paul in the second reading. The second reading is amazing! It's so obvious and clear what Paul is trying to share with you and me about the way the world is, now that it has been redeemed, that everything is somehow connected, and everyone is part of everyone else and that we are somehow *one.* It seems like the rejoicing in the New Testament is all about connection, union, communion, oneness—we're all a part of something much bigger than each of us individually, and we all have a role to play and a part to play. Instead of being basically told in this reading what it is we have to do in terms of the Law, it's more like the Law is presumed to already be in our hearts and that we are already somehow intuitively knowing that we shouldn't steal or lie or harm each other. We should respect each other; we should respect our God for all that he does for us; we should honor him. The ten rules are pretty simple.

So we're invited to see in this second reading then that beyond just the call to become loving, forgiving human beings, we're also invited to imagine ourselves as all inter-connected and every one of us has a part to play. I love the image that we're all different parts of the body. (If it wasn't a religious program, I might talk about some people being parts of the body [chuckles], but you know what I mean.) It's like such an interesting image. Some parts of the body are much more attractive than others. "I'd rather be your eye than your toe," or something like that. But it's so beautiful because it's saying every single part is valuable. No single part can exist without the others, and then the line I love: when the body's sick, everyone, all the parts feels bad. What an incredible sense of community when you feel that you are a part of something so much bigger. And whenever you think about things getting better or life being better, we have to understand that we're a part of *making* it better. And the people who might have the gift of mighty deeds and the gift of wisdom will be the spokesperson for us who are other parts of the body, but they couldn't speak without us. It's an amazing, beautiful image of *connection*. We should *never* feel alone.

And then we get to the gospel. And I want to talk about the gospel first just for a moment about these first few lines of Luke's gospel because they give me an insight into why this gospel is a canonical gospel. By "canonical," I mean it's part of the Bible. There were *many* gospels written: the gospel of Thomas, the gospel of Mary Magdalene, the gospel of Peter. *All* of those and many more were out there; yet there are only four that are part of this core teaching of the Bible. And the reason they were included is I think clearly stated by Luke because he said, "I wrote this gospel for this very purpose—that I'm going to look over everything that happened in the life of Jesus that I experience, and out of my own experience—not because someone told me—I'm going to tell you the story in a way that organizes it and helps you to understand as clearly as possible what Jesus is teaching." So it's interesting that the canonical gospels, the four that we have, were written with an *intention* to be used in the way they are, where the others may not have been. Probably weren't. And so we give much more priority to these four. It doesn't mean the others are without any value, but it means they aren't the ones that we would go to to get the core teaching of Jesus. So we're looking at the core teachings of the gospel, always.

Now let's look at this gospel. It's powerful. Jesus goes back to his hometown. Now the thing that might be interesting to know: Before he goes to his hometown in Luke's gospel, he has gone out to the desert for forty days, and he comes to the point at the end of those forty days that the devil comes and tempts him. You know the three temptations: to turn stones into bread, to use everything to make yourself comfortable, to nourish yourself, to feed yourself. It's a kind of image of self-centeredness that he's tempted to have. And then there's the one about jumping off the parapet of the Temple to test God so that we always want to be certain. So test everything. Don't just trust in God, but *test* to be sure he's going to be there when he promises. So lack of trust. And then the temptation to be just like the world, just control everybody, use power over people. It's a great way to live, a great way to make things happen. And he fights all those temptations, and he comes back, and he wants to free you and me from those same exact temptations. So he stands up in his hometown and he reads this reading from the Old Testament, from the book of Isaiah. And listen to it, it's awesome: Someone's come that's anointed. The Spirit of God is in him. And he's got something that he's going to tell you that's so sweet, so good, so fantastic that there's no other word for it but *gospel*—*good news*. Because here's what he's going to do: He's going to heal the brokenhearted, and that's not about helping people go through a bad romance, and have God come into them and say, "It's OK, you're going to find somebody else." No. Healing broken hearts has everything to do with changing hearts from hearts of stone to hearts of flesh, to write the Law on our hearts, so that we *become* the Law, so that we can think with our heart, feel with our heart, connect with our heart, nurture each other through our heart. And then he says, *I want to release everyone that's captive*. And I think that's so connected with the other thing he says: *I want to free people from their blindness*. Free them from their blindness—that's what holds us captive. To not know, to not see, to not realize the things that we do that cause us pain is to imprison us in that pain. The interesting thing about divinity, when it comes into our life, it's like a mirror that holds up, before the ego, the *truth*, and the truth is not always what the ego wants. You know how this gospel story ends, and you'll hear about it for next week. These people have no sooner seen this Jesus announcing this incredible promise than they want to destroy him, kill him, because he shows them by his very presence who they really are. They *weren't* open to him; they *weren't* ready to be healed by him.

And then the last thing that is promised is called being released from prison, but I found in the Bible used by the Eastern Church, it quoted this phrase about being released from prison in this way, and I think it's so beautiful: Jesus announces that when he comes, and he is here now, that he's going to strengthen, with forgiveness, those who are bruised—to strengthen with forgiveness those who are bruised. *Bruised* sounds so much like *abused*. Imagine. All the things that have been done to us that have blinded us, that have kept us in prison, not able to see what we need to see, not able to be as free as we need to be—whether it's spiritual abuse, sexual abuse, whatever kind of abuse it is, it's giving us something bigger than we can handle, more than we can cope with, so we don't know what to do with it, so we're blinded by it and we can't see the effects of it. And to imagine that we have a God who has come into our life to strengthen the forgiveness that we need to work with that, to see that.

So we have then in this reading the proclamation of a new time, a new era, the time that you and I live in, and we need to be unlike those who were in his hometown; we need to be capable of believing that he is able to do what he promises. He said it so often to Catherine of Siena: *People don't believe I'm strong enough to do what I promise; or that I'm loving enough to be with them in their imperfection; or I'm forgiving enough to free them from everything that's happened to them.* But that's the *key* to our faith, to *have* that kind of trust.

Father, you over and over again tell us that we are loved, that we have nothing to fear, and that we are part of a wonderful, wonderful plan that you have designed, and empowered us to accomplish. Bless us with the joy that comes and the praise that is in our heart when we understand fully all that you are and all that you are doing. And we ask this in Jesus' name. Amen.

Nehemiah 8: 2-4A, 5-6, 8-10
[2]Accordingly, the priest Ezra brought the law before the assembly, both men and wom-
en and all who could hear with understanding. This was on the first day of the seventh
month. [3]He read from it facing the square before the Water Gate from early morning
until midday, in the presence of the men and the women and those who could understand; and the ears of all the people were attentive to the book of the law. [4]The scribe
Ezra stood on a wooden platform that had been made for the purpose; [5]And Ezra
opened the book in the sight of all the people, for he was standing above all the people;
and when he opened it, all the people stood up. [6]Then Ezra blessed the Lord, the great
God, and all the people answered, 'Amen, Amen', lifting up their hands. Then they
bowed their heads and worshipped the Lord with their faces to the ground.
[8]So they read from the book, from the law of God, with interpretation. They gave the
sense, so that the people understood the reading. [9] And Nehemiah, who was the gover-

nor, and Ezra the priest and scribe, and the Levites who taught the people said to all the
people, 'This day is holy to the Lord your God; do not mourn or weep.' For all the people wept when they heard the words of the law. [10]Then he said to them, 'Go your way,
eat the fat and drink sweet wine and send portions of them to those for whom nothing
is prepared, for this day is holy to our Lord; and do not be grieved, for the joy of the
Lord is your strength.'

1 Corinthians 12: 12-30

[12]For just as the body is one and has many members, and all the members of the body,
though many, are one body, so it is with Christ. [13]For in the one Spirit we were all baptized into one body—Jews or Greeks, slaves or free—and we were all made to drink of
one Spirit. [14]Indeed, the body does not consist of one member but of many. [15]If the foot
would say, "Because I am not a hand, I do not belong to the body," that would not
make it any less a part of the body. [16]And if the ear would say, "Because I am not an
eye, I do not belong to the body," that would not make it any less a part of the body. [17]If
the whole body were an eye, where would the hearing be? If the whole body were hearing, where would the sense of smell be? [18]But as it is, God arranged the members in the
body, each one of them, as he chose. [19]If all were a single member, where would the
body be? [20]As it is, there are many members, yet one body. [21]The eye cannot say to the
hand, "I have no need of you," nor again the head to the feet, "I have no need of you."
[22]On the contrary, the members of the body that seem to be weaker are indispensable,
[23]and those members of the body that we think less honorable we clothe with greater
honor, and our less respectable members are treated with greater respect; [24]whereas our
more respectable members do not need this. But God has so arranged the body, giving
the greater honor to the inferior member, [25]that there may be no dissension within the
body, but the members may have the same care for one another. [26]If one member suf-
fers, all suffer together with it; if one member is honored, all rejoice together with it.

[27]Now you are the body of Christ and individually members of it. [28]And God has appointed in the church first apostles, second prophets, third teachers; then deeds of power, then gifts of healing, forms of assistance, forms of leadership, various kinds of
tongues. [29]Are all apostles? Are all prophets? Are all teachers? Do all work miracles?
[30]Do all possess gifts of healing? Do all speak in tongues? Do all interpret?

Luke 1: 1-4; 4: 14-21

Since many have undertaken to set down an orderly account of the events that have
been fulfilled among us, [2]just as they were handed on to us by those who from the beginning were eyewitnesses and servants of the word, [3]I too decided, after investigating
everything carefully from the very first, to write an orderly account for you, most excel-

lent Theophilus, [4]so that you may know the truth concerning the things about which
you have been instructed.

14 Then Jesus, filled with the power of the Spirit, returned to Galilee, and a report about
him spread through all the surrounding country. 15He began to teach in their synagogues and was praised by everyone.
16 When he came to Nazareth, where he had been brought up, he went to the synagogue
on the sabbath day, as was his custom. He stood up to read, 17and the scroll of the
prophet Isaiah was given to him. He unrolled the scroll and found the place where it
was written:
18 'The Spirit of the Lord is upon me,
  because he has anointed me
    to bring good news to the poor.
He has sent me to proclaim release to the captives
  and recovery of sight to the blind,
    to let the oppressed go free,
19 to proclaim the year of the Lord's favor.'
20And he rolled up the scroll, gave it back to the attendant, and sat down. The eyes of all
in the synagogue were fixed on him. 21Then he began to say to them, 'Today this scripture has been fulfilled in your hearing.'

FOURTH SUNDAY IN ORDINARY TIME

Jeremiah 1:4-5, 17-19; 1Corinthians 12:31–13:13; Luke 4:21-30

Grant us, Lord our God, that we may honor you with all our mind and love everyone in truth of heart, through our Lord Jesus Christ, your Son, who lives and reigns with you in the unity of the holy Spirit, one God for ever and ever. Amen.

The gospel for this Sunday picks up where the gospel from last Sunday ended. It's when Jesus has come back to his native place, he's in the synagogue, and he's been handed a scroll. The scroll is from Isaiah, and he reads the prophecy about the Messiah coming and the effectiveness of that Messiah and what he's going to *do* for people, how he's going to transform things, transform *people*, open them to this incredible gift called God's healing, where everything that binds us, everything that imprisons us, everything that holds us in darkness can be broken apart, and we can be set free.

I think it's interesting that the idea of a Messiah is so ingrained in everyone; it's that *hope* that we have that things will be better and somehow whatever I'm struggling with will come to an end, and I will *survive;* I will make it. So let's just imagine that Jesus is the hope that every human being has, in the sense that he has, within his teaching, within his very presence, that thing that we so, so deeply long for. It's a way of being in the world, a way of seeing the world and seeing ourselves that somehow enables us to deal with all things, and not be destroyed or harmed.

So let's go back to the first reading. One of the things we see in it is that this Messiah who is prophesied to come into the world is going to be *up against* something; let's just call it *resistance*. And the Messiah himself, and anyone who wants to follow the Messiah and be all that he is seeking to be for us, when we want to continue his work through us, what we need to be ready for is some kind of resistance, some kind of thing that "works against the work." And the beauty of this first reading is the God who created us, who knows us from the beginning, who knows everything about us, is saying, "What I want to do—not just for the Messiah, but for *all* of you—I want somehow to become, for you, like a pillar of iron, of steel, a wall of brass; just this amazing, strong resistant thing that keeps that which would destroy us from doing it! It's interesting that when he tells us that we are going to be empowered, you'll notice that the image is one of *protecting* us, not destroying the enemy. Be careful. Whenever you think about getting rid of something, destroying it, blowing it up, like how many times would you like the world not to have anything negative in it; wouldn't you like all the things that you find as obstacles, for all of them to go away? And it would be nice if that could happen, but really more likely what is planned by God is not so much that the enemy goes away, but the enemy can't penetrate *us*. So we don't get rid of all the negativity, we just are protected from it by this amazing, powerful God who will not let anything harm us.

Now let's go back to the gospel. In this gospel, we see that Jesus has come into his hometown, and if you follow the story, it makes a very, very abrupt shift from the moment that Jesus has finished reading the prophet Isaiah and says, *Now this is being fulfilled in your hearing. This is what's going to happen now. I am the one who's come to show you the way, to empower you to live the way I'm going to show you.* And they are moved by his eloquence, his voice, his demeanor. They are impressed. Many times people will say of the teaching and preaching of Jesus, that he taught unlike the scribes and Pharisees. He taught with great authority. He was just so convinced of what he was saying. Just the tone of his voice, the inflection of his words, gave those who listened to him a sense that he knew exactly what he was talking about—unlike the scribes and Pharisees, who were notorious for talking the talk but not walking the walk.

So Jesus has this positive response from these people and then all of a sudden someone makes a comment that says, "Well, isn't this Joseph's son, the one we grew up with?" And that doesn't seem to be enough to have everything turn, but if you play with the story the way I'm inviting you to, it may be that Jesus already knew that this was going to be a tough audience. And I would say that if you've ever been up in front of a group of people, you know when they're with you or against you, whether they're really receiving or things are bouncing back to you, unaccepted. He *must* have had that intuition, so the real change in their attitude came when Jesus reminds them that there were other prophets in their history that came along that were there, sent by God to the Israelite people, but they couldn't do the work for the Israelites because of some kind of block, some kind of stubbornness, some kind of closed disposition that wouldn't receive what is being offered.

So Elisha came hoping to do something wonderful for the Israelite people but could only do it for foreigners and outsiders. Well, when they hear this, they know that they're being equated with the other Israelites, those who were blocked and unable to receive the gift that God wanted to give them, and a phrase that I used last Sunday that I like so much: When divinity comes, when the truth comes, it holds a mirror up to your ego and you see what you don't really want to see, what you haven't been willing to see, you'll see yourself as you are. If it flies in the face of what you are comfortable with, what you think you should be, it's threatening and you feel attacked, and this human nature that we have is hard-wired, in the reptilian brain that we all share. So if you appear to attack, you get attacked back, or the person who feels attacked flees. And these people decide to attack back, so they decide to kill Jesus. I just find this amazing, you know? Leaving the temple, leaving the church, and deciding to kill the speaker [chuckles].

Anyway! I love the image of Jesus walking against the flow of their hatred and their anger. He's got this wall of brass around him, this pillar of steel holding him up, and he just walks right through their midst and says, *You're not going to stop me, and you're not going to be able to silence what I'm saying. And if you won't receive it, then I'll go and give it to someone who will.* I'd like you to imagine with me what it is that Jesus ultimately, ultimately was offering them that they couldn't receive. I'm going to take a stab at this, and it may not be exactly right, but I'm praying it will resonate with something in you that's truthful and that then has its power to change you. It seems to me that the Israelite people, their greatest problem was, they had a religion that basically worked on their mind and their will. Telling them what to do and then frightening them into doing it by the threat of punishment so that they would find the energy in their will to protect themselves because it's the most basic instinct that we have. "Rather than being killed, I'll do anything to protect myself, to save myself!" It obviously has an overshadowing side that's saying, "It's all about *me*." And Jesus was anything but all about himself. He was all about doing something for someone, freeing someone, opening their eyes, their ears, helping them to see, to speak, to hear—all those things.

And what was it that he was doing? What was at the heart of what he was doing? Well, the second reading gives us an indication that one of the most basic things, the core thing of all Christianity, is the image of love. Love is what it's all about, and there isn't any word that probably has more meanings when we hear it than that word, *love.* Everything from the most lustful desire for someone to the most altruistic desire to heal and change; and everything in between. "It's what I like." "I love it." "I hate it." But when you really get to the heart of the message of Jesus, you know that he had a gift, sometimes called *grace*, given to those who deserve it; *mercy*, given to those who don't deserve it. What *is* this grace? What is this mercy? What is it that he's trying to pour into the hearts of people that has a unique promise, and the promise of this mysterious thing that God longs to pour into us is that it enables us to transcend our human nature? *Transcendence* is what this whole Christian thing is about, becoming aware that we have the power to transcend our humanity. Now often when I use that word, I talk about it as Jesus being able to transcend *his* human nature, being able to heal people, give sight to the blind, being able to raise people from the dead. Those are dramatic examples of something that is much more common, much more experienced by people, and that is when we are somehow capable of being vehicles through which this mysterious thing called *love*, the love that Paul describes so beautifully—never boastful, never self-centered, not prone to anger, it's not jealous, it's not envious. It's this mysterious thing that you might describe as the capacity to connect with everything without judgment. And to somehow not just connect, but to somehow bring with that connection a strength and a power that enables something to happen in that person. And I'm thinking about our human nature and how it responds so *positively* to being affirmed, loved, treated with enormous respect; told over and over again that just as we are, we are so beautiful and so powerful and so wonderful. And how devastating it is when any abuse comes into our life that confuses us and makes us feel that we're objects and only need to *perform* to please someone else in order to be of *any* value. So it strikes me that this thing that Jesus was carrying is this new heart that he had, this amazing, sacred, life-giving, burning heart of love. He's trying to awaken in all of us this center of our body that is called "the heart" that can resonate. It can literally be photographed, this electromagnetic resonance of the heart, which actually goes out about 15 feet. We have this mysterious power inside of us to convey this transforming energy that enters into people and enables them to go beyond the self-centered, self-important thing that we all get caught up in, and the anger and the envy and the jealousy about other people, and the resistance that we often have to anybody having more information than we do—and all that stuff that the ego and the will are so caught up in.

So let's imagine that this gift, this thing we call love, grace, mercy is in this Messiah. He longs to give it to us, and the only way we can receive it is if we allow him to love us, and believe and have confidence that we are loved, which awakens I think even more the power of the resonance of the heart to be able to reach out and do the same thing for other people. And we do it in ways beyond our imagining and ways that don't even need to be done with any kind of real action. It's a kind of force that is just so healing and so life-giving in this world. So I'm asking you, and I want myself so much to believe, in this awesome power of a God who has the power to love and through his love for us as we are and we accept it and we become the resonance of that kind of transforming love that gives others the capacity to be the miracle workers that Jesus was so gifted in being—the source of new life for people.

The Enthusiastic Heart

Father, the miracle of love is all around us. It is your power in us that is enabling those around us to find the peace that is the promise of the kingdom, so bless us with an awareness of this gift we offer. But help us also to recognize that our task is to receive it as well and to be receptive and open to those around us whose love inspires us and moves us to the core of what you've made us to be, and that is your body and your hands and your eyes in this world. Amen.

Jeremiah 1: 4-5, 17-19
4 Now the word of the Lord came to me saying,
5 'Before I formed you in the womb I knew you,
and before you were born I consecrated you;
I appointed you a prophet to the nations.'

17But you, gird up your loins; stand up and tell them everything that I command you.
Do not break down before them, or I will break you before them. 18And I for my part
have made you today a fortified city, an iron pillar, and a bronze wall, against the
whole land—against the kings of Judah, its princes, its priests, and the people of the
land. 19They will fight against you; but they shall not prevail against you, for I am with
you, says the Lord, to deliver you.

1 Corinthians 12: 31–13:13
31But strive for the greater gifts. And I will show you a still more excellent way.

1If I speak in the tongues of mortals and of angels, but do not have love, I am a noisy
gong or a clanging cymbal. 2And if I have prophetic powers, and understand all mysteries and all knowledge, and if I have all faith, so as to remove mountains, but do not
have love, I am nothing. 3If I give away all my possessions, and if I hand over my body
so that I may boast, but do not have love, I gain nothing.
4Love is patient; love is kind; love is not envious or boastful or arrogant5or rude. It does
not insist on its own way; it is not irritable or resentful; 6it does not rejoice in wrongdo-
ing, but rejoices in the truth.7It bears all things, believes all things, hopes all things, en-
dures all things.
8Love never ends. But as for prophecies, they will come to an end; as for tongues, they
will cease; as for knowledge, it will come to an end.9For we know only in part, and we
prophesy only in part; 10but when the complete comes, the partial will come to an
end. 11When I was a child, I spoke like a child, I thought like a child, I reasoned like a
child; when I became an adult, I put an end to childish ways. 12For now we see in a mir-

ror, dimly, but then we will see face to face. Now I know only in part; then I will know fully, even as I have been fully known. 13And now faith, hope, and love abide, these three; and the greatest of these is love.

Luke 4:21-30

21Then he began to say to them, "Today this scripture has been fulfilled in your hearing." 22All spoke well of him and were amazed at the gracious words that came from his
mouth. They said, "Is not this Joseph's son?" 23He said to them, "Doubtless you will
quote to me this proverb, 'Doctor, cure yourself!' And you will say, 'Do here also in
your hometown the things that we have heard you did at Capernaum.'" 24And he said,
"Truly I tell you, no prophet is accepted in the prophet's hometown. 25But the truth is,
there were many widows in Israel in the time of Elijah, when the heaven was shut up
three years and six months, and there was a severe famine over all the land; 26yet Elijah
was sent to none of them except to a widow at Zarephath in Sidon. 27There were also
many lepers in Israel in the time of the prophet Elisha, and none of them was cleansed
except Naaman the Syrian." 28When they heard this, all in the synagogue were filled
with rage. 29They got up, drove him out of the town, and led him to the brow of the hill
on which their town was built, so that they might hurl him off the cliff. 30But he passed
through the midst of them and went on his way.

FIFTH SUNDAY IN ORDINARY TIME

Isaiah 6:1-2, 3-8; 1Corinthians 15:1-11; Luke 5:1-11

Keep your family safe, O Lord, with unfailing care, that relying solely on the hope of heavenly grace, they may be defended always by your protection, through our Lord Jesus Christ, your Son, who lives and reigns with you in the unity of the holy Spirit, one God, for ever and ever. Amen.

I'm always looking for the connections in readings when I work with the set of readings that is given to us as the source of the wisdom we long to be filled with each week. And in this particular set of readings, there is the same theme in each one of them that's really clearer than usual, where it's not so obvious—the connection. In the first reading, we see someone who is in touch with the presence of the glory of God, his awesomeness and his beauty and his power, and the reaction to being in the presence of God is to, in a way, turn to the other direction and to feel that one is not capable of being in this presence of goodness because we, human beings, know our human nature, know that we fail, and so there's the image in this first reading of a man who says, "Get away from me. I am a man of lying lips. And I *live* with people with lying lips." It's a great image of human nature. It's hard for us to speak the truth, and we tend to create a world that is filled with illusions. Often, if you have two or three people agree that an illusion is real, then it *becomes* real.

In the second reading, we see Paul, who is describing what happened to him in terms of *his* experience with the holy, when Christ appeared to him on the road to Damascus, he was overwhelmed, became blind, and had this amazing transformation. And one of the things now as he speaks about it much later, he's saying very clearly he was gifted with this presence. Not because of anything he did; in fact, he says, "I am the one who is probably the least of all the apostles in terms of being chosen, because I'm the lowest candidate because my work was to work *against* the church." And he didn't have a conversion and then say, "No, I shouldn't be persecuting these new Christians. I now see the truth" and then God comes to him. No, God comes to him in the person of Jesus *while Paul is in his sin.* A very important point. And he's aware of it. He knows that this was a gift to him. It is called *grace.* Now think of grace as unmerited love. And it transformed him. He says something so beautiful that it gives me a little bit of a chill. He said, "I've been transformed by this experience of being loved in my imperfection, being filled with God's Spirit as I was still in my sin. And who I am is because of grace, because of this love, this forgiveness that comes from our Father."

And then he says very clearly, *What I'm doing is preaching that. As I preach, you will believe.* It always gives me a chill when I think about myself, preaching right this moment to you, to your heart, and realizing that when anyone preaches, and they try to describe the God who is, it's such an awesome responsibility, and yet when one is open to being used by God, God's certainly not going to depend on the individual to be so smart or so clever but will fill that preacher with the teaching that he longs for his people to believe in. And so I can be in a sense in this position without great anxiety. What I *need* to believe is that God comes to me in my imperfection, in my egocentricity, in all my narcissistic sides, that he comes and says, *I will use you.*

And then we have in the gospel passage, you know, this experience of Jesus revealing to people who he really is by his mighty works, by his miraculous capacity to make things happen. And when he creates this large catch of fish, Simon's first response—it's so interesting!—his first response when he's in the presence of something that we can call the holy, he immediately thinks about his imperfection. "Get away from me. Get away. I'm a sinful man." So all this seems to me to be pointing to one simple truth that I'm asking you to look into yourselves and ask yourselves this question: Where are you with your imperfections in terms of where God is with you *because* of them? In other words, how do you feel that God sees your weaknesses? Now one of the things I find fascinating about the way God intends for us to receive his grace and what God intends for us to *do* with his grace—which is his love, his forgiveness, his mercy—what is he doing with that? How does he expect that to work in us?

Well, it would seem to me that when you look at everything that the Incarnation represents or taught, it's that God who loves us is the God who wants to come and dwell within us and enable us to treat each other as he treats us. Now that last statement, that we're going to treat each other as God treats us—it seems to me so crucial that we understand how God treats us in our imperfection—because nothing is more dangerous and more destructive than when people in relationships with each other somehow demand more than a person can give, and when that person can't produce—and I'll use a *strong* word—there is a *rejection* of them, a condemnation of their sin.

And all I want to tell you is that there is nothing in God that wants to condemn your sinfulness. Does that mean he's OK with sin? Not at all. But he has this amazing capacity to understand that our choices, that often include something destructive to ourselves and to someone else, that so often that's not something that's so much *willed* as it is about a *weakness* inside of us, or a missing part of us, or a lack of trust in the way God loves us. There's a powerful, powerful statement in a book that St. Catherine of Siena wrote about her visions, and she says that God came to her and said, *My problem with human beings is that they don't think that I really love them enough or that I can love them enough, or that I can be strong for them, or that I can accomplish all kinds of things within them. They don't believe that I can convert them to the truth; they don't believe that I can open their eyes and help them to see.*

And think about that. If there is anything in us that allows us to imagine that when we are weak, God backs away or does not choose then to be with us, we're in a very, very dangerous place. Because what happens is that without realizing it, we have this sense that God condemns our weaknesses and therefore we should condemn the weaknesses of the people around us. So we become hypercritical, demanding, judging, saying things to people like "Your behavior is unacceptable. And if your behavior is unacceptable, then *you* are unacceptable to us." And nothing would be further from the way God longs for us to treat one another because there's nothing in God that would do that to a human being—because he knows us so perfectly, that for us to be condemned for our weaknesses is the *antithesis* of how we're converted. It's his grace, unmerited love, his forgiveness that comes to us when we're at our worst, when we're weak.

And when we can feel that love coming into us, when we in a sense don't deserve it, then there is this mysterious thing I call *transformation.* It frees us. Forgiveness frees us. Think of it. If you feel responsible to shape yourself up in order to be pleasing to God, then you're under a lot of pressure. And there are probably a lot of things you would say to yourself like, "I hate myself when I do this. I can't stand this part of me. I want to destroy this part of me."

If you're ever caught in saying those kinds of things to yourself about your imperfections, as you fear they may be separating you from God, then just think of what you're doing to the people around you—whether it's done literally, out loud, or whether it's a feeling inside. Isn't it interesting that we actually feel justified in rejecting people because they can't shape up to what we want, and then feeling like, "Well, I'm not responsible for them anymore because they simply haven't proven to me that they are worthy of my love." Now nobody would probably really *say* that, but that's really what's going on.

And when we say that someone is not worthy of our love, then we have to look inside of ourselves and ask, "Am I saying that to myself about my God? Am I saying that he won't come to me when I'm imperfect, so the one way I could try to achieve perfection is to become a tremendously strong-willed person who simply denies myself any kind of freedom to make a mistake, and that's a pretty tense, rigid life. Or are we just doing something that somehow *denies* that we're doing something wrong? That's another way we get away with thinking we're acceptable to God. We just won't *look* at our weaknesses, and when you don't look at your weaknesses, then the *last* thing you're going to be able to deal with is the weaknesses of somebody else.

So look deeply into your relationship with holiness, divinity, perfection—and your human nature, which is anything *but* those things. And if you don't see those as two things that are *made* for each other, perfectly designed, so that the one enters freely into the other, and there's where the transformation happens—the ability for divinity to enter into broken, sinful, dirty humanity (if you want to call it that)—that whole thing is what we call forgiveness, mercy, grace. That's the heart of what it means to be a believer, to know that that's where we stand with God. And if we can stand in that place with God, we're much more likely to be able to open our hearts to everything that is imperfect in us and still feel the love of God, and that love of God is the thing that transforms. So I hope you can feel this with me, because it's such a major issue. I see all around me judgmental people, critical people. I hear people saying things about themselves that—as far as the way they feel about themselves and their humanity—they can be *so* condemning. Self-condemnation, and that just flows over to everything else. Let me tell you: Condemnation does nothing but *injure*. It *never* heals. It keeps wounds wide open, and it's *abusive*. It's *spiritual* abuse.

Our challenge is to enter into the kingdom that God has created for us. He made it so clear in everyone he chose and everyone he spent time with on this earth. He wanted to be around people who were honest, imperfect sinners—those are the people he loved. Does that mean he loved sin? Absolutely not. But he loves the part of human nature that can believe that someone can love them even though there's nothing they're doing that would give them the sense that they've earned it.

Father, your mercy is beyond anything we can imagine—its depth, its power to see past our faults and to penetrate into our hearts, and there awaken the potential that we have for goodness. So bless us with a greater awareness of this gift, help it to free us from so much of the bondage that criticism and judgment and condemnation create, and we ask this in Jesus' name. Amen.

Isaiah 6:1-2, 3-8;

In the year King Uzziah died, I saw the Lord seated on a high and lofty
throne, with the train of his garment filling the temple. 2Seraphim were
stationed above; 3One cried out to the other:
"Holy, holy, holy is the LORD of hosts!
All the earth is filled with his glory!"
4At the sound of that cry, the frame of the door shook and the house was
filled with smoke.
5Then I said, "Woe is me, I am doomed! For I am a man of unclean lips,
living among a people of unclean lips, and my eyes have seen the King,
the LORD of hosts!"6Then one of the seraphim flew to me, holding an em-
ber which he had taken with tongs from the altar.
7He touched my mouth with it. "See," he said, "now that this has touched
your lips, your wickedness is removed, your sin purged."
8Then I heard the voice of the Lord saying, "Whom shall I send? Who will
go for us?" "Here I am," I said; "send me!"

1 Corinthians 15: 1-11

1Now I am reminding you, brothers and sisters, of the gospel I preached to
you, which you indeed received and in which you also stand. 2Through it
you are also being saved, if you hold fast to the word I preached to you,
unless you believed in vain. 3 For I handed on to you as of first importance
what I also received: that Christ died for our sins in accordance with the
scriptures; 4that he was buried; that he was raised on the third day in accordance with the scriptures; 5that he appeared to Cephas, then to the
Twelve. 6After that, he appeared to more than five hundred brothers at
once, most of whom are still living, though some have fallen asleep. 7After
that he appeared to James, then to all the apostles. 8Last of all, as to one
born abnormally, he appeared to me. 9For I am the least of the apostles,
not fit to be called an apostle, because I persecuted the church of God.
10But by the grace of God I am what I am, and his grace to me has not been
ineffective. Indeed, I have toiled harder than all of them; not I, however,
but the grace of God [that is] with me. 11Therefore, whether it be I or they,
so we preach and so you believed.

Luke 5: 1-11

1 While the crowd was pressing in on Jesus and listening to the word of
God, he was standing by the Lake of Gennesaret. 2He saw two boats there

alongside the lake; the fishermen had disembarked and were washing
their nets. 3 Getting into one of the boats, the one belonging to Simon, he
asked him to put out a short distance from the shore. Then he sat down
and taught the crowds from the boat. 4 After he had finished speaking, he
said to Simon, "Put out into deep water and lower your nets for a catch."
5 Simon said in reply, "Master, we have worked hard all night and have
caught nothing, but at your command I will lower the nets." 6 When they
had done this, they caught a great number of fish and their nets were tear-
ing. 7 They signaled to their partners in the other boat to come to help
them. They came and filled both boats so that they were in danger of sinking. 8 When Simon Peter saw this, he fell at the knees of Jesus and said,
"Depart from me, Lord, for I am a sinful man." 9 For astonishment at the
catch of fish they had made seized him and all those with him, 10 and likewise James and John, the sons of Zebedee, who were partners of Simon.
Jesus said to Simon, "Do not be afraid; from now on you will be catching
men." 11 When they brought their boats to the shore, they left everything and followed him.

FIRST SUNDAY OF LENT

Deuteronomy 26:4-10; Romans 10:8-13; Luke 4:1-13

Grant, almighty God, through the yearly observances of holy Lent, we may grow in understanding of the riches hidden in Christ and by worthy conduct pursue their effects, through our Lord Jesus Christ, your Son, who lives and reigns with you in the unity of the holy Spirit, one God for ever and ever. Amen.

We've just begun the season that I think all of us know as one of those times when we're invited to go deeper, to reflect, to wonder more about what this whole task is, when we think about our God calling us to wholeness, to fullness. So my prayer, for you and for me, during this season is that we grow in awareness, in full consciousness of what we're engaged in, what we're really working on, what we're working *for*. There's been a long tradition that the First Sunday of Lent deals with the temptations that Jesus received from the devil. I think they're the most important things to look at as we begin a journey of more intense spiritual growth—because it reveals to us something very, very essential about our human nature, what our weakness is, what we're asked to deal with.

But I want to begin my thoughts with the first reading, because it's a beautiful description of the human condition as we see it in the Old Testament, and what we see is that human beings after the fall of Adam and Eve were wandering around as if they were, in a sense, separated from their God, and they were aliens in a strange world. And as they moved about this world, what they were longing for is to grow and to become something strong and good—because that's one of those gifts that's deep inside each of us, the gift of longing for goodness and wholeness and freedom. So God entered into the lives of these people and made them into a community, a great nation. And then they found themselves as they were formed into a community and found themselves the victim of oppression, a spirit that was somehow against their very human nature. Instead of building them up, instead of helping them to become all that they could be, they were oppressed, burdened, weighed down. And then the story is that God somehow entered into their lives, and with terrifying power and signs of wonder and a strong outstretched arm, he freed them from their slavery and brought them to the land of milk and honey. That's our story. That's every human being's story. I come into the world, I find myself at odds often with who I am, where I am, what should I do? We long to become great and strong, but often when we work hard at becoming great and strong, we find ourselves choosing things that instead of freeing us, oppress us and burden us. And then there's the *real work*: freedom from the heaviness and the burden that we so often get entangled in as we seek to find fullness on this planet.

In the second reading, from Romans, he talks about a way to find salvation and this way to find salvation is in two ways: to confess with your mouth that Jesus is Lord and to believe in your heart he's been raised from the dead. That's an easily over-simplified formula for salvation. I can believe that Jesus is the Messiah. It's not that hard for me to somehow believe in my heart also that he rose from the dead. So it's not just two things that we're asked to be convinced of or believe. It's two things we're asked to *experience*. To be able to confess something with our mouth, it's necessary for us to have experienced it. That gives our words authority. For me to say something to you because I've been told to say it is one thing; for me to say something to you because I've experienced it is something quite different.

So we have to understand and know Jesus as Lord. What kind of lord? What is he lord over? What does his lordship mean to me? And in terms of his rising from the dead, it seems we have to have some sense of what it means and how it feels to be lifted up out of our human condition, to be somehow not just converted, changed, redirected, but to be truly transformed, changed, radically changed from the core. That's what it means to believe that Jesus rose from the dead; that he's given us something that bypasses, that over-rides all of the logic that we sometimes have about the way life is—because death has always been seen, still is feared to be the end, and yet we see in the resurrection of Jesus that the way he lived his life, the death that he endured was not the end but the breakthrough, the beginning, the key to entering into the fullness of life. So he came back and made it clear, fully clear, what he was teaching.

So that's the thing that we're engaged in, this amazing journey to find this wisdom, this truth that God has hidden in Jesus. Notice the opening prayer was, we're asking God, as a community, to please bless us with wisdom that has been hidden in Christ. And that just says to me that it must be something much more complicated, much more complicated than what the Old Testament gave us. And that's not to say that the Old Testament was inappropriate or wrong. It was *perfect* at the time, but all it could really do is call us to a kind of conversion. Turn away from evil and turn toward the good. Just think about that for a minute. If I want to turn away from evil and turn to the good, that means the *goal* that I'm after has shifted from something self-centered and damaging to me and to others. The goal is now to be something that is *helpful* to me and helpful to others. It *pleases* my God. And in a way you could use the same ego and the same human energy to move from doing evil to doing good, because you can do good for your *own* good. You can do evil for your own good. When I say you can do good for your own good, it means, if you look at it, if you see at the heart of our human condition that we have a kind of egocentricity, a kind of narcissistic side, we're going to see in a few moments what is worked on by the devil, on Jesus in the desert. But when you look at that, you say, "Well, OK, if that's our weakness, our kind of Achilles' heel, then if I turn around and decide that I'm going to use that same kind of self-centered, narcissistic energy to say, 'I'm going to now do the *right* thing, for *me,* because I get *rewarded* for it.' And instead of saying maybe, 'I'm going to get what I can from people and use them,' I'm going to say, 'No, I'm not going to use them, but I'm going to do something for them so I can get from God what I need.'" Reminds me of a story of a very successful businessman, and very aggressive. Always worked harder than anybody else in the office. He always wanted to be the best, the best salesman, the best record. He had a tremendous drive to be successful and somehow he was converted from the business world to a monastery and felt that, "No, I want to give my life to God." And he got into the monastery and checked everyone else out, and said "I can out-fast these people. I can out-do them in goodness. I can be the best one in this monastery. Watch me. I will be the king of the monastery!" I wouldn't call that a transformation. I'd call that a simple shift. From one goal to another, but using the same means.

Having *transformation,* the thing that God has planned for us from the beginning, the thing we call redemption, the thing that Jesus came into the world to accomplish, this transformation is something much more radical. It's a re-shifting of the way we are, the way we see. It creates something *awesome.* And what it creates is a human being who transcends his human nature. Not condemns it or destroys it, but goes beyond it.

So let's look at these temptations. They're really interesting. I love the way that in the gospel of Luke, different from Matthew, they're arranged in a different order, and I think this order seems more appropriate because the first two are really the same temptation. Here's Jesus, he's just been baptized, and he's getting ready to begin his spiritual journey of awakening people to the transforming power that he is going to win for them. So the devil comes to him at the end of forty days of reflection. I can't imagine what those forty days were like, what Jesus had to think about, what he had to focus on. But if you look at it simply as a typical human experience or something like it, it would be,

"Here I am, about to begin this journey and this work, and it's an awesome work, and I'm committed to it, and it's going to be really difficult and it's maybe not going to turn out—I have no guarantee it's going to turn out the way I want it to turn out." So he must have known intuitively that "I have to let go of all of my expectations as I do this. I've got to be free of anything in this that's coming from simply my human nature—in all of its goodness." We have human nature that is weak and prone to evil; we have human nature that at the same time is very prone to good. So he is looking at this and he's saying, *Alright*. The devil comes along and says, "Here's the deal. You're going to have amazing powers. You know that you're a gifted human being. You know that you can make changes in people that are going to be phenomenal. It's like you can change one thing into another. So let's look at that power. How about changing these stones into bread? And I know how hungry you are and how in need your body is for nourishment. And you've got this human longing. Why don't you use this gift you have of being able to transform things and use it for you, for your own needs, for your own satisfaction?" And Jesus says, "No, I'm not going to do that. I'm not going to do what I know you want me to do when that's going to be feeding my ego, my self, my needs." Then he takes him and puts him on a high mountain and shows him the world in all of its glory and says, "You know what? Everything that human beings long for in terms of power, control can be yours." And let me tell you, there's something in all of us that loves power and control. And we do respect it. When we're with somebody who has ultimate power, we have a different feeling about who they are, how much more important they are. Take anybody who's in charge of something—the president of anything, from the United States down to the president of the parish council—they have more authority, we treat them differently and the ego *loves* that. And the devil says, "I can give you all of this. ALL of it. You are going to be so talented and so charismatic, and I can give you more power to accomplish that." And maybe he was subtly saying, "Use that power to change people. Don't do this thing that you're getting, this instinct about what you're *supposed* to do, which is to forgive everything and not to fight everything and not to try to destroy all that is evil." Jesus must have understood that there was a call here that was different from the way the world works. So he says, "No, I'm not going to do that." And the last one, it's a shift. "OK. If you're not going to be self-centered and narcissistic, you're going to trust in something outside of yourself to take care of you. Alright. Let's test it. You've got a God who you think is going to take care of you, and you're going to do things that are going to be misunderstood and you're going to be asking people to go through some radical change that is so over their head, beyond their imagining, and you know it's going to be tough and you may not make it, but you say you're going to trust in God. Well, let's test him." And Jesus says, "No, I'm not. I'm never going to test him. I trust him, implicitly." So it's like Jesus is experiencing this transformation out of humanity into full divinity. I should say that his moment now is that he's just been anointed in his baptism. He's ready to experience this task that's before him. And he's setting the stage for the way it's going to work. He's not going to do it for anything that is basically about *him*. He's not going to do it in the way the *world* does it. And he's going to do it in a way that is not fearful, but one that he trusts implicitly that he's going to make it. It's almost like he's having this overwhelming sense that "my God, who has created me and called me to be this Messiah who is not the messiah that people expected." People expected a messiah who was going to be wielding this sword and destroying evil, cutting out all the bad people. And just think about how many times you see that in an individual who's a believer who wants to destroy, get rid of everything that's not right. Somehow that's *not* the issue. It's not destroying evil. It's somehow, mysteriously, *surrendering* to it, which doesn't make *any* sense to the mind; *forgiving* it, which seems to almost say then that you're giving it power and somehow when you do that, there's a mysterious transformation that happens, a shift, a radical capacity to enter into a new place. It's called *the kingdom*, the place of peace. And that's the joy that we're looking forward to at the end of Lent, the joy of a resurrected life after Easter.

Father, help us to see what is hidden, to enter into the mystery of who you are and who you've called us to become. Draw us out of the ways of the world and into the ways of your heart. Make our hearts like yours so that we can truly profess, with our very presence, the wisdom and the mystery that we celebrate during this season, and we ask this through Christ our Lord. Amen.

Deuteronomy 26: 4-10

[Moses said to the people:]
4 The priest shall then receive the basket from you and shall set it in front of the altar of the LORD, your God.
5 Then you shall declare before the LORD, your God, 'My father was a wandering Aramean who went down to Egypt with a small household and lived there as an alien. But there he became a nation great, strong and numerous.
6 When the Egyptians maltreated and oppressed us, imposing hard labor upon us,
7 we cried to the LORD, the God of our fathers, and he heard our cry and saw our affliction, our toil and our oppression.

[8]He brought us out of Egypt with his strong hand and outstretched arm, with terrifying
power, with signs and wonders;
[9] and bringing us into this country, he gave us this land flowing with milk and honey.
[10] Therefore, I have now brought you the first fruits of the products of the soil which
you, O LORD, have given me.' And having set them before the LORD, your God, you
shall bow down in his presence.

Romans 10: 8-13

[Brothers and sisters:]
[8] But what does it say? "The word is near you, in your mouth and in your
heart" (that is, the word of faith that we preach),
[9] for, if you confess with your mouth that Jesus is Lord and believe in your
heart that God raised him from the dead, you will be saved.
[10] For one believes with the heart and so is justified, and one confesses with
the mouth and so is saved.
[11] For the scripture says, "No one who believes in him will be put to shame."
[12] For there is no distinction between Jew and Greek; the same Lord is Lord of
all, enriching all who call upon him.
[13] For "everyone who calls on the name of the Lord will be saved."

Luke 4: 1-13

[1] Filled with the holy Spirit, Jesus returned from the Jordan and was led by the
Spirit into the desert
[2] for forty days, to be tempted by the devil. He ate nothing during those days,
and when they were over he was hungry.
[3] The devil said to him, "If you are the Son of God, command this stone to become bread."
[4] Jesus answered him, "It is written, 'One does not live by bread alone.'"
[5] Then he took him up and showed him all the kingdoms of the world in a
single instant.
[6] The devil said to him, "I shall give to you all this power and their glory; for it
has been handed over to me, and I may give it to whomever I wish.
[7] All this will be yours, if you worship me."
[8] Jesus said to him in reply, "It is written: 'You shall worship the Lord, your
God, and him alone shall you serve.'"

9 Then he led him to Jerusalem, made him stand on the parapet of the temple,
and said to him, "If you are the Son of God, throw yourself down from here,
10 for it is written: 'He will command his angels concerning you, to guard
you,'
11 and: 'With their hands they will support you, lest you dash your foot
against a stone.'"
12 Jesus said to him in reply, "It also says, 'You shall not put the Lord, your
God, to the test.'"
13 When the devil had finished every temptation, he departed from him for a
time.

SECOND SUNDAY OF LENT

Genesis 15:5-12, 17-18; Philippians 3:17 – 4:1; Luke 9:28-36

O God, who have commanded us to listen to your beloved Son, be pleased, we pray, to nourish us inwardly by your Word, that with spiritual sight made pure, we may rejoice to behold your glory, through our Lord Jesus Christ, your Son, who lives and reigns with you in the unity of the holy Spirit, one God for ever and ever. Amen.

We continue our journey during the season of Lent. I want to go back to the very beginning of the scriptures that we constantly, week after week, turn to for wisdom, understanding, insight. We go back to the very beginning of the story about how sin entered the world, the story of Adam and Eve. In that story, there's much to ponder, but one of the things that I'd like to focus on is, what was it that God really didn't want Adam and Eve to do? Why did he give them the ability to eat of all the trees in the Garden, but not that *one* tree?

It's like every good fairy tale: when a story starts like that, you know that somebody is going to eat of that tree. And what I'd like you to imagine with me is that what was happening to them was that they were growing in their consciousness of who they are as human beings, and God gave us this amazing gift that is both our glory and, in a way, our shame—that we can think, we can reflect, we can imagine, and the other creatures that God created cannot do that. One of the things, it seems to me, that they began to wonder about was—and certainly there was someone there to pose it as a lie—what God would really like you to do is to figure everything out, or *know* everything; to know what should be and what shouldn't be, to know what's right, to know what's wrong. It's like that capacity that you and I have to say, "This is the way I should be. This is the way *you* should be. This is the way the *world* should be." And how *dangerous* that is, because what it leaves out is *mystery*. What it leaves out is the thing that Jesus came to reveal to us: the mystery of how it is that we enter into the kingdom.

So I want to begin my thoughts with the idea that we are to be careful of how we see God, how we see ourselves, and how we see the world, because we are prone, because of original sin, to imagine things that are not real. Or maybe a better way to say it is that they're only *half true.*

Now the story we have in the first reading is the story of the beginning of our faith, when God called Abram and told him that he would make a promise to him that he would have posterity, that he would have many children. Now that may not strike you and me as powerfully as it did for Abram, but Abram was childless, and his wife Sarai had no children, and one of the things that was considered in the imaginations of those who lived at that time—and this is surprising to a lot of people, but in the Old Testament there is really nothing—except there in the end there might be some allusions to it, but there's nothing in the Old Testament coming from God to his people that says that God has created a place for them called *heaven,* and when they die, they don't cease to exist but they will continue to live. They *did* not believe that. They thought that when their life was over, it was *over. Sheol,* the place where you would go, was more like a graveyard where life was terminated, and it just *stayed* terminated.

The only way you had any sense of any kind of longevity was that you would have *children* and in your children you would live, and in *their* children's children you would live because you were a part of them. So posterity had *everything* to do with that instinctual feeling every human being has: "I want to make a difference, and I don't want to go away. I want to live. I want to continue to live."

So this is an amazing promise. It's almost like he says to Abram, in the language Abram would understand it, *I am the God who is entering into your life, and what I want to do is to awaken in you a way, a way to achieve what your human nature is longing for: fullness, wholeness, eternity, love.* And what he says, basically, in the story is *I will ask you to trust me in this seemingly strange promise I'm making* (because already Abram was old). And Abram says, "How can I trust you? What sign will you give me that I can trust in you?" And God says, *I'll make a covenant with you. I'll make a promise.* So he used what people at that time knew, that there was a ritual that would be like signing a contract in a mortgage place today when you sign fifty sheets of paper. What he's saying is, *I will promise you that I will not break my part of the bargain without my—in a sense—being destroyed, who I am.* What he's saying is, *My* ***promise*** *is who I am. If my promise is not real, then I'm of no value.* So the idea of cutting the animals in half, and usually two people who made an agreement would walk between the two animals. And the idea was, if you broke the promise, you would have the same fate as the animals. It would split you in half. You would die. So here's the commitment that he makes. Now I'm just going to take the story on quickly.

You know that eventually, many years after Abram was called to leave Ur for

Canaan, God did keep his promise with Abram and Sarai, and said that you're going to have a *son*. By this time Abram was ninety-nine and Sarai was in her nineties, so Sarai laughed. And that's how the word "Isaac" was translated: as "laughter." It was also at this time that God renamed them Abraham and Sarah. And they entered into the covenant with Isaac. So even though that promise was made, it sounds like there were many years that went by where Abram wasn't sure how it would unfold. When he finally saw it happening, he was sort of incredulous. That was when Abram was ninety-nine and wouldn't die until he was 175. So let's say he was just a teen-ager still. [chuckles]

Anyway, he grows in his understanding of who God is. He keeps his promise, and then comes the *test*, which is really weird to me. Here's the gift of longevity, here's eternal life in the image of the son. And then God says to Abraham, *I want you to kill him. So take him out on a mountain, build a little fire, get out your knife, and stab your only son in the heart.* What was going on in him? The fascinating thing to me was that Abraham was willing to do it; willing to do it. As he lifted the knife, the Voice comes and says, *No. Don't do this. You have proven to me that you trust me.*

So let's just say the story is about God making a promise, fulfilling that promise in one sense, and then almost asking us to imagine letting go of the fulfillment of that promise, as a sign that we believe he'll keep his promise. How's that for a paradox? He promises to take care of us, but it's almost like he sets us up that we are in a situation where it doesn't *seem* like he's taking care of us, and then he wants to say, *Do you trust me?* Look at the life of Jesus. It's amazing! This man comes into the world and knows that he's called to save the world by teaching them what it means to be a follower of God, what it means to be fully human, what it means to love. And one of the things that he goes through, the most obvious thing he goes through is this horrific disappointment of starting this ministry and in three short years, it's all falling apart, and the very things that he hoped to accomplish, convincing people of who he was, turning the church around so they weren't so hypocritical and so phony and so fake—all of that that he was promised by God, the Father, that he would be able to accomplish—he goes through a sequence of events that would make *anyone*—outside observer, the person involved in it, saying, "I failed. It didn't work. Completely failed. My disciples are scattered; the people I came to save have humiliated me, killed me."

And then an explosion, an amazing transformation, that Jesus then enters into a new way of being. We call it his resurrected body, but just think of it as a transformation that happens when anyone can do what Abraham was asked to do, but didn't have to follow through. Jesus was asked, and he *had* to follow through. What *is* that mystery that we are invited to imagine that we have before us, that there is something we're asked to do, that doesn't make a lot of logical sense, but it's almost as if we're asked to be able to trust that when we're in that disposition of finding nothing going on in our life as the way in which we thought God promised it would be, when we're in that, where are we? That's the question: Where are we at that moment?

For me, I get scared. I get angry. I get depressed. I don't know what's going on because I don't see anything happening like I thought it was going to happen, and things go really south for me. So I'm listening to Paul in the second reading, and he's talking to people, and he's saying, "I want to make sure there isn't anybody out there who's an enemy of the cross of Christ. An enemy of the cross is the enemy of what I'm trying to talk about." The enemy of anyone who can trust through the fact that life is *nothing* like we hoped it would be, and it's *all* going the wrong way, and yet we have this absolute, deep conviction that it *is moving* in the direction it's supposed to.

And he says there are a lot of people out there, and they're all caught up in the world. Their stomach is their god, their glory is their "shame," which is a really tricky thing, but all the research I did on it, it means that they're probably the people who are just worried about the Law, following the Law, and if they're following the Law, they expect everything to work out. There were so many dietary laws that the Pharisees followed to the letter, yet their hearts were far from what they were supposed to be. "Their glory is their shame" is probably reference to the fact there are people who were glorying in their circumcision—the sign of the covenant between God and his people—and what they're saying is, "God has made this promise to me, so I'm saved. I'm fixed, and I'm doing everything right, and I can't feel the pain of the people around me. I can't sense things that are wrong with people." So I can feel that instinct inside of me that says, "I know what that feels like when I'm not engaged in the real work. I'm just working hard at being clean and fixed and perfect."

So then we look at the gospel. And the gospel is that incredible moment in the life of the disciples when they were shown for the first time the cross. And the cross was the words of Jesus saying to them: *I'm going to tell you something. I'm going to go to Jerusalem, and I'm going to turn myself over to these people who are so antagonistic towards me as I try to break them out of their enclosed, selfish, tiny little world. I'm going to let them destroy me, and then I'm going to rise again.* Well, they didn't understand "rising again," so they were completely perplexed and confused. It's almost like Jesus is saying, *OK. This is the cross, this is what I'm asking you to embrace. And that's what we all have to embrace, so I want to show you something about me so that you can somehow understand, because this is what you really want me to be in the world, this glorious light that everybody bows down to, and everybody turns to, and I fix all the problems.*

You know the image of the Messiah forever in the Old Testament was that somebody was going to come in to *fix* everything. How many of us, how many times have I, wanted God to fix everything in my life. Well, accepting the cross means we don't expect everything to be fixed. In fact, things perhaps are supposed to fall apart and *never* get fixed here. How do we deal with that? Do we blame people because they haven't done what they're supposed to? Do we get angry? Do we blame God because he's not really there? Do we blame ourselves because we didn't do what was right? What happens if you're like Jesus—you did *everything* right, and still everything goes wrong. That's the key. That's what Jesus was discussing with Moses and Elijah. They were discussing *the cross*. And I imagine Moses and Elijah saying, "Wow! I didn't know this is what it's going to be." And Jesus is radiant, and the disciples—Peter, James, and John—who are there don't know what to make of it. They can't even *fathom* it. But just *pray* that we all will understand more fully the mystery that this is all pointing to, because we will be sticking with this image through the next couple of weeks until we get to the point where we re-enact that cross, that surrender, that allowing everything to somehow, as crazy as it is, as broken as it is, as sinful as it is, as harmful as it seems to be for everybody—all those things are going to be subjected to Jesus being there, all going to work together for the good.

Father, so often on this journey that you give to us, we experience darkness, and we experience the doubt that comes from our anxiety that the world you have given us, the people in our lives that you've given us, somehow are not going the way we want them to go, or becoming the people we want them to become, or they're causing us pain instead of joy. So bless us when this darkness overwhelms us, that we will have the faith of Abram and this amazing wisdom of Christ so that we can experience the cross. And instead of destroying us, it lifts us up to the fullness of eternal life. And we ask this through Christ our Lord. Amen.

Genesis 15-5-12, 17-18

5 [The Lord God] took Abram outside and said: Look up at the sky and count the stars, if
you can. Just so, he added, will your descendants be. 6 Abram put his faith in the LORD,
who attributed it to him as an act of righteousness.
7 He then said to him: I am the LORD who brought you from Ur of the Chaldeans to
give you this land as a possession. 8 "Lord GOD," he asked, "how will I know that I will
possess it?" 9 He answered him: Bring me a three-year-old heifer, a three-year-old female goat, a three-year-old ram, a turtledove, and a young pigeon. 10 He brought him all
these, split them in two, and placed each half opposite the other; but the birds he did
not cut up. 11 Birds of prey swooped down on the carcasses, but Abram scared them
away. 12 As the sun was about to set, a deep sleep fell upon Abram, and a great, dark
dread descended upon him.

17 When the sun had set and it was dark, there appeared a smoking fire pot and a flaming torch, which passed between those pieces. 18 On that day the LORD made a covenant with Abram, saying: To your descendants I give this land, from the Wadi of Egypt
to the Great River, the Euphrates . . .

Philippians 3:21 – 4:1

17 Join with others in being imitators of me, brothers and sisters, and observe those who
thus conduct themselves according to the model you have in us. 18 For many, as I have
often told you and now tell you even in tears, conduct themselves as enemies of the
cross of Christ. 19 Their end is destruction. Their God is their stomach; their glory is in
their "shame." Their minds are occupied with earthly things. 20 But our citizenship is in
heaven, and from it we also await a savior, the Lord Jesus Christ. 21 He will change our
lowly body to conform with his glorified body by the power that enables him also to
bring all things into subjection to himself.
1 Therefore, my brothers and sisters, whom I love and long for, my joy and crown, in
this way stand firm in the Lord, beloveds.

Luke 9: 28-36

28 About eight days after he said this, he took Peter, John, and James and went up the
mountain to pray. 29 While he was praying his face changed in appearance and his clothing became dazzling white. 30 And behold, two men were conversing with him, Moses
and Elijah, 31 who appeared in glory and spoke of his exodus that he was going to accomplish in Jerusalem. 32 Peter and his companions had been overcome by sleep, but becoming fully awake, they saw his glory and the two men standing with him. 33 As they
were about to part from him, Peter said to Jesus, "Master, it is good that we are here; let
us make three tents, one for you, one for Moses, and one for Elijah." But he did not
know what he was saying. 34 While he was still speaking, a cloud came and cast a shadow over them, and they became frightened when they entered the cloud. 35 Then from
the cloud came a voice that said, "This is my chosen Son; listen to him." 36 After the
voice had spoken, Jesus was found alone. They fell silent and did not at that time tell
anyone what they had seen.

THIRD SUNDAY OF LENT

Exodus 3:1-8, 13-15; 1Corinthians 10:1-6, 10-12; Luke 13:1-9

Father, you've promised to all of us that you would come to save us and to bring us into fullness of life. Bless us during this season of Lent as we open our hearts to your teaching, that we can drink of the beauty of your Son, who awakens us to the goodness that you have placed in each of us and the way to follow you that brings that goodness to fullness, and we ask this in Jesus' name. Amen.

We continue now our Lenten journey, that is moving us ever closer to the experience that Christ had that was so powerful, so overwhelming to all those who saw it and witnessed it. He surrendered himself to his enemies and then was somehow mysteriously transformed into something so much more than he was when he simply walked this earth. He returned in this glorious state and had the most profound impact on those who witnessed his resurrection. So it tries to awaken, I believe, in our imaginations that that same kind of transformation is what we are destined for. And religion, when it's healthy, when it's all that it should be, leads us into that kind of experience.

Now the work of God, working with his people, has a long tradition—the Old Testament *and* the New Testament. And one of the things we're looking at in the first reading, the reading from Exodus, is the call of Moses. We had the call of Abram last week. What's interesting about this image is that there is something mysterious that draws Moses, draws his attention to the fact that there is something divine in his midst. And it's interesting that the divine is almost always going to reveal itself as something that doesn't make sense to the mind. So here's a bush that is burning but is not being burnt. It seems like it should be destroyed by this fire, but it's *not* being destroyed.

As Moses gets closer to this mysterious thing that he's looking at, he hears the voice of God, and he hears a *call.* And what he's listening to is the *intention* of God, the *will* of God, what he longs for. And these words are spoken to every human heart that's ever, ever been born into this world: *I want to free you from everything that enslaves you. I want to take you to a place where you are no longer under the pressure of something that keeps you from being who you are. I want to bring you to a place of great liberty. I want to see you flourish and become who I created you to be.* That's the promise, always, that God makes to everyone who is born into the world.

When Moses realizes, yes, there is this need, he knows that the Israelite people are enslaved by the Egyptians, and so he's aware that there's a need for him. Then, when he's asked to go and to proclaim this message, he wants to know, How will people even begin to give me any kind of credence? What kind of authority am I going to say that I have that is going to make them listen to these words about liberty and freedom? God says, *Just tell them my name.* And the word *Yahweh* is best translated in this mysterious way as *I AM*, as *I am who I am.* The way I'd like you to feel that with me is God is saying, *I am revealing to you who I am by telling you my intention, what I exist for, what I long for, where my heart is, where my energy goes. I AM the one who wants to free you. I AM that. If I say that I AM that, then I AM that. I AM who I AM* is the way to understand it.

So what I'd like you to feel from this first reading is that we see Moses being called to take on a role of being an intermediary between God and the Israelite people, to lead them to a better place, a land of milk and honey, and somehow what we're seeing is actually the revelation of the intention of God: *I want to save my people.*

Since we're talking about the name *Yahweh, I AM who I AM,* the name *Jesus* means *Yahweh saves*. So the call of Moses into this role is in a way the beginning of the call of the Church into the same kind of role. The Church's role is to free people from everything that enslaves them.

Now we know the journey that the Israelites then embarked on with Moses as their leader, and we know that one of the things you could say about it is that it was a miserable failure on the part of the Israelites—because they could never, ever really keep their part of the bargain. They were told that if they followed the Law, that Moses was able to share with them, the Ten Commandments, if they could do that, if they could have the right relationship with God, that God wants; if they could have the right relationship with each other—the other seven commandments as to how they were to treat each other—if they could do this, they would *find* this land. Because the land isn't really about geography; it's about *being*, a way of being in the world.

So they were miserable in their track record. They failed. There were those famous moments when God was so frustrated with their inability to do what he was asking, that he decided he would kill 'em all, punish them, destroy them. And there was a side to God in the Old Testament that was very much about punishment, about wanting to destroy that which is bad, that which is evil. And of course it ended up with the "bad ones" being the people who couldn't follow the rules.

Now throughout the Old Testament there was no belief in a life after death. Glimmers of it come at the end, but basically the Israelite people believed that they had this life, this life only, and when they died, it was all over. So maybe that gives us some insight into why punishment is so much a part of the Old Testament, because in Justice there is this idea that if you do something wrong, you need to make up for it, and since there wasn't any time to make up for it after death, as the images of heaven and hell give us, then people had to be punished and corrected during the time that they lived on this earth. So one of the ways in which that image of a God who punishes, the way it was supposed to work on the imaginations of those who were invited to follow the laws but couldn't, there was a clear indication that, well, these are not neutral. These are not rules that you can forget and still get to the goal that they promise. You have to *do* these things. In other words, there isn't any way to this inner kingdom of peace unless you have these right relationships.

But listen to Paul in the second reading, because he's using the way in which God used punishment in the Old Testament to remind people: "Look. You can see that if you don't do the things that God is asking you to do; if you don't follow the way that he's calling you to live, all these negative things are going to happen to you. And when you see those, as Paul says, you should take them as an image, a sign that you need to be smart and wise enough to say, "Look, if it's hard for me to do these things, and I'm tempted not to do them, I have to realize there are consequences." And much as you deal with a four-year-old or five-year-old, or even a teenager, you have to say, "Look. If you don't do it, there are consequences. So think again about doing it." So why do we do it? Because we're afraid of the punishment, OK? So the Old Testament is basically working around that whole image: God comes into your life to tell you what to do, and if you don't, you'll be sorry.

Then comes the New Testament, something radically different. Jesus, in this particular passage, talks about, and goes into the imagination of the people he's listening to, and he's saying, *You know, you all believe that whenever anybody is having real struggles and has setbacks or something horrible happens to them, or to someone they love, you all believe that's because they're sinners.* And Jesus says, *I want to tell you something. That's not true. That's not the way it works.* So think about how radical that must have been to those who listened to Jesus. This is their whole system. Their whole system is, "I have the energy to do what I'm supposed to, because if I don't, I'll be punished. And everybody I see around me that's being punished, well, they obviously haven't done what they're supposed to. God hates them, and I hate them, and we condemn them, we cut them out of the community." And Jesus is saying, *No, that's not true.* That's what people needed to believe perhaps at that time, but now what he wants to say to them is, *There's something different. So if you think those people*—Pilate somehow executed them and mixed their blood with the blood of sacrifices—so there was some kind of torture and murder for those people. And there was a tower that fell and killed another bunch of people. And he said, *You think those things happened because they weren't following the rules or the laws? No,* he said. *That's not it. But I will tell you this: You've gotta repent.* So what Jesus is saying is, *It's not punishment that I'm going to use or that you really need in order for you to do what you're supposed to do. It's* ***awareness****. Not punishment, but awareness.*

What does "repent" mean? When Jesus says "to repent," it means somehow to be conscious of something that happened in the past, and you see it for what it is, and it was not able to give you what it promised. So you see *through* it. "What I thought I was getting when I did what I did, I'm *not* getting. So I regret doing it." That's the heart of repentance. Seeing through the things that we choose, that *we* think are going to bring us to this place where Christ says *I am going to be the fulfillment of that place of milk and honey, that core inner place of inner peace, that wonderful place that you all long for. I'm going to do that, but I want you to join me in this process of getting there by being not so much under the pressure of fear but under, in a sense, the pressure of awareness. I want you to see, I want you to see what you're doing.* It's almost like we've grown up. It's like we've moved from childhood and adolescence into adulthood, and now it's time for God's presence, God's saving love and action to take flesh in Jesus and to reveal to us the fullness of the mystery of what this whole thing is about.

So look at the parable he throws in. He throws in a parable about a gardener with a fig tree, and the owner of the farm comes and says, "You know, this thing isn't working, so cut it down." It's almost to say that in the Old Testament that's basically the way things went. If you didn't perform, you were cut out, cut down, destroyed. That was the way it seemed that God worked. Now comes Jesus, and just think about this: The farm owner might be the image of those who were leading the people in the Old Testament, and their disposition was, If they don't produce fruit, we'll cut 'em down, cut 'em off. But Jesus says, *What I'd like you to do is to dig around it and fertilize it.* And there's something about the three years that this fig tree has been watched, to see if it changes and transforms. And it's three years that Christ ministered on this planet, and I think there's some connection there. What I *sense* in this is that Jesus is trying to help re-imagine, help others to re-imagine this whole notion of how God is going to save them. It's not through punishment, it's not through shaming, it's not through anger, but through a loving disposition of wanting to fertilize, to give each of us everything that we need so that we're able to somehow *see* what's really there, *understand* what's really going on. And the way we understand that in our Christian tradition is called *redemption;* it's called sending of the holy Spirit. So think of that as the fertilizer that's coming into this figure that is not fruitful, and when one believes that that fertilizer is there, and Jesus is saying, *I've come to give to you everything that you need, that you will then be able to take up a different task—with the same end, but a different task.* By "different task," it means not so much to be "in pain," so that you change. That's not "the work." But rather to be moved out of illusion, half-truth, not knowing who we really are, not knowing who God really is. *I am here finally to reveal to all of you what is really going on here. And my Father is who he says he is. He's the savior. I am the means that God the Father has chosen to reveal to human beings how this change is going to take place.* It's not going to take place by your ability to follow rules and laws. It's not your discipline, your will frightened into action because of the possibility of punishment. That's not going to work, and that's the tendency that you all will have, so be sure to weed that out of your imaginations and then place back into your imagination—or for the first time put into your imagination—something radically different. Someone who comes to feed us, to nurture, to awaken, so that we can actually *see, see* what's going on, see *through* the ways in which we live so that we can somehow get in touch with that core that's in us that *knows* what to do. It doesn't need to be *told* what to do. It *knows*. It *understands*. It *sees* what needs to be done.

What a gift awareness is! And what a grace! And what a wonderful way for all of us to work towards this feast of Easter: *longing for that gift.*

Father, bless us during this season of Lent, that we grow in our ability to become all that you call us to be, particularly that you open our eyes that we become aware of who we are, who you are, and what you are doing in our life. And we ask this in Jesus' name. Amen.

Exodus 3: 1-8, 13-15

1 Meanwhile Moses was tending the flock of his father-in-law Jethro, the priest of Midian. Leading the flock beyond the wilderness, he came to the mountain of God, Horeb.
2 There the angel of the LORD appeared to him as fire flaming out of a bush. When he
looked, although the bush was on fire, it was not being consumed. 3 So Moses decided,
"I must turn aside to look at this remarkable sight. Why does the bush not burn up?"
4 When the LORD saw that he had turned aside to look, God called out to him from the
bush: Moses! Moses! He answered, "Here I am." 5 God said: Do not come near! Remove
your sandals from your feet, for the place where you stand is holy ground. 6 I am the
God of your father, he continued, the God of Abraham, the God of Isaac, and the God of

Jacob. Moses hid his face, for he was afraid to look at God.
7 But the LORD said: I have witnessed the affliction of my people in Egypt and have
heard their cry against their taskmasters, so I know well what they are suffering.
8 Therefore I have come down to rescue them from the power of the Egyptians and lead
them up from that land into a good and spacious land, a land flowing with milk and
honey. . .

13 "But," said Moses to God, "if I go to the Israelites and say to them, 'The God of your
ancestors has sent me to you,' and they ask me, 'What is his name?' what do I tell
them?" 14 God replied to Moses: I am who I am. Then he added: This is what you will
tell the Israelites: I AM has sent me to you.
15 God spoke further to Moses: This is what you will say to the Israelites: The LORD, the
God of your ancestors, the God of Abraham, the God of Isaac, and the God of Jacob, has
sent me to you.
This is my name forever; this is my title for all generations.

1 Corinthians 10: 1-6, 10-12
1 I do not want you to be unaware, brothers and sisters, that our ancestors were all under
the cloud and all passed through the sea, 2 and all of them were baptized into Moses in
the cloud and in the sea. 3 All ate the same spiritual food, 4 and all drank the same spiritual drink, for they drank from a spiritual rock that followed them, and the rock was
the Christ. 5 Yet God was not pleased with most of them, for they were struck down in
the desert.
6 These things happened as examples for us, so that we might not desire evil things, as
they did.

10 Do not grumble as some of them did, and suffered death by the destroyer. 11 These
things happened to them as an example, and they have been written down as a warning
to us, upon whom the end of the ages has come. 12 Therefore, whoever thinks he is
standing secure should take care not to fall.

Luke 13: 1-9
1 At that time some people who were present there told him about the Galileans whose
blood Pilate had mingled with the blood of their sacrifices. 2 He said to them in reply,
"Do you think that because these Galileans suffered in this way they were greater sinners than all other Galileans? 3 By no means! But I tell you, if you do not repent, you will
all perish as they did! 4 Or those eighteen people who were killed when the tower at Si-
loam fell on them—do you think they were more guilty than everyone else who lived in

Jerusalem? 5By no means! But I tell you, if you do not repent, you will all perish as they
did!"
6 And he told them this parable: "There once was a person who had a fig tree planted in
his orchard, and when he came in search of fruit on it but found none, 7he said to the
gardener, 'For three years now I have come in search of fruit on this fig tree but have
found none. [So] cut it down. Why should it exhaust the soil?' 8He said to him in reply,
'Sir, leave it for this year also, and I shall cultivate the ground around it and fertilize it;
9it may bear fruit in the future. If not you can cut it down.'"

FOURTH SUNDAY OF LENT

Joshua 5:9, 10-12; 2Corinthians 5:17-21; Luke 15:1-3, 11-32

O God, through whom your Word reconciled the human race to yourself in a wonderful way, grant, we pray, that with prompt devotion and eager faith the Christian people may hasten towards this solemn celebration to come, through our Lord Jesus Christ, your Son, who lives and reigns with you in the unity of the holy Spirit, one God for ever and ever. Amen.

We're moving ever closer to the great Feast of Easter, and the focus of that feast is the mystery of transformation. Christ's death on the cross led to an amazing transformation in the person of Christ. He moved from a human being limited by his body into this Spirit that entered into the world and somehow was able to do what he *couldn't* do while he walked this earth, because if you look at his ministry, it's pretty obvious that things did not go very well. I've often been perplexed by that. I mean, I think of all the things I want to do, all the things I want to achieve; I think of the times when I'm depressed and not feeling very good because nothing seems to be working right. And somehow when things are not working right, I have this sense of shame, I have this sense that somehow something's wrong with *me,* because things aren't the way people expect them to be who are around me. And when I get into that place, I'm realizing that somehow I'm *expecting* myself to be *successful.* And I think we live in a culture where people around us expect us to be successful. But here's Jesus, whose life on this planet, while he walked as a human being filled with divinity, he was anything but successful. In fact, he failed miserably. At the end of three years, he had nobody really understanding fully his message. He had no one there with him except a very few—his mother, some women, one of his disciples—were there with him when he went through this deepest, darkest period. And then the Church that he longed to change and transform, the minds of these men who were running the Church, who were so far from what God wanted them to be, so disconnected from the people they were serving, they treated him as if he was a common criminal. And they humiliated him and spit upon him and laughed at him and murdered him. How can we miss that there's something in that that is absolutely crucial for us to fathom? How do we deal with failure? How do we deal with our sin?

One of the most common things that happens to me when I fail is three things: I'm most likely to be angry. And generally I'm angry at the people who expect me to be more than I was or more than I am, and I blame them often for the discontent that I feel because I feel like they have somehow attacked me. So I'm angry. And then also it seems that I'm *afraid*, because I wonder if I'm going to make it. I wonder if I'm *good enough*. I wonder if there's something that's going to be taken from me because of my mistakes, because of my failures, that I *need* desperately, and therefore I'm threatened and I'm afraid. And then another way it often happens to me, I look at myself and I say, "Alright, there's something core wrong with *me*. I am not enough. I'm ashamed of myself. I'm filled with this thing called *shame*." So, anger and shame and fear are often the things that race into me when I'm aware of my sin, my failures, my faults, my weaknesses, my not reaching the goal.

So what is this set of readings trying to tell us about that? And how is it that we're supposed to deal with that? Well, listen to this phrase. It's really strange. It comes from the second reading. St. Paul says, as he's talking very much about the mystery of Christ in the world and how he's come to *do* something. The thing that it *doesn't* say he's here to do is to take away the sin, take away all the faults, so that none of us make any mistakes any more. That's not at all the essence of the ministry of Jesus. The essence of the ministry of Jesus, in Paul's mind, is *reconciliation. Reconciliation*—what does that mean? Well, maybe to oversimplify it, it means *connecting*. Somehow connecting with ourselves, our God, and each other.

The Pharisees were really interesting characters, and one of the things that I sense so much about the way they're depicted in the lives of those they were serving is, there was no real connection between them and the people they served. They were laying burdens on people without ever realizing what they were doing to them. They didn't seem to lift a finger to do anything to help them. They were spewing out what people had to do. They were completely self-centered. They were all wrapped up in their own life. They were looking for all kinds of ways to make *themselves* feel better. So the only real connection they had was with their own self, their egos. And that's who they were serving.

And Jesus comes into the world to say, *This is the greatest sin.* This autonomy, this separation we get caught up in. Look at the first sin. It's very interesting! It's all about Adam and Eve somehow saying, "We can be autonomous from God because we can be *like* him. So that means that God is in charge of *his* universe. I'll be in charge of *my* universe. I'll be my own god. I'll take care of everything. I'll make sure everything is the way it should be." And that creates isolation, separation, disconnection. And that's what Jesus came to change. I want everything to be connected because of the greatest mystery, the mystery of Christ becoming part of you, entering into you, resonating through you, and that resonating spirit of Christ in me can't reach the people that it's designed to help unless there's connection. So anytime we feel separate and isolated from people, we're in trouble spiritually.

So what causes this kind of separation that we often feel between ourselves and other people? It's often when we fail. And we feel all these things coming from the other, so that we feel that we've been rejected. We're separated. And in this state of isolation, all kinds of negativity thrives. So in this reading from Paul, it says this: Jesus, who was not sin, was made sin for us. Was *made* sin for us. So that we might be freed from sin, that we might be connected again to God. We might be connected to God, made *righteous* in the mind of God, OK?

So that means that Jesus, if he *became* sin for us, we could look at the crucifixion and say, "Alright, this is what sin, when we sin, this is what the experience is like. We have this sense of being rejected, isolated, and separated, and being punished." Now that's where Jesus is. He plays a role, in a sense. Like alright, even though he's innocent, he goes through this experience. Now it's one thing to be isolated and punished because we've done something wrong, but think how hard it is to do that when we're innocent! When we *haven't* done anything wrong. So here's what he does. He takes on this role, and we watch what he does when he's in that place called *crucifixion*, where he's experiencing the effects that we often experience when we fail. And here's his response. Number one: He knows, deep inside of him, he knows, with all his very being, that whatever this painful, awful place that he knows he's in, the pain he's feeling as a human being, that somehow he's absolutely convinced that no matter how intense that pain is, somehow it is not going to destroy him. So he has this *amazing* trust in God. *I'm going to make it. I'm going to get through this. I know I am.* The second thing: You never hear him doubting his goodness. Well, you could say that he knew in his heart that he *didn't* do anything wrong, alright? But go back to, he took on this role so that he could show us how to *deal* with this role. So what he's saying to us is that one of the things when this is going on that we need to feel and hold onto is our own dignity and our own value. So he refuses to fall into shame. He separates, he teaches us how to separate our faults from who we are. And he never blames anybody. He's not angry. You would think he would be *so angry* at the Church and these people jeering and laughing at him because they're putting him in this situation, but what does he do? He turns around and is connected with them and says, *All I want to do is help these people, and they don't un-*

derstand what they're doing. And don't hold this against them, and I won't hold it against them.

Imagine! Something comes down on ourselves and we want to say when we're going through the pain of being rejected and feeling the weight of our faults and—whether they're real or not, we're feeling the weight of separation. And what he's saying is, the way through that, the way to be transformed by that and not destroyed by it, to rise from it as a new person, is to not have that sense of anger or resentment, to not in any way, shape, or form doubt your goodness. And to somehow know, when I go through this, it is going to bring me to an amazing place! An amazing place!

So you look at the story of the gospel, and the gospel is this beautiful story about the father's forgiveness for the son. And the interesting thing about that is the issue where the son comes to his senses, he realizes he's failed, he sees the effects of all the destruction that's come to him. He's in a pigsty. He's not hanging on a cross, but he's in that crucifixion mode, and then he sees that there's something in him worth saving; his father is going to take care of him when he comes back, and he knows he doesn't deserve anything, but he has a sense he's going to receive something wonderful. And then the father says, "Oh, my God. He's got it. He was dead, and now he's alive."

And the key figure is the older brother, who's done everything right, never gone through anything like he's feeling that he's failed; he's never gone through any kind of crucifixion of having to face his own shadow and his own darkness and his own mistakes. And one of the things he doesn't have is any compassion, any connection, anything that would tie him to his brother. In fact, he doesn't even call him "my brother," he calls him "my father's son." So he *can't* celebrate transformation because he's the master of his own universe. He's created his own universe, he's created his own isolated world that he feels is fine, and he doesn't go through the thing that all of us are called to go through, so he doesn't feel one with the human race. He's not engaged in this mysterious process of facing our shadow and our brokenness over and over again and coming through it, through a kind of death and resurrection. *That's* the heart of the season, to learn what that means, and to somehow *fully* embrace it and enter into it. That's the challenge. And that's the gift of the Christ.

Father, your mercy is what our hearts long for; your unmerited love transforms us, enables us to believe in ourselves, in you, and forgive our brothers and sisters, to bless us consistently with this gift. And let us drink of your mercy, as we in turn are then able to pour it out on those around us. And we ask this in Jesus' name. Amen.

Joshua 5: 9, 10-12
9 Then the LORD said to Joshua: Today I have removed the reproach of Egypt from you.
. . .
10 While the Israelites were encamped at Gilgal on the plains of Jericho, they celebrated
the Passover on the evening of the fourteenth day of the month. 11 On the day after the
Passover they ate of the produce of the land in the form of unleavened cakes and
parched grain. On that same day 12 after they ate of the produce of the land, the manna
ceased. No longer was there manna for the Israelites, who that year ate of the yield of
the land of Canaan.

2 Corinthians 5: 17-21
17 So whoever is in Christ is a new creation: the old things have passed away; behold,
new things have come. 18 And all this is from God, who has reconciled us to himself
through Christ and given us the ministry of reconciliation, 19 namely, God was reconcil-
ing the world to himself in Christ, not counting their trespasses against them and en-
trusting to us the message of reconciliation. 20 So we are ambassadors for Christ, as if
God were appealing through us. We implore you on behalf of Christ, be reconciled to
God. 21 For our sake he made him to be sin who did not know sin, so that we might become the righteousness of God in him.

Luke 15: 1-3, 11-32
1 The tax collectors and sinners were all drawing near to listen to him, 2 but the Pharisees
and scribes began to complain, saying, "This man welcomes sinners and eats with
them." 3 So to them he addressed this parable.

Then he said, "A man had two sons, 12 and the younger son said to his father, 'Father,
give me the share of your estate that should come to me.' So the father divided the
property between them. 13 After a few days, the younger son collected all his belongings
and set off to a distant country where he squandered his inheritance on a life of dissipation. 14 When he had freely spent everything, a severe famine struck that country, and he
found himself in dire need. 15 So he hired himself out to one of the local citizens who
sent him to his farm to tend the swine. 16 And he longed to eat his fill of the pods on
which the swine fed, but nobody gave him any. 17 Coming to his senses he thought,
'How many of my father's hired workers have more than enough food to eat, but here
am I, dying from hunger. 18 I shall get up and go to my father and I shall say to him, "Father, I have sinned against heaven and against you. 19 I no longer deserve to be called

your son; treat me as you would treat one of your hired workers."' [20]So he got up and
went back to his father. While he was still a long way off, his father caught sight of him,
and was filled with compassion. He ran to his son, embraced him and kissed him. [21]His
son said to him, 'Father, I have sinned against heaven and against you; I no longer deserve to be called your son.' [22]But his father ordered his servants, 'Quickly bring the finest robe and put it on him; put a ring on his finger and sandals on his feet. [23]Take the
fattened calf and slaughter it. Then let us celebrate with a feast, [24]because this son of
mine was dead, and has come to life again; he was lost, and has been found.' Then the
celebration began. [25]Now the older son had been out in the field and, on his way back,
as he neared the house, he heard the sound of music and dancing. [26]He called one of the
servants and asked what this might mean. [27]The servant said to him, 'Your brother has
returned and your father has slaughtered the fattened calf because he has him back safe
and sound.' [28]He became angry, and when he refused to enter the house, his father came
out and pleaded with him. [29]He said to his father in reply, 'Look, all these years I served
you and not once did I disobey your orders; yet you never gave me even a young goat
to feast on with my friends. [30]But when your son returns who swallowed up your property with prostitutes, for him you slaughter the fattened calf.' [31]He said to him, 'My son,
you are here with me always; everything I have is yours. [32]But now we must celebrate
and rejoice, because your brother was dead and has come to life again; he was lost and
has been found.'"

FIFTH SUNDAY OF LENT

Isaiah 43:16-21; Philippians 3:8-14; John 8:1-11

By your help, we beseech you, Lord our God, may we walk eagerly in the same charity with which out of love for the world your Son handed himself over to death, through our Lord Jesus Christ, your Son, who lives and reigns with you in the unity of the holy Spirit, one God for ever and ever. Amen.

The musical piece was written by Hildegard von Bingen, performed by *Sequentia.* The translation of that prayer has opening lines I want to point out: *I am a pilgrim, and where am I? On what path am I journeying?*

We're coming to the end of this series of Sundays during Lent, and the next Sunday we begin Holy Week, with Palm Sunday. Then we go through the Triduum (Holy Thursday, Good Friday, Holy Saturday Night, Easter Sunday). So the work we've been doing together has been *intended* by those who chose these readings for us to ponder—the intention has been that we would grow in our wisdom and our understanding of who Christ is and what he is doing and what he has done for us. The question of "Who am I? Where am I going? What path am I on" is a good one to listen to and to ponder, a good question to think about, because it certainly reveals to ourselves what it is that we really believe at the heart of the message of Jesus—What *is* the heart of that message? And why was it so violently rejected? Why were human beings, particularly the institutional church, so *frightened* by this Christ, this Anointed One? Why did they kill him? Why did they try to humiliate him? Why did they try to make him look like a failure?

Well, let's go to the first reading, because it's from Isaiah, and it talks about the coming of a messiah, and the interesting thing about this coming of a messiah is that he says I'm coming to do something new, something new. What would be new? We know that the Old Testament writings cover the history of the human race, let's say, for three thousand years. And we know that Christ came two thousand years ago, so we're looking at, five thousand years ago, God breaking into human beings' consciousness in a way that had never happened before. And he began to reveal to them what he longs for them to see. And what he longs for them to see has something about learning how to live according to our nature. God created us; the Old Testament is filled with such interesting stories where you can get a sense, when you listen to the story, that God looked at what he created and saw so many problems! After sin entered into the world, he saw people—at times, he even said, *Everything about them, even their hearts, are dark and corrupt*. And the response of God to that situation was, *I just want to kill them all. I'll start over again. (Well, maybe if you found a few that were good, would you kill them all?) Well, find a few? How about Noah and his family*? So at the time when God destroyed everyone except for just a very few, *Maybe I can start again with this few. Maybe I can begin to form them into what they are called to be.* He *loves* what he created, and he gave them all the most amazing gift, free will, so it's the first time God ever created anything that had the capacity to go against its own nature. And that, I would say, in the Old Testament, seemed to anger God. In the New Testament, in Jesus, we see how sad it makes the Christ, who embodies the Spirit of God the Father.

So a move from anger and maybe even punishment to sadness. It's an interesting change, doing something new. But it seems that what the Old Testament is based on is God giving his wisdom to human beings in the form of the Law, so he gave them ten commandments and told them not to take any away. And then the one part we *really* ignored was his statement, *Don't take any of these rules away, and don't add anything to them!* So much for that! The Israelites added another 603 laws and rules to live by. And when you *broke* those rules and laws, there was a condemnation if you failed. In fact, there was this image in the Old Testament and in many books that implied that when the messiah would come, because they always had this instinct—I call it an *instinct*—deep inside of them that there's more coming than this. There's got to be something more than a bunch of rules and laws that we have to follow, and if we don't, we're going to be punished. That's the hope of a messiah. But they really believed the messiah would come with this sword and he would destroy *all* that is evil and save all that is good.

So that's what they expected, and they're living in a world that has laws and rules and when you *keep* those laws and rules, you're safe and you are respected and honored; and if you *fail* to keep those rules, you are garbage, you are worthless; you are going to be punished. Now the Israelites didn't have any nice, neat categories like heaven and hell, as we do, a place of reward or punishment after death, so all the punishment had to be taking place in this world, and all the rewards had to be taking place in this world. So you have this institution that was formed, this way of seeing God and the rules and the laws where it was a set of people who felt they were absolutely justified in receiving all the good things that God was giving them because they *earned* it by doing what was right.

And there was a kind of selfish side to that—they did things right because they would not be punished; they would not have a bad life. So we have an instinct deep inside all of us as human beings that self-preservation is the core of what it means to be human. "I'm going to take care of myself. I'm going to make sure I'll be OK." Well, the rule promises that if you do what you're told, you *will* be OK. So there's a *great* motivation to do what's good. "I do good so I'll be taken care of. Who am I serving in that? I'm serving myself, alright?" So there's a sort of core selfishness in human beings that God created. And anyone that's embarrassed that's there hasn't understood what it means to be human. That's who we are. Even so many of the things Jesus said, you know, If you treat your brothers well, they'll treat *you* well. So when you're treating your brothers well, you're really doing something for yourself. How about this? I'll forgive you if you forgive your brother and sister, but if you don't forgive your brother and sister, I won't forgive *you*. Well, then what's my motivation for forgiving my brother and sister? *I* want to be forgiven, you know?

So we have that kind of thing in us. The system was set up so that it was basically designed for us to take care of ourselves, so I would say that would be working with human nature at its most basic instinctual level, OK? That's about as far as the Old Testament could ever go.

But somehow something else was coming on the scene, something radically different. Paul talks about it in the second reading. He's saying, "Something happened to me. Something mysterious, something awesome. What happened to me is, something came to me in terms of an insight and I saw something and understood something. And the very thing I thought I was doing that was so wonderful and so pleasing to God, was not." And what was he doing? Condemning the people who were "bad." Now they happened to be good, but in *Paul's* mind they were bad. So here's a man who's a religious man, formed in the school of Pharisees, rigid in everything, and his major force in the world for good was to condemn *bad*. Now what if this Jesus, who comes into the world, has another plan, something new, something different from condemning the guilty? Something radically different.

So let's go to the gospel. Here is Jesus; it's getting close to the time when he knows he's further and further from a place of safety; he knows more and more that his life is moving in a direction where it doesn't look good at all. And I don't know how you feel about how much Jesus knew about his life, but I think you would do something radically wrong if you would take away from Jesus the struggle that he was having, and that he was working toward a goal that he wanted to succeed at, and yet it wasn't going well, so he had to be dealing with a lot of sense of shame, failure. I mean, did he know that he was going to die in that short of a time? He knew that he was going to do what God called him to do. He knew that; he surrendered, he was willing to do that, but did he know *everything* that was going to happen? If he did, it would be like he was going through a play where he knew the ending, knew the final scene was crucifixion, would kind of look forward to that scene because it was the most dramatic. He'd just go through it and it would be painful, but you know it's just part of the show, part of what I have to do. I think that that would be to take something away from the experience that Jesus had, that he's trying to show us, teach us, that he went through that as *we* would go through it—as a human being. He was terrified and frightened, and it was real to him that that would happen. He begged and begged the Father not to be crucified. Twice. But it had to be, so he gave in.

But back to his place. He was knowing that things were getting tougher and tougher, and he was really frustrated that he couldn't reach the Pharisees and the scribes. And this is one of the few stories, maybe the *only* story, where he *got* to them. He finally broke through. A woman is brought to him who has broken the law. She is a prostitute. Now the thing I find ironic is that here's a woman who has chosen to give herself to someone, and the very act of giving yourself in sexuality is—the ideal is that that's an act of self-giving to someone who will care for you and love you and support you. It's a beautiful image, two human beings coming together as one. Well, prostitution—you can't get oneness out of that. It's not even designed for that, alright?

So this woman who's caught in the sin of going to something that isn't really going to take care of her, fulfill her, is I think the way Jesus sees the Pharisees using the Law and trying to become one with the Law, and it's not going to produce the oneness that they want. They were made for something more than the Law. We're made for a divine Spirit to enter into us and to transform us—not simply to be told what to do—we're made for something much more than that.

Anyway, this woman is condemned for that, and that's exactly the sin of the Pharisees. They're all prostitutes, in a sense—giving themselves over to the Law and not to God. So they say this woman has to be executed. This is what the Law demands.

And Jesus looks at first disinterested in the whole argument. That's one way of saying that this is not the issue at all. *Let me tell you, the new thing I've come to do, the new thing I'm doing in this world, I want to free the entire world from a spirit of condemnation. I am not here to condemn anyone who's done anything wrong. That's not my work. My work here is to affirm every single thing in everyone that is good, and help them to embrace that goodness that is their inheritance, that is there by nature. And what they need, and what I want to share with them is that the God who created them wants to enter into them and give them the ability to do something that in human nature they're not able to do.*

The call of the Gospel is not simply to become the most complete, full human being, in terms of just using our human nature. The gift is for us to accept and embrace exactly what our human nature is, to surrender to it. Once we surrender to it, and see its limitations, then we know that we need something *beyond* that. So what enters into us is this divinity that Christ won for us through his act of surrendering to his human condition. That's what he did. He surrendered to the way life is, and he didn't condemn anyone for doing what they did to him. He said to his disciples, and it frightened them, and it still frightens people, he said the only way to deal with evil is to give in to it—not to fight it, not to condemn it. What a strange message! And yet it somehow slips through our fingers, and we're not aware that that's the mystery of Easter.

Father, your gift of forgiveness, your gift of longing to awaken in us the power that your way of life, your teaching gives us to deal with our weaknesses and not let them lead us to shame, but to lead us to an openness to your power, your strength, your ability flowing through us to make us all that you've called us to be through the truth of the Gospel, and we ask this in Jesus' name. Amen.

Isaiah 43: 16-21

16Thus says the LORD,
who opens a way in the sea,
a path in the mighty waters,
17Who leads out chariots and horsemen,
a powerful army,
Till they lie prostrate together, never to rise,
snuffed out, quenched like a wick.
18Remember not the events of the past,
the things of long ago consider not;
19See, I am doing something new!
Now it springs forth, do you not perceive it?
In the wilderness I make a way,
in the wasteland, rivers.
20Wild beasts honor me,
jackals and ostriches,
For I put water in the wilderness
and rivers in the wasteland

for my chosen people to drink,
21The people whom I formed for myself,
that they might recount my praise.

Philippians 3: 8-14

8More than that, I even consider everything as a loss because of the supreme good of
knowing Christ Jesus my Lord. For his sake I have accepted the loss of all things and I
consider them so much rubbish, that I may gain Christ 9and be found in him, not having
any righteousness of my own based on the law but that which comes through faith in
Christ, the righteousness from God, depending on faith 10to know him and the power of
his resurrection and [the] sharing of his sufferings by being conformed to his death, 11if
somehow I may attain the resurrection from the dead.
12It is not that I have already taken hold of it or have already attained perfect maturity,
but I continue my pursuit in hope that I may possess it, since I have indeed been taken
possession of by Christ [Jesus].13Brothers and sisters, I for my part do not consider myself to have taken possession. Just one thing: forgetting what lies behind but straining
forward to what lies ahead, 14I continue my pursuit toward the goal, the prize of God's
upward calling, in Christ Jesus.

John 8: 1-11

. . . 1while Jesus went to the Mount of Olives. 2But early in the morning he arrived again
in the temple area, and all the people started coming to him, and he sat down and
taught them. 3Then the scribes and the Pharisees brought a woman who had been
caught in adultery and made her stand in the middle. 4They said to him, "Teacher, this
woman was caught in the very act of committing adultery. 5Now in the law, Moses
commanded us to stone such women. So what do you say?" 6They said this to test him,
so that they could have some charge to bring against him. Jesus bent down and began
to write on the ground with his finger. 7But when they continued asking him, he
straightened up and said to them, "Let the one among you who is without sin be the
first to throw a stone at her." 8Again he bent down and wrote on the ground. 9And in
response, they went away one by one, beginning with the elders. So he was left alone
with the woman before him. 10Then Jesus straightened up and said to her, "Woman,
where are they? Has no one condemned you?" 11She replied, "No one, sir." Then Jesus
said, "Neither do I condemn you. Go, [and] from now on do not sin any more."

PALM SUNDAY

Isaiah 50:4-7; Philippians 2:6-11; Luke 23:1-49

Almighty, ever-living God who, as an example of humility for the human race to follow, caused our savior to take flesh and submit to the cross, graciously grant that we may heed his lessons of patient suffering and so merit a share in the resurrection. Amen.

Today begins the holiest week of the year, and it's called holy because the truth that is found in this week that celebrates the death and resurrection of Christ has the power to create in us a kind of wholeness, a kind of completeness, to bring us to the place of fullness. The great theme of Scripture is God taking his people on a journey, through something deep, into a new land. That basic image of God calling people to a new life is the thing that you and I are invited to ponder from one very particular perspective: What is it that we need to go through? What is it that we need to enter into? What is it that we need to go down into in order to find this new place, this new freedom, this new life, freed from fear, freed from shame, freed from excessive anger? How do we get there? What do we do?

Well, the mystery of Christ's death is the key. It's the secret. There are a couple of things I want to say about our way of looking at it that are important to make sure we're not carrying a misconception. And two misconceptions that I think are very, very easy to slip into our imaginations when we look at the death of Christ on the cross, that block us from really understanding the fullness of what it means: One is that we still cling to a misconception that the God who created us, when we sin, has one basic reaction: He is angered, and he wants to punish us. He's disappointed; he wants to punish us. He did so much for us and we don't seem to be grateful; he wants to punish us. The thing that's so interesting about that is that the way in which that was always presented to me was in a kind of—I'm sure the people who gave this to me wanted so much for me to be a good boy. And they wanted to create in me some kind of disgust and horror around the fact that I would willfully sin. So as I grew up in my faith as a Roman Catholic, I knew that the worst thing I could do was sin; it was the thing that made God angry; it was the thing that caused all the pain in the world. And I was told this: Every time I had sinned, somehow I had participated in the crucifixion of Christ. So my sins were like driving nails through the flesh of Christ. (I hope *you* didn't get that, but I got it "big time.")

So that image that we see on the cross is Jesus representing humanity, and he is acting out for us a scene in which we feel that God's anger will somehow be appeased. So God is furious at human beings for not being who they are; he demands some kind of retribution. "Somebody needs to pay for this." So Jesus says, "OK, I'll do it." And then we add to our guilt and our shame about having been a bad little boy by the fact that not only was I bad and made God mad, but I was bad and caused an innocent, beautiful man who was nothing but love to be tortured. *Wrong!* Totally wrong.

Another thing that gets in the way of our fully understanding what this image of Christ dying on the cross means for us is that we sometimes feel that Christ was God as well as man, so he went through this scenario of going through his life, his death, his resurrection with complete, total understanding of everything that was going to happen. He knew it would all turn out all right. He knew that he was only supposed to do certain things because that's the way he could see it in the future. So he's sort of like an actor. He comes onto the scene and goes through the actions so that we can watch this thing. That interpretation seems to me to minimize the human side of him, the "son of man."

There isn't a lot of understanding of what Jesus is *really* trying to do, which is to show you and me what it's like to be human, to be human. He's there to reveal who God is, and who *we* are. So the first thing that he wants to reveal to us about God, in terms of punishment, is that he comes onto the scene with a completely different image of sin. He doesn't seem to have a problem with sin as much as we *thought* God did—because we thought that God was always punishing those who had a bad life; and those who had a bad life were called sinners, and they were considered to be outcasts. God didn't care about them. So Jesus comes onto the scene and he *is God*, and he's living the life that God wants him to live as a human being and his whole nature is to be drawn to sinners and to want to *be* with them. It's almost like he likes them better [chuckles] than the Pharisees and scribes who claim to be so perfect. It's like he *likes* human nature. He understands it. He has compassion for it.

I want you to feel this: God created you, made you, basically as you are, and one of the core things about being human is that we have a deep, deep drive inside of us to protect ourselves. We have natural reactions to when we're afraid or when we're made fun of, or when things go wrong, we have these natural reactions. They're like shame and fear and anger, and that's the way we are. And those things *don't make God mad*, any more than you would look at an infant always putting things right in their mouth or a two-year-old who won't do what you say. You don't look at them and say, "I've got to go *punish* this child." No, you say, "This is a child, and this is the way children act." God has enormous compassion for your struggles and my struggles, whatever we're going through. He understands us; he created us; in a way it's his fault [chuckles] that we're human. Somehow he *wanted* this. He wanted this great experiment where he would try this out, where he would allow people to go through all kinds of difficult things and know that those difficult things would be a challenge for them, because when things aren't the way that human beings like, we're often angry. When we don't think we're enough, we're ashamed. When somehow we think we're going to be destroyed, we're in fear. Those are natural human experiences, and when we're in them, chances are we don't necessarily surrender, but we necessarily attack!

And that's the nature of sin, the insidious nature of sin. It's always contagious. When you're sinned against, you're most likely to sin back. Or to sin against yourself. What is sin? Sin is any action, it seems to me, that we choose to do, that instead of building us up and making us whole, it destroys us and fragments us. And there's a reason for it in the world. It's called evil, and evil wanted this whole experiment to fail. Lucifer, the great angel that was destroyed, decided, "I am going to make sure that people are going to make all the mistakes that they're prone to." So Lucifer is the accuser. He's always the one who's going around accusing, accusing, accusing. Somebody does something wrong, and they accuse them, through you, and then you feel you have a right to destroy them or hate them. Or if things aren't going right and say they accuse you, "It's your fault. You've not done something right. You're a mistake. You're no good." Or the accuser comes along and says, "You're not going to make it; you're not going to make it." So we have to be careful of these things.

So what is Jesus doing then, on the cross? He isn't being punished, but somehow he is showing us, being by his very essence, the way in which we're invited to be, when it comes to dealing with all the imperfection and all the sin and all the pain in the world. He's the model of what we should do. And notice, there's nothing in him, nothing in him that retaliates. He's not angry because his life didn't turn out the way he hoped—because I would say, as a human being, he was probably hoping he'd have more time than he did. He didn't have any kind of real success in his life, so he must have felt ashamed at times, and he *felt* that shame; he *felt* that anger. And when he was in the Garden of Gethsemane, he prayed with his whole heart to not have to go through this because he feared it might destroy him. I don't know that it was just the *pain* of the suffering, but as a human being, could he have worried about being destroyed, if he's fully human? And he had the quality, also in you and in me, of trusting in God. You know, you put that trust to a test, and it's really tough! I'm not saying he doubted God would take care of him, but knowing God will take you through whatever you're going through does not immediately take away all the pain and the fear and the shame that is involved in it, and that's where Jesus showed his humanity and gave us *the model*, because he was sweating blood, and he said, *Please take it away*, and God said, *No*, and what was his response to that? *Please take it away!* He said it again. So here's a human being, *fully* human, filled with divinity, knowing that he is cared for, that he's loved, that somehow he knows this is going to work—on some level—but he holds that as tenuously as anyone could in a human form, and he says, *I'm hanging in here, I'm hanging in here, I'm hanging in here, and I refuse to do anything wrong. I'm not going to resist it; I'm not going to feel it's my fault; I'm not going to believe it's going to destroy me. But I will* <u>*allow*</u> *it. I allow it.*

Now there's a *tension* in his allowing—When I tell you our task is to allow things to be as they are, I don't mean we should be like people who simply act as if "Everything is fine. It doesn't matter who's been murdered, who's been hurt. Doesn't bother me. Nothing matters. I know God's in charge." That's not the way it works! It's somehow this *tension* between the human nature that longs for certain things and God's divinity, who is in us, that can enable us to deal with those things that are so difficult, but at the same time *not* to retaliate with "sin for sin." *That's* the key; that's the mystery of the cross. And that's what this week is about. Until we see it, until we believe it, until we understand it, we will not experience resurrection.

I'd like to end this program simply with that thought, that powerful image, of Christ on the cross as we move into this holiest of all weeks. Amen.

Isaiah 50:4-7

4The Lord GOD has given me
a well-trained tongue,
That I might know how to answer the weary
a word that will waken them.
Morning after morning
he wakens my ear to hear as disciples do;
5The Lord GOD opened my ear;
I did not refuse,
did not turn away.
6I gave my back to those who beat me,

my cheeks to those who tore out my beard;
My face I did not hide
from insults and spitting.
7The Lord GOD is my help,
therefore I am not disgraced;
Therefore I have set my face like flint,
knowing that I shall not be put to shame.

Philippians 2: 6-11
6[Christ Jesus], though he was in the form of God,
did not regard equality with God something to be grasped.
7Rather, he emptied himself,
taking the form of a slave,
coming in human likeness;
and found human in appearance,
8he humbled himself,
becoming obedient to death, even death on a cross.
9Because of this, God greatly exalted him
and bestowed on him the name
that is above every name,
10that at the name of Jesus
every knee should bend,
of those in heaven and on earth and under the earth,
11and every tongue confess that
Jesus Christ is Lord,
to the glory of God the Father.

Luke 23: 1-49
1Then the whole assembly of them arose and brought him before Pi-
late.2They brought charges against him, saying, "We found this man
misleading our people; he opposes the payment of taxes to Caesar
and maintains that he is the Messiah, a king."3Pilate asked him, "Are
you the king of the Jews?" He said to him in reply, "You say
so."4Pilate then addressed the chief priests and the crowds, "I find
this man not guilty."5But they were adamant and said, "He is inciting the people with his teaching throughout all Judea, from Galilee
where he began even to here."
6On hearing this, Pilate asked if the man was a Galilean;7and upon

learning that he was under Herod's jurisdiction, he sent him to Herod who was in Jerusalem at that time.[8]Herod was very glad to see
Jesus; he had been wanting to see him for a long time, for he had
heard about him and had been hoping to see him perform some
sign.[9]He questioned him at length, but he gave him no answer.[10]The
chief priests and scribes, meanwhile, stood by accusing him harshly.[11][Even] Herod and his soldiers treated him contemptuously and
mocked him, and after clothing him in resplendent garb, he sent him
back to Pilate.[12]Herod and Pilate became friends that very day, even
though they had been enemies formerly.[13]Pilate then summoned the
chief priests, the rulers, and the people[14]and said to them, "You
brought this man to me and accused him of inciting the people to re-
volt. I have conducted my investigation in your presence and have
not found this man guilty of the charges you have brought against
him,[15]nor did Herod, for he sent him back to us. So no capital crime
has been committed by him.[16] Therefore I shall have him flogged and
then release him."[17]

[18]But all together they shouted out, "Away with this man! Release
Barabbas to us."[19](Now Barabbas had been imprisoned for a rebellion that had taken place in the city and for murder.)[20]Again Pilate
addressed them, still wishing to release Jesus,[21]but they continued
their shouting, "Crucify him! Crucify him!"[22]Pilate addressed them a
third time, "What evil has this man done? I found him guilty of no
capital crime. Therefore I shall have him flogged and then release
him."[23]With loud shouts, however, they persisted in calling for his
crucifixion, and their voices prevailed.[24]The verdict of Pilate was that
their demand should be granted.[25]So he released the man who had
been imprisoned for rebellion and murder, for whom they asked,
and he handed Jesus over to them to deal with as they wished.

[26]As they led him away they took hold of a certain Simon, a Cyreni-
an, who was coming in from the country; and after laying the cross
on him, they made him carry it behind Jesus.[27]A large crowd of people followed Jesus, including many women who mourned and la-
mented him.[28]Jesus turned to them and said, "Daughters of Jerusalem, do not weep for me; weep instead for yourselves and for your
children,[29]for indeed, the days are coming when people will say,
'Blessed are the barren, the wombs that never bore and the breasts
that never nursed.'[30]At that time people will say to the mountains,
'Fall upon us!' and to the hills, 'Cover us!'[31]for if these things are
done when the wood is green what will happen when it is

dry?"32Now two others, both criminals, were led away with him to
be executed.
33When they came to the place called the Skull, they crucified him
and the criminals there, one on his right, the other on his left.34[Then
Jesus said, "Father, forgive them, they know not what they
do."] They divided his garments by casting lots.35The people stood
by and watched; the rulers, meanwhile, sneered at him and said, "He
saved others, let him save himself if he is the chosen one, the Messiah of God."36Even the soldiers jeered at him. As they approached to
offer him wine37they called out, "If you are King of the Jews, save
yourself."38Above him there was an inscription that read, "This is the
King of the Jews."39Now one of the criminals hanging there reviled
Jesus, saying, "Are you not the Messiah? Save yourself and us."40The
other, however, rebuking him, said in reply, "Have you no fear of
God, for you are subject to the same condemnation?41And indeed,
we have been condemned justly, for the sentence we received corresponds to our crimes, but this man has done nothing criminal."42Then he said, "Jesus, remember me when you come into your
kingdom."43He replied to him, "Amen, I say to you, today you will
be with me in Paradise."
44 It was now about noon and darkness came over the whole land until three in the afternoon45because of an eclipse of the sun. Then the
veil of the temple was torn down the middle.46Jesus cried out in a
loud voice, "Father, into your hands I commend my spirit"; and
when he had said this he breathed his last.47The centurion who witnessed what had happened glorified God and said, "This man was
innocent beyond doubt."48When all the people who had gathered for
this spectacle saw what had happened, they returned home beating
their breasts;49but all his acquaintances stood at a distance, including
the women who had followed him from Galilee and saw these
events.

EASTER SUNDAY

Acts 10:34, 37-43; 1Corinthians 5:6-8; John 20:1-9

O God, who on this day brought your only begotten Son to have conquered death and unlocked for us the path to eternity, grant, we pray, that we who keep the solemnity of the Lord's resurrection may through the renewal brought by your Spirit, rise up in the life and the light of life, through our Lord Jesus Christ, your Son, who lives and reigns with you in the unity of the holy Spirit, one God for ever and ever. Amen.

Today is the greatest feast of the Christian faith. It is the one that focuses most clearly on that which we need to see, understand, grasp, live, enjoy. It's all about something happening to you and me, happening to the human race through an action that took place on a cross that created in us something new, something that's never been there before; some insight, some power, some grace. And my only desire, this morning, talking with you, is how can I help you see it, how can I help you feel it, how can I help you know it more fully?

Something that the second reading talks about, the "yeast" in our life, this sort of undercurrent of something that penetrates everything, can move from the place we're so often in, of negativity, fear, shame, anger—*all* that, you know? What is it that we need to see and understand so that those things no longer rule and somehow infect everything about us, but instead we have this thing called *sincerity* and *truth*? Life, grace?

I love the promise. I love the promise that God has made to us from the very beginning. The Old Testament, filled with so many stories of the failure of human beings to be all that God wanted them to be; story after story about them failing and wallowing in their self-pity, in their own selfishness; being not so nice to each other—that whole destructive thing. And every time that would happen, God would go back to them and welcome them back and try to call them back and say, No, I want so much for you to experience something that he called "the promised land," the place of peace, this inner core of peace—*that's* what we're all destined for. God placed us on this planet, I believe, with an intention that we would find *joy* in who we are, and he gave us a *challenge*. He said, *Everything in my world that I've created is in a harmonious place with what it does and how it exists. It doesn't seem to want to be anything other than what it is.*

So then he gave human beings free will. I know this is going to sound silly to say it this way, and I don't mean it literally, and theologically this is going to be sounding incorrect, but it's almost like God, along with human beings, is learning how to deal with these people who have this thing called free will. And the first, most logical way it seemed right to deal with it was, *Here is what you should do, and this is my law.* And it's all about right relationships with God, with each other, and *I want you to do it because that brings you wisdom.* It's like, *I'll take your human nature, which I created, which has a core value of self-preservation, and I'm going to take that and I'm going to try to explain to you that if you try always to take care of yourself, and you do that by harming other people, and turning away from the Source that's there to help you, you're going to be miserable. But what I really want to tell you, I want to build on that longing that you have for fullness and life, and say that you* <u>*can*</u> *get it, but don't try to get it by using and abusing people, taking from them. But you can find it by being all that you need to be for other people, and you're going to find that so satisfying!*

So it's like in the beginning, when God is working with his people—even Jesus uses this tactic—he will say, *Do the right thing because it really does help you. The good things you do to somebody else, they're going to be done back to you. So do them not just for their sake but for* <u>*your*</u> *sake. Forgive your brothers and sisters as often as they need, and don't do that just because you're letting them off the hook. Know that if you don't do that, I won't let* <u>*you*</u> *off the hook. So you've got to forgive your brothers and sisters because if you don't, I won't forgive you.* That's pretty much of a selfish motive, you know? And there doesn't seem to be anything in Jesus, God, that seems to be embarrassed by the fact that human beings respond best to doing what is best for *them*. And yet sometimes Christianity seems to say, "No, all that part of us that is self-centered, everything about being self-protective, that's all the enemy. We should be willing to destroy ourselves. That's a good, solid, healthy way to live. Destroy yourself." How many people, in the name of religion, have set out to destroy their human nature? How many times in religion have you sensed or felt that the religious teaching you're receiving is somehow either embarrassed by or not pleased at all with all these human things we need? These messy things, these smelly things. All that, you know?

So, what is it that this Feast of Easter is trying to get us in touch with that frees us from that negative leaven that is infecting everything, that opens us up to a love of

God and the world and me and you, opens us up to seeing something so beautiful in all of it—instead of a spirit of condemnation, it seems that the whole notion of Easter is to bring us into a spirit of the *antithesis* of condemnation.

And I'm going to use a word for it. It's not *acceptance*, though that's a good word. I want to use the word *allow*. Jesus' death on the cross empowers us to *allow* God to be God, me to be me, you to be you, the world to be what it is—but not in the way we might suspect, that he would take away any longing or desire for anything and make us sort of like, "It doesn't matter what happens, nothing matters. Doesn't matter if my life is miserable or not, I'll be happy." That's just too naïve.

Somehow, there's a tension. There's always going to be a tension in our human nature that is being asked to surrender to things that are difficult, things that make us feel bad about ourselves, things that anger us, things that frighten us. It's *natural* to have a resistance to that. Somehow, when we're in that resistance—and I hope I can describe this because I see it on the cross—in that resistance to all that in human nature, and it was in Jesus, too. I mean if he was human, he had to resist being made a fool of, looking like he was put to shame. So many scriptures talk about the suffering servant, prophesying about Jesus, and God promising, *I won't let you be put to shame.* Yet here he is, experiencing the most shameful death. He's saying, *I won't let them destroy you; you cannot be destroyed.* And yet they're doing something that looks and feels, to those who are watching it and perhaps to Jesus, who's experiencing it, it certainly *looked* like destruction. Though I know Christ understood all that was promised by God, but please, don't take away the humanity of Jesus and put him on the cross as if he's going through a play that's painful, but he's just not in the least bit worried, that he doesn't feel any of the negativity of it. His pain was *intense;* his fear was *intense.* Look at the Garden of Gethsemane. He sweats blood, begging God not to allow this to happen. So there was a *tension* in that figure Jesus on the cross that is a beautiful image for you and me to hold onto. When we see the cross, we say, "Yeah! There's my struggle. That's it."

So when you're in that struggle between accepting things as they are, and you don't *want* them to be that way, *that's* the place you *want* to be in. *That's* the place you want to be in. And here's what happens in that place. I can't describe it, but something new is born out of that friction, out of that heat, out of that tension; something explodes. And what explodes is a new insight, a new awareness, a new understanding. One of the things that the disciples kept saying over and over again when Jesus described that he was going to have to go through something like this, he knew that this was going to be the fundamental struggle that he would go through to show people how *they* had to go through it, because this *is* the fundamental struggle of being a human being. My will versus the will of God. Another way to say that: My way versus the way it just is, just that is. *That's* the tension. So in that moment when we're called to look at that, Jesus says, *This is what I want you to look at; this is the key.*

So the thing that happens when he goes through that is that he rises from the dead. And there's one thing that's said over and over about the disciples. They kind of got the part where Jesus said, *I have to go through this terrible thing.* They didn't want it to happen, but whenever he said, *And to rise from the dead,* they had no idea what he was talking about. Even in the gospel that I just read, Peter and John standing there and looking at the tomb and just kind of going, "What?" Because they didn't understand "rising from the dead."

They didn't understand that new life, new birth, can come out of this kind of tension, this kind of struggle that human beings are invited into by God, who gives us the wisdom to say, "It's here that it all happens; it's here where it's going to work itself out." I know that there are a lot of people, and I don't mean to take anything away from anyone or any religion that's struggling to give the truth. We're all doing that, but one of the things that we often hear is that to be saved is somehow a moment where you just say, "I accept Jesus as my savior, and he's going to take care of me, and everything is going to be all right," and that certainly is an absolutely crucial step. But it doesn't *end* there; that's not the work alone, just to say, "I accept him as the one who can save me, whose will I will surrender to, whose help I will ask for constantly." Because *my* experience of Jesus in my life is not that he's taken away every painful situation. He's not made my life easy. He's certainly given me a major struggle with my own ego. I'm always worried about how I'm performing, I'm always trying to be great. I love it when people tell me I'm good. I hate it when people tell me I'm bad. All those struggles have been part of my life—from the very beginning. So there's no promise in this Easter celebration that you and I will *not, will not* be in struggle. But look at this man on the cross! Look at what he's doing. As a human being, he *had* to feel that somehow his ministry could have been, should have been, would have been successful! Doesn't it make sense that as a human being—again, don't make him God; he *is* God, but he says so clearly in Scripture: *My divinity was nothing that I wanted to cling to; I wanted simply to be human. So my experience is, I want to be a human being, struggling like every other human being.* So he was prone to sin, just like you and I are. He was tempted to sin in every way that you are. You get out there and try to do something, some major task, trying to achieve something, and after three short years, and after thirty years of training—after three short years, it's all falling apart. Are you going to say, "Oh, this is just so nice! I guess this is the way it's supposed to be!"? He *must* have felt frustrated. His disciples didn't fully believe in him; the people he tried to convert—they wouldn't even listen to him, so he really at times screamed and lost his temper and turned tables over, wasn't exactly the most "politically correct" guy, working with people with strong egos—like the Pharisees. Maybe he wondered if that was good enough, so he *had* to be struggling with, "Is this *my* fault? Is this a mistake that *I* did?" He *had* to feel something like that. And he had to be angry at the people who were accusing him because he was innocent. I mean, how do people feel when they're accused constantly of something, when they haven't been guilty of it—they're bound to be angry at their accusers! And going through that horrible death—he must have had some kind of fear! "This might destroy me." So unless you get into that mindset, you're not going to quite feel what he's inviting you and me to go through—because it's that time when we're struggling and feeling that, *that's* the time when new birth happens. That's the place of friction and heat and power.

And then he's changed, because he *didn't* get angry. He *didn't* give in to shame. And he *knew* he wasn't going to be destroyed. That was it. He knew all that deep inside of him, but he didn't necessarily feel that belief taking away the *pain* that he was in at the time. Got that? He didn't have a faith that took away pain. But he had to go *through* the pain, and on the other side of the pain, there's the birth. That's the cross. That's what he's trying to teach us. It's a beautiful, beautiful moment for us to look at, ponder, wonder about. And you know, we're told *we* have to go through something like that. Well, I don't know any of my friends who've been hung on a cross, but I know *every* friend I've had has been in pain over something that wanted to rob them of their dignity, their worth, something that they hated and didn't want to see happen; and made them angry, something that just scared them to death that they were going to be destroyed. Yes. All those things happen over and over again. And we have this incredible model. Allow it, allow it, allow it. Because you're going to rise; there's going to be new birth. There's going to be a new beginning. Birth after birth after birth into the fullness of life.

Father, this feast is filled with the wisdom that your grace, only your grace can infuse into our hearts. Bless us with this wisdom so that we might engage as fully as possible in the transforming work of surrendering to all that you have offered to us in growing in an ability to find peace that is your greatest gift. And we ask this through Christ our Lord. Amen.

I have a special dedication for this program, and I want to say a little bit about it. There's a wonderful young woman by the name of Juliette Turner, who is a friend and listener, and she's probably the youngest listener ever to take her own money that she saved—she's still in high school—and put together the money it takes, the thousand dollars, to dedicate a show. And she wanted me to dedicate it to a special person, unnamed, but also, I think, to everyone who struggles with faith, who has a hard time seeing the beauty of this God and opening their heart to him and being transformed by him. So Juliette, thank you so much for your donation, for making this program possible. And my prayer, with yours, is that this special person, as well as the world, opens their heart to his grace.

Acts 10: 34, 37-43

[34]Then Peter proceeded to speak and said . . .

[37][You know] what has happened all over Judea, beginning in Galilee after the baptism that John preached,[38]how God anointed Jesus of Nazareth with the holy Spirit and power. He went about doing good and healing all those oppressed by the devil, for God was with him.[39]We are witnesses of all that he did both in the country of the Jews and (in) Jerusalem. They put him to death by hanging him on a tree.[40]This man God raised (on) the third day and granted that he be visible,[41]not to all the people, but to us, the witnesses chosen by God in advance, who ate and drank with him after he rose from the dead.[42]He commissioned us to preach to the people and testify that he is the one appointed by God as judge of the living and the dead.[43]To him all the prophets bear witness, that everyone who believes in him will receive forgiveness of sins through his name."

1 Corinthians 5: 6-8

[6][Brothers and sisters] . . . Do you not know that a little yeast leavens all the dough? [7]Clear out the old yeast, so that you may become a fresh batch of dough, inasmuch as you are unleavened. For our paschal lamb, Christ, has been sacrificed.[8]Therefore let us celebrate the feast, not with the old yeast, the yeast of malice and wickedness, but with the unleavened bread of sincerity and truth.

John 20: 1-9

[1]On the first day of the week, Mary of Magdala came to the tomb early in the morning, while it was still dark, and saw the stone removed from the tomb. [2]So she ran and went to Simon Peter and to the other disciple whom Jesus loved, and told them, "They have taken the Lord from the tomb, and we don't know where they put him."[3] So Peter and the other disciple went out and came to the tomb.[4]They both ran, but the other disciple ran faster than Peter and arrived at the tomb first;[5]he bent down and saw the burial cloths there, but did not go in.

SECOND SUNDAY OF EASTER

Acts 5:12-16; Revelation 1:9-11, 12-13, 17-19; John 20:19-31

God of everlasting mercy, who in the very recurrence of the Paschal feast re-kindles the faith of the people you have made your own, increase, we pray, the grace you have bestowed, that all may grasp and rightly understand in what font they have been washed, by whose Spirit they have been reborn, by whose blood they have been redeemed. Through our Lord Jesus Christ, your Son, who lives and reigns with you in the unity of the holy Spirit, one God for ever and ever. Amen.

We linger on this awesome feast of Easter. The heart of what it means to be a believer is to somehow enter into this mystery, to allow it to change us, to transform us. And if you, like myself, had gone through the Triduum, and many of you have, and yet many of you, in your own religions and places have wondered and pondered and looked carefully at this image that Christianity holds so dear, a crucifix, and wondered what it all means. What is that image that we're asked to look at and understand and take in and receive the power that is in it that enables us somehow to enter into a new place, a new life, to become a new creation?

So my thoughts this morning, I pray, will be some thoughts that will help you understand more fully the mystery of the cross. And to be honest, I'm digging as deeply as I can, and I'm not sure that my words that I feel I need to speak are even understandable by myself! [chuckles] But I keep feeling there's a mystery here that we *must* ponder, we must get into it and understand it. Probably the worst thing that happened to me in my own upbringing was, I looked at the cross, and somehow people told me that the reason Jesus was hanging there is because of what *I've* done, because of *my* sins, and every time I sin I sometimes drive another nail into the flesh of Christ. So there's an image of my sins somehow causing God, who's on the cross in the form of Jesus, to *suffer*. And somehow, when he says, "OK, I'll suffer for *you*," then I'm supposed to feel even *worse* about my sins.

And I don't know. Mercy, unmerited love, that incredible image that's all over the crucifix somehow went out the window, as I saw it as a place where I could see how horrible sin was and how I should feel even worse about committing it, and shame would just rush in like a dam breaking, and it just would overwhelm me; a tsunami just taking me away. Shame is not the place we want to be, ever. It's the lowest form of consciousness, to imagine that the problem with the world is how bad each of us are.

The cross is actually the opposite: It's leading us out of shame into a place of enormous love, mercy, acceptance. But let's take a broad-brush approach here, looking at this whole thing that has happened between humanity and divinity. It started, obviously, in a garden, where there was a wonderful relationship between human beings and God—a oneness, a comfort level, described as a beautiful garden of openness and receptivity; in the image of nakedness, being ourselves completely, not embarrassed or ashamed of any part of us. And there we are, in this wonderful place.

It's almost as if, it seems to me, that there is a way that God did not want to leave the relationship between what he created in terms of humanity and himself. He didn't want to have that kind of almost innocent, childlike relationship you might describe as a parent of a very, very young infant child. He wanted something "grittier," more real; so what we have in the story, it seems to me, is that the sin of Adam and Eve is a growth in awareness and consciousness—it's almost, if you've ever raised an adolescent, you know what adolescence is like. It's all of a sudden, "I don't need rules and I don't need people, and I don't need anything. I just want to go off and do what *I* need to do." Kind of this sense of being filled with the *autonomy* that comes with realizing that you're a human being and you've got enormous potential. So human beings fell into that trap, and that was "the sin," to be autonomous, to be separate from God, to be on our own. "We don't *need* God."

So in a way you look at the story, and God was most upset with the *serpent*, because he was the liar, and people were pretty vulnerable back then (as we still are). The real punishment goes to the serpent, but it's clear that if people are going to go off on their own, what God is saying to those leaving the Garden, the place of innocence: "This is going to be tough. Life is going to be hard. And I'll do everything I can to help you." And all that he really did do is basically evaluate them and find them wanting, and so often said, "I just want to destroy all these human beings and start over again. They are *so* far from what I want them to be."

And then he realized they needed something, so he gave them the wisdom of the Law, and the Law was going to give them the guidance they needed, and they would work out of their own stuff to follow this wisdom of God, and the more they tried—they were at times successful—but mostly you have the whole series of Old Testament stories where they fail over and over again.

So let's just say that at the time that Jesus came into the world, it was time for a radical change in the way that human beings related to God, and the way God related to human beings. In the Old Testament, it was about God telling us what to do, and we struggling with our own selfish, self-centered humanity that is *designed* to be self-preserving—so if you feel that sometimes you've been selfish about taking care of yourself, don't feel that. That's who we were created to be. That's why the species survives.

So as human beings we have this kind of weakness of being pretty self-centered, and it is the issue that I think keeps us from surrendering to God. But we didn't realize, I don't think, until the time was right for Jesus to come into the world, that this surrendering to God was also something that God was feeling a need to somehow surrender to us. Now it may sound strange to say "God surrendering to us," but if you look at something very clear in the teaching of Christianity: When you look at Jesus on the cross, we see humanity hanging there in the form of the son of man, Jesus, and we see *God* hanging there, for we believe that God and Jesus are *the same.*

Now this is really tricky, but listen in the gospel again to the struggle that Thomas had. He was the doubter; he was a pessimist kind of guy, and one line about Thomas in John's gospel: When Jesus is talking about how we have to give in to evil, we have to go and face the dark side of this whole thing; it's not working; it's not turning out the way we thought; we're not going to succeed as human beings in terms of hoping to create a whole new world and fix all the problems of the world. It's not going to work. The only way this is going to go is that we're going to have to surrender to the power of evil.

And it didn't make *any* sense to the disciples, and when it came time to go to Jerusalem, where Jesus knew things were going to go *really* bad, I *love* Thomas' response to that: "OK. Let's *all* go, and then we'll *all* die." It wasn't "we'll all go and all die together." No, it's "OK, this thing is looking really dark and we'll all be killed, and it's a mess." So it's so interesting that at the end of the ministry of Jesus, which was only, say, three years, there was a clear indication that everything that they hoped for and longed for—and I'd like you to imagine this—Jesus was 100% human, and he had a divine nature, but he kept saying, *I put that aside, and I'm really experiencing this as* <u>*you*</u> *would experience it as a human being.* So it makes sense to me that Jesus perhaps did not *know* that there was going to be just three short years of his ministry. He didn't *know* for sure at the beginning of it that he wasn't going to be more successful. He must have had nights where he struggled, *I wonder if I'm doing this right. Was I too hard on the Pharisees? I shouldn't have lost my temper in the Temple, when I turned the tables over. Maybe that was the wrong thing.* So just imagine him as a human being going through the same things you do when you're struggling to do what you feel is your calling—whether it's being a good husband or wife or good parent, good at whatever you do—all those things we feel at times, you know,

"I'm messing up. I'm messing up!" So think of Jesus going through that, his disciples looking at him, wondering if this whole thing has gone wrong, and it's not going to work. So here's Jesus, the man, having to face the fact that it didn't turn out the way his humanity would have hoped. Even though he had a deep conviction, when it started going wrong, that it wasn't really something he could change, or maybe even *should* change, so he had to surrender.

So we had the Garden of Gethsemane, which is such an important element in our understanding of Jesus, because he—think of this. It happens after the Lord's Supper, he's in the Garden, and even though he's told the disciples, "Everything is going to work out, it's going to be OK, I'm going to be with you. Don't worry." And he goes into the Garden and says, *I want out of this; I don't want to do this; I really don't want to do this! Is there any other thing we can do besides this? This is too hard, too painful, too difficult.* And I don't think the pain was so much the beating of his body and the hanging on the cross—that was *horrible*—but think about it, how many people suffer for years and years and go through excruciating pain; and Jesus went through his passion in one morning, beaten in the morning, then taken to the cross, and it started in the morning and ended by 3 o'clock. I'm not diminishing the horror of the pain, but it wasn't the pain of his body; it was the disappointment of his ego and his humanity that he *thought* he was going to be much more successful than this, and there he is, hanging there, as a failure with his disciples nowhere around except for one of them, John, who really understood him and "got" him; and then there's Mary, his mother, and Mary Magdalene. All those crowds and all those adoring people—where were they? They were there on the Sunday before, but none of them were there now. If you can imagine that Palm Sunday was the height of his popularity, and it looked like everything might work out so well, even though he knew things were risky when he went to Jerusalem, and he was worried, and his worries came true, and there he is, hanging on the cross.

And you think of it, you know, his temptations in the desert were really interesting. They were almost the temptations that are in every single human being in some form. You know, that temptation that you want life to be just comfortable, and you want all your needs met. That was one of the temptations, about turning stones into bread. Then there was the temptation of wanting to be certain—there are a lot of us—that's the only security we have, to be certain, to figure things out. Or the most common one we all get caught up in is *success*. That's the third temptation. So to be comfortable, to be certain, to be successful—that's in *all* of us. And that's the part in humanity that is being crucified. Give up on that. It's not the goal. There is a way to have your needs satisfied, and there is a way to be certain, and there is a way to be successful, but it's not in the ways of the world. So everything that Jesus had to endure was, OK, let go of *that* system and now enter into a *new* system. So we see *human-*

ity giving in and doing what it is called to do, but it's just so against simple human nature.

And then you look at Thomas in the gospel, and he says something so powerful when he sees who Jesus really is. He says, "You're my Lord, and you're my God." So Thomas and the disciples knew it was *God* hanging on the cross, and what God was doing—and this is the mystery that I have never seen before—it was *God* hanging on the cross, too; and *he's* surrendering, *he's* giving in, saying, "I can no longer demand of you that you follow my Law. What I have to do is *forgive* you." And so that image of a majestic God demanding all the honor and all the adoration and all the sacrifices; "No, I'm going to sacrifice for you. I'm going to hang here and show you my divinity at its greatest. The *power* of my divinity is my love for you, my desire to feel what you feel. And when I feel it, I don't ever want you to be in this pain again. I'll do *everything* I can to change that." There's an image in the cross of humanity going through a transformation, and I know this sounds strange, and don't take it too literally, that you'll get all messed up in the theology of divinity, but it's God somehow expressing that which was always in him, that he said, "I am not there to demand from you as much as I'm there to *give* you something so powerful and so beautiful—my love, my mercy, my understanding. I know what it's like to go through what you're going through. I know how tough it is, and I'll be there."

So when we look at that cross, we see *two* mysteries unfolding: the mystery of God revealing himself finally *fully* to us, and we see finally humanity in its greatest hour—not taking care of itself, not being certain, not being successful in the eyes of the world, but somehow finding the place of vulnerability and openness to God so that he is now in us and we are in him in such a new way. We need him, and we just had to admit that. And he needs us. Without us, he can't save the world. Without him, we can't be fully who we are. What a mystery! What a union! What an awesome thing to ponder.

Father, the mystery of the cross is the heart of your teaching. Bless us with the wisdom we find in this image. Help us to let it penetrate every part of our body and resonate through our heart to those around us. It's about you; it's about each of us coming together in a union that was destined but hidden and now found. And we ask this in Jesus' name. Amen.

I'd like to dedicate this program to two really beautiful women in my life, people I met when they were in college and I was the chaplain. Teacy Thompson then, Teacy Bernardy now, was a friend and a wonderful support for me when I was going through my first years at the University of Dallas. She was and is a great friend. And a mutual friend of ours was Pat Ryan then and now Pat Ryan Brown. And Teacy would like to dedicate this program to Pat, and I would just like to thank both of them for everything they've been in my life. Pat, it's your birthday, so from Teacy and also from me, *happy birthday*, and I ask God to bless you.

Acts 5: 12-16

[12]Many signs and wonders were done among the people at the hands of the apostles.
They were all together in Solomon's portico.[13]None of the others dared to join them, but
the people esteemed them.[14]Yet more than ever, believers in the Lord, great numbers of
men and women, were added to them.[15]Thus they even carried the sick out into the
streets and laid them on cots and mats so that when Peter came by, at least his shadow
might fall on one or another of them.[16]A large number of people from the towns in the
vicinity of Jerusalem also gathered, bringing the sick and those disturbed by unclean
spirits, and they were all cured.

Revelation 1:9-11, 12-13, 17-19

[9]I, John, your brother, who share with you the distress, the kingdom, and the endurance
we have in Jesus, found myself on the island called Patmos because I proclaimed God's
word and gave testimony to Jesus.[10]I was caught up in spirit on the Lord's day and
heard behind me a voice as loud as a trumpet,[11]which said, "Write on a scroll what you
see . . ."[12] Then I turned to see whose voice it was that spoke to me, and when I turned, I
saw seven gold lampstands[13]and in the midst of the lampstands one like a son of
man, wearing an ankle-length robe, with a gold sash around his chest.

[17]When I caught sight of him, I fell down at his feet as though dead. He touched me
with his right hand and said, "Do not be afraid. I am the first and the last,[18]the one who
lives. Once I was dead, but now I am alive forever and ever. I hold the keys to death
and the netherworld. [19]Write down, therefore, what you have seen, and what is happening, and what will happen afterwards.

John 20:19-31

[19]On the evening of that first day of the week, when the doors were locked, where the
disciples were, for fear of the Jews, Jesus came and stood in their midst and said to
them, "Peace be with you."[20]When he had said this, he showed them his hands and his
side. The disciples rejoiced when they saw the Lord.[21][Jesus] said to them again, "Peace

be with you. As the Father has sent me, so I send you."[22]And when he had said this, he
breathed on them and said to them, "Receive the holy Spirit.[23]Whose sins you forgive
are forgiven them, and whose sins you retain are retained."
[24]Thomas, called Didymus, one of the Twelve, was not with them when Jesus came.[25]So
the other disciples said to him, "We have seen the Lord." But he said to them, "Unless I
see the mark of the nails in his hands and put my finger into the nailmarks and put my
hand into his side, I will not believe."[26]Now a week later his disciples were again inside
and Thomas was with them. Jesus came, although the doors were locked, and stood in
their midst and said, "Peace be with you."[27]Then he said to Thomas, "Put your finger
here and see my hands, and bring your hand and put it into my side, and do not be un-
believing, but believe."[28]Thomas answered and said to him, "My Lord and my
God!"[29] Jesus said to him, "Have you come to believe because you have seen me?
Blessed are those who have not seen and have believed."
[30]Now Jesus did many other signs in the presence of [his] disciples that are not written
in this book.[31]But these are written that you may [come to] believe that Jesus is the Messiah, the Son of God, and that through this belief you may have life in his name.

THIRD SUNDAY OF EASTER

Acts 5:27-32, 40-41; Revelation 5:11-14; John 21:1-19

May your people exult forever, O God, in renewed youthfulness of spirit, so that rejoicing now in the restored glory of our adoption, we may look forward in confident hope to the rejoicing in the day of the resurrection, through our Lord Jesus Christ, your Son, who lives and reigns with you in the unity of the holy Spirit, one God for ever and ever. Amen.

It's been just two weeks since we celebrated the great feast, the heart of the Christian faith, the great feast of Christ's death and resurrection. And I want, as I believe these readings long to do, I want to awaken in us more and more an awareness of what this all means. What is it that we're supposed to see, feel, understand, experience from this event? Paul says, If you don't *believe* that Jesus rose from the dead, your faith is worthless. And that can't simply mean this one doctrine of faith, this one thing as an item to put on your "I must believe" list. If you say *yes* to that, then that's all that it requires. No, it requires more than just believing in it. It really depends upon *experiencing* what it promises. To *feel* it, to *know* it.

The reading that we started with, from the Acts of the Apostles, gives us a really good indication of what it is that Jesus is leading us into through this action of his resurrection. And you know that for most of the Jewish people that lived at the time that Jesus walked this earth, some believed in the resurrection, that there was life after death; others didn't believe it, and there was some inconsistency in that, but the most interesting thing is that none of them had an image of what we now know as *heaven*, and hell—a place of punishment. Heaven as a place of eternal life. And think of eternal life more as *abundant life*.

So the people that seemed to be the most interested in stopping this message of Jesus were not ordinary people that walked the streets. It really was the leadership of the Church that had the hardest time with it. And we have in this particular first reading an image of the Sanhedrin, which was the group—usually twenty-one people, though it could be as large as seventy, like the Supreme Court of every city that the Israelites lived in. It was the body of advisors and guides that would say, "We have decided this is what is right; this is what is true." So the Sanhedrin call the disciples in and say, "You've got to stop talking about this man Jesus. Just stop it." And what's so interesting to me, it seems they were intuitively wanting it to stop because it really did undercut their power. What is clear that the disciples say to them: "We're not here to follow the Sanhedrin; we're not here to follow the leaders of this religious group. We're here to follow God." Well, that's threatening to *any* religion, to say, "I'm not going to listen just to you. I'm going to listen to God who is *in* me, who is a part of me that reveals himself to me, who walks with me."

So it's easy to see that the thing that's really threatening is the thing that the resurrection of Jesus so powerfully reveals—that when Jesus dies and seemingly is gone, he is there again in a way that could not be ever expected. And he teaches this and makes it clear through his post-resurrection appearances—we had one last week, and we have one this week—what I want you to feel in this is not just that Jesus is saying, "Death does not end one's existence." It *does* mean that, but it's not *just* that. It's more exciting than that. It's saying that death opens up, for the one who dies, the capacity to enter more fully into our life.

And then as you look back on what Jesus is describing, as far as his life with the disciples—and he is a human being, remember, 100% human—and so he's setting a precedent for how it is that you and I relate to each other. And this is what he's saying to his disciples; this is what he said before he died; this is what he tends to go back over again and again when he appears again after his death: "Look. I *love* you. I have always loved you. And my love for you is not going to engage with you in terms of judgment and condemnation, but my love is going to engage with you as forgiveness, acceptance. And somehow, through that acceptance and through that forgiveness, you are empowered, *empowered,* to believe and to feel something about yourself and about me that is so amazing!" It goes something like this: Jesus talking to his disciples in John's gospel before. The night before he's arrested, and he's got this conversation with them, and it's so amazing. He's saying, "Look, I want you to understand something. The Father lives in me, and I live in the Father. That's the relationship I have with divinity. And I want *you* to know that I have this gift in me that I know is so powerful. It heals, it transforms, it never judges, it lifts up; it doesn't condemn or destroy. It's in me. So you let me in you; if I can come into you, I'll bring this power with me into you, and that will ignite something in you called the divinity in you. It will grow, it will flourish." It's an amazing teaching!

So he says, *I'm in the Father; the Father*

is in me. I want to be in you. And the reason I want to be in you is because I want you to be in each other. I want you to be one, like the Father and I are one. So I've come to create something that unifies people in a way that's beyond anything we could imagine. It goes way, way beyond normal human activity.

I know what it's like to be loved. I know what it's like to love someone, I know how that is sometimes a wonderful experience of receiving, and I know how sometimes love can sometimes turn into something that isn't anything like receiving—it can suck life out of us. We call it *co-dependency.* So we know that connections with human beings are not always the most positive things. We've had experiences both ways. But there's something unique about the way Jesus is inviting you and me to love each other. And he's saying it this way. He's saying, "What I want you to realize is that if God dwells in you, the *way* he dwells in you is for you to let him love you. But you have to realize that his love is only that which *gives* life. It never demands too much of us; it never robs us of our freedom; it never causes us pain in that kind of negative sense where someone is abusing us. *It is all about giving life.* And what we have to do is believe that he loves us that way. He's a servant, not a taskmaster. Then, that's when he can enter into us. That's the only way we let anyone in, if we think they're safe, that we'll let them in to be a part of us. And then when he's a part of us, he's saying, "Alright, now I'm in you; you have this sense that you are loved, that you are forgiven, that life is good, that all things will work out. I am in you with that kind of power to take care of you. Now, when you feel that security and that sense of strength, then I want you in turn to bestow your love on other people, but I want you to love them with a sense that what is happening when you love them is that this confidence and this presence of God in you somehow reaches out and seeks to awaken in the other person this amazing sense of God's loving presence."

All this makes sense to me in terms of this appearance we've just listened to in the gospel, because here's Jesus, he's coming back for the third time in this gospel of John, the third time Jesus appeared. And it's morning, and the disciples have gone back to their ordinary work. They're back to doing their fishing. They don't fully yet understand what they're called to do because they haven't yet received the holy Spirit on Pentecost. So they're in this kind of liminal, borderland space. They ponder and they wonder what this whole thing is about. But they really are just still wondering more than they are understanding. So what happens in this encounter is that *Peter* becomes the focus. When Jesus gives them that kind of intuition that enables them to be so much more fruitful in their decisions, I think they recognize . . . John says, "Oh, oh! This is Jesus." This is the kind of thing he does for us. He gives us this kind of insight and wisdom, and we can be so fruitful. Then this dialogue with Peter. It's clear that many people will say, "Well, he's asked to answer the question three times, 'Do you love me?' because he *denied* him three times, and it's sort of making up for that." Well, that could well be. If you understand how much I love you, you will love me back. If you understand how much I love you, you will love me back. So "Do you love me?" is another way to say, "Do you understand how much I love you?" And Peter says, "Yes, I know you love me, because I do love you for who you are and what you're doing for me." Then Jesus says three things: *I want you to feed my lambs and tend my sheep.* Feed and tend, feed and tend. "Feed," to me, is giving to other people this incredible sense of the presence of God in them. "Feed them; awaken in them this awesome power that I am, in them." And then *tend them.* Tending is an interesting word because to tend someone to do something is not to force them to do it or tell them how to do it. It's to try to direct them in a particular path. We say that someone is "tending" towards this. They're sort of leaning in that direction. They're going. He doesn't say *control* them; he doesn't say to *shame* them into doing what they're supposed to—the things that we might say are the things of the world; to judge and condemn is the way the world works. The way the Spirit works is to forgive and to free. So he's saying, "I want you to have a ministry that is radically different from the institutions that so often run religions, countries, people. It's not power *over* people, but it's somehow *empowering* people." And that's what Peter is asked to do, and it's what it means to *follow* Jesus, which is the third thing that Jesus says. So he's saying it to Peter and to you and to me: We've got to do something different from the way we sometimes see the world working, even religions working, institutions working. We have to get out of that incredibly negative environment of condemnation and criticism, judgment; enter into the place of feeding and tending; loving and guiding, mostly through example, through encouragement. But notice if one is *tending,* it seems that they have already inside of them a sense of the direction they need to go. And to treat that with respect and to believe in that. That's the key to tending. So a reminder today then in this post-resurrection experience is, if we're going to follow Jesus we need to believe in his love, know that he dwells in us, share that with others, and watch them grow with that spiritual food, and watch them change from the desire to be like him.

Father, you are the shepherd; you are the one who knows us, guides us, stays with us in all things. Bless us with the greater awareness of this gift of you in us, and as we sense it, as we believe in it, as we trust in it, let it be the source of life and light that we share with our brothers and sisters. And we ask this in Jesus' name. Amen.

Acts 5: 27-32, 40-41
27When they had brought [the apostles] in and made them stand before the Sanhedrin,
the high priest questioned them,28"We gave you strict orders [did we not?] to stop
teaching in that name. Yet you have filled Jerusalem with your teaching and want to
bring this man's blood upon us."29But Peter and the apostles said in reply, "We must
obey God rather than men.30The God of our ancestors raised Jesus, though you had him
killed by hanging him on a tree.31God exalted him at his right hand as leader and savior
to grant Israel repentance and forgiveness of sins.32We are witnesses of these things, as
is the holy Spirit that God has given to those who obey him."

40After recalling the apostles, they had them flogged, ordered them to stop speaking in
the name of Jesus, and dismissed them.41So they left the presence of the Sanhedrin, rejoicing that they had been found worthy to suffer dishonor for the sake of the name.

Revelation 5: 11-14
11I, John, looked again and heard the voices of many angels who surrounded the throne
and the living creatures and the elders. They were countless in number,12and they cried
out in a loud voice:
"Worthy is the Lamb that was slain
to receive power and riches, wisdom and strength,
honor and glory and blessing."
13Then I heard every creature in heaven and on earth and under the earth and in the sea,
everything in the universe, cry out:
"To the one who sits on the throne and to the Lamb
be blessing and honor, glory and might,
forever and ever."
14The four living creatures answered, "Amen," and the elders fell down and worshiped.

John 21: 1-19
1After this, Jesus revealed himself again to his disciples at the Sea of Tiberias. He revealed himself in this way.2Together were Simon Peter, Thomas called Didymus, Na-
thanael from Cana in Galilee, Zebedee's sons, and two others of his disciples.3Simon Peter said to them, "I am going fishing." They said to him, "We also will come with you."
So they went out and got into the boat, but that night they caught nothing.4When it was
already dawn, Jesus was standing on the shore; but the disciples did not realize that it
was Jesus.5Jesus said to them, "Children, have you caught anything to eat?" They answered him, "No."6So he said to them, "Cast the net over the right side of the boat and
you will find something." So they cast it, and were not able to pull it in because of the

number of fish.7So the disciple whom Jesus loved said to Peter, "It is the Lord." When
Simon Peter heard that it was the Lord, he tucked in his garment, for he was lightly
clad, and jumped into the sea.8The other disciples came in the boat, for they were not far
from shore, only about a hundred yards, dragging the net with the fish.9When they
climbed out on shore, they saw a charcoal fire with fish on it and bread.10Jesus said to
them, "Bring some of the fish you just caught."11So Simon Peter went over and dragged
the net ashore full of one hundred fifty-three large fish. Even though there were so
many, the net was not torn.12Jesus said to them, "Come, have breakfast." And none of
the disciples dared to ask him, "Who are you?" because they realized it was the
Lord.13Jesus came over and took the bread and gave it to them, and in like manner the
fish.14This was now the third time Jesus was revealed to his disciples after being raised
from the dead.
15When they had finished breakfast, Jesus said to Simon Peter, "Simon, son of John, do
you love me more than these?" He said to him, "Yes, Lord, you know that I love you."
He said to him, "Feed my lambs."16He then said to him a second time, "Simon, son of
John, do you love me?" He said to him, "Yes, Lord, you know that I love you." He said
to him, "Tend my sheep."17He said to him the third time, "Simon, son of John, do you
love me?" Peter was distressed that he had said to him a third time, "Do you love me?"
and he said to him, "Lord, you know everything; you know that I love you." [Jesus]
said to him, "Feed my sheep.18Amen, amen, I say to you, when you were younger, you
used to dress yourself and go where you wanted; but when you grow old, you will
stretch out your hands, and someone else will dress you and lead you where you do not
want to go."19He said this signifying by what kind of death he would glorify God. And
when he had said this, he said to him, "Follow me."

FOURTH SUNDAY OF EASTER

Acts 13:14, 43-52; Revelation 7:9, 14-17; John 10:27-30

Almighty and ever-living God, lead us to share in the joys of heaven so that the humble flock may reach where the brave shepherd has gone before, who lives and reigns with you in the unity of the holy Spirit, one God for ever and ever. Amen.

The piece of music we just listened to (*Oh Cruz Fiel*) is what is often played during the veneration of the cross on Good Friday. And the Church continues its reflections on this greatest of all mysteries. For those of us who believe in the Christ as our savior, it's the mystery of his acting in a way that renewed the very essence of who we are. Christ's death on the cross is a *great* mystery, and we know that it refers to a new union between divinity and humanity, but it also is that moment in which human beings are able finally to reach their fullness because they now have this amazing strength that dwells *inside* of them. It's *divinity* inside of them. It's a divinity that becomes their guide, their shepherd.

I'm always fascinated by the fact that in the early church, the image that was so comforting to people was not the image of the crucifixion but rather the image of Christ, the Good Shepherd. And in a sense they are reflections on the same mystery. So we again pursue, as we have last week, and we'll continue for a while on this image of, *Who* is the Christ that is resurrected? *Where* is he? What is his work? How do we experience him? We're getting ready as we move along, with two more Sundays, to the feast of the Ascension, Jesus rising and returning to the Father after the days that he spent on this earth being with his disciples, and then the great feast of Pentecost, which is the feast that we celebrate as a way of keeping in mind the presence of God coming as a fire into our hearts.

So let's look at this set of readings, with the hope that in them we find a kind of wisdom that puts us more and more in touch with this greatest of gifts: God's presence in us, God shepherding us. In the first reading, we go back to the time when the disciples were first preaching, and I want to give you a little background because I think it's fascinating when we look at the Jewish faith that was being lived at the time Jesus walked the earth. It was anything but a unified group of people all believing the same thing. There were many different groups within the Jewish community that had different focuses, different emphasis. As I say these words, they'll sound familiar to you because we have the Pharisees as a group, the Sadducees, the Essenes. We have the Zealots, we have the scribes. Who were they? What was their role? What do we learn from the fact that these different elements live side by side within this great religion called Judaism.

Let's look at the *focus* of each of them because in a way they're religious movements; in another way they're kind of political powers. (There wasn't much of a distinction between religion and politics back then.) So let's look at them carefully. I'm going to oversimplify it just to make my point. The Pharisees were in a way the movement that was most in touch with the ordinary folks, with the poor. And their primary focus was, you find God by listening to his law and following his law. The Sadducees were another group, and they had a lot to do with temple worship, so their *primary* focus was to tell people that they can get in touch with God through the rituals of the temple, and they were much more in tune with the more sophisticated and wealthier members of the community. And you had the scribes, and the scribes were the people who were always translating and rewriting the Torah, the scriptures, so they were in a way the scripture scholars. They were the ones who said, the way to find God is to understand the Law, understand the scriptures. And then you have the Essenes, and they were an interesting group because they felt the way to find God was to separate yourself from the world and to live in the desert, to live a kind of *mystical* experience of God, to *have* that mystical experience. And they had many rituals, like the bathing every day, kind of like a daily baptism they would go through. And there were also the Zealots. The Zealots were interesting. They were the radicals. They were the ones who believed the way we can experience God is to use force and power to destroy all the enemies of the Israelite people.

It's amazing to me—*that* sounds like a good cross-section of almost every single religion. So you take all those parts, all those different things, and you try to grab hold of what it is that, ultimately, *our* God is asking us to focus on, because all those are different ways of focusing on different things to come to the same end—to find this mysterious thing called *the kingdom,* which is a place of being *satisfied,* having that which quenches our thirst, that which satisfies our longing for food, that which takes away our anxiety and fear. That's what human nature is designed to accomplish. It's called our most basic human instinct—called *self-preservation*—

we *all* have it. We should honor it and recognize it for what it is, but realize that when we work for that goal simply out of our mind, we end up in one of those categories that I just listed.

So in *place* of that, we have something radically different. And let's go to the second reading to look at the radical difference because we see again in one of the visions of John in the book of Revelation, we see something that's again the image of Jesus, who is the one who is here, who's come into the world to open for us the key to finding the fullness of what God longs to share with us. We have him being placed on a throne, and all these people are standing around him, giving him all kinds of praise and awe. They're just totally in love with this figure because of what he's been able to accomplish in them. They have mysterious language. Their robes are white because they've been washed in the blood of the Lamb. All these people realize that no matter what they were doing, no matter where they have been, no matter how far off they'd gone from having the right means to accomplish the goal of finding this kingdom—they've all been forgiven. *It's all the past. Don't worry about where you've been. Just delight in the fact that I am here with you, and I'm here to save, to heal, to transform. But the way I'm going to do it is so amazing!* He reveals, *The way I'm going to do it is to enter into you and to live inside of you, to be a part of you.*

So that means we no longer simply rely upon the Law. We don't simply rely upon rituals. We don't simply rely upon separating ourselves from the world in order to find peace. We don't necessarily go after all the enemies and try to destroy them—even as sometimes we try to destroy the weaknesses inside of us, and somehow when we use destruction to try to bring about transformation and healing, it never works. No matter what all those things were, we have this new image of a God who dwells in us so that in a way all those things have their place, all those things have their role, but we need something more *core*, something more basic, something that holds all that other stuff together and keeps us balanced. And it is this amazing promise: that when Jesus leaves this world, he says so clearly to his disciples, and he's saying it to everyone: *The only way for me to be who God has called me to be—and my name, Jesus, means "God saves"—the only way I can save you from the confusion and the extremes of all these different parts is to somehow be your shepherd, be your guide. I want to come inside of you. And I'll live there, and I'll be with you.*

I know you hear me say this over and over again, but somehow it's a mystery we should ponder, I think, every single day. What does it mean that God is inside of me? How do I work with that? How do I know that that's what I'm working on? What's interesting to me as I used all those images of different ways in which we tend to find the Spirit, find the kingdom, it seems to me that what we need is something that is going to be able to guide us on a moment-by-moment basis of being able to use all those different means to come to this conviction that this God of ours is there primarily *for us*, and that his guidance is so *personal*. I've said this to you often, that the problem with Christianity is that it's so amazingly simple and so intensely personal. And we have this God who says, "Look. Just trust me. I'm here inside of you. Listen to me. I'll tell you everything you need to know. I'll show you everything you need to see, how to open your heart, understand everything that's out there that you can't figure out. I am absolutely here to be your guide. And all I need for you to do is to become this incredibly powerful, empty vessel; *empty vessel*." It means I'm not filled with one particular way of thinking I can find God. I'm not looking to something outside of myself, other than the God who is inside of me, to save me. I'm empty in the sense that the place, the core of my being, my heart, is there to hold this incredible, guiding presence of a God who wants to dwell there. He wants to dwell there and guide us *from* there. And he does it by truly entering into us. I mean it's like, "I want to marry you. I want to come and live with you. I want to be in your house. I want to hang out with you." I mean, it's like it seems silly for me in a way to say that; it seems silly in my mind to think of God as this *intimate*, because he's so great, so mighty, so powerful. So how can he be so intimate and so personal? Well, he can! That's all I can tell you. He *can*! It's what he does best. And when he does it, he does it in a way that is so *natural*. I guess that's what I want to say. So *natural*! I think about times—I was saying this to a friend the other night—I think about the way I used to pray, and I'd say, "God, you don't really know everything that's going on in my life, so let me bring you up to date." And I'd tell him what I'm struggling with, as if he didn't know, and then I'd say to God, "Wherever you are—I know you're out there somewhere, wherever you are—now that I've told you what my needs are, would you do something to enter into that? Would you come and be a part of this?" As if he's not already there! I'd say, "Come down if you can and kind of help me out. And if you can't take care of it right away, I'm consciously knowing that you *can*. I mean, I'd *like* to believe that you can, but if you don't, I guess that really you're too busy. So excuse the interruption because I guess you've got bigger things on your plate than *my* needs." That's a little exaggerated, but I think that's pretty much the way I used to pray. Now it's so different. I go inside, I say, "You see everything. You know everything I need before I even ask for it, and I don't even want to tell you what I would like to see happen. I *can* say, I want to do something to be an instrument of healing, so what I want to be is someone that *you* can use to accomplish whatever it is that I'm longing to see happen." So I become a *full* vessel in that sense, full of God's wisdom, full of God's grace, God's presence, God's love, to enter into whatever personal situation *I'm* struggling with, or wherever I want to bring it—into a friend's situation, into a tragedy that happens in our country, into a violent act against innocent people. I want to be an instrument of being there for them, and we can *do* that by simply *intending* it, by wanting God to use me and my care and concern, and it's almost like God says, "Don, I want *you* to manifest my care, my love for these people by your intention to love and care for them." *That's* the way it works. What a beautiful image, to know I have that power, to know I have that wisdom—which is not mine, but comes through me. So the challenge, always, is just for us to continue to trust. And a shepherd who is so personal and so real, so much inside of us that he can resonate through us the most amazing gifts to the people around us. And there we are with this great reservoir of energy and life and food and drink for those who are thirsty and longing for more. We, by our intention, can bring that to them. *That's* the challenge; that's the belief that God has called us to through his death and resurrection, through his cross—so we can find the places where we truly long and need to serve.

Father, your life, your presence, is within each of us. Help us to grasp the depth of this mystery as we learn more and more to turn to you for all that we are called to be. Help us to feel the peace that comes from trusting in one who guides so carefully, so wisely. Help us to give in to you, our good shepherd, and we ask this in Jesus' name. Amen.

Acts 13: 14, 43-52
[14][Paul and Barnabas] continued on from Perga and reached Antioch in Pisidia. On the
sabbath they entered (into) the synagogue and took their seats.

[43]After the congregation had dispersed, many Jews and worshipers who were converts
to Judaism followed Paul and Barnabas, who spoke to them and urged them to remain
faithful to the grace of God.
[44]On the following sabbath almost the whole city gathered to hear the word of the
Lord.[45]When the Jews saw the crowds, they were filled with jealousy and with violent
abuse contradicted what Paul said.[46]Both Paul and Barnabas spoke out boldly and said,
"It was necessary that the word of God be spoken to you first, but since you reject it and
condemn yourselves as unworthy of eternal life, we now turn to the Gentiles.[47]For so
the Lord has commanded us, 'I have made you a light to the Gentiles, that you may be
an instrument of salvation to the ends of the earth.'"
[48]The Gentiles were delighted when they heard this and glorified the word of the Lord.
All who were destined for eternal life came to believe,[49]and the word of the Lord continued to spread through the whole region.[50]The Jews, however, incited the women of
prominence who were worshipers and the leading men of the city, stirred up a persecution against Paul and Barnabas, and expelled them from their territory.[51]So they shook

the dust from their feet in protest against them and went to Iconium.[52]The disciples
were filled with joy and the holy Spirit.

Revelation 7: 9, 14-17

[9]After this I had a vision of a great multitude, which no one could count, from every nation, race, people, and tongue. They stood before the throne and before the Lamb, wearing white robes and holding palm branches in their hands.

[14]He said to me, "These are the ones who have survived the time of great distress; they
have washed their robes and made them white in the blood of the Lamb.
[15]"For this reason they stand before God's throne
and worship him day and night in his temple.
The one who sits on the throne will shelter them.
[16]They will not hunger or thirst anymore,
nor will the sun or any heat strike them.
[17]For the Lamb who is in the center of the throne will shepherd them
and lead them to springs of life-giving water,
and God will wipe away every tear from their eyes."

John 10: 27-30

[27]My sheep hear my voice; I know them, and they follow me.[28]I give them eternal life,
and they shall never perish. No one can take them out of my hand.[29]My Father, who has
given them to me, is greater than all, and no one can take them out of the Father's
hand.[30]The Father and I are one."

FIFTH SUNDAY OF EASTER

Acts 14:21-27; Revelation 21:1-5; John 13:31-35

Almighty, ever-living God, constantly accomplish the Paschal mystery within us, that those you are pleased to make new in holy baptism may, under your protective care, bear much fruit and come to the joys of life eternal; through our Lord Jesus Christ, your Son, who lives and reigns with you in the unity of the holy Spirit, one God for ever and ever. Amen.

In our tradition, we have two testaments. The Judeo-Christian tradition came in two parts, and it is so important to understand what each of them was about and how they interface. The Old Testament is the first revelation from God to his people, and it is focused on, I'll say, two major themes. One is monotheism, God revealing to his people that he is the one and only God, the most powerful one; and the other is the whole notion that this God is a God of *justice*. And what he wants so much to do is to give his people a wisdom so that they will make the right decisions. He gives them a law that is a revelation of who they really are, what their nature is like; and he's trying to teach them that they have, basically in them, a longing to be connected to a higher power than themselves. They need to honor and worship this being, called God. And then, they are to treat each other in a certain way. The ways are very fair and make a lot of sense: to not lie, to not cheat, to not steal, to not murder, to respect each other's commitments. All those things make total sense.

But that's basically, in a way, as far as it could go. (I know I'm oversimplifying, but just stay with me.) Then comes the New Testament. It's called "the good news." It's not that the Old Testament is "bad news," but there's something in the New Testament that people have longed for forever. And there is that long tradition in the Old Testament of waiting for a messiah, waiting for a message, waiting for an insight that would come, that would change everything, that would answer all their longings and all their needs. They so often thought this messiah would come and straighten out the political system and make the Israelite people the leaders of the world. They had a very oversimplified notion of what this messiah would reveal. But if we ponder and enter into the New Testament and we enter *deeply* into it, we recognize the *heart* of the message of the Messiah is something that is so radical, so different, so beyond anything that anyone could imagine—that so many of us who are more steeped in the Old Testament because it's so much easier to understand, so much more practical—in a sense, you can understand it if you're in a much lower level of consciousness, and that's where people were then. But in the new age of the New Testament, as we continue to move in this process of our own human development, and deepening our awareness of what is, we grow in our consciousness; we're more and more capable of grasping *the good news*, the incredible mystery revealed to us in the New Testament.

So in my reflections today, I want to hopefully draw you into a greater understanding of how different life is for all of us when we completely understand and accept and begin to live the teaching of the Messiah. It's not that it's contradictory to all the prophets of the Old Testament; it's just that it fulfills it. It brings it to completion. And at the *heart* of this message is the difference between how God dwells with his people—how he dwells with his people.

In the Old Testament, it's very clear that God dwelt with his people through his teaching, particularly his message of justice, the message of the Law. The wisdom God gave to his people was his presence. And so to emphasize that the wisdom of God, the presence of God, was *the Law*, there was an Ark of the Covenant, and in that Ark was kept the tablets upon which the Law was written. So the Law was then honored; the presence of the Law in their life was honored through this Ark that was kept in the center of the Temple. And only the special men who were assigned to this role, the priestly class, were the ones who were able to enter into this special place, and draw from this Law the wisdom, and they in turn then taught and preached to the people and told them how to live. And because the message was basically one of justice, it meant that if you followed the Law, you were rewarded with a good life; if you didn't follow the Law, your life was less than what you had hoped for. OK? Real simple.

We move to the New Testament. How does the Messiah reveal to us the new information, this wonderful news of a *new* way that God longs to dwell with his people? When Jesus, the Messiah, revealed this message, he was called a blasphemer. He was ridiculed, laughed at; he was condemned—primarily because he spoke of a relationship with God that was so intimate, so personal, so beyond anyone's imagination as to who God really is.

Jesus said, *My Father, the God who is, lives in me, dwells in me.* God no longer dwells among his people in his Law, or *as* Law, but he dwells *personally* with us. He's *in* us—the indwelling presence of God in our hearts. That's the heart of everything I long to teach to all of you who listen to me.

Now listen to these readings. It's interesting: the first reading, from the Acts of the Apostles, is all about the work of the early church, and I love the language that's in it, and the language is—listen to this—when they were going around doing all this work of somehow feeding the followers of the Christ, helping them understand the gift that they had been given; let's say they were going around affirming the presence of God in each of their hearts, and he comes back and as they gather the church together and they say, "We want to tell you something. We want to tell you . . . (And they could have said, "We want to tell you what we've done for these people. We were so effective. We went out there and we opened their hearts to the mystery of God, and we did some fantastic things!" No. They don't say that.) Here's what happened: When they arrived, they called the church together and reported what God had done with them. Interesting! What God had done *with* them. So that statement reveals that they were under the clear understanding that what they were now doing was not their work but God somehow in them working through them, accomplishing the most amazing things through them. They saw it; they understood it.

Let's look at the second reading, from Revelation, a very interesting, kind of complicated book. It's more metaphorical and allegorical than almost anything else in Scripture, and here it is. It's John having this vision, and what he's seeing is the effect of God entering into the world in a new way. And John, being the mystic that he was, realizes that God is not just entering into human beings in a new, special way, but he's entering into Creation in a new and special way, into the earth in a new and special way. And just as a human being is radically transformed by this indwelling presence of God, so is the earth, so is all of Creation. And John sings out, "Now, *everything* is new! There's a new earth, a new heaven." This whole kingdom that God has come to establish, which is symbolized in the holy city, Jerusalem, is now like a bride ready to receive her husband, God coming into her, filling her with life and the abundance of life. And when this presence of God is felt and known inside of a human being, there's something that shifts. And the image is: Every tear is wiped away, no more mourning, no more death, no more wailing, no more pain. We *know* those things still exist in terms of our existence in the world. There *is* pain and suffering, but remember this is allegorical, this is metaphorical. It's talking about something that might not be the thing that we usually call pain, but you've heard me say over and over again how I know that the presence of God in my life and in your life is there to open you up to the fullness of life so that we can enter into it and draw from it the richness and the beauty that's there. And what we find ourselves doing when we're soaking in this goodness, we're somehow being released of shame and fear and anger. *Those* are the painful things in life! That's what kills us. That's where the mourning is.

There's something about knowing that all things work together for the good, knowing that you have the power to accomplish anything that God needs you to accomplish, knowing that he's on your side; he will help you do whatever it is—whether it's overcoming some kind of addiction; whether it's knowing enough to be a source of life to the persons that you love; raising your children in a way that brings them life; being a partner to your spouse in a way that helps them and helps you; all of that. And when you have that awareness, somehow there's a pain in life that goes away.

So then you listen to the words in the gospel, because this is a very intense moment for Jesus. He's at the Last Supper; he loves so much his disciples; he wants so much for them to realize that *he is with them, and will be with them.* But he's going to be gone for a little while. That waiting, that time between Good Friday and the resurrection of Jesus and his *clarity* in speaking of what had happened to him, that his Spirit is now in a unique way capable of coming and dwelling in them. Just as he says so often, *The Father is in me, and I'm in the Father, and if I come into you, the Father will come into you, and we will dwell there, forever.*

So when Jesus comes back from the dead, he's making it so clear that what he's doing is coming back *into* this world in a form that then goes through locked doors (fear, shame, anger) and enters into the presence of his disciples and gives them this awareness that dispels all their fears, all their shame, all their anger that locked them into that space. What an amazing image! The Spirit coming into human beings.

And listen to *these* words. He says, *Now God is glorified in me, and I am glorifying God in myself.* That's the way I'm reading this. What is that? What is *glory*? *Glory* is an interesting word because when you look it up in the Oxford English Dictionary, it has so many meanings, but it means basically the best that a person is is "their glory"; the highest they can achieve in terms of becoming fully who they are meant to be is their glory. It's like the thing that gives them the most importance, the most prestige, the most fame. And it's interesting here because I think what Jesus is saying is that the "son of man," human beings, are glorified in this moment that Jesus is in when he is recognizing that what he's being asked to do is to surrender, to give in, to allow God to fulfill what he wants to fulfill through Jesus. He's probably at the lowest point of his ministry because his disciples don't really understand him. They're really not "with" him. The work that he came to do is not working, and now the final blow, one of his own goes about the process of turning him over to his enemies. So Judas has just left the room, and Jesus must have felt: Now, this is the moment for all human beings to look at and to watch and to see what *we* are capable of. Human beings are capable of allowing God to fulfill his plan within us when it *doesn't make any sense and it doesn't seem to be right,* in terms of what our own human mind has figured out or what our will wants. The greatest thing about human beings is their capacity to be a *vessel,* an open, empty vessel to God. And that's when you let go of your ego and you let go of everything that is so naturally oriented in us to self-preservation. You *trust* in something way beyond yourself. That is the greatest act that a human being can accomplish, and the greatest act of divinity is to rush into that place, to come into that place without any judgment, without any condemnation, and without any need for that person to change—because the change that will come about when a person is able to say, "I give up. I give in. I'll let it go. I'll let it be done the way you want." When you do that, that's not going back over all your faults and straightening them out, and then coming to God after you're all squeaky clean. No, it's just an admission of need and an acknowledgment of the glory of God that he is that kind of God.

So when Jesus said, *I'm giving you a new commandment: It's to love as I love.* It's not a commandment that says, "Do more than being nice. *Really* love your brothers and sisters. Really gotta love 'em." Love isn't that kind of emotional feeling you have towards someone. Love is understanding the mystery of divinity inside of us, and that resonance of divinity *is* the love that we're called to give to one another. That's what Jesus was doing when he *loved* his disciples. He was not just warmly attracted to them! He was resonating the love of God the Father that was in him, and that love is beyond our imagining, beyond anything that is like human nature, limited as it is. It's an amazing, transforming power. So when we get a new commandment to love each other as Christ has loved us, it's not about feeling warmer and closer to those around us. It's about the awesome power that we have dwelling within us that can make everything new, can make everything free of that which destroys, and fills us with only that which gives life.

Father, during this season that we continue to return over and over again to the mysteries of Easter, your incredible death and resurrection, the invitation you give us to move from death to life, we long for wisdom, we long to understand, as fully as we can, what you've done for us so that we can drink of its power, its grace, its peace. And we ask this through Christ our Lord. Amen.

Acts 14: 21-27

21After [Paul and Barnabas] had proclaimed the good news to that city and made a con-
siderable number of disciples, they returned to Lystra and to Iconium and to Anti-
och.22They strengthened the spirits of the disciples and exhorted them to persevere in

the faith, saying, "It is necessary for us to undergo many hardships to enter the kingdom of God."[23]They appointed presbyters for them in each church and, with prayer and
fasting, commended them to the Lord in whom they had put their faith.[24]Then they
traveled through Pisidia and reached Pamphylia.[25]After proclaiming the word at Perga
they went down to Attalia.[26]From there they sailed to Antioch, where they had been
commended to the grace of God for the work they had now accomplished.[27]And when
they arrived, they called the church together and reported what God had done with
them and how he had opened the door of faith to the Gentiles.

Revelation 21: 1-5
[1]Then I, John, saw a new heaven and a new earth. The former heaven and the former
earth had passed away, and the sea was no more. [2]I also saw the holy city, a new Jerusalem, coming down out of heaven from God, prepared as a bride adorned for her husband.[3]I heard a loud voice from the throne saying, "Behold, God's dwelling is with the
human race. He will dwell with them and they will be his people and God himself will
always be with them [as their God]. [4]He will wipe every tear from their eyes, and there
shall be no more death or mourning, wailing or pain, [for] the old order has passed
away."
[5]The one who sat on the throne said, "Behold, I make all things new."

John 13: 31-35
[31]When [Judas] had left, Jesus said, "Now is the Son of Man glorified, and God is glorified in him.[32][If God is glorified in him,] God will also glorify him in himself, and he
will glorify him at once.[33]My children, I will be with you only a little while longer. You
will look for me, and as I told the Jews, 'Where I go you cannot come,' so now I say it to
you.[34]I give you a new commandment: love one another. As I have loved you, so you
also should love one another.[35]This is how all will know that you are my disciples, if
you have love for one another."

SIXTH SUNDAY OF EASTER

Acts 15:1-2, 22-29; Revelation 21:10-14, 22-23; John 14:23-29

Father, grant that we who have celebrated with heartfelt devotion the resurrection of our Lord, bless us with the remembrance of the mysteries that it celebrates so that we might hold fast to all that you teach us and all that you ask us to be, and we ask this through Christ our Lord. Amen.

We dwell on the same theme during these weeks of Easter: the mystery of what happened to the world, what happened to us, when Jesus died on the cross. What we're saying is that something *radically* changed; something is created new; something has *changed* us. The fact that we could use that piece of music [*Create in me a clean heart*, performed by John Michael Talbot] as an image—something has been created new inside of us, in our heart. And I'd like you to imagine that the awakening of the heart as a result of the death of Christ is to open us to a new understanding. Not just a new understanding of our faith, but in a way a new *connection* with the *source* of that which makes us who we're called to be.

I would say that one of the greatest things we learn from the Old Testament was that we learned about a God who was different from all the other gods, and he's come into our life, and he's so powerful. He has ways in which he's called us to live, and he tries to get us to live that way by giving us the Law, asking us to follow it. And the track record of human beings with this loving God who asks us to live a certain way—and the track record is not so good because in a sense, we were working, I would say, with simply our understanding at that time of who God is and who we are; and understanding the relationship at that time was to understand that God is out there, over there; he is telling me, here, what I need to do, and I need to do it in order to find favor. If I find favor, I find life; if I don't find favor, if I don't do what he asks me to do, I find nothing other than condemnation. And I can't tell you how sad it makes me to keep hearing people over and over describing the work of the Church or describing their life of faith, and it sounds just like that, you know? "God's laying these burdens on me, asking me to do these things, and I just try, and I fail, and the more I fail, the less I feel I can do it, the less enthusiasm that I have; I don't feel the encouragement that I need, and somehow it just seems like a futile task, and so why go to church, why be involved in any religion? It just doesn't seem to *work*!" But the truth is, what isn't working in that vision of God telling us what to do and we trying to muster up the ability to do it, the thing that doesn't work is the part where we are seeing ourselves as the one who has to produce something in order to be in right relationship with God.

So along comes the New Testament, along comes a complete, radical shift. Something new. Something new is created. And it was created in human beings—not a mind that is anxious, worried, afraid, ashamed; but rather a *heart* takes over, and the heart somehow knows the mystery that has been hidden for so long, and that is that the beginning of any real relationship, any healthy religion, will draw us to this first place, and the first place is to recognize in God not someone who's demanding something of us, but rather a God who wants to do something *for us*. He's a *servant* God; he's the one who is here to do whatever *we* need so that we in turn can live the life that he's calling us to. In other words, the way it's expressed in the New Testament over and over again, and John is the most often quoted for this great mystery, is that *God loves us first*. And because of his love for us, because of his affirmation of who we are through that love, and because that love is a dynamic force that says, "I'm there to help you to accomplish anything I ask you to do; I'm the one who will enable you and help you to do it," once we see that and understand that and embrace that, then there's nothing left but to *love* a God like that. So he loves us *first*, and then we in turn fall in love with him. He does something awesome for us, and in response to that, we do something for him, and the primary thing he's asking you and me to do for him is to *lean* on him, trust in him, believe that he's strong enough, powerful enough, willing enough, caring enough, to enter into your personal situation *with* you and make a difference. That's the heart of what we call the New Testament. The new good news! The *gospel*. The word means *good news*.

So in that first reading we listened to, there's that transition period, and I love this reading because it seems so perfect in reminding us that we don't want to carry over from the Old Testament the same burden of the Law that's there and bring it over into the New Testament. And the image that we have in that first reading is that so many of those who lived in the old system wanted the people who are now being baptized into the *new* system to be obligated to the same things that were a part of the old system, and the old system was really burdensome. I love that image where Jesus talks to the religious leaders of his time and says, "You know, the problem with you guys is that you're laying so many burdens on people, and you're not doing a *thing* to help them deal with those burdens." Does that sound familiar? Does that sound like the church that you might feel is the church that Jesus founded? That it's always laying restrictions and limitations and taking away some kind of core freedom that you have, that you feel like you're being so restricted that you can't be who you are? I mean, that would be a very common thing that I would find in people who have rejected religion. Why would I submit myself to something that robs me of the needs I feel I have to become fully myself? So when they were told they had to follow all those dietary laws and also had to be circumcised in order to be part of the church, and they were disturbed by this, thank God there was—and this is the *power* of the church—there was a core center that could respond to this. Not the guy out there in the field trying to continue living the way they always had lived; those are the people who laid these burdens on the Gentile converts that they had to go back and do everything that the Jews had to do. So it's interesting that we see in this story the kind of temptation that is in so many church leaders to go back to something that puts us in the position of trying to do what we have to do in order to get in right relationship with God, and it has something to do with living according to the rules. In the Old Testament, when God gave those ten commandments, he said, "Don't take anything away from these," and they absolutely didn't. But then he also said, "Don't add anything *to* them," and boy, did we ever! So the *excessive* rules and laws are what we are freed from. Does that mean I'm telling you that as a believer in Christ and the New Testament, as a redeemed person, that you're able to choose anything you want to do and then do it, because you feel it's fine, even though it breaks the rules? No, I'm not saying that. It's not that simple. The core of the rules, the Ten Commandments, are the core, are nothing other than a way of living that is in absolute sync with our human nature. Every moral rule in the Catholic Church, or any church, any healthy, moral rule is nothing other than a rule that invites people to look carefully at their nature and to feel that this rule is somehow guiding them into the most natural way of dealing with the situation the law is talking about. But the experience of many people is that the rules and laws are not always *that,* and sometimes they do what the first reading talks about: They simply seem to lay a burden on us.

So what do we do with that? Well, look at the second reading. The second reading is talking about the "*new* Jerusalem," the kingdom of God, different from the way it used to be. And if you look at the way that God was present to the Israelite people—and this is not because God was stingy or didn't want to give everything to them that he longs to give to you and me; it's only that those people at the time, that's as far as God could take them. You don't take a third-grader and give them an intense workshop on the intricacies of conscience and moral laws. You just tell them what has to be, and it works. It gives them order, it gives them a sense of security. They know where they stand. It's *healthy*, for someone who's not fully developed, to have that kind of order. But now we're different. We're more mature. We're capable of greater understanding than we ever had before, and that's called *evolution.*

And so we see, in the second reading, an image of the Church where no longer is it in one building, where the holy things are kept and there's a sort of entourage of men who are in charge of it, circling it, so the inner part of the temple is where the holy of holies was, where the Ark was, where God dwelt, and then the men who represented him were around that, and the outer court around that was where the men could stay, and outside that where the women could stay, and you can see the hierarchical form. And in this vision of the new church, the new way, I will call it, the "good news," is that God is no longer limited to that temple. He no longer works and just lives there, but he somehow has broken through that. The veil that separated the holy of holies from the rest of the temple was ripped in two when Jesus died, and that meant that somehow the holiness of God entered into *everything*. And I love the image of the holiness and presence of God in everything—it's like that city, that new Jerusalem, that kingdom we're called into, is filled with light, life, energy. So there's no need for a sun or moon because the light is *in* us.

So we listen to Jesus, and he's talking so clearly, in the gospel. He said, "You know, the thing is"—and this is the statement he's saying to his disciples at the Last Supper, and so we go back to that moment, and he's just saying: "You know, if you love me, you will keep my word." And I think it's interesting that he says, "If you love me," because he says that with the recognition that the *way* you love him is knowing what he's done for you, so I'll add this to it: "If you see what I'm doing for you, if you know what I'm going to do for you through my death and resurrection, you will love me, and when you fall in love with what I am and who I am for you and how I want to enter into you and guide you with interior guidance where you no longer need the Law—if you understand the freedom that gives you and how personal my guidance is going to be, the problems with the rules and the laws—they cannot, they *cannot* cover every situation." And in most religions, you know, we have this notion of conscience, and the conscience is that we have an insight into who we are and where we are and what is the right solution in this situation, and sometimes that breaks a religious law. And if that seems scandalous, then you don't understand the incredible gift that we now possess, and that is, as Jesus says, "I'm going to come and stay with you, and the form I'm in is an Advocate, the holy Spirit." And the *Advocate* is an interesting word because it means a *lawyer*, so "I'm going to be in you, arguing your side of the case. I'm inside of you as the holy Spirit. You know, looking at the Law, looking at you, and defending you when I see you have not really broken the Law, because the

Law can only accuse the guilty and condemn them, or find someone innocent and free them." And that's so *limiting* when we understand the uniqueness of every situation that we find ourselves in.

So it strikes me that religion loses all of its attractiveness when it resides too much in that old way of religion being the *binding force* that robs you of any kind of negotiation that has anything to do with the struggle that you're in right now. And religion blossoms and becomes what it's intended to be when you recognize its fundamental role is to connect you and me with an Advocate inside of us, the holy Spirit, God himself somehow mysteriously guiding us, defending us, encouraging us, and wanting nothing more than for you and for me to know how much he is on our side and how much of *his* strength and *his* wisdom he'll share with us if we open ourselves to this incredible gift of redemption.

Father, your gift of yourself is beyond anything we could have imagined was possible, but you said to us over and over again that your deepest longing is for us to grow and to become who you've called us to be. And it's clear that you see that we cannot do that on our own. So we give you praise and thanks for your presence within us, your guidance. Keep us calm, open, receptive to the ways in which you teach us individually and personally, and we ask this in Jesus' name. Amen.

Acts 15: 1-2, 22-29
[1]Some who had come down from Judea were instructing the brothers, "Unless you are
circumcised according to the Mosaic practice, you cannot be saved."[2]Because there arose
no little dissension and debate by Paul and Barnabas with them, it was decided that
Paul, Barnabas, and some of the others should go up to Jerusalem to the apostles and
presbyters about this question.

[22]Then the apostles and presbyters, in agreement with the whole church, decided to
choose representatives and to send them to Antioch with Paul and Barnabas. The ones
chosen were Judas, who was called Barsabbas, and Silas, leaders among the brothers.[23]This is the letter delivered by them: "The apostles and the presbyters, your brothers, to the brothers in Antioch, Syria, and Cilicia of Gentile origin: greetings.[24]Since we
have heard that some of our number [who went out] without any mandate from us
have upset you with their teachings and disturbed your peace of mind,[25]we have with
one accord decided to choose representatives and to send them to you along with our
beloved Barnabas and Paul,[26]who have dedicated their lives to the name of our Lord Jesus Christ.[27]So we are sending Judas and Silas who will also convey this same message

by word of mouth:[28]'It is the decision of the holy Spirit and of us not to place on you any
burden beyond these necessities,[29]namely, to abstain from meat sacrificed to idols, from
blood, from meats of strangled animals, and from unlawful marriage. If you keep free
of these, you will be doing what is right. Farewell.'"

Revelation 21: 10-14, 22-23

[10]He [the angel] took me in spirit to a great, high mountain and showed me the holy city
Jerusalem coming down out of heaven from God.[11]It gleamed with the splendor of God.
Its radiance was like that of a precious stone, like jasper, clear as crystal.[12]It had a mas-
sive, high wall, with twelve gates where twelve angels were stationed and on which
names were inscribed, [the names] of the twelve tribes of the Israelites.[13]There were
three gates facing east, three north, three south, and three west.[14]The wall of the city had
twelve courses of stones as its foundation, on which were inscribed the twelve names of
the twelve apostles of the Lamb.

[22] I saw no temple in the city, for its temple is the Lord God almighty and the Lamb.
[23]The city had no need of sun or moon to shine on it, for the glory of God gave it light,
and its lamp was the Lamb.

John 14: 23-29

[23]Jesus answered and said to him, "Whoever loves me will keep my word, and my Father will love him, and we will come to him and make our dwelling with him.
[24]Whoever does not love me does not keep my words; yet the word you hear is not mine
but that of the Father who sent me.
[25]"I have told you this while I am with you.[26]The Advocate, the holy Spirit that the Father will send in my name—he will teach you everything and remind you of all that [I]
told you.[27]Peace I leave with you; my peace I give to you. Not as the world gives do I
give it to you. Do not let your hearts be troubled or afraid.[28] You heard me tell you, 'I
am going away and I will come back to you.' If you loved me, you would rejoice that I
am going to the Father; for the Father is greater than I.[29]And now I have told you this
before it happens, so that when it happens you may believe.

ASCENSION OF THE LORD

Acts 1:1-11; Ephesians 1:17-23; Luke 24:46-53

God our Father, make us joyful in the ascension of your Son, Jesus Christ. May we follow him into the new creation, for his ascension is our glory and our hope; and we ask this through our Lord Jesus Christ, your Son, who lives and reigns with you in the unity of the holy Spirit, one God for ever and ever. Amen.

These next three Sundays are very important feasts that we're focusing on, and this one is the feast of the Ascension. Then next Sunday is the feast of Pentecost, and we close this Easter time with the feast of the Holy Trinity. What I can sense the Church is doing is trying to put us into the right disposition, the right place, to begin what we call Ordinary Time throughout the summer months and through to the time of Advent when we listen attentively to the teaching and the experiences that people had of this figure, Jesus. So I want to start with a kind of broad-stroke picture of this mysterious thing we call *redemption*. God came and became one of us and saved us from something horrific. So let's look at it.

First of all, I want to start with the image of God creating human beings and setting them on this earth and taking a risk, a chance in giving them the one thing he didn't give to any other thing that he created, and that was *free will*. So he has now created these beings that can actually turn away from him and reject him and do anything they want to do, if they set their mind to it. And he started with them in a beautiful, idyllic kind of place, much like we begin our own lives in this world in childhood, and everything is in harmony and everything seems one and it's a beautiful time.

Then, as we develop, and as the story developed, we see that all of a sudden, *independence and autonomy* begins to fill the human race, which is symbolized in Adam and Eve. What we see in them is this choice that they make to basically be autonomous from God. That's one of the fundamental things we see in the story in Genesis, that they thought they could be equal to God, they could know what God knows and have what God has, but not necessarily because he's steadily giving it to them, but because they can possess it. And that was the lie that was given to them. The result of that is that they had to struggle on their own if they chose to *be* on their own. God said, *Okay, I'll sew you some clothes and I'm going to send you out into the world and it's going to be tough!*

So he gave them the Law, and the Law was something to help them in their choices and to guide them. They struggled and struggled to follow the Law and really, basically, couldn't do it very well at all. Then there were those very powerful moments when God looks at the human race and just says, *This is such a mess. I'm going to start all over again. I'm going to get rid of them all!* He saves a family and then continues the work, and so it's an interesting story, not unlike our own stories of struggle with understanding who God is and how we surrender to him. It took the course, eventually, where God said, *The only thing I can do is come down and show them more dramatically, more clearly, who they can be.* That's what Jesus came into the world to do, to show them who they can be, human beings filled with Spirit. For this, they needed something. They needed something that would break open their hearts and their souls to the presence of God, because Jesus, it seems to me, came to teach—more than anything else—the teaching of *presence.*

So he came into the world to do something, to open men and women to this mysterious power of God dwelling within them, partnering with them and enabling them to do this work in a new context. *A new creation* is the way it's described in Scripture. So the work of Jesus is to come in the form of a human being and then to say, *Look, this is what, potentially, human beings have within them, this capacity for divinity to dwell within them. It's what you rejected back in the Garden, and it changes everything.* And so we have this thing called *redemption.*

Then Jesus himself went through the process of redemption. The interesting thing about redemption is that it has something to do with surrendering and submitting to a destiny that God calls us to, and there is a kind of dying to it that is so essential, and that's what Jesus did—he gave into a plan. And the plan seemed so ridiculous to the disciples that they thought it was not a good plan at all! So they really basically felt that this was a stupid idea. But Jesus gave in to his destiny and he gave in to what it is that God was calling him to, even though it looked to the world as if he was truly destroyed. But he wasn't, and it was in the act of surrender that he gained all this ability to come back and be with his disciples. What he wanted so clearly to show them is that when we do the grieving and the suffering that is so much a part of our lives, when we go into that and accept it, we come out of it a new person. We come out of it, in a sense, in a risen form.

Jesus makes sure that they understand that those things that are destiny for us can never destroy us. They can only bring us to fuller life. So Jesus comes back and spends forty days with his disciples. And they're absolutely, totally convinced that he isn't gone, that he wasn't destroyed. Forty days with a person who was dead in a bodily form would convince anybody! This is a mysterious, marvelous, wonderful thing that they are experiencing.

Then, when he gets ready to leave the time he spent with them with a resurrected body, that's where we pick up the story today and in both the Acts of the Apostles and in the gospel, he told them there was going to be something given to them. This is the part that I can't explain. I don't know exactly how it worked, but what Jesus was saying was, *I have to return to the Father so that when I return to the Father, then it's possible for my Spirit, the holy Spirit, the Spirit of my Father and myself, to come and dwell within you. So, I have to do all these things. You watched me go through all the things that I had to do in terms of my death, suffering, and passion, and then you see me rise. But now I must go back to the Father. And what I'm going to do when I'm with the Father is that I'm going to be your advocate. I'm there for you. I'm there to continue to be a source of grace and teaching for you. And the way it comes to you is in the form of Spirit. So the Spirit is going to come.*

What's important about the second reading, from Ephesians, is that it says what is promised is *wisdom*, wisdom that brings knowledge of who God is. So what is the work of the Spirit in you and in me? (We're going to celebrate that next week at Pentecost.) What is this gift that God's Spirit in us is producing? Well, let's look at that. Wisdom is something that goes beyond logic and goes beyond cause and effect. It's a kind of understanding of something where we're wide open to allowing something to happen that doesn't make a lot of logical sense, but we believe it, we know it's true. So, this wisdom is given to us and the wisdom is regarding the full nature of who God is, and if you're going to look at who God is, you're looking at what he's doing for you. So, the Ascension is the invitation on the part of Jesus to his disciples, to all of us, to be open, radically open, ready to receive this gift of wisdom that is going to show us who he is.

I'm thinking to myself, this is such an interesting image! Who is God? Who is he to you? I have a sense of who he is to me, which has radically changed since I was 18, 19, 20 years old when I went into the seminary. I knew God existed and I knew that he was a personal God and I believed in Jesus, but what I think I basically felt about God is that he came into my life to tell me all the things that I needed to do in order to please him, so that I could get the reward of eternal life, or the reward of a good life. It seemed to me that primarily what I was looking at in my thought about God, what I was grasping in my imagination, was a kind of good teacher who would tell me what to do in order to get what I needed. And what I realize now is that Jesus *is* a good teacher, but who so often is not understood, and what I think we need is the Spirit to help us understand—because the way it unfolds is *totally* mysterious—that we have a God who has created, for you and for me, an entirely new world. A *new* world! Something radically different. And that we, if we understand it fully and we surrender to it, enter into a new creation. There are dimensions to this new creation, and one of them is a kind of unity, a oneness. I love those images in the Old Testament, in Genesis, of Adam and Eve in the Garden. There's always this sense of such harmony and oneness and walking with God, and everything is connected. And yet, in this world that I live in, so often, I can go through a day and I feel nothing more than being scattered, my attention is being pulled in twenty directions, and I try to cover all the things that I'm responsible for. Then I hear things that are going on in the world that worry me. There's oil spilling in the Gulf and then there's this war and there's this economy and then there are these problems on Wall Street and, you know, it doesn't seem to have any kind of oneness or any kind of unity or connection.

What I'd like to see happen to us is that we would be open to this idea that there is a gift that is given, called the Spirit, that comes into us when we're open to it. Notice that St. Paul, in this letter, says that we need to open the eyes of our hearts to see it. That's so much the image of wisdom—*the eyes of your heart*. Not the eyes of your mind, but the eyes of your heart. And that just says to me that it's more in the area of feeling, it's more in the area of intuition, it's more in the area of something you kind of know without knowing how you know it.

But if you could believe that this promise is real, that God is really creating for you and for me a way of seeing the world where everything is interconnected, it's not that you can figure it out first and then say, *Oh, now I believe it*. No, *assume* that it is, and then wait to begin to sense and to feel the connections. It's a very, very important exercise in terms of our spiritual lives, to have some way of sensing that every single thing that's going on is somehow connected to the other things that are going on, that are connected to the needs that your soul has, that your heart has, that the culture has, that everything has, that it's all working together for the good. That's the promise. Because if you don't have that sense, if you *don't* have a sense of God as an agent in the world who is working *for* you and doing radical things *for* you, then it seems to me he ends up simply being a tour guide through this whole thing—the teacher that tells you what you have to do and not do in order to get to the goal. And that's such an over-simplified, impersonal, short-sighted way of imagining this God.

Jesus says, in a way, *I've come into the world to give to you something so radically new that it changes everything, and there's a unity in the universe because of what I've done. There's a oneness that we need to be aware of.* That kind of language is all through the New Testament. I often wonder what it was that so electrified the converts to Christianity, and I don't think it was the fact that there was just this story of a man who died and came back. I don't think that would have changed that much. It would be such an interesting thing to believe that it happened, but it's got to be that that event did something more than just present a human being who was dead and then came back and then somehow went up to heaven. There's something that he did in that act that is so essential. If you think of it as divinity coming down and entering into this whole, messy sort of thing we call life and somehow charging it with connection and grace and unity, then you begin to sense something that's very exciting, very challenging to be a part of.

So my prayer with you today is that we somehow open our hearts, the eyes of our hearts—I love that image—and somehow enter more fully into this place where we're more conscious of what this God has done and is doing for us. And what it means that he dwells within us and what this wisdom really is that helps us to see exactly what he is doing within us. You know, it's like first we believe and then we experience; not experience and then believe. So, believe with me in this most amazing promise, that as this figure, Jesus, ascended into heaven, he made a promise, and the promise is real and has everything to do with the new life he's inviting you and me to live. We cannot possibly live without his help and without his teaching and without his presence.

Father, on this feast of the Ascension, we ask you to awaken in us a longing for what it is that you promise so that our hearts will be open to the mystery of your gifts, especially the way they mysteriously work in our lives and draw us into a place of oneness and wholeness, and we ask this in Jesus' name. Amen.

Acts of the Apostles 1: 1-11

In the first book, Theophilus, I dealt with all that Jesus did and taught[2]until the day he
was taken up, after giving instructions through the holy Spirit to the apostles whom he
had chosen.[3]He presented himself alive to them by many proofs after he had suffered,
appearing to them during forty days and speaking about the kingdom of God.[4]While
meeting with them, he enjoined them not to depart from Jerusalem, but to wait for "the
promise of the Father about which you have heard me speak;[5]for John baptized with
water, but in a few days you will be baptized with the holy Spirit."
[6]When they had gathered together they asked him, "Lord, are you at this time going to
restore the kingdom to Israel?"[7]He answered them, "It is not for you to know the times
or seasons that the Father has established by his own authority.[8]But you will receive
power when the holy Spirit comes upon you, and you will be my witnesses in Jerusalem, throughout Judea and Samaria, and to the ends of the earth."[9]When he had said
this, as they were looking on, he was lifted up, and a cloud took him from their
sight.[10]While they were looking intently at the sky as he was going, suddenly two men

dressed in white garments stood beside them.[11]They said, "Men of Galilee, why are you
standing there looking at the sky? This Jesus who has been taken up from you into
heaven will return in the same way as you have seen him going into heaven."

Ephesians 1: 17-23

[17] . . .that the God of our Lord Jesus Christ, the Father of glory, may give you a spirit of
wisdom and revelation resulting in knowledge of him.[18]May the eyes of [your] hearts be
enlightened, that you may know what is the hope that belongs to his call, what are the
riches of glory in his inheritance among the holy ones,[19]and what is the surpassing
greatness of his power for us who believe, in accord with the exercise of his great
might,[20]which he worked in Christ, raising him from the dead and seating him at his
right hand in the heavens,[21]far above every principality, authority, power, and domin-
ion, and every name that is named not only in this age but also in the one to come.[22]And
he put all things beneath his feet and gave him as head over all things to the
church,[23]which is his body, the fullness of the one who fills all things in every way.

Luke 24: 46-53

[46]And he said to them, "Thus it is written that the Messiah would suffer and rise from
the dead on the third day[47]and that repentance, for the forgiveness of sins, would be
preached in his name to all the nations, beginning from Jerusalem.[48]You are witnesses of
these things.[49]And [behold] I am sending the promise of my Father upon you; but stay
in the city until you are clothed with power from on high."
[50] Then he led them [out] as far as Bethany, raised his hands, and blessed them.[51]As he
blessed them he parted from them and was taken up to heaven.[52]They did him homage
and then returned to Jerusalem with great joy,[53]and they were continually in the temple
praising God.

THE FEAST OF PENTECOST

Acts 2:1-11; 1Corinthians 12:3-7, 12-13; John 20:19-23

O God who by the mystery of today's great feast sanctifies your whole Church in every people and nation, pour out, we pray, the gifts of the holy Spirit across the face of the earth. And with the divine grace that was at work when the Gospel was first proclaimed, fill now once more the hearts of believers, through our Lord Jesus Christ, your Son, who lives and reigns with you in the unity of the holy Spirit, one God for ever and ever. Amen.

This feast of Pentecost is the culmination of what we began on Ash Wednesday, weeks and weeks ago. What we're looking at here is the fullness of what it is that God longs to share with you and me. The journey has been long, the work of God, drawing human beings back into a place of wholeness, a place of peace, a place of freedom. And I suppose in order to understand more fully where we have been led, where we are now after this great feast of Pentecost, we need to look at where we began, and certainly where we began is in the Garden when there was a lie presented to human beings; and the lie was, "Why not go it on your own? Why not do what *you* want to do? Why not be separate from God, and yet not turn your back on him?" It's subtle, that lie. It's, "Why not be strong, like he wants you to be, but be that on your own?" It's almost like asking God, "Make me into something autonomous and capable of taking care of whatever you want me to do, and then I'll be rewarded for that, and I'll feel good because *I'll* be the one that made it all happen."

That image of separation, isolation, is the key problem that human beings have, and in place of it, there is a call to unity, to oneness, to community. All religions, all religions, have in a sense the same goal: to bind us to the God who created us—not in any kind of bondage sense but in a sense of being connected and through that connection to find fullness, to find wholeness. We're *made* for a relationship with divinity. It's not really an option if we're going to evolve and develop into fully who God has created us to be.

So we're looking at this moment now, we're going back to a historical moment in the Church, and Jesus has walked this earth for three years, he has gone through his—confusing to many people—the end of his life. It was nothing like people expected. Everyone thought the messiah would come into the world and be the great wielder of justice and would conquer all evil and would destroy all those who are evil and would save all those who are good, and it would be some kind of triumphant experience of good over evil. And that's the way everyone thought the world would be saved, and *should* be saved. And then in comes this strange figure who doesn't have any real credentials for power, in the sense that he came from a very simple background in this small, little town of Nazareth. And he comes onto the scene and instead of wielding a great sword of justice, he seems to almost be soft on evil, and instead of forcing people to see what they have done and to change or to be killed, he does something radically unexpected. He seems to engage himself in the lives of those who are failures, with a sense that that's the way he gets *into* their life; that's the way he *enters* them—through their weakness—and then when he's there, he teaches them that the only way to deal with evil is through forgiveness. It's the *only* way to deal with evil. The only way to *conquer* it is forgiveness. This doesn't make any sense to our logical minds, that believe the way to deal with evil is to destroy it, to attack it.

With that transformation in mind, we see this experience that the disciples and the Church were having. On Pentecost Sunday it was all the Church together coming into the place where there was this strong, overpowering sound of a Spirit that rushed into people, and it took the form of tongues of fire over each individual. And that's all very mysterious and miraculous, and I can't imagine what it would have been like to have been there to see something like that. Yet the *real* mystery, the real miracle was not that, but that something happened *between* human beings. People from everywhere, who spoke different languages, were all present, and somehow, even though they did not speak the same language, even though they weren't on the same page, perhaps didn't have the same culture and therefore did not approach the world in the same way, one thing they could all agree on and feel and communicate between each other is this awesome thing that God has done—the awesome act of a God who redeemed us—not by "converting" us from evil to good—because you can work against evil with the same energy that you formerly worked against good. You can be totally separated from everyone and be the great warrior and decide that you're going to go out there and conquer all the evil around you and in you, and you're doing it on your own. That *seems* like a conversion from going around and trying to *use* people. I mean, you went from evil to good, but doing good in the same way that we achieve evil is *not a real transformation*. It may be a *conversion*, but not a transformation. And God's gift, through Christ, is a *transformation*, called *redemption*. And its effect is transcendence, and we become someone else. Not someone foreign to our nature, but someone, because divinity dwells in us, we have the capacity to go beyond our human limitation, and that means we go beyond logic, beyond our way of thinking, beyond the way our culture has trained us. We don't fall into the temptation that was presented to Jesus when the devil took him to a high mountain and placed him before the world and said, "Look at this, how it all works. People have power over people, and they have authority, and people look up to them, and they're frightened of them, and they can make people do anything! Why don't *you* change the world by using the tactics *of* the world?" And Jesus' response was, *I'm not going to worship your way. I'm not going to surrender to your way of the world, but I'm going to use something radically different. I'm not going to save the world by forcing people to do things, by frightening them into doing things, by using my power over them. I'm going to enter into them, forgive them, dwell with them, and in partnership with them, we're going to be a force, an awesome force in the world that is not a violent force, but is a powerful force for transformation.* That's what we want. That's the goal.

We call that the gift of the Spirit, people being filled with this unique Spirit that filled Jesus, that transformed the world, and as the second reading makes clear, there are different forms of it, so there again you're seeing that there's a way in which the world, when it uses its own worldly power, is almost always going to work toward some kind of uniformity—everybody marching to the same beat, everybody doing the same thing, all the moral laws being followed exactly the same by everyone. That's a great "shadow" of religion—laying the same moral responsibilities on everyone, no matter who they are or what their situation is—sort of bypassing individual stories and just wanting everything to be the same. And when we see religion doing that, we know that it's trapped in the ways of the world.

So when we look at the Spirit's manifestation in people, what is clear that Paul is saying in the letter to the Corinthians is that we have to look very carefully into the way the Spirit works so that we don't fall into the trap of trying to evaluate everyone as if they have to have the same gift, the same spirit, the same qualities of life. Some people, their destiny maybe is to be weak throughout their life, to even be a burden to people. Maybe *that's* their role. It makes sense to me. Now why doesn't everybody just shape up, and why hasn't religion worked over 2,000 years where we just start doing the right thing? If that were the call, if that were the reason that Jesus came to the world, to make everybody do the right thing while they lived here, then he's a miserable failure. But if it was something more hidden, more mysterious, more subtle, if it's all about us living in relationships that are both positive and negative and learning how to deal with the positive and negative, how to support and enhance and encourage the positive and to meet the negative—not with force or demands but with this mysterious thing called *forgiveness.*

And that's what we see in the gospel, this awesome story of that moment between Easter and Pentecost, the moment that I think clarifies for us—in ways that we couldn't imagine without it—clarifies for us what Jesus was really about when he suffered, died, rose. He comes back! Awesome thing! He comes back, and speaks to his disciples. Wouldn't you love to have been living at that time and seen that experience? The way it's described in scripture in one of the writings of Paul is that when Jesus came back, he first appeared to his disciples. Incidentally, Paul doesn't mention the women, but that's more of a cultural problem. But he appeared to Mary Magdalene, to the women, to his disciples, and then he appeared to 500. Imagine that! Being in a room with 500 people or in a field with 500 people and there's Jesus, resurrected, and he looked different. People never recognized him at first, but there he was, radiating this amazing wisdom and radiating this presence, that was transforming by its very nature, the presence that he longs for you and me to have in this world—it must have been an awesome experience! And then he appeared to *all* of his apostles. So he's appearing to them, and what is he saying? If you look at the heart of this message that is in the gospel, it's a simple message. *I have come into the world to save it, and the way I'm saving it is to go through an experience that unites humanity and divinity,* and that is to be able to live in this world in a way that goes way beyond human nature—*way* beyond human nature. Jesus was truly transformed from his simple human nature to divine nature, to be connected so deeply to divine nature in that baptism where he was filled with the Spirit, becoming the Anointed One, the empowered one. He said, *What a power looks like in the kingdom is nothing like how power looks in the world. I've not come to wield a sword, to kill and destroy that which is evil, to condemn and to scream at people. I've come to be in them, with them, support them, love them, forgive them. And that's what I'm asking you to do.* Jesus is saying this in the gospel passage when he says to his disciples, *What I want you to do is realize something. My Spirit in you, my gift of redeeming you, my invitation for you to live not just with your humanity but to be connected naturally and comfortably with divinity, to be comfortable with God in you.* And then to do exactly what Christ did: fight evil with the most amazing, surprising "ammunition," and that is to forgive it.

And he makes a simple statement. He doesn't say, "Go and forgive everybody, or I'm going to be really upset, and I'll condemn you if you don't." He says, *No, just realize, recognize, be aware that when you forgive another person, when you forgive them, you release them from their sins. And when you don't do that, somehow their sins are retained.* What does that mean? Does it mean if we try to remove someone's sin by hating them, wanting them to be destroyed, yelling at them, condemning them, we're doing nothing but allowing their sin to be there? But if we do forgive them, somehow they are freer to be freed from it? It's a great, great mystery, but I think everyone knows the difference between being loved into wholeness or being judged and condemned into wholeness. Why is it that we think so quickly, or why is it so easy for us to imagine that if I just tell everybody where they're messed up, and tell them how messed up they are and how screwed up they are, that they'll turn around and say, "Oh, wow! I didn't realize I was that bad. Of course I don't want to be bad. I want to be good." There's so much guilt and shame in people who are not doing it well. There's a burden, there's a wound, there's a heaviness, and then you come on them and affirm all their negative feelings about who they are. Where are they going to have the stuff to pull themselves up and say, "I want a greater power than myself to transform me because I'm worth it"? No, they've got to be loved. They've got to be supported, and the way you do that is understanding and compassion and empathy. Those are things that are so underestimated in their power to transform, so we can transcend the kind of wound inside of us that keeps us in places of darkness and imprisons us in places where we don't feel that we're worth even working on. And you know, most people don't go around and say, "I'm not worth it; I'm not going to change; I'm not going to develop." No, they just go into a state of unconsciousness and get distracted with a whole bunch of other stuff. So it's easy. It's *easy* for people, I think, to somehow miss the most amazing gift that God has prepared for us, and the greatest gift he's empowered us with, and that's the gift of forgiveness and the gift of being a source of awesome, awesome power to the heart and to the soul of someone struggling. And that is a good model, I think, for the way God's forgiveness works. And when somebody's weak, and there's something broken, we don't put stress on it. We rather take it, clean it, open it, bandage it, support it, try to leave the pain of it, and wait for something—not coming from us, but something coming from deep inside of every human being, this gift of God that will always, always achieve the healing we allow it to do.

Father, on this day that we consider the birthday of the Church, the Christian Church that you founded, bless us, bless us with an awareness of the gifts that have been given, with a keen sense that as we surrender to your way, the way of the Spirit, we will find the goal that this great faith has always promised us, and that's the goal of wholeness, the goal of peace, and the goal of entering fully into your kingdom. And we ask this through Christ our Lord. Amen.

Acts 2: 1-11
[1]When the time for Pentecost was fulfilled, they were all in one place together.[2]And
suddenly there came from the sky a noise like a strong driving wind, and it filled the
entire house in which they were.[3]Then there appeared to them tongues as of fire, which
parted and came to rest on each one of them.[4]And they were all filled with the holy
Spirit and began to speak in different tongues, as the Spirit enabled them to proclaim.
[5]Now there were devout Jews from every nation under heaven staying in Jerusalem.[6]At
this sound, they gathered in a large crowd, but they were confused because each one
heard them speaking in his own language.[7]They were astounded, and in amazement
they asked, "Are not all these people who are speaking Galileans?[8]Then how does each
of us hear them in his own native language?[9]We are Parthians, Medes, and Elamites,
inhabitants of Mesopotamia, Judea and Cappadocia, Pontus and Asia,[10]Phrygia and
Pamphylia, Egypt and the districts of Libya near Cyrene, as well as travelers from
Rome,[11]both Jews and converts to Judaism, Cretans and Arabs, yet we hear them speaking in our own tongues of the mighty acts of God."

1Corinthians 12: 3-7, 12-13
[3] . . .Brothers and sisters, no one can say, "Jesus is Lord," except by the holy Spirit.
[4]There are different kinds of spiritual gifts but the same Spirit;[5]there are different forms
of service but the same Lord;[6]there are different workings but the same God who produces all of them in everyone.[7]To each individual the manifestation of the Spirit is given
for some benefit.

[12]As a body is one though it has many parts, and all the parts of the body, though many,
are one body, so also Christ.[13]For in one Spirit we were all baptized into one body,
whether Jews or Greeks, slaves or free persons, and we were all given to drink of one
Spirit.

John 20: 19-23
[19]On the evening of that first day of the week, when the doors were locked, where the
disciples were, for fear of the Jews, Jesus came and stood in their midst and said to
them, "Peace be with you."[20]When he had said this, he showed them his hands and his
side. The disciples rejoiced when they saw the Lord.[21][Jesus] said to them again, "Peace
be with you. As the Father has sent me, so I send you."[22]And when he had said this, he
breathed on them and said to them, "Receive the holy Spirit.[23]Whose sins you forgive
are forgiven them, and whose sins you retain are retained."

TRINITY SUNDAY

Proverbs 8:22-31; Romans 5:1-5; John 16:12-15

Father, you sent your Word to bring us truth and your Spirit to make us holy. Through them we come to know the mystery of your life. Help us to worship you, one God in three Persons, by proclaiming and living our faith in you. Grant this through our Lord, Jesus Christ, your Son, who lives and reigns with you in the unity of the holy Spirit, one God, for ever and ever. Amen.

This feast, the Feast of Trinity, feels weighty and filled with awesome mystery and the fullness of God. Sometimes when we get into that image of the fullness of God, we can get kind of serious and heavy, and I think that's why I chose the joyful "If I Got My Ticket," performed by Jubilant Sykes, to start off with. There's a kind of energy in it that's filled with life. Not so much a reverence of life somewhere else, but a joy that life has *entered into us*. Not that we don't have enormous reverence for God, don't misunderstand me, but it's something that, when you look at the Gospel, you look at the whole salvation history, you're realizing that what is going on is that there is a God revealing himself to us, much like in any relationship—friendship, partnership, whatever—it's a constant process of getting to know each other, revealing to each other who we are.

And that's what God wanted so much: to open the hearts and minds of those he created so they could really see him for who he is, not just to know him, but so that he can be who he wants to be in our life. He wants to be something *for* us, and what he wants to see is you and me coming into glory, *coming into glory*. And that image of glory is simply nothing more than a human being fully alive, fully awake, fully alert, fully who God wants us to be.

So, let's look at this feast then, as a way of imagining that what we're celebrating is the fullness of the process that God has chosen to reveal himself to us.

And he's so big—I love that phrase—he's so big, he's so amazing and enormous, and we have these small minds. Even though our mind is a fabulous thing, it can only grasp so much, and that's why we have to learn how to live with mystery and live in that disposition of awe about things that we can't fully comprehend.

Let's look at this picture of the Trinity of God—the Father, Son, and holy Spirit. One of the things that I want to look at is this whole sense of *wisdom* that the first reading starts with. Wisdom is depicted often in Scripture as a person, as something that is human-like. And the thing that is so interesting about this image is that this God, who is creating the world, is creating it *with* Wisdom, so there's enormous wisdom in every single thing that God has done. If you think about that, it's a really amazing thought because it means that so often we look at the limitations of time, we look at the limitations of physical or human nature and how we resist and how things don't go smoothly and how things fall apart and how we get up and start again. It's as if Wisdom was there in the beginning and what Wisdom was doing was dancing and sort of laughing and playing. It's a beautiful image of the playfulness of the Spirit, the Spirit of Wisdom. And what's happening in that story, it seems, is that Wisdom is watching God create the world. And what is clear about the world and about human nature is that it's limited. And so you see the story of Wisdom watching God set up the different parts of the earth, the sky, the earth, and the seas within limits and then everything has its balance and its place in the picture, and it's all interrelated. It's like Wisdom is just playfully watching all this and saying, *Isn't this wonderful!* I love the way the passage ends where it says, *And I just love human beings! I really like them! They're limited; they have these interesting, complex processes that they're caught up in.*

What I want you to take from that reading is that there's something beautiful about this whole wonderful thing we call the world, and yet, if you're like me, you can put on a judgment, you can put on a kind of prejudice, you can work out of your brain solely, and all of a sudden you can be really frustrated because it's not the way *you* would like it to be.

I wonder, if you listed prayer requests to God, I wonder, if you had in one column all the things people were asking God to do, where they were requiring him to change the way things are in the world right this moment; and then how many prayers are offered to accept and surrender to exactly the way things are. I guarantee you the first list is *much* bigger than the second list! But it seems like the second list or the second prayer is so important if Wisdom is saying that all of this is so good, so beautiful, and that it has a kind of playfulness to it. Then the seriousness of having to judge it and evaluate it and plan it and figure out whether it's right or wrong is just too much work.

And so the first image we have in this Feast of the Trinity is to be more open to the world that God has created, and that's the image of the Father. He's the creator; he made this whole thing with great, great wisdom and great understanding.

And then Saint Paul, in the second reading, is recognizing that we have, through the second person of the blessed Trinity, through Jesus, this amazing gift called grace, peace, and we received it through Jesus Christ. We've gained access to a way of seeing God, a way of knowing God that became possible because we saw him incarnate in Christ. So Paul is very, very much appreciative of this dimension of God coming into the world, revealing to us not only who he is, but in the most unique way showing us what it's like when you look at someone who is both human and divine—a human being partnering with God. What a beautiful image that figure Christ is. Yes, he's God incarnate, but he's also flesh incarnate. He's human. And so we see in Christ the most powerful example we could have of what it is that we are destined to be when we open ourselves to God, his creation, his ways, his purposes.

And then you can hear Paul realizing that when he's saying all this, he's realizing that this is a very different way of thinking. This isn't the way the world thinks. So he's going on to say not only are we people who trust and surrender to God and his will, but we also notice that there's a kind of mysterious power in surrender and acceptance of things. He's talking about afflictions that we have to surrender to and knowing that they lead to endurance and endurance to character and character to hope and hope doesn't ever disappoint us, because we have this—and this coming right from the experience of seeing Jesus—we have God poured into us, God poured into us. And so the second person of the blessed Trinity is that mysterious example of the presence of a God in our midst so that we could see him and sense him and know that this is what it's like to be in a relationship with him, a relationship that is going to bring us into glory.

And then we have in the gospel passage the image of the holy Spirit. And this is the one that we've been spending a lot of time on, because we just celebrated the Feast of Pentecost. But let's look at the way in which this particular gospel describes the Spirit's work, because it's clear that Jesus said something to human beings, and he said it not simply with words but with his very being. He was showing them who we are to be. And he says that the Spirit of Truth, which is the holy Spirit, is going to take that experience of hearing Jesus, seeing him, understanding him; and it's going to do something for us. And what it's going to do is somehow enable us to sense it and know it so that we can understand it, so we can grasp its fullness. And it's like everything that Jesus did came from the Father. And then what he's saying is, *I'm going to turn everything I received from the Father over to the Spirit, and the Spirit will take care of it and make it understandable to you.* It's like we have this creation we surrender to, we have this extraordinary figure, Christ, who we surrender to; and now we have God the Spirit, who is simply there to be the instrument of enabling you and me to grasp and to understand what this all means.

This is the part that I find most fascinating: *that we live in the age of the Spirit.*

We weren't there at the very beginning when God created the world. We have not lived at the same time that Jesus walked the earth, so we live in the time of the Spirit, and one of the things it seems to me that we need to be aware of, more than perhaps we are, is the work of the Spirit. So it seems essential that our prayer life and our intention should be very much in this disposition of radical openness to whatever it is the Spirit is trying to reveal to us about what is going on. And if you think it's the Spirit revealing to us just who Jesus is or going back and revealing the Scriptures to us, then that's just too limited. We're talking about the Spirit who is there to be able to interpret for us the things that are going on in our lives, so that we somehow have a way of entering into them, not as victims, or not as frustrated people who are begging God to *change* what's going on, but somehow we have the promise of a Spirit that will help us to integrate what's going on and somehow surrender to it and be fed by it, be fed by it in a really powerful, effective way.

The fruit of that, if you want to look at it—does it mean you're going to be really smart? Are you going to be able to tell people what's really going on? No, it's not that kind of knowledge exactly. It's much more a kind of unity, a kind of *oneness* with what's going on.

You know that feeling when you're alienated, you're separated, you don't have any connection with anything; you're feeling isolated, alone, and it's a very, very uncomfortable feeling. And one of the ways that we hide it is to stay really busy or fill ourselves with all kinds of activities. There's never been a generation that has had more opportunities to fill themselves with something to distract them than we do. With the technology that we have, it's like we can be bombarded with information and images and entertainment—whatever, it's just a couple of clicks and there we are, we have something given to us.

So we have to be careful that we're also taking time to be in a disposition of receptivity, not just to images and information of the world and what's going on, but to sit back and to say, *Give me, please give me, some kind of context, some kind of understanding, some kind of ability to put all this together and see it as unified, see it as one.* That's what I think is so interesting about God's creation. He kept saying, *This creation that I've done is beautiful and it's wonderful!* Wisdom saw it as beautiful and wonderful.

And it's *one*—it's all unified, it's all connected. What's happening to you is also happening to everybody. What's happening to the earth is happening to us. What's happening in politics, in everything, there's a way of seeing it and a way of interpreting it that's trying to say to us, *Do you understand what is happening and can you surrender to that and can you be a part of that when you believe*—and this is the tricky one—*when you believe that somehow wisdom is behind all of this, all of this?* And it's more like play than it is like bad news. It's more like a kind of wonderful story that is going to end in a really good way, but it has so many struggles in it, so many difficulties in it, and so many disappointments if we're not filled with this capacity to receive the gift of the Spirit, which is to interpret things in a way that helps us to really feel and know that there's something, something really, really good going on. And that leads to what has always been the sign of believing.

The sign of a believer is not that they're morally sharper and more perfect than other people. In fact, often the most rigidly moral people are very, very, very far from the life of faith that I think God is calling them to, because it's all about will and ego and forcing themselves to be perfect and being really upset when no one else is. You can always tell somebody who's forcing themselves to do something and resents it deep down because they'll be so angry at everybody else that's not doing what they're doing. Another way to say that is, they're really upset that somebody seems to be getting away with something that they can't give themselves permission to get away with—like a joyful openness to life.

But there's that image that the life of faith is not so much something that makes us into these righteous people as much as it makes us into a kind of peaceful, playful, hopeful, loving human beings, who just don't have that high, high anxiety or that excessive fear and worry about things being all so terrible. *Gee, the world is so much worse than it ever was!* I always think that's so amazing, that anyone would think that the world is continually being sucked into the hands of evil, and it's just getting worse and worse and worse until it's going to self-destruct. Well, that blows away every promise that God has made to us. He's made a promise that he's going to save us. He's made a promise that he's going to use all things to bring about something good. He made a promise that he would love us till the end and take us with him wherever he is. Those are promises that aren't just made to the men in the early Church, the disciples! But they're promises to all of us, and if we don't have that conviction deep inside of us, that this all has purpose and meaning and is leading to glory, then it's going to be a dark, dark time going through the short years that we have in this world. And then our eyes will be opened. But how wonderful it is to have your eyes opened *now*, eyes opened *here*, eyes opened so that you can see the glory of this Trinitarian God, a God who created a world that's so beautiful and rich for you and me. He's created an opportunity for us to see him in the flesh and to know what it's like to live with him and then he's given us this extraordinary interpreter of all things, God the Spirit, who guides us in all wisdom, and so we give praise and thanks to the holy Trinity.

Father, we give you praise for this life that you have given to each of us, and we offer our minds, our hearts, our wills, in service to the plan that you have created for each of us. Bless us with the capacity to surrender to that plan and to find the peace and the joy, the playfulness, that comes from truly a life of faith, and we ask this in Jesus' name. Amen.

Proverbs 8:22-31
[Thus says the Wisdom of God:]
22 The LORD created me at the beginning of his work,
the first of his acts of long ago.
23 Ages ago I was set up,
at the first, before the beginning of the earth.
24 When there were no depths I was brought forth,
when there were no springs abounding with water.
25 Before the mountains had been shaped,
before the hills, I was brought forth—
26 when he had not yet made earth and fields,
or the world's first bits of soil.
27 When he established the heavens, I was there,
when he drew a circle on the face of the deep,
28 when he made firm the skies above,
when he established the fountains of the deep,
29 when he assigned to the sea its limit,
so that the waters might not transgress his command,
when he marked out the foundations of the earth,
30 then I was beside him, like a master worker;
and I was daily his delight,
rejoicing before him always,
31 rejoicing in his inhabited world
and delighting in the human race.

Romans 5:1-5
1Therefore, since we are justified by faith, we have peace with God through our Lord
Jesus Christ,
2through whom we have obtained access to this grace in which we stand; and we boast
in our hope of sharing the glory of God.
3And not only that, but we also boast in our sufferings, knowing that suffering produces
endurance,
4and endurance produces character, and character produces hope,
5and hope does not disappoint us, because God's love has been poured into our hearts
through the holy Spirit that has been given to us.

John 16:12-15
12"I still have many things to say to you, but you cannot bear them now.
13When the Spirit of truth comes, he will guide you into all the truth; for he will not
speak on his own, but will speak whatever he hears, and he will declare to you the

things that are to come.
[14]He will glorify me, because he will take what is mine and declare it to you.
[15]All that the Father has is mine. For this reason I said that he will take what is mine and declare it to you.

THE MOST HOLY BODY AND BLOOD OF CHRIST

Genesis 14:18-20; 1Corinthians 11:20-26; Luke 9:11-17

Lord Jesus Christ, we worship you living among us in the sacrament of your body and blood. May we offer to our Father in heaven a solemn pledge of undivided love. May we offer to our brothers and sisters a life poured out in loving service of that kingdom where you live with the Father and the holy Spirit, one God, for ever and ever. Amen.

This time of the Church year is filled with some marvelous feasts. Last Sunday we celebrated Trinity; the week before that, Pentecost; the week before that, Ascension. And one of the things that it seems to me that we could learn from the way the Church has carefully placed these celebrations is that there's a connection between them. There's a teaching that flows from one to the other.

I want to go back to the Feast of the Ascension, because it was there that we listen so often during that season, around that feast, we listened in the scriptures to words of Jesus praying for his disciples. And he used language that was so interesting, so fascinating when you think about it, because he would say things as he was leaving them, not about "Be sure you do this, be sure you do that. Don't forget this, don't forget that." You would think he might be giving instruction after instruction on what to *do*, but instead he talked over and over again about the *unity* that was now possible between Christ and his disciples. He would talk about the unity first that he had with the Father: *My Father lives in me; I live in the Father. The Father loves me. And we want to dwell with you.* And then he would say to his disciples things like, *I want to live inside of you. I want be there with you, inside of you. And the Father, who loves me, is going to be in there with us. We are going to love you, and just as the Father loves me, his love for me is going to dwell in you.* It's amazing language! Intimate language of lovers. So one of the things that we can clearly see—

the core message of Jesus, and you would think at the end he would talk about the core, what's he's leaving them with, he would say, over and over again—*I want you to understand the relationship that is now possible between us, between God and man.*

In the Feast of Pentecost, we look at this event that happened in the beginning of the Church, this descent of the Spirit upon the disciples. It's like Jesus had spoken all these words about *I want to dwell in you, and I want my power to be in you.* And on Pentecost there was a manifestation very similar to the manifestation that happened at the baptism of Jesus when John was baptizing him. There was this sense of the Spirit breaking through heaven, coming, descending upon this man in the form of something like a dove. And it dwelt there, and there were words of affirmation: *You are my Son. I love you. My Spirit dwells with you.* So at Pentecost we see a similar descent of Spirit upon now, not Christ, but those that Christ has somehow liberated through his death and resurrection so that they can receive this same Spirit.

And they're *intoxicated* with this awareness that they now have of divinity—this life, living inside of them, animating them, enlivening them, enabling them to be in union with others in the form of communicating in language that is not normal—meaning, they were speaking one language and everyone heard them in their *own* languages. So it has something to do with some kind of amazing communication that goes beyond words that's now possible between people.

And then in the Feast of the Trinity, we talk about the *fullness* of who God is—Father, Creator; the Son, who manifests the fullness of who the Father is; and then this God entering intimately into each of our lives. It's *one* God: It's a God who creates; it's a God who communicates; it's a God who touches us; and then it's a God who lives inside of us.

So all this leads us then up to this Feast of the Body and Blood of Christ, and then we go to Ordinary Time. This feast is obviously focused on the Eucharist, but what I want us to consider this morning is, how this extraordinary gift of the Eucharist, which to me is at the heart of every Christian community's understanding of the presence of God in their life, is such a key element—yet we all see it a little differently perhaps. The technical words we use are different, but it seems impossible to read the scriptures and understand the scriptures without having a very similar view of this thing, the Eucharist, that this is something extraordinary! This is God's Spirit entering into us. We, coming and eating and drinking. From the beginning, it's been clear that God wants this intimate relationship with us. And one of the effects of the relationship we have with God is that we're strengthened, we're empowered. Food is such a powerful image of that. If you don't have food, you don't have energy. Without the Eucharist, you don't have this mysterious *spiritual* energy. And by that I don't mean just literally "the Eucharist." I mean the understanding that the Eucharist *celebrates* is that God is *with* us, God is inside of us. This *essence* of God is part of us. And one of the things I'd like us also to get to this morning is, when you think about this as such an essential part of the Christian message, then let's make sure we don't fall into too literal or too oversimplified an understanding of it because what are we really saying when we say that Christ is coming to dwell within us? Is that to say that without the Eucharist there is no spark of divinity inside of us? That seems hard to believe. That doesn't seem right. It's more like this celebration is some mysterious participation in a reality that when we celebrate it, it becomes more real. And it is more powerful. But it also is a kind of extraordinary remembrance of something that God is already accomplishing in each and every human being, that inside of us there is already this *life force*, this divinity, that is us. We *are* that. You know, we have to understand that everything that is alive, everything in the world is somehow participating in divinity, or it wouldn't exist.

Now it's interesting, in the second reading, when Paul is talking to the Corinthians, he's really concerned about abuses of the Eucharist. It's interesting, right now in the Catholic Church, since we've had so many changes in our liturgical norms, there's a lot of concern on the part of the Church about the way in which we are celebrating the Eucharist. And I think what's important to see in these norms that the Church is trying to work through that what She, the Church, is trying to do is to make sure that we really act in a way that reflects what we really *believe* about the Eucharist. What we *believe* about it is that it's not just a piece of bread and not just a cup of wine, but it is somehow a piece of bread and a cup of wine that is the body and blood of Christ. One way to work with that is that it is an element *filled* with divinity, and it needs to be honored and respected, and we treat it with great reverence. And that's like an incredibly interesting exercise because what we're really supposed to do with that is not treat the *Eucharist* in such a way—we do need to treat it as divinity, that's true, but also everything *else*. It's almost like an exercise in belief: Can you believe that in this tiny flat piece of bread, there is divinity? Can you really believe that? I can. I've *grown* to believe that. I believe that with all my heart. But how insane it is when I would turn around then and say, "But I don't believe it's in *you*." And it would be even sillier to say, "It's not in you until you receive the Eucharist." That would be kind of crazy. What we're supposed to do is recognize in this incredible gift that Jesus has given to us is a message to us of who we are, how we are to deal with this whole notion of God's presence in our world—and *especially* in human beings. We are to honor them, reverence them. The care that we take in the way we treat the Eucharist, the gold cup, the white linens, touching it with reverence, receiving it with reverence—this is the way we should treat everything that God has created, in particular, human beings. We should treat them with *enormous* reverence, and that's not always there. And that's why this abuse that we see in the second reading is so interesting, because what Paul is upset about is that the Corinthians were gathering together to celebrate the Eucharist, and one of the things that they were doing was treating each other with very little respect, and the rich would come early and they would get all the food; the poor would be treated as secondary and "less than." Just think about any way in which a human being—and we're all guilty of this on some level—classify, categorize, judge other people as less than us, whether it's a race, a group of people, a certain lifestyle, whatever it is. We might say to that, to ourselves, to that person, "You're not *worth* anything!" It's hard to believe that we would say that, but in a sense there is some degree of that when we judge and categorize people that way. It seems to me that if we understand Eucharist and what it's supposed to be, and what it's supposed to teach us, and how it's supposed to deepen our awareness of divinity, the *presence* of divinity, then we should have, *through* the Eucharist, extraordinary sensitivity to the value and the dignity of every human life.

In the gospel we see Jesus performing the miracle of the multiplication of the loaves, and you know, I've said this to you so often, it's the most often repeated miracle in the scriptures, so it had to be one of the favorite miracles of the Church in terms of its early teachings. And what I think that's all about is that it touches so deeply into the core of what we're supposed to be engaged in when we talk about a Eucharistic life. This miracle has these marvelous elements: A group of people are in need; the people who are aware of the need come to God, as we often do, and say, "We better do something to help these people," and Jesus' response is always the same: *Well, you take care of it.* And they say, "Well, we don't have *enough* to take care of it." And Jesus says, *What do you have?* And they say, "We have just a few loaves and a few fish, and with 5,000 men (and with women and children, maybe 15,000-20,000 people), and there's no way we can do this." And he says, *Well, do it! Just give them what little you have.* There's something about that moment, in the minds of the disciples that would have been so interesting to be with them as they listened to those words. They know that was absolutely impossible, and yet they went ahead and started working with and feeding these people. How did they imagine it was working? I don't know, any more than I realize when I do my work or you do your work, and when we're in the disposition of taking care of each other, or when we're in the disposition of trying to save a world that seems to be insane and constantly killing each other in this world, how do we fix that? How do we feed the problem with that which *heals* the problem? And I think if we turn to God and say, "What can *I* do? Nothing!" And he says, *Well, do what you can do!* What *can* we do? Well, it's like you do what you wish the world was doing. You know, you recognize the goodness of every single human being, the goodness that's in every single thing that God has created, and you honor that, and you want that to flourish, and you want that to grow, and you do something that honors it, that supports it, that encourages it—whenever you're looking at a human being, if you're looking truly, as I think Christ looked at human beings, and as he's inviting *us* to look at human beings, when we look at their *essence*, what we're looking at is *divinity*. We're looking at God's Spirit in this world in the form of a human being. We honor that, we recognize that as so valuable; and all the other things that go into a human being—their actions, the way they look—all that is not their *essence*. And that doesn't mean that we don't protect ourselves against things that are negative. We *name* things for what they are, we try to change things that are negative and turn them into things that are positive, but it seems to me that the world would be such a different place if at the heart of our work with each other we were always recognizing and honoring and reverencing this life spark, this essence that's in every human being, and honoring that. And then in honoring that, we'd work *with* the "accidental" issues, the bad behavior, the good behavior, the good looks, the bad looks, the habits, which are all conditioned on people. Sometimes they're their fault and sometimes they're not their fault. We're all responsible, but I mean we have to look at people's lives and see how often someone is damaged, severely damaged by their environment, by what's happened to them to the point that they're not able to act in ways that we would like them to act. What I'm saying is that the reverence that we have for the individual goes beyond that kind of judgment and condemnation, so I think all of this gets back to the heart of what this feast is about. It's about the exercise that you and I have of being able to recognize the divinity in something where God simply says, *This is Life in this piece of bread; this is Life in this cup. If you receive it, if you take it in, if you drink it, that's the thing that is going to bring you into a different way of understanding and seeing the world.* I remember reading a book, Morton Kelsey wrote it many years ago, and he was talking in one of his stories about a man who wanted to *be* Eucharist for people, and I loved it because just as the Eucharist in the assembly draws our attention to something that is so life-giving and so loving, just as we're invited to come up and take it inside of ourselves and then leave the room with a sense of something that we tend to forget as we get involved in our daily existence, this figure wanted to *be* that for people. He just wanted to be something that people would experience as something loving and life-giving and they would somehow be able to take it in, and having taken it in, would therefore be changed. And it's a beautiful way of taking this theology of Eucharist and using it in exactly the way that I think Jesus would want us to use it. One of the saddest things in Christian communities today is that we don't all *share* in the Eucharist. Someday, I pray that that will work out, that somehow we'll be able to come together and celebrate in a way that brings great unity to our celebrations. But even without that unity, with separate celebrations, in a sense, there is still the possibility that the theology, that the understanding of Eucharist has this tremendous unifying element in our Christian life. So we pray for that on this Sunday that is the Feast of the Body and Blood of Christ, that we grow in our awareness of this gift, we live it, we become it, and somehow we take joy in sharing in it together.

Father, bless us with a greater understanding and awareness of the gift of the Eucharist. Help us to see it as a source of understanding of the world in which we live. And help us truly to be drawn as communities all over the world into greater unity because of this great gift, and we ask this in Jesus' name. Amen.

Genesis 14: 18-20
In those days, Melchizedek, king of Salem, brought out bread and wine,
and being a priest of God Most High,
he blessed Abram with these words:
"Blessed be Abram by God Most High,
the creator of heaven and earth;
and blessed be God Most High,
who delivered your foes into your hand."
Then Abram gave him a tenth of everything.

1 Corinthians 11: 20-26
Brothers and sisters:
When you meet in one place, then, it is not to eat the Lord's supper,
for in eating, each one goes ahead with his own supper, and one goes hungry while another gets drunk.
Do you not have houses in which you can eat and drink?
Or do you show contempt for the church of God and make those who have nothing feel ashamed?
What can I say to you? Shall I praise you? In this matter I do not praise you.
I received from the Lord what I also handed on to you,
that the Lord Jesus, on the night he was handed over,
took bread, and, after he had given thanks,
broke it and said, "This is my body that is for you.
Do this in remembrance of me."
In the same way also the cup, after supper, saying,
"This cup is the new covenant in my blood.
Do this, as often as you drink it, in remembrance of me."
For as often as you eat this bread and drink the cup,
you proclaim the death of the Lord until he comes.

Luke 9: 11B-17

Jesus spoke to the crowds about the kingdom of God,
and he healed those who needed to be cured.
As the day was drawing to a close,
the Twelve approached him and said,
"Dismiss the crowd
so that they can go to the surrounding villages and farms
and find lodging and provisions;
for we are in a deserted place here."
He said to them, "Give them some food yourselves."
They replied, "Five loaves and two fish are all we have,
unless we ourselves go and buy food for all these people."
Now the men there numbered about five thousand.
Then he said to his disciples,
"Have them sit down in groups of about fifty."
They did so and made them all sit down.
Then taking the five loaves and the two fish,
and looking up to heaven,
he said the blessing over them, broke them,
and gave them to the disciples to set before the crowd.
They all ate and were satisfied.
And when the leftover fragments were picked up,
they filled twelve wicker baskets.

TENTH SUNDAY IN ORDINARY TIME

1Kings 17:17-24; Galatians 1:11-19; Luke 7:11-17

O God from whom all good things come, grant that we who call on you in our need may at your prompting discern what is right and by your guidance DO it; through our Lord Jesus Christ, your Son, who lives and reigns with you in the unity of the holy Spirit, one God for ever and ever. Amen.

There's a fascinating image in both the first reading and the gospel. In them, we see a prophet, Elijah, and the prophet, Jesus, who was God, doing the same thing. They are giving life to someone who is dead. We know that Jesus was noted for his powers, particularly his miraculous powers of being able to effect healings in people. And it's one of the things that drew people's *attention* to him, and for obvious reasons. But whenever I see him doing something like this or know that here's the prophet Elijah doing it, and then Peter did it in the Acts of the Apostles, bringing somebody back to life, it's like *Whoa!* I mean, how does a human being do that? And what I'm trying to help you see and what I long to see is what is this kind of power that we see in a human being? What is it trying to teach us? What is it trying to say to us? Because if it were just simply saying, "Now this is the thing you should expect to happen, so all of you, once you follow Christ, you can go around and bring people back from the dead." All you've got to do is what Elijah did in the first reading—he just lay on this young man and breathed onto him and told God, "Don't do this! Don't kill him! Save him." It almost sounds like talking God out of what he's doing. That's what it almost sounds like. That *can't* be right!

So let's look at it more in the way it was intended. There is something in this particular kind of *power*, the power to bring life back into someone that has *everything* to do with what God *intends* to do with every single one of us, that his presence in your life and in mine, his work in us, is to bring us from death to life, to give us life. And what that *means* is that there is something in us that is not fully developed that he longs to be a part of developing, and a way we could think about it is this: One of the things that people did not have throughout the Old Testament, it seems to me, or even that people had at the time of Jesus—they did not have the level of consciousness and awareness that we have today. We hadn't matured, we hadn't grown enough into the truth of who we are and what this world is about and who God is. And when we're in that more unconscious state—I'll call that "lesser life"—maybe when we're completely unconscious, we're almost dead, that into that comes this gift of God, this work of God, that that's what he's doing in the world. He's trying to awaken in us the fullness of who we are, and then he wants us to see the fullness of who *he* is and wants to see this perfect companionship, this perfect connection that we're made for. We can't *live* without it.

And isn't it interesting that in both these healings, it's the *son of a widow* that is being brought back to life? What would it be like to be a widow at the time that both these stories took place? Well, women had *no* rights, no education, no way of taking care of themselves. If they didn't have a husband, they were in deep trouble if they didn't have a family to go to. So let's imagine that both of these women, who didn't have family and only had a son, and this son was dead. Try to imagine that as you, your soul, this part that is you, this eternal part of us—let's call it a feminine part of us, because it needs something to fulfill it; it needs a complement, it needs a force inside of it, and God has been considered masculine for a long time. So just imagine that God uses that language: *I am the Father. I created you. I want to marry you.* All those images tend to be masculine. Doesn't mean that God is really a man, like we think of men. He's everything, he's fullness, he's all men, he's all women. But just imagine that what we're hearing in this story is that this gift of God in the world that is made manifest to us in Jesus—when it's received, when it's understood, when it comes into us, it is like something being born inside of us, or something that was dead being brought to life. And it's that part that sustains us and keeps us going in this existence that we have. Just like the widow could not exist without her son. And when Jesus sees it, in the gospel passage, it's almost like he wasn't *planning* on doing this, but he's walking through the gate into a city and all of a sudden he sees a funeral, and he looks at this woman and he sees in her the anguish of being left without what she needs, and he knows that's the condition of human beings, and he's there to awaken them to what he wants to bring to them in terms of *partnership* and *care*. So he cannot *not* heal!

So how do we live in a world where that's what we imagine is happening—that we have a way of being in the world that is dangerously void of that which we *actually* need. And what do we tend to think that we need? Well, I think we tend to *think* we need what Paul, in the second reading, is talking about: What *he* felt that he needed to do was to be in this world to correct what was wrong, to condemn what's wrong, and to reward what's right. In fact, that was basically the mentality of the Old Testament because in a way, the Old Testament's primary role was to teach monotheism, so in the Old Testament, God *is* the only God. And that means that *everything* comes from him, both good and evil. So God punishes, God destroys, God saves. Well, something happened with Paul, who was in that mindset of going into the world with his energy and strength and saying, "I'm going to get rid of everything that's bad, destroy it because that's what God wants, and save everything that's right." He saw all these people, these Christians, as somehow Law-breakers and they were wrong, so he was absolutely justified in destroying them. That whole image that the way you deal with evil is to destroy it.

Then something new comes into Paul's life, and what that is is the Christ. And listen to the way it enters into Paul—it's so fascinating! He says, "Something happened to me. I was living the life that I thought I was to live. I was conscious of what I thought was the fullness of what is, so I knew what our role in this world was—to condemn everything that's bad and get rid of it and attack it. And then we'll make this perfect life." It's like Nazi Germany. "Let's get rid of everything that's bad and we'll have this perfect race." It's *insanity*, but it doesn't *feel* insane to the people who are unconscious. So let's say that Paul's in that unconscious state, but then something breaks through his consciousness. He has this *awakening*, this mysterious light that goes off and blinds him for a while. It's almost like that insight that's so big, so different that everything you knew doesn't make any sense any more, and you're lost and you're *blinded* by this new insight. And what I love about Paul's story is that he's saying, "Nobody sat down and explained this to me. Nobody did that. It was given to me through grace. God entered into me; Jesus entered into me; the Spirit entered into me, and revealed this to me. And I didn't know what to do with it, so I stayed with it. All I did was stay with this image and went over it and over it in my imagination until it took root in me and became part of me, and that took three years." And he never went to anyone who was officially part of the Christian church to find out if he was right or wrong. He didn't go and check it out. He didn't ask, "What do you think about this?" It's almost like God said, "I don't want you to listen to anybody else but me for a while. *Listen* to me." I think God is saying that to you and me over and over again. "I want to talk to you. I want to reveal myself to you, I want to show you where you might be caught in something that isn't in any way, shape, or form the place I *want* you to be." And the most common place most of us are is hating that which is bad. I mean, shame is one of the most debilitating things that can happen to a human being. And shame is usually based on some kind of disposition where that which isn't what it should be is considered to be bad! Trash! Worthless! But what if God has created you and me as human beings in such a way that by our very *nature* we're *imperfect*, right? Does anybody really *think* they're perfect? We *are* imperfect. So when Jesus says to his disciples, *I have to give myself over to evil in order to save the world,* it's a tricky statement because what he's really saying is, *I have to give myself over to the way things are, the way things are, the way it's written.*

"I, Don Fischer, have to give myself over to who I am. With my own set of weaknesses, with my own set of areas where I'm blind. I have to somehow befriend that. I have to not want to condemn it. I have to not want to destroy it. I don't want to hate myself for being who I am."

And yet, shame has some element in that that is so debilitating. If you get caught up in any kind of feeling that God's work in this world is to enter into it to destroy all evil, all ordinariness, all humanness, make us all into angels or something, then we're in deep trouble, you know? [chuckles] And it would mean that God somehow looks at what he created and said, "This was a horrible mistake." But he *doesn't* believe that we're a mistake because we're human, because we fail, because we doubt, because we hate, because we fear, because we get angry. All he wants you to do and wants me to do is to embrace that and understand that, and that's part of who I am. And what I need is to be in a right relationship with that, and that is that I've got to forgive myself for everything, for every failure. I've got to do the same thing for my brothers and sisters.

And that's the core message of Jesus: *Forgive everything.* That means be at one with everything. It doesn't mean we're not growing, not challenging ourselves to grow and change, but it means there's this radical acceptance of the way things are, with no hatred and no disgust, but rather a kind of humble acceptance that this is who I am, and I'm not enough, and I have a God who's going to use me whenever he needs me to be an extraordinary carrier of something that is so beyond my human nature that when it works through me, it is not just something like information that I give to someone, or advice, but it's this powerful, transforming, resonant thing called *grace,* unmerited love, that flows through me. And it can't flow through me to someone else unless it's first filled me. And that's what *happened* to Paul. He was filled with an overwhelming sense of God's love for him—*in his imperfection*! He was destroying people who were following Christ. He was holding the coats of people who were *killing* people. I wouldn't say that's the best place to be if you would look at a God, if you think of a God who is interested in only destroying that which isn't what it's supposed to be.

Jesus is not interested in condemning; he's interested in transforming, changing; and the shock, the surprise is that changing begins—it can *only* begin—after acceptance of imperfection sets in in a way that begins to refocus all that human energy that's so God-given and good. We have a *lot* of human energy to make things happen, but when that energy is directed towards destruction, *of anything,* we're in trouble. We're not to use God's power to destroy; we're not to use our own power to destroy; we're only asked to transform. To first connect, and through the connection, the understanding, the forgiveness, then we transform. But *we* don't do that; God does that though us. That's the mystery of what it means to live in this kind of world that Jesus won for us on the cross. What a gift! What a powerful, awesome gift, to have on board, inside of you and me, this marvelous, accepting, forgiving—there's a word I'm trying to reach, and I don't want to make it sound too weird, but I almost want to say, Is it possible to *delight* in the mess that we are, and the whole world—it's all crazy—not delight in the sense that it doesn't need to change. It's just what is. It's the given. It's what God created. This is what he expects life to be; it's this way. And then he's saying, "OK, now, can you accept all that, and get over all your resistance and hatred and condemning spirit? And say, 'OK, this is what is. I'll accept it and then I'll become an instrument, through my acceptance, of being at peace and calm and then, be used, be used to transform.'"

Father, your wisdom is beyond our human understanding, yet it is your gift. Open our minds, open our hearts, to this wisdom of how it is you long for us to live in this world. Called both to accept and embrace all that we are, all that the world is, at the same time to become an instrument, a vehicle, a way, of helping the world to grow, to change, and to become more and more the place you intend it to be, in all of its fullness. And we ask this in Jesus' name. Amen.

1 Kings 17: 17-24

Sometime later the son of the woman, the owner of the house, fell sick, and
his sickness grew more severe until he stopped breathing.18So she said to
Elijah, "Why have you done this to me, man of God? Have you come to me
to call attention to my guilt and to kill my son?"19Elijah said to her, "Give
me your son." Taking him from her lap, he carried him to the upper room
where he was staying, and laid him on his own bed.20He called out to the
LORD: "LORD, my God, will you afflict even the widow with whom I am
staying by killing her son?"21Then he stretched himself out upon the child
three times and he called out to the LORD: "LORD, my God, let the life
breath return to the body of this child."22The LORD heard the prayer of Elijah; the life breath returned to the child's body and he lived.23Taking the
child, Elijah carried him down into the house from the upper room and
gave him to his mother. Elijah said, "See! Your son is alive."24The woman
said to Elijah, "Now indeed I know that you are a man of God, and it is truly the word of the LORD that you speak."

Galatians 1: 11-19

Now I want you to know, brothers and sisters, that the gospel preached by me is not of human origin.[12]For I did not receive it from a human being, nor was I taught it, but it came through a revelation of Jesus Christ.
[13]For you heard of my former way of life in Judaism, how I persecuted the church of God beyond measure and tried to destroy it,[14]and progressed in Judaism beyond many of my contemporaries among my race, since I was even more a zealot for my ancestral traditions.[15]But when [God], who from my mother's womb had set me apart and called me through his grace, was pleased[16]to reveal his Son to me, so that I might proclaim him to the Gentiles, I did not immediately consult flesh and blood, [17]nor did I go up to Jerusalem to those who were apostles before me; rather, I went into Arabia and then returned to Damascus.
[18]Then after three years I went up to Jerusalem to confer with Cephas and remained with him for fifteen days.[19]But I did not see any other of the apostles, only James the brother of the Lord.

Luke 7: 11-17

Soon afterward he journeyed to a city called Nain, and his disciples and a large crowd accompanied him.[12]As he drew near to the gate of the city, a man who had died was being carried out, the only son of his mother, and she was a widow. A large crowd from the city was with her.[13]When the Lord saw her, he was moved with pity for her and said to her, "Do not weep."[14]He stepped forward and touched the coffin; at this the bearers halted, and he said, "Young man, I tell you, arise!"[15]The dead man sat up and began to speak, and Jesus gave him to his mother.[16]Fear seized them all, and they glorified God, exclaiming, "A great prophet has arisen in our midst," and "God has visited his people."[17]This report about him spread through the whole of Judea and in all the surrounding region.

ELEVENTH SUNDAY IN ORDINARY TIME

2 Samuel 12:7-10, 13; Galatians 2:16, 19-21; Luke 7:36 – 8:3

O God, strength of those who hope in you, graciously hear our pleas. And since without you, mortal frailty can do nothing, grant us always the help of your grace, that in following your commands we may please you by our resolve and our deeds, through our Lord Jesus Christ, your Son, who lives and reigns with you in the unity of the holy Spirit, one God for ever and ever. Amen.

We begin our Liturgy of the Word this week with the image of a relationship that is so interesting in the Old Testament. It's the relationship between David and God. David was the king that God chose from all the brothers. He was the youngest, and God's *favor* was with him. So just imagine, the God that this story is talking about is a God who is deeply in love with and connected to David. And then David becomes a very fascinating character as he lives out his role of being king. It could make a great miniseries on TV [chuckles]. It's filled with all kinds of corruption and failures and infidelities and murders. So in this passage, we see that God is stating very clearly to David: *David, you have just so disappointed me. There's so much intrigue and so much anger and so much hatred and so much violence in your family and in what you've created. I want to tell you, that sword is going to stay in your family. You failed.*

And so it's interesting that then Nathan the prophet, after he gets David's reaction to God's condemnation of what he's been doing, David says, "I really messed up. Now I know God hates me, and he's not going to be with me anymore." Nathan says, "No, he forgives you." But the punishment that is due to happen in terms of the effects of these negative things is going to *be* there, but what's interesting is the statement that is so clear. God is saying, *No matter how many times you mess up, I'm still committed to you; I'm still there for you.* Now that's not unique to the relationship with David. It is the thing that you and I have to believe with all our hearts. That's the relationship that God has with you and me, with everything he creates. His support, his love, his attention—his *intention* is that whatever he creates flourishes. That's what he wants, and he will never, ever not be there for us.

How do I know that? It's because that's what Jesus came to teach. It's called *forgiveness*, and forgiveness has everything to do with not allowing the faults that we commit, the mistakes that we make, to destroy in any way God's commitment to us. And yet I know—I hear over and over again, the words, "Jesus came into the world to conquer sin, so why doesn't that mean that we're not going to sin anymore?" Well, the conquering that Jesus did when he died on the cross to free us from sin was not to free us from the potential of sinning, but to free us from the destruction, the *destruction*, that happens to the human being when they get caught in sin. Sin can no longer destroy us. In fact, the irony is, and the thing that must make evil really, really upset, is that God figured out a way to use sin, our weaknesses, to deepen our commitment to him, to each other; and to grow. The way we *deal* with sin is the crucial thing.

So we have in the second reading, from Galatians, an image of what Paul is saying here: "Look. God's desire is not that you and I, through his grace, are never making mistakes, that we follow every rule, every law." (It may sometimes sound like that's exactly what Christianity is asking of us.) But he's saying that anybody that does that, does everything right—if that's all it takes to be justified, if that's all it takes, just to do everything right, then you'll please God and everything—well, then this whole thing that Jesus went through, called his death and resurrection, it means nothing! We didn't need it! Because all we needed was the strength from God to make sure that we did everything right!

Well, it seems to me—and this may sound weird, but I don't think God's intention is ever to make you and me so strong, so loving, so perfect that we never make a mistake and we never fail anyone else, that we never fail him—that just doesn't seem to be the plan. What *is* the plan? The plan is that we go through what Jesus went through. The plan is that we go through crucifixion. And listen to Paul. He said, "If following the Law is all that we're required to do, then the death of Jesus means nothing." So since that *can't* be, and the death of Christ means *everything*, it's what changed the world, transformed everything, what is at the *heart* of that act of Christ dying on the cross? Well, there's a mystery involved, which we cannot fathom, and it means that in that act, somehow something radically changed in human nature and we now are able to do something we couldn't do before. What *is* it? Well, if we think the thing that was supposed to change in us is that we no longer ever sin, *that* certainly wasn't it. So what is it? God, through the death and resurrection of Jesus, redeemed us, and somehow redemption has something to do with you and I being capable of dealing with our weaknesses and our sins in a way that can only deepen and strengthen our ability to be who Christ wants us to be. So mistakes, sins, are essential to the whole process.

We listen next to the gospel passage about Jesus, who comes to this man's house, the Pharisee's house. And there were images of welcoming someone to your house, rituals. And the rituals would be that since you were walking on the street, your feet were probably dirty, and when you reclined at table, your feet probably weren't under the table, under the tablecloth, so your feet were exposed, and they were washed and sometimes people didn't smell so good, so they anointed you—which was kind of a way of adding a fragrance. And they would kiss you in the welcoming, so you'd be kissed and washed and perfumed. Beautiful images of hospitality!

Well, the Pharisee didn't offer any of those things to Jesus, so you know that something is amiss, something was going on there that they didn't welcome him because they *resisted* him, resisting what he was inviting them to do, which was of course to stop living the lie they were living by pretending that everything they were doing was fine, and they were justified by the Law—he's seeing through that, and they *know* that, so they're not drawn to him at all, because what they *don't* want to see, which is absolute anathema to them, is to see anything in them that is not good. So just think about that. Think how seductive it is that you and I, when we believe that God's call to you and me is to not make mistakes, how easy it would be for us not to face them and to not look at them and to develop this skill, called *being a hypocrite, acting* as if everything is fine, but it really isn't. I'll just say, we go *unconscious*. We're not very conscious of what's going on. We're not very connected. And we certainly don't *need* anybody. So what is it with the woman in the story? She *knows* she needs forgiveness. She *knows* that she has failed miserably; in fact, she's sort of the town sinner. Tradition says it's Mary Magdalene, who was noted for not such a great past. So what we see in the story is Jesus showing the Pharisee that her desire, her longing for forgiveness, flows out of her understanding of the debt that she owes, or the thing that needs to be healed or transformed in her. She's needy, and she knows that this Christ, this Anointed One, has the capacity to get her through what she's done, and not to be weakened by her failures but to be strengthened by them. And she goes through, in a sense, the crucifixion. She goes through the crucifixion. What's the crucifixion? We go back to Paul. He said he's been crucified with Christ. *He* lives no longer, but Christ lives *in* him. What is in him that wasn't there before, that he learned from and received from Christ's death on the cross? Well, I've said it to you before, but it's this mystery that when Christ is on the cross, what he's doing is giving us an indication of how we need to deal with our sin and our weakness. And this is what he does. He first of all recognizes that the place he's in, the dark place that he's caught in in this moment of being rejected and spit upon and laughed at, and somehow whenever we fail, there's a voice in *us*, there's a voice *around* us, putting us down, telling us we're not worth anything; and so the first thing we see in Jesus, when he's in this position of being rejected, he knows in his heart that he has a God who's on his side, and he never doubts that he will take him through this, and he will survive. It's amazing when I'm in a place of being rejected and told that I'm a failure or realize that in the depths of my being that I've deeply failed to be what I want to be, somehow the fear is that I'm going to *die*, that I'll be *destroyed* by this. Guilt and shame and fear rush in. So right away, Jesus on the cross is saying, *I'm not afraid to do this. I thought it through. I'm not afraid. God is going to take me through this, and I am going to rise.* And then he realizes also that he's looking at these people jeering and laughing at him, and he never, ever implies in any way, shape, or form that he feels somehow that he failed. Wouldn't that be a natural thing for Jesus as a human being to feel when he tried for three years to change the minds of people and to awaken in people a way of seeing and he wasn't able to do it? Maybe he *did* say that over and over again. "I just didn't do it well enough. I'm *not* good enough." But there's nothing in him, nothing that gives us any indication that he ever doubted his goodness. And that's what you and I have to hold onto when we're being put down, when we're being rejected, when we're told we're no good. We have to believe, "No, maybe what I *did* is no good, maybe what I did was not at all what I *should* have done, but I, *myself*, the core of me that God created is good." And the most *beautiful* thing that Jesus did on the cross, which is what we all need to do when people are "on" us, judging us, condemning us (and sometimes legitimately so), it's so easy to be angry at those people and to make *them* "the problem" and to sometimes say it's all unfair, and what they're doing to me is unfair, and I shouldn't be rejected and I shouldn't be put down. So we often find ourselves that we might be angry, angry, angry when things are not the way they should be. Angry at some situation, somebody that we can blame. And Jesus doesn't do that either. In fact, he has this most awesome thing of saying, you know, *Father, forgive them. They don't know what they're doing.*

We're looking at somebody who has to deal with all the effects of sin, even though he's innocent. *We* have to deal with all those things because we're guilty, but the same thing that we see witnessed in Christ on the cross are the things that *we* have to be involved in. We have to have those dispositions. And to die with him, to be one with him on the cross is to go through that kind of experience and then to experience resurrection. That's the mystery of the cross; that's the thing that Paul is so clearly saying: "I want to die with him, I want to rise with him. It's what *I* want to do; it's what I want *you* to do." That's the challenge of the *message* of Christ. Learn how to do this. Learn that there's life, abundant life, on the other side of our darker side, our weakest side, the side that we often will not embrace. Christ embraced it on the cross; we need to embrace it in ourselves, and live the life he's called us to live.

Father, the plan that you have for us includes our struggles, our weaknesses, our human nature. Over and over again, you teach us that you are the God who is faithful, and you ARE forgiveness. So take from us anything that would give us the sense that we are somehow separated from you by our weaknesses or that you somehow lose hope or trust in us, so we never feel, never feel isolated from you. For you are the source that enables us to deal with our sins in the way you've called us to. We thank you for that gift of your fidelity. And you're always there for us. We ask this in Jesus' name. Amen.

2 Samuel 12: 7-10, 13

[7] . . . "Thus says the LORD God of Israel: I anointed you king over Israel. I delivered you from the hand of Saul.[8]I gave you your lord's house and your lord's wives for your own. I gave you the house of Israel and of Judah. And if this were not enough, I could count up for you still more.[9]Why have you despised the LORD and done what is evil in his sight? You have cut down Uriah the Hittite with the sword; his wife you took as your own, and him you killed with the sword of the Ammonites.[10]Now, therefore, the sword shall never depart from your house, because you have despised me and have taken the wife of Uriah the Hittite to be your wife.

[13]Then David said to Nathan, "I have sinned against the LORD." Nathan answered David: "For his part, the LORD has removed your sin. You shall not die . . ."

Galatians 2: 16, 19-21

[16][Brothers and sisters] we who know that a person is not justified by works of the law but through faith in Jesus Christ, even we have believed in Christ Jesus that we may be justified by faith in Christ and not by works of the law, because by works of the law no one will be justified.

[19]For through the law I died to the law, that I might live for God. I have been crucified with Christ;[20]yet I live, no longer I, but Christ lives in me; insofar as I now live in the flesh, I live by faith in the Son of God who has loved me and given himself up for me.[21]I do not nullify the grace of God; for if justification comes through the law, then Christ died for nothing.

Luke 7:36 – 8:3

[36]A Pharisee invited Jesus to dine with him, and he entered the Pharisee's house and reclined at table.[37]Now there was a sinful woman in the city who learned that he was at
table in the house of the Pharisee. Bringing an alabaster flask of ointment,[38]she stood
behind him at his feet weeping and began to bathe his feet with her tears. Then she
wiped them with her hair, kissed them, and anointed them with the ointment.[39]When
the Pharisee who had invited him saw this he said to himself, "If this man were a
prophet, he would know who and what sort of woman this is who is touching him, that
she is a sinner."[40]Jesus said to him in reply, "Simon, I have something to say to you."
"Tell me, teacher," he said.[41]"Two people were in debt to a certain creditor; one owed
five hundred days' wages* and the other owed fifty.[42]Since they were unable to repay
the debt, he forgave it for both. Which of them will love him more?"[43]Simon said in reply, "The one, I suppose, whose larger debt was forgiven." He said to him, "You have
judged rightly."[44]Then he turned to the woman and said to Simon, "Do you see this
woman? When I entered your house, you did not give me water for my feet, but she has
bathed them with her tears and wiped them with her hair.[45]You did not give me a kiss,
but she has not ceased kissing my feet since the time I entered.[46]You did not anoint my
head with oil, but she anointed my feet with ointment.[47]So I tell you, her many sins have
been forgiven; hence, she has shown great love.* But the one to whom little is forgiven,
loves little."[48]He said to her, "Your sins are forgiven."[49]The others at table said to themselves, "Who is this who even forgives sins?"[50]But he said to the woman, "Your faith
has saved you; go in peace."
[1]Afterward he journeyed from one town and village to another, preaching and proclaiming the good news of the kingdom of God. Accompanying him were the Twelve
[2]and some women who had been cured of evil spirits and infirmities, Mary, called
Magdalene, from whom seven demons had gone out,[3]Joanna, the wife of Herod's steward Chuza, Susanna, and many others who provided for them out of their resources.

TWELFTH SUNDAY IN ORDINARY TIME

Zechariah 12:10-11, 13:1; Galatians 3:26-29; Luke 9:18-24

Father, guide and protect your people, grant us an unfailing respect for your name, and keep us always in your love; and we ask this through our Lord Jesus Christ, your Son, who lives and reigns with you in the unity of the holy Spirit, one God for ever and ever. Amen.

The gospel this morning has a very interesting theme. And to put it in its context, I want you to realize that Jesus had just performed probably his most famous miracle. It's the one most often recorded in scripture, and that was the feeding of the 5,000. What's interesting about that particular miracle is that of so many of the miracles that Jesus performed, some were done in private; most of the time they were done in small groups or just between Jesus and the person being healed. But this is probably his most *public* display of this unique power that he possessed, so it's right after that experience—and I'm sure that Jesus was wondering, "What do people think about me? What are they imagining?" And knowing human nature as he did, he could conceive that they were probably thinking of a million different things, as far as how they saw him and who they thought he was. So he asked his disciples, after he's had this experience with the crowd, *Who do you think these people are saying I am? Who do you think?*

And then of course come the different answers: "Some think you're John the Baptist come back, some think you're Elijah." But it's not hard to imagine this in a contemporary context, where you could get a group of people together—say a large group of people who are in a church—and they listen to stories of miracles, and they have community experiences of Spirit, and they have the personal spiritual life that they have, where they have experiences. In each of those situations, it would be amazing to me if you ever found a 100% consistent image of who God is. Everyone has a slightly different image.

But the point is, how *do* we find who this God really is? How do we answer the question of who Jesus is, because Jesus is so clear to say, *I am the Father's presence in the world. When you see me, you see the Father.* Well, to know who Jesus is, you somehow have to know who *God* is. So how do we find that? How do we find this wisdom, this insight? Well, one thing that's interesting to do is to think about how many different images that people have of God that are in nice, neat categories; and I'll just mention a couple, because they're the ones that come to mind first.

A lot of people see God as the most amazing sort of rich uncle, rich relative, who's going to bail them out of every situation, take care of them, make life easy. There are so many people who see God as the one who is to take *care* of them, help them avoid all kinds of pain and suffering. You know that that's where they are because they don't often say that directly, but when they experience something negative, they're so quick to say something like, "I don't know where God was. He wasn't there to help me. I called on him and nothing happened, so I'm not really very happy with God right now." Or you see people who go through a traumatic experience of losing a loved one, and then you hear something like, "I'm through with God, because if he's supposed to be love, and he's supposed to take care of people, well, he's sure not taking care of me!" So there's that one image of a God who's supposed to take *care* of everything, pay for everything, pick up the tab, you know? [chuckles] And that can get us into real, real trouble.

The other extreme is the one where God is just an idea, just a distant idea that he exists. "Yes, I guess he exists. It's hard to explain the universe without some kind of intelligent design in it all, and I suppose there is this divine power, but it doesn't seem to have any impact on me." So it's that sense of a God who is so impersonal.

There's a great line from a movie I always liked, *Come Back to the Five and Dime, Jimmy Dean, Jimmy Dean.* It's a Robert Altman film and one of the characters is in there, and they're praying for rain. It's been a really hot, dry summer in Texas and this woman is just thinking, (and it's wonderful the way it's done), she's just kind of thinking, "Well, of course God's not going to answer our prayers for rain because there's just too many people in the world now. How can he possibly keep up with everything?" So it's that putting human limits onto God, but either he seems too distant or it seems that he's supposed to be there to take care of everything.

Those are the two extremes I want to talk about, because if I take those two extremes and try to put us in the middle, I think I might be able to help us to see, as clearly as we can, who God really is. And the first thing I want to say is, the only one who can *know* God, the only way we can get to know God, is if he's *revealed* to us. He has to be *shown* to us. So one of the dispositions that would make this work, of seeing God as he really is, answering the question as Jesus poses it to his disciples, and Peter does say, "You are the Christ," and that's the right answer, but there you see also that Jesus is saying to Peter and to the rest of the disciples, *You're right. I am the one who's come into the world to show you who God really is, but don't talk about it yet because you have no idea yet who I really am.*

So just to say Jesus is the Messiah is not enough. You have to know *who* the Messiah is. You have to understand him. And there is one major hurdle that everyone has to get over in order to really see him and understand him, and that is the whole issue of suffering. What is that about? Why do we have to suffer? Why do we have to go through painful stuff?

Well, I want to start with two things. One is, it seems so clear that if you look at life carefully, you will see that the things that are most difficult and the things that are most painful seem to carry within them the most potential for changing us. Nothing seems to change us like suffering. Joy is a wonderful experience, and it has a wonderful impact on us, but going through something really difficult and really painful is always the most transforming experience.

And one of the reasons I think that is is because one of the things we carry within us all the time is a kind of anxiety and a fear that things are not going to work out. We carry it like a low-grade anxiety. What if *this* would happen? What if *that* would happen? And we carry that all the time, and one of the things that happen so often to us when we then go through one of these experiences that are really painful and we begin to sense and experience that there's something in this *for* me, there's something in it that's *transforming* me, there's something in it that makes me feel stronger and more capable, it's sometimes this real experience of confronting that anxiety and fear that if this happened, I couldn't take it. You *can* take it! You can take it with God's help. You *can* go through it. I *had* that experience once, of an anxiety and a fear that I always had, and it happened, and all of a sudden, in the midst of that, I said, "Where's this *strength* coming from? Why do I feel all of a sudden *strong*?" And what I realized is, I was still alive! This thing didn't kill me! I could *do* this! So there's something in the experience of suffering that helps us confront this low-grade anxiety that always makes us long for this God who's going to take care of us and make sure we never stumble or fall.

There's an image in scripture that says that, but the stumbling and falling is not stubbing your toe or falling down and breaking your leg or something. It's more about saying: Spiritually, if you follow me, you will never fall into the trap of this worry and anxiety and fear that we often get caught up in, you know? So one of the things we have to look at so carefully then is this mystery of what it means to suffer and how much power and how much strength there is coming to us when we go through something like this.

Alright. Then another thing, it seems to me, that this set of readings is talking about, and especially you find it in the first reading, is this idea of when you grieve, even when you mourn, when you go through that experience, then a fountain will come over you that cleanses you, that purifies you, that releases you from all kinds of negative and difficult things.

So I guess that one of the things we want to work on then, in terms of finding that middle place between a God who takes care of us and keeps us safe from *everything*, or a God who's not even around and just too impersonal, we end up with a God who is very much involved in our lives personally—because he is the one who determines the way things go. That's another, absolutely essential ingredient to understand who God is. It seems to me, if you don't have that *sense* that in the death and resurrection of Jesus that all things have been placed under his feet, that he is now champion of the world, he's conquered all evil—and that means he's conquered the power of evil to somehow be able to destroy us. It's always interesting to me that Jesus said, *I've destroyed evil, but it's still around*. Well, what he's saying is, *I've destroyed its power. I am stronger. I have something that I offer you that is stronger than anything out there that might destroy you.*

So it seems like if you have two things on board, then you have this *sense* that suffering is an important ingredient and a transforming ingredient that brings you to a place that nothing else can bring you to, and it's a place you really want to be; and you also believe that this God who created the world and has set us in the world, that he gives each of us a destiny, and he's guiding that destiny—it's not predestination; it's not that we don't have choices, it just means that somehow his hand is in each thing and he has one primary concern, one deep desire, and that's for you and me to reach our full potential. Makes so much sense to me that a God who created you, created me, in the way that he created us, a unique, eternal being that will someday know him and see him face-to-face; that our destiny, this work that we are engaged in on this earth, has some major part to play in the overall plan. And if there is this amazing plan, then we need to trust in it and we need to trust in it in a way that brings us to a really peaceful place in the process of going through what we go through.

So the question, "Who am I?" is a very, very important question when the person asking is God incarnate. Because he knows that without that knowledge, without that awareness, without that sense, we are not going to be able to engage in what he longs for us to engage in, which is a transforming process, a growth process called *life*.

Now we have one other thing that I want to tie this together with. Not only do we need to get into the center between those two extremes, the distant impersonal God and the God who takes care of us like a doting grandfather; we have this mystery that we celebrated a couple of weeks ago, Pentecost, and that is the mystery of an Advocate being given, a most extraordinary Advocate, the holy Spirit, who has one primary role. And this is a really comforting thought for me always, to realize that this Spirit of God, who is somehow the presence of God in me; and the one focus I want to stress right now, is that *it longs to reveal to us who God really is.*

So, if we have a trust in our destiny; we trust in things being somehow important and connected, and if we believe in a God who says, "I want you to go through an experience that's going to be so life-giving for you even though it's difficult. Trust me." And then we have the sense of the Spirit that's guiding us and working with us and helping us see all these things, then it seems to me there ought to be a deep confidence in us that we would be able to accomplish this goal of really seeing who God is. Seeing him as he really is and knowing him for who he is. And feeling his presence.

Jesus says in the gospel today, there's a line that's so important, that I want to end the homily with: *If you try to save your life, you'll never find it. You've got to go through something that is letting go of that which you think is really you.* And if you can just imagine, that statement is reminding us that there are *two* of us. There's the person that God has created and the person *we* think we are. And the person who thinks the world is the way they think it is, or thinks that God is the way we think he is—and that's that egocentric sort of focused figure that is, well, let's just say they're formed by their culture, their family of origin, all this stuff. And so when you can't let go of that, when you're so self-identified with the way you see the world, you know, that's the self that you have to let go of. You have to "lose" that self; then you find your *true* self. It's an interesting image that we have, that we have these two selves, you know? The one that perceives the world as we see it, or the way we think it is, and the person who sees it as it really is. And what a beautiful prayer to the Spirit, to say, "Help me, help me, help me to be able to see this wonderful, wonderful self that you have created—because as you see God as he is, you'll see yourself as you are. And that's the *moment*, it seems to me, that the spiritual life has really reached the maturity that it's called to reach, and we've reached the place that God wants us so much to be.

Father, we praise you for the gift of your Spirit, the Advocate that continues to open our eyes and open our hearts to who you truly are. Bless us with this knowledge so that we truly can cooperate with all that you send to us, so that through our acceptance and surrender to your will, we find life and fullness. And we ask this in Jesus's name. Amen.

Zechariah 12: 10-11; 13:1

10 I will pour out on the house of David and on the inhabitants of Jerusalem a spirit of mercy and supplication, so that when they look on him whom they have thrust through, they will mourn for him as one mourns for an only child, and they will grieve

for him as one grieves over a firstborn.
[11] On that day the mourning in Jerusalem will be as great as the mourning for Hada-
drimmon in the plain of Megiddo.

[1] On that day a fountain will be opened for the house of David and the inhabitants of
Jerusalem, to purify from sin and uncleanness.

Galatians 3:26-29

[26][Brothers and sisters,] through faith you are all children of God in Christ Jesus.[27] For all
of you who were baptized into Christ have clothed yourselves with Christ.[28]There is
neither Jew nor Greek, there is neither slave nor free person, there is not male and female; for you are all one in Christ Jesus.[29]And if you belong to Christ, then you are
Abraham's descendant, heirs according to the promise.

Luke 9: 18-24

[18]Once when Jesus was praying in solitude, and the disciples were with him, he asked
them, "Who do the crowds say that I am?"[19]They said in reply, "John the Baptist; others,
Elijah; still others, 'One of the ancient prophets has arisen.'" [20]Then he said to them, "But
who do *you* say that I am?" Peter said in reply, "The Messiah of God."[21]He rebuked
them and directed them not to tell this to anyone.
[22]He said, "The Son of Man must suffer greatly and be rejected by the elders, the chief
priests, and the scribes, and be killed and on the third day be raised."
[23]Then he said to all, "If anyone wishes to come after me, he must deny himself and take
up his cross daily and follow me.[24]For whoever wishes to save his life will lose it, but
whoever loses his life for my sake will save it.[25]

THIRTEENTH SUNDAY IN ORDINARY TIME

1Kings 19:16, 19-21; Galatians 5:1, 13-18; Luke 9:51-62

Father, you call your children to walk in the light of Christ. Free us from darkness; keep us in the radiance of your truth; and we ask this through our Lord Jesus Christ, your Son, who lives and reigns with you in the unity of the holy Spirit, one God for ever and ever. Amen.

The theme of the readings today has something to do with urgency, a willingness to make a decision *now,* not to put it off, not to wait. If you're like me, there are many times when I feel something is important that I need to do—something I should get engaged in that would make my life better, whether it's physically like through exercise or diet, or whether it's a spiritual exercise that I really know I should do. I don't know what it is! Call it *procrastination*! [chuckles] But there's this kind of resistance. You sometimes *feel* it. It's almost *physical,* like you feel something is stopping you from doing this. I don't know what that is, exactly—whether it's a negative spirit or whatever, you know? But it's an inertia that comes over you.

So I find that often when there's something I know I should do, but I really *don't* want to do it, maybe one of the things we have to check out when we feel this inertia is, "Do I really *want* to do this, or do I just think it's a good *idea* to do this?" And the really *wanting* to do it, that's the freedom that I think the scriptures are talking about in today's set of readings. We're called into a place of *freedom,* not slavery. If I'm being a slave to whatever thing I think I should be doing, if I feel like I'm going to be obligated to this thing forever and forced to do it against my will for a long period of time, I can see why that inertia might be there. "Oh, come on, let's not get into all this. Let's just watch some TV, have a beer."

It's interesting that this call that Jesus gives us is something that we have the potential to want freely and to be able to go after freely—if we surrender to this mysterious thing we call *grace.* Let's look at grace, because grace is always connected to a call. So when we're *called* to do something, then the grace is given to do it. So let's imagine that grace is not just a power that's given to you to use any way you want, but it's rather a force that's given to you to help get past the resistance that we often have to things, to enter into a place where we feel this *oneness of mind and will and heart*—whatever it is we're called to do. And it's *natural* to do it. It's something that we *want* to do.

Let's look at the first reading. It's about a call, it's about Elijah, who wants to retire. (I think I can identify with that [chuckles], since I've done it recently.) He wants to retire from his work, and he needs someone to take over after him. And God says, "Elisha is the one." So he goes to Elisha, and he asks him to do it, and that symbol of "Let me go and say good-bye to my parents" is something that has to do with that resistance I'm talking about. I mean, literally, there's nothing wrong and it seems right and just that you should go and say good-bye to your parents. So don't take this as literally as it might sound, but realize that what Elijah is saying to Elisha is, "You need to do this right now. This is not about procrastinating or putting it off. I want you to do it right now."

And the symbol of what's happening to Elisha is interesting. Everything in the story is a little exaggerated. I can't imagine a plow with twelve oxen. I mean, that's one big plow! Twelve oxen pulling this plow that he's guiding into the earth. But the thing that's interesting is that this job is helpful. It's a *good* thing for the soil, and planting, and all that stuff. But symbolically, it's interesting that the story goes on to say that what Elisha does is slaughter the twelve oxen, takes the plow and burns it to boil all the meat, and then he gives it to his friends. Well, literally that would have to be one big plow, to make enough heat to boil flesh from twelve oxen! So again, it's not so literal as much as it's saying, "I want you to take whatever you're doing and make sure that it's transformed into food for people." That's God's will, that every plan that he would give you or me is somehow a plan that somehow leads to being something that feeds other people. That's to me the mind of God. He's calling us into this world, into a process where we are sources of life for each other. So that's the thing we want to be as freely responsive to as possible. And that's one of the images we have of redemption and grace. It gets us past the inertia.

Now when Jesus is on his way to Jerusalem, and we know that that's the image of the second part of his ministry. The first was the "Galilean ministry" and the second is when he goes to Jerusalem in that particular gospel. And on his way to Jerusalem, the Samaritans, the dreaded Samaritans [chuckles], were not very sympathetic with the Jews, and they particularly didn't like them using their territory to get to Jerusalem, and so the resistance to hospitality is what starts this particular passage. It's a resistance to welcoming Christ. When Jesus then has someone ask him, "I want to follow you. I want to go where you're going," Jesus seems to focus very clearly on, "There's going to be some resistance to following me because of one very simple thing. I don't exactly have a place I'm going that's very clear." What he's saying is that this journey of ours is not something that can take us into nice, neat places that are predictable and comfortable. It's about being radically open to whatever is coming. So that's why he's saying, "I don't have a place to lay my head; I'm on a journey and the journey is continuing, and the *journey* is what I'm involved in, not getting to a particular place." And that's a beautiful image of the call to be "in service" to the world; and to be food for the world, to say, "I'm open and ready to go and be involved in whatever it is that is needed at this moment." So it's a kind of *freedom* to be wherever and whatever the circumstances demand of us. I think that's *one* of the things that Jesus is teaching in this gospel passage. It's not as fixed and predictable and easy to grasp as one might think.

And then again, we have the next two images of people who want to take care of something else when they decide that they *are* going to follow Jesus, and the first one is a very interesting phrase that Jesus uses when the person says, "I need to go and take care of burying my father." Well, we don't know whether the father has just died, but he's saying, "I need to hang around until my father dies, and then I'll be able to come with you when Dad dies." Well, if that's the case, then it's interesting, because Jesus' response is kind of scary. "Well, let the 'dead' bury the dead." And what I think he's saying is, if you don't respond, if you can't respond to me now, in my call, there's a lack of spiritual life. There's a lack of grace-life in that person. So he's saying, people who hang back, who are always waiting to take care of something before they really do this work that God calls them to, are spiritually dead. So he's saying, "If you hang back, the spiritually dead can bury the dead. I want you to come now with me." So it's a symbol of readiness to enter into whatever plan that God has for us. And to hold back is a kind of death to the process.

The last one's interesting. It's about single-mindedness. If you know anything about plowing, the way they used to plow, the plow was something the person had to guide with their hands. Then the oxen produced the *force* of the plow into the ground, but it was up to the person who was doing the plowing to make sure that the rows were straight, with the first row the most important. So if you turned around and looked back while you were doing that, chances are you wouldn't have a straight line, because you have to have your eye fixed on one point ahead of you so that you could make this straight line. It's so interesting that Jesus knew all these things about the agrarian culture he grew up in, and he uses all those examples. We wouldn't use those examples so much today in Dallas, Texas, but maybe if I was in a farming community I might. Anyway, the issue is, Keep your mind focused on what you're called to do, and that's part of the genius of what God is calling us into.

And then we look at the *second* reading, and it's about *the flesh,* and its resistance to this work of following God and doing this work, and I want to make a really important point here. When you hear the word "flesh," the first thing I always thought of was sexual sins, you know. "Sins of the flesh" are the sins of sex. But that's *not* what this is. This word "flesh," in Paul's Greek, is *sarx,* which means just human nature without Spirit. It's the willful side of us. All about our mind, all about our will. There's no openness to mystery or to God or divinity. That's "living in the flesh." And it's opposed to "living in the Spirit," for obvious reasons. One is, *you* make the decisions, *you* make the judgments, *you* get things done, *you* look at yourself and you thank yourself for whatever you did, and you know that that was what you had to do. Often, that kind of person is driven by "the law"; it's the law of their own desires, the law of what they feel they have to do; their working *for* that. They're kind of a slave to that, because if you're *not* working in the Spirit, you have to produce a lot of stuff, you know? You have to figure things out, you have to plan, you have to work at it. It's very clearly cause-and-effect, but you know, when you're working in the Spirit, cause and effect is there but not quite as rigid. Things can happen with one little tiny thing that doesn't seem to be able to cause much, and it can have an *enormous* effect on someone, if it's done "in the Spirit," if it's done *with* the Spirit.

So there's a very important challenge, then, if we're going to be followers of the Christ and we want to do this work of bringing life into the world. We have to realize that the world of "the flesh" is dangerous. Procrastination is one thing, because we put it off. But again, if you heard me earlier, it's like saying that procrastination is often going on because we're afraid to feel like we're going to be slaves of doing this thing. If somebody tells you, "I want you to be in service to other people," you go, "Oh, man! The rest of my life I've gotta serve people. I'm like a slave." It's *not* that kind of service. It's not slavery. It's a joyous experience of participating in something that not only brings life to the other people, but it gives *you* abundant life and *enormous* satisfaction. And that's life in the Spirit. That's what we're made for. That's what human nature is built for.

And when you look at the gospel and when you look at what it's calling us to, it's not calling us to some kind of super, supernatural world that is completely devoid of the human. It's this mysterious integration of divinity and humanity that works inside of a human being, so that I would say a truly spiritual person seems to be the most natural and the most human, as well as the most capable of bringing life and goodness to someone. We have a strange image sometimes of spirituality where it ends up sounding like truly spiritual people have given up having anything to do with the *physical* world.

Maybe that's what the danger of the reading from Paul is, this whole idea that spirit is *opposed* to the flesh, flesh is opposed to the spirit. That's like saying, "Well, that means my humanity is opposed to my spirituality and the divinity in me." And the two are absolutely *perfect* partners. But "the flesh," as it's used in this reading, is not our humanity. It's our stubborn, willful, fixed, autonomous, separate kind of disposition that we often have toward this thing we call life. So if religion is a set of rules and laws that you have to follow, then what Paul says is, "Be careful. Don't become a slave! Don't be a slave to these things that God is calling you to, but instead of being a slave, I want you to be some kind of wonderful, wonderful partner in a relationship with God that is very, very, very exciting!"

So in summary, the work of this particular set of readings is to open us to two things: Open us to the call that God is calling us into places where we need to be food for other people. And second, that that call is something that needs to be responded to—not later [chuckles], not next week, next month—not "take care of everything else first and then I'll get to that." But what he's looking for is hearts that are eager and excited to surrender to a plan that is *for us* as well as it's for the world. It's for us *and* for the world. And then when you realize that that is something you want to give yourself over to, then you need to realize that this *process* of giving yourself to it is something that can be done in full freedom and full communion and connection with Spirit so that there's a really natural way in which Christianity calls us to live out our years on this planet with a kind of joyous, wonderful sense of being engaged in something that is playful—not heavy, burdened work, but playful, life-giving and really very, very exciting. It's a beautiful way to spend your life in terms of service, and that's the major message of God, who became one of us, and served us in the most extraordinary ways.

Father, unite our wills, our hearts, and our minds so that truly we can respond most generously to your gifts that call us into service to our brothers and sisters. Help us to taste and experience the joy that you experienced in bringing life and fullness to those that you loved; and we ask this in Jesus' name. Amen.

1 Kings 19: 16, 19-21

The LORD said to Elijah: 16You shall also anoint Jehu, son of Nimshi, as king of Israel, and Elisha, son of Shaphat of Abel-meholah, as prophet to succeed you.

19Elijah set out, and came upon Elisha, son of Shaphat, as he was plowing with twelve
yoke of oxen; he was following the twelfth. Elijah went over to him and threw his cloak
on him.20Elisha left the oxen, ran after Elijah, and said, "Please, let me kiss my father
and mother good-bye, and I will follow you." Elijah answered, "Go back! What have I

done to you?”[21]Elisha left him and, taking the yoke of oxen, slaughtered them; he used
the plowing equipment for fuel to boil their flesh, and gave it to the people to eat. Then
he left and followed Elijah to serve him.

Galatians 5: 1, 13-18

[1]Brothers and sisters: For freedom Christ set us free; so stand firm and do not submit
again to the yoke of slavery.

[13]For you were called for freedom, brothers. But do not use this freedom as an opportunity for the flesh; rather, serve one another through love.[14]For the whole law is fulfilled in one statement, namely, “You shall love your neighbor as yourself.”[15]But if you
go on biting and devouring one another, beware that you are not consumed by one another.
[16]I say, then: live by the Spirit and you will certainly not gratify the desire of the
flesh.[17]For the flesh has desires against the Spirit, and the Spirit against the flesh; these
are opposed to each other, so that you may not do what you want.[18]But if you are guided by the Spirit, you are not under the law.

Luke 9: 51-62

[51]When the days for his being taken up were fulfilled, he resolutely determined to journey to Jerusalem,[52]and he sent messengers ahead of him. On the way they entered a Samaritan village to prepare for his reception there,[53]but they would not welcome him because the destination of his journey was Jerusalem.[54]When the disciples James and John
saw this they asked, “Lord, do you want us to call down fire from heaven to consume
them?”[55]Jesus turned and rebuked them,[56]and they journeyed to another village.
[57]As they were proceeding on their journey someone said to him, “I will follow you
wherever you go.”[58]Jesus answered him, “Foxes have dens and birds of the sky have
nests, but the Son of Man has nowhere to rest his head.”[59]And to another he said, “Follow me.” But he replied, “[Lord,] let me go first and bury my father.”[60]But he answered
him, “Let the dead bury their dead. But you, go and proclaim the kingdom of
God.”[61]And another said, “I will follow you, Lord, but first let me say farewell to my
family at home.”[62][To him] Jesus said, “No one who sets a hand to the plow and looks
to what was left behind is fit for the kingdom of God.”

FOURTEENTH SUNDAY IN ORDINARY TIME

Isaiah 66:10-14; Galatians 6:14-18; Luke 10:1-12, 17-20

Father, through the obedience of Jesus, your servant and your Son, you raised a fallen world. Free us from sin, bring us the joy that lasts forever, and we ask this through our Lord Jesus Christ, your Son, who lives and reigns with you in the unity of the holy Spirit, one God for ever and ever. Amen.

The problem that God has with revealing himself to us is that he had to work with us at different stages of our development. Who we are today is not who we were 2,000 or 3,000 years ago. I believe that most people have a problem with God because of the way he is revealed in the Old Testament. He seems to be a God who is enormously close and comforting and also seems to be a God who is distant and dangerous. Anyone who has raised children knows that there's a time to hold a child and comfort a child—and there's also a time to tell a child that what they've done is wrong and to punish them. Perhaps we could look back on that kind of relationship God had at the time of the Old Testament with the human race, when it was much like a father or mother with a child. In trying to understand who this God is, we ask, "Is he a loving God or a punishing God?" The absolute key ingredient in moving toward a full understanding of God is not to take any one period of revelation as if that is the total picture, but to wait for the fullness of the revelation of who God is in the person of Jesus.

We have a long, thousands-of-years process of finally understanding who this God really is. The most extraordinary thing about him is his intimacy with us, his desire to be with us, his desire to share his life and his power with us. In that image in the Old Testament reading, we see a mother fondling and caring for her child. This is a beautiful image of the way in which God longs for us to see him as a

God that nurtures, that supports, and that feeds us. Another one of my favorite images in the Old Testament and the New Testament is one of relationship: God wants to *marry* us. One is a kind of feminine figure; one is a kind of masculine figure. In either case, we need to understand in this revelation of God that we have a most comforting message of a God who wants to serve us, to minister to us, to heal us. He wants somehow to make us aware of his deep, abiding presence that is connected to the deep reverence he has for us.

Let's take the first reading and glean from it that there is a wonderful way in which, if we understand this God, something happens to our hearts. They rejoice. So we should be people who are rejoicing in our God. We should not be afraid of him in the sense of hiding from him our weaknesses or fearing he is going to punish us—but somehow being open to the beauty of this God and knowing that our hearts leap for joy when we see him as he truly is.

St. Paul, in the letter to the Galatians, is trying to awaken his people to an understanding of who this God is. Typical of so many of us trying to understand our God and our religion, it's clear that there were problems. One of the two major problems Paul saw was whether or not grace was the key issue, meaning God's gratuitous gift of salvation—or was it the law that saved people? Was it the law or was it simply God's goodness that gets us into heaven? The other was the importance of ritual. How important was circumcision? That was one of the major rituals of the Old Testament. Without circumcision, could people still be saved? What I love about this passage from the end of Galatians is that Paul just looks at the people and says, "It's not really the issue of grace or the law. It's not about the issue of circumcision or what rituals are required. What it's really about is becoming *a new creation*." What is that new creation we are supposed to become? It has something to do with what the first reading is saying when it comes to rejoicing.

The new creation is a human being who is filled with an awareness of the goodness of God to the point that they experience the goodness of God flowing through them. The real rejoicing that comes to the heart of a believer is when they realize that God is acting through them and the action of this God through them is healing, serving, and reverencing everything around them. It's to be in a place where we sense the immediacy of that kind of power flowing through us. That's what it means to be a new creation. That's what Paul was so aware of. Imagine Paul, who was so immersed in the law and all those things that he was required to do. He had to listen to all the controversies going on around him and to see through all of it. He wanted so desperately for people to understand what God was doing in Christ. This incarnate God wanted people to know and understand that his Spirit dwells within them and empowers them. Listen to that phrase at the end of Galatians: "The grace of our Lord Jesus Christ be with your spirit." We're so used to saying, "The Lord be with you." But he says, "The grace of our

Lord Jesus Christ be with your spirit." The new creation has something to do with this Spirit of God mingling with our spirit. That's called the spirit of God's grace, this mysterious power that, when connected to our actions, adds to our actions an amazing power to heal, to serve, and to reverence.

I think you and I both know when we are with a person and their actions are much more than just nice things they do. They are much more than kindness. They seem to have this ability to be nurturing to our very soul. They seem to give us a sense of value, purpose, and meaning beyond the actions themselves. That's what grace is: It's the power of God connected to our human spirit, co-mingling with it in such an intimate way that it's impossible to distinguish which part is God and which part is us. It flows into the world, and it does something extraordinary.

We see this same image in the gospel, where Jesus is calling seventy-two to go out and to proclaim the kingdom. Make sure you understand that this is not the sending out of the disciples to start the church. This is a different kind of image. This is sending out ordinary people, seventy-two—we don't know who they are—and they are being sent out into community. They are being asked to go into the world and to not fix or do anything except to announce *what is being done.* That is so important to understand. That's what it means to be a true believer. We are not called to fix situations we find ourselves in. We work to do that, but the spiritual work is not to imagine that we go into each situation to fix or repair it or make it better ourselves, but somehow to proclaim to whatever is going on that there is a power that is available that can heal and can transform and can even take the most difficult situations and turn them into something mysteriously healing and transforming. That's not a human power; that's *divine* power.

Human power goes into situations and tries to fix everything. We try to make everybody understand something that we think they should. All of that is good and well-intentioned—but so dangerous. I love that image we have in the work of St. Catherine of Siena. She asks Jesus, "Why do you ask us not to judge each other?" And he replied, "I'm not asking you not to judge. I'm just telling you that you can't. You can never fully know the heart of another human being." When I walk into an emotional situation as a priest trying to help a couple work through something or when I am trying to help an individual see something, I am guessing sometimes that if I go in there and say, "I think I see what's wrong," and I push what I sense is the healing work, maybe if I'm lucky I hit it. But what is so much more exciting about ministry is to somehow walk into a situation where there is conflict and to announce to that situation that we possess a power inside of ourselves that can do something to transform it. It's called grace. We bring grace into that situation, and we do it with great determination.

The pairs of disciples go out; they are given a work to do. They are given a kind of focus to get to where they're supposed to go. As they work toward getting to that place of announcing salvation, this great news of grace flowing through us to the situation, if the people who are there in that situation are open to it—they get it. If they don't get it, we just walk away. This is so important. It's such a strange way of imagining helping and healing people. But it implies that unless there is some receptivity to grace, it can't work. If grace can't work, then isn't it better just to move on? Isn't it better just to go on to the next place? The image of "shaking the dust off our feet" is a very negative image in some ways, but what I think Jesus is trying to say is that the whole issue of grace and salvation working in our lives means that if we close ourselves off to it, we haven't got it. It's not a punishment. God is not punishing somebody for not receiving a gift he is offering. He is just trying to make it clear that when you don't receive it, some very negative, destructive things can happen to you.

The challenge is to be open to telling the world, not so much in words, but in the way we respond to situations, that this power is available and it's working—and we believe with all our hearts, minds, and souls that it can transform situations. When we see that, somehow Satan is done. That image of Jesus saying he saw Satan fall like lightning from the sky is a very curious, interesting thing. What Jesus is trying to say is that Satan rules in situations where people refuse to believe that there is anything greater than themselves to help them through a situation. That's what Satan needs, because Satan is stronger than we are. But Satan isn't nearly as strong as God is. So if we want to go up face to face with Satan and every evil inclination inside of us and decide we are going to take care of it ourselves, that's a dangerous place to be.

Here's a God who is saying, "I want to nurture you. I want to marry you. I want to be inside of you. I want to be a part of you. I want to share my life with you. Just believe with all your heart, mind, and soul that I am giving you this power, this grace—to mingle and mix with your human desires and spirit that is good and loving—and something extraordinary then happens."

This co-mingling of grace with our human spirit is a very tricky thing and a very important thing to be in touch with. But one of the things we need to understand is that grace is awakening this spiritual center inside of us, our heart. The heart is an interesting organ. It's a physical organ, but also in our tradition, it's a *spiritual* organ. It's where we always believe that this grace of God dwells in a unique, special way. We see images of the Sacred Heart or the Immaculate Heart of Mary. The heart is such an interesting image to work with. What I would like you to believe in and trust with me is that there is this wonderful way in which grace, God's Spirit, dwells within our hearts, and somehow out of that comes this powerful force that is a kind of glow. It's a kind of light. It's a kind of thing that affirms, supports, and awakens insight into other people. It's a marvelous thing to be able to be in touch with that, without feeling that *we* are doing the work.

The work we do is belief, openness, trust, allowing this partner to enter into our hearts—allowing our hearts to be awakened as spiritual organs to be able to bring life into the world. That is work. That takes a lot of selflessness, faith, and trust. But when it happens, there is an amazing, amazing transformation.

The theme throughout this Liturgy of the Word is the idea of *rejoicing*. If we follow the passage into the next chapter of the gospel, we see the image of Jesus rejoicing with the seventy-two over what's happening. It's the only time in Scripture we have Jesus rejoicing. That doesn't mean he wasn't happy. But what is the greatest joy that the incarnate God would feel in this world as he looks at the world he is trying to minister to? It would be that they have received his ministry and they are continuing it.

In the same way, Jesus was so aware of his human nature being filled with divinity, he sees in the seventy-two that they are doing the same thing. They finally got it. Divinity dwelling in humanity. Their human heart, with all of its deep desires to heal and to strengthen other people, receives grace that enables them to be a real source of service, of healing, a real source of reverence and love and connection for other human beings and to other situations, to the world God has created. It's a beautiful image of what this ministry of Christ is all about, and yet it can be so buried in so many other things that are moralistic and legalistic and bound into all those same things that Paul struggled with. Let's end this reflection on these readings with that one, wonderful invitation on the part of Paul: Let us move not into something that is binding us, but into something that is freeing us—into the new creation.

Father, we ask you to awaken in our hearts the joy that is our destiny as we experience the beauty of your grace flowing through us, helping us to be all that you have called us to be. We ask this in Jesus' name. Amen.

Isaiah 66: 10-14

10Rejoice with Jerusalem and be glad because of her,
all you who love her;
Rejoice with her in her joy,
all you who mourn over her—
11So that you may nurse and be satisfied
from her consoling breast;
That you may drink with delight
at her abundant breasts!
12For thus says the LORD:
I will spread prosperity over her like a river,

like an overflowing torrent,
the wealth of nations.
You shall nurse, carried in her arms,
cradled upon her knees;
[13]As a mother comforts her child,
so I will comfort you;
in Jerusalem you shall find your comfort.
[14]You will see and your heart shall exult,
and your bodies shall flourish like the grass;
The LORD's power shall be revealed to his servants,
. . .

Galatians 6: 14-18

[14]But may I never boast except in the cross of our Lord Jesus Christ, through which the
world has been crucified to me, and I to the world.[15]For neither does circumcision mean
anything, nor does uncircumcision, but only a new creation.[16]Peace and mercy be to all
who follow this rule and to the Israel of God.
[17]From now on, let no one make troubles for me; for I bear the marks of Jesus on my
body.
[18]The grace of our Lord Jesus Christ be with your spirit, brothers and sisters. Amen.

Luke 10: 1-12, 17-20

[1]After this the Lord appointed seventy [-two] others whom he sent ahead of him in pairs
to every town and place he intended to visit.[2]He said to them, "The harvest is abundant
but the laborers are few; so ask the master of the harvest to send out laborers for his
harvest.[3]Go on your way; behold, I am sending you like lambs among wolves.[4]Carry no
money bag, no sack, no sandals; and greet no one along the way.[5]Into whatever house
you enter, first say, 'Peace to this household.'[6]If a peaceful person lives there, your
peace will rest on him; but if not, it will return to you.[7]Stay in the same house and eat
and drink what is offered to you, for the laborer deserves his payment. Do not move
about from one house to another.[8]Whatever town you enter and they welcome you, eat
what is set before you,[9]cure the sick in it and say to them, 'The kingdom of God is at
hand for you.'[10]Whatever town you enter and they do not receive you, go out into the
streets and say,[11]'The dust of your town that clings to our feet, even that we shake off
against you.' Yet know this: the kingdom of God is at hand.[12]I tell you, it will be more
tolerable for Sodom on that day than for that town.

[17]The seventy [-two] returned rejoicing, and said, "Lord, even the demons are subject to us because of your name."[18]Jesus said, "I have observed Satan fall like lightning from the sky.[19]Behold, I have given you the power 'to tread upon serpents' and scorpions and upon the full force of the enemy and nothing will harm you.[20]Nevertheless, do not rejoice because the spirits are subject to you, but rejoice because your names are written in heaven."

FIFTEENTH SUNDAY IN ORDINARY TIME

Deuteronomy 30:10-14; Colossians 1:15-20; Luke 10:25-37

God our Father, your light of truth guides us to the way of Christ. May all who follow him reject what is contrary to the Gospel. We ask this through our Lord Jesus Christ, your Son, who lives and reigns with you in the unity of the holy Spirit, one God forever and ever. Amen.

Probably one of the most common questions a priest receives and one I have certainly received over and over again goes like this: *Tell me what I am supposed to do. Tell me what the law requires. Tell me what the church says I must do.* Not a bad question—an important question. But one of the things I think that is so interesting about our relationship with the law and the rules of the church is that these guidelines give us direction—but in some way, we are supposed to outgrow our need for the law. St. Paul says we no longer need the law, because there is something given to us in place of it.

We need to believe and trust in this wonderful insight. It's awareness, understanding, a kind of attention we develop that enables us to perceive in every situation what basically we are called to do. It's not so much a case of going outside ourselves to ask: *What are we supposed to do? What am I to do? Someone tell me what to do.* Rather, it's looking inside and saying, *I need to discern in this situation what I am called to do.*

The image of discernment is highlighted in today's set of readings. I want to see if I can draw from these scriptures some understanding of what they contain in terms of a teaching. Let's go to the first reading, from Deuteronomy, a powerful reading from the Old Testament. What it basically says about the law is that there is something we should always recognize. It's something we already know. We're called to follow the Commandments, which gives us wisdom. That's the way the church began. In the Old Testament, there's a strong emphasis on God giving his wisdom to his people by telling them how they should act—the law. That's a great gift, a way of making sure people are thinking in a way that is close to their nature. The interesting thing about the law is that it's something already known. The law God asks us to follow is not something difficult to grasp. It is not something we have to search or work for.

We don't have to go somewhere to find the law. It's already inside of us. What an interesting image to use—that the law is already "in your mouth" and "in your heart." What does that mean, the law is already in our mouths? It means we don't necessarily have to be told by some outside force or source what to do. We already know, and we can articulate what we know we are supposed to do.

The fact that it's "in the heart" signifies that the heart is the spiritual organ inside us that helps us to feel and be in touch, to connect with others. It's the place of our soul. We know that the soul's basic work is connection. When there's connection, and attention to what is needed, then it seems to me we don't need an outside source to tell us what to do. We are attentive to what is going on. We have a sense of what is needed. The law is somehow in our hearts already.

The direction the law tries to put us in as it guides our actions is something that takes its place eventually: If we understand fully the mystery of who we are, we recognize that we have to look deep inside for our own inner discernment. Why is that important? The law is always going to be for the general situation. It cannot fit every conceivable situation. So to say that we are always going to be able to follow the law in every situation is to miss the point that I think the Scriptures always try to put before us. The law is an important guideline, but it cannot take care of every situation. The only thing that can take care of every situation is a loving, attentive heart that longs to do what its destiny is calling it to do. It longs to give life. That's what we are here for—to give life.

In the second reading, St. Paul says that what we have in this figure Christ is an incredibly important model, someone we look at and see the fullness of everything. *In him, all fullness was pleased to dwell.* He says something else: *In him, everything holds together.* What I think he points to is that there is a way for us to know that when we are looking at the figure Christ we are looking at the best clue we have as to who God is and who we are. The most beautiful thing about this figure Christ is his ability to invite our imaginations into a place where we see an incredibly beautiful connection between humanity and divinity.

Humanity and divinity are made for each other. Sometimes we think humanity is the antithesis of divinity. We see our humanity as something broken, evil, and corrupt. God is good and perfect, and so the two can't get together. But that's not the way it has been planned by God. Yes, a human being can fill themselves with so many attitudes and dispositions that are the antithesis of who God is and create distance. But that's not the nature of what it means to be human. The nature of what it means to be human is found in Christ's fullness, and what Paul tries to say is that we have the power to participate in the indwelling power of Spirit so that we have the capacity to be in the world just as Christ was. How many times did Jesus say to his disciples: *I am giving you an example of who you are. I want you to understand that you can do the same exact thing I am doing. I am empowering you to go out and do my ministry. I am sending you forth.*

Last week Jesus sent out the seventy-two. During daily Mass this week, we had mention of Jesus sending out his disciples. In both cases, he tells them the same thing: *I want you to go into a town and heal the sick, raise the dead, cure the lepers, and expel demons.* That's amazing! He doesn't go in and say, *I want you to establish a church by giving them the rules and the laws.* He doesn't say, *I want you to set up ministries and teams of ministers. I want everybody to go to classes and learn what the rules and laws are.* He just says, *I want you to go into these places and be a source of life. Cure the sick.* In every situation, there is always something dysfunctional. We are caught up in some aspect of seeing things that is not clear. There is *dis*-ease, discomfort. We have the power to go into a situation, and through our presence, cure that sickness.

To "raise the dead" is a little dramatic. It would be an extraordinary thing to be able to go into morgues and bring people back, but what I think Jesus is really talking about here is not so much that action. "Death" is so often an image in Scripture of being in a place where we are not fully alive, fully alert, or fully attentive. What he's saying about raising the dead is really lifting people out of their unconscious state and making them more aware, making them more conscious.

"Healing the leper" is Jesus saying that leprosy is the image of sin that disfigures us. Leprosy as a disease disfigures people; it takes away all of their features. The image of leprosy being like sin makes sense because when we sin, we are not being who we really are. I don't know if you have ever had the experience of someone coming along and doing something you never expected and your reaction is: *I don't know you anymore. I don't know who you are.*

The last example speaks of expelling demons. I would like you to think of demons as all those voices, all those influences, all those things in our culture that are grabbing at us and trying to get us to think in ways that just don't really make any sense. Demons try to get us to buy into things that we think will make us happy when they have no real capacity to do that. We have the capacity to walk into a situation, anywhere that we are, and we have been given the power to raise the dead, to heal, and to expel demons because we have the mysterious quality of divinity living inside us. God is with us. He's not leaving us to deal with things on our own.

A man comes up to Jesus in the gospel reading, and he wants to make a point. He's a lawyer. One translation says: *He is a great observer of the law.* Here we are with Jesus, and he is being asked, *Where does the law fit in this new place called the king-*

dom that you came to establish? I love when Jesus does this. People ask questions, and he realizes that the question they are asking is not really the issue. He always refines the question. The lawyer asks Jesus, *What do I have to do to gain everlasting life?* The wisdom at the time was that people had to do what the law required. The man says, *I know that the heart of the law is to love God with all your heart, mind, and soul and to love your neighbor.* He knew that was the heart of the law, and he was saying, *I am willing to follow the law.* Jesus says, *Great. That's a good way to do this.* Then the man goes on and says, *By the way, who is my neighbor?* We have to understand that in the culture these people lived in there was a very clear distinction between those you should care for and those you didn't need to care for—and even *shouldn't* care for. When anyone was a sinner or an outcast, you were not responsible for them and, more than that, you weren't supposed to do anything for them. You were supposed to simply cut them out.

Jesus takes this opportunity to undo that conventional way of seeing. He goes on to describe who the neighbor is. He does something else as well. He tells a story about the Good Samaritan. He is not so much describing who a neighbor is, who we are supposed to be responsible for—but what a neighbor *does*. It's not so much the object Jesus is focused on but the subject: *Who are you? What does the law empower you to be? When you say that you love God with all your heart, mind, and soul, what is it that you are being asked to become?* When we love someone, we become like them. It's the most natural thing in the world. One of the things I think we see is the invitation on the part of Jesus to get the lawyer, who was very legalistic in his way of thinking, to begin to shift and recognize that there is something very important to see when it comes to the power to minister to each other, how we are to be *neighbor*. I think the subtext of this is: *Be careful, because the law can only go so far and when it no longer functions in a positive way, it backfires and functions in a negative way.*

The two people, the Levite and the priest, will not go near a man injured by the side of the road, beaten and left half-dead. They won't go there for one reason: the law. The law kept them from entering into a place where someone was dying because it would make them impure to go to the temple. Here is a story where two good, law-abiding people, who are assumed to be doing exactly what God wants by following the law, don't do what God wants. They aren't neighbors. They are *limited* by the law.

The law has its limitations, but this Spirit of Christ inside us, this awakening of our hearts to the needs of those around us—has no limitations. The heart can enter into every situation. It is flexible; it is able to adjust however it needs to so that it can be with the source of raising the dead, healing the sick, curing the leper, expelling the demon. That's what the law can't control. It can't control a person's behavior in a way that enables them to reach every situation where they are needed. What Jesus is doing is genius. He's trying to get people to realize that we have to be careful when we are dealing with the law. The law is the heart of a way of life, and that heart is always somehow about loving—loving God with our hearts, minds, and souls and loving our neighbor. If love is the essence of the law, can the law be wise enough, flexible enough, particular enough to take care of every situation in which a person needs to be loved? The answer is no, it can't. What takes its place? That which is in our mouth already; that which is in our hearts already: the awakening of the soul to the promise of being in God's kingdom. That—and only that—can take care of the needs around us. It's liberating to listen to this wonderful message of Jesus and the Good Samaritan. It's also interesting that the one who ends up being everything he is supposed to be is one who is *outside* the law. That's another thing we can't miss in the story. The Good Samaritan, being outside the Jewish religion, was not required by the law to do *anything*. But without the law, he had everything he needed to do what he was called to do. People with "too much law" weren't able to reach the man on the side of the road who was half-dead. It's up to us to make this very important distinction in our working with the needs around us so that we are able to make sure we are not bound by the law but that we have it as the base. Our spirit, soul, and our love can take care of each and every particular situation.

Heavenly Father, we ask you to continue to awaken in us the presence of your Spirit that enables us truly to reach out and to do the work that you call us to do, the work that we long to do within our hearts for those that we love, for those who are in need around us. We ask this in Jesus' name. Amen.

Deuteronomy 30:10-14
10[Moses said to the people] . . .when you obey the LORD your God by observing his
commandments and decrees that are written in this book of the law, because you turn
to the LORD your God with all your heart and with all your soul.
11Surely, this commandment that I am commanding you today is not too hard for you,
nor is it too far away.
12It is not in heaven, that you should say, "Who will go up to heaven for us, and get it
for us so that we may hear it and observe it?"
13Neither is it beyond the sea, that you should say, "Who will cross to the other side of
the sea for us, and get it for us so that we may hear it and observe it?"
14No, the word is very near to you; it is in your mouth and in your heart for you to observe.

Colossians 1:15-20
15[Christ Jesus] is the image of the invisible God, the firstborn of all creation;
16for in him all things in heaven and on earth were created, things visible and invisible,
whether thrones or dominions or rulers or powers—all things have been created
through him and for him.
17He himself is before all things, and in him all things hold together.
18He is the head of the body, the church; he is the beginning, the firstborn from the
dead, so that he might come to have first place in everything.
19For in him all the fullness of God was pleased to dwell,
20and through him God was pleased to reconcile to himself all things, whether on earth
or in heaven, by making peace through the blood of his cross.

Luke 10:25-37
25Just then a lawyer stood up to test Jesus. "Teacher," he said, "what must I do to inherit
eternal life?"
26He said to him, "What is written in the law? What do you read there?"
27He answered, "You shall love the Lord your God with all your heart, and with all your
soul, and with all your strength, and with all your mind; and your neighbor as yourself."
28And he said to him, "You have given the right answer; do this, and you will live."
29But wanting to justify himself, he asked Jesus, "And who is my neighbor?"
30Jesus replied, "A man was going down from Jerusalem to Jericho, and fell into the
hands of robbers, who stripped him, beat him, and went away, leaving him half dead.
31Now by chance a priest was going down that road; and when he saw him, he passed
by on the other side.
32So likewise a Levite, when he came to the place and saw him, passed by on the other
side.
33But a Samaritan while traveling came near him; and when he saw him, he was moved
with pity.
34He went to him and bandaged his wounds, having poured oil and wine on them. Then
he put him on his own animal, brought him to an inn, and took care of him.
35The next day he took out two denarii, gave them to the innkeeper, and said, 'Take care
of him; and when I come back, I will repay you whatever more you spend.'
36Which of these three, do you think, was a neighbor to the man who fell into the hands
of the robbers?"
37He said, "The one who showed him mercy." Jesus said to him, "Go and do likewise."

SIXTEENTH SUNDAY IN ORDINARY TIME

Genesis 18:1-10; Colossians 1:24-28; Luke 10:38-42

Father, let the gift of your life continue to grow in us, drawing us from death to faith, hope, and love. Keep us alive in Christ Jesus; keep us watchful in prayer and true to his teachings until your glory is revealed in us. We ask this through Christ our Lord. Amen.

In all religious traditions, there's always a theme that goes something like this: There's a power greater than ourselves, and this power's glory, this power's beauty, in a sense, is its desire to connect with us, to be a companion-presence with us. I'd like to begin the thoughts for this homily with an image. We do have in our tradition a very, very strong sense that our task in this life is twofold: It's about receiving something and about giving something. The receiving we are called to be engaged in is somehow about opening our hearts and minds to this companion-presence, this gift of God inside us, this mysterious place in which we are called to live where we are in constant contact with a source of energy, life, and power. As the opening prayer said, "that this indwelling presence leads us away from death into life, hope, and love." Today's gospel, a very well-known and comforting one, is all about the task we have of being in a disposition where we can truly be open to this beautiful companion-presence of Spirit, of God, of Christ living within us.

We could say that the work of being open to God is about hospitality. It's about welcoming. The first story, a wonderful one from the Old Testament book of Genesis, is about Abraham encountering God. Abraham has an experience of God's presence. God's presence seems to move into this image of three men walking along the road. As Abraham notices them, there's an interesting Trinitarian image of the three, who turn out to be angels. Abraham is not aware of them being anything other than mortals. He sees them, and I love the image of great hospitality that follows. Abraham says, "Please, would you do me a favor? Would you let me serve you? Would you let me invite you into my house where I will wash your feet and prepare something for you? Let me just take care of you for an hour or two so that you can rest, and I can feed you a wonderful meal. Just let me take care of you for a while. It would be a great privilege and a great joy for me to do this."

Abraham is obviously a man of great hospitality. Remember that he is our father in faith. There is something about Abraham and his qualities that every man or woman needs to have in order to be men and women of faith. He is wide open to strangers. He doesn't know these people. It turns out they are very special guests; they are messengers from God. That's what an angel is. Abraham puts himself in a disposition where he is wide open to receive whatever God longs to send to him. Lo and behold, one of the angels has a very special message: "Your wife Sarah is going to have a baby." When Abraham heard this in an earlier story, he laughed. When Sarah hears this in the story today, she laughs because the tradition is that she was well past the age of being able to conceive a child. She was considered to be in her late 80s or 90s. Imagine telling an 80 or 90-year-old she is going to have a baby, even though Abraham and Sarah had longed for a child throughout their lives.

Sarah does conceive a child, and we sense that the story is about Abraham, a man of faith, being radically open to receive whatever is sent to him by God. When he receives what God sends, it produces new life. It's a pretty clear image that we are called to be people open to receive whatever God longs to send to us—with the conviction that as we open ourselves to whatever he teaches or wants to show us, whatever he wants this companion-presence to effect within us—we are ready for it. We are open for it, even though it may happen in ways that do not make logical sense and are not even possible in the physical world. I love the image in the story of receiving something that could not be conceived out of a logical pattern of thinking. That's being wide open. I don't know that I have been that wide open when it comes to being able to receive the things God wants to send to me. That may be true for you also.

The second reading, from Paul's letter to the Colossians, talks about the mystery of God's full revelation in Jesus. One of the things Paul is so excited about, which we find in the other two readings as well, is simply the image that this God of ours has come to all people—even to the Gentiles, to those who "don't deserve it." He's come to dwell within them and he is "the awesome revelation of God with us," this companion-presence inside of us. Its glory—meaning its purpose for being there and what it came to accomplish—is the ability for us to continue the same work Christ was doing. This is an interesting reading because at first it might seem to imply that what Christ did wasn't enough to save the world—and Paul had to step in and finish the work. That's not what he is saying. That doesn't fit any theology we would support. It's not that Paul is trying to make up for what Jesus wasn't able to do. Jesus did everything he needed to do. He saved the world through his act of self-sacrificing love. The point is that if we are going to follow this Christ, if we are going to be his companion in the world, then we are going to continue a similar work. We are not going to make up for it in the sense of doing what Christ didn't do, but we embody this work of his redemption—we give it flesh and bone, we give it action in the world. When we are called and moved to be a source of life for someone else, that's a reflection of the action of Christ being a source of life for the world. We continue the work; we're not making up for it. We are expected to participate in its unfolding. It's as if Christ saves the world but he then needs instruments, his presence within us, to help accomplish the task of moving people into the place of life and truth and out of the places of death and destruction.

In the gospel passage, we find the story of Mary sitting at the feet of Jesus. Martha is very concerned about hospitality. In Luke's gospel, we have to understand that he always gives two examples for whatever he is trying to teach. Usually one example involves a male figure and the other example involves a female figure. Last week, we had the image of what it means to be a follower of Christ, with the lawyer coming up and asking Jesus, "What must I do to be saved?" The story is about doing what the law requires—but going beyond the law and basically doing what *mercy* requires. It's a story about action.

This companion-presence inside of us allows us to be compassionate and to go out and do things for other people. But there's another aspect of the spiritual life we are called to live—and it really has little to do with going out and doing anything. It has to do with resting. It has to do with stopping, emptying ourselves, so that we can receive something. Both are essential. A life of constant action, constant "doing" for other people, might seem like the ideal. But it's not. It has to be balanced with some kind of quiet emptying of all the things that preoccupy us and being able to sit with and be with this "companion-presence" that allows it to speak to us. One of the difficult things about this is that the language of the Spirit, of this companion-presence, is always silence. There may be images that come to us, there may be words we sometimes hear, but most of the time what we are dealing with when we are in this disposition of silence and quiet receptivity and hospitality to this companion-presence, is that we are sitting simply in this wonderful place called *silence*. It's not a kind of emptiness; it's a kind of fullness. It's a place that is so effective when we are there that once we *are* there and recognize its power to help us to be in dispositions that are truly life-giving, it's almost addictive. We *have* to be there.

That's what I think Jesus is trying to say to us in this beautiful little story. When Martha is anxious and worried about so many things, Jesus says, "It's wonderful that you are being hospitable, but there's a lot of worry, anxiety, and tension inside of you. That's a sign that you probably are not in touch with this wonderful companion-presence. It's a sign that you are mostly working out of your sense of responsibility to take care of things." It's a wonderful thing to be responsible to other people and situations. But it's deadly if that's only in a kind of "locked-on" position, and all we think about each day is taking care of the needs. I don't know if you get caught up in this, but sometimes I get caught up in "production-mode," wondering if I have enough time to get everything done. A good day is when I put in 26 hours of work in a 24-hour day and everything gets done. Then I can sit back and say, "I was very responsible."

That kind of frantic activity is important, but there is something more important. There's a better place. That's not to say the other goes away completely. But there's a companion piece to the activity we are called to live in, this acting responsibly and with mercy to take care of the needs of others. It's a companion piece about being still and clearing ourselves of all kinds of preoccupations in terms of getting things done—and simply being able to sit in the presence of this God of ours who longs to reveal to us not only who we are and what we are called to do—but he longs to reveal to us the *way* in which we are called to live.

I think it would be very naïve and dangerous to think that we are responsible for every single need we come in contact with. In a parish the size of the one I was serving, it's impossible to even begin to take care of every single need that's out there. And yet, I think there are times when I get so caught up in "wanting to be successful" in the way we think of success of getting everything done, that the frustration of not being able to get to everything robs me of any kind of real sense of value or peace. It's so destructive.

This is so much more than talking about spending 20 minutes in silent meditation. It's about being somehow in a disposition throughout the day where there is a kind of stillness available in our psyche where we can be *receiving*. I think about the way God speaks to us and his presence in us. It's one thing to imagine that we are sitting alone and God is present in us. He speaks to us. That's true. But if we also believe that God's presence is in everything, if God's presence is in creation and individuals, then there's a way in which we need to have a certain amount of stillness while still being present to what is going on around us.

We can then receive what's being offered. There's a beauty in the world, in individuals, and in situations that are loaded with presence. The world is then loaded with this gift of life. If we are so focused on taking care of things, so focused on doing things, then we miss it. When we miss it, we are running on empty. We have the awful experience of saying, "All I see is the work before me. There's never enough time to do it all." Oftentimes I don't have the energy to do it, and that leads to shutting down, going numb, doing just a few things and trying not to feel bad about the things I can't reach.

This presence of God is something necessary not only to give us the energy we need to do the work, but it is also what keeps us balanced, rooted in a reality God has called us to live in.

It's a reality that struck me this week. We have the wonderful gospel where Jesus says, "My burden is really light. My yoke is easy." When I look around, I see that some people's lives are extraordinarily difficult. They are dealing with all kinds of things. Does that mean those people didn't get what God promised? No, I think in everything, in every situation we are in, if we sense this companion-presence within us and if we are there to listen to what every situation—as bad as it may be—has to tell us, there is a gift for us in some mysterious way. We can recognize that it's not too much of a burden. It's not too difficult. It promises us something good. The prayer of this liturgy is for all of us to be open to this great gift of God's presence so that we can feel the nurturing support of a God who is love.

Father, open our hearts and our minds to a greater awareness, attentiveness to this beautiful gift of your companion-presence in our lives. Help us never to lose sight of this gift of wisdom, this source of power, to enable us to live the life you have called us to. Give us peace in all that we do. We ask this in Jesus' name. Amen.

Genesis 18: 1-10

1The LORD appeared to Abraham by the oak of Mamre, as he sat in the entrance of his
tent, while the day was growing hot.2Looking up, he saw three men standing near him.
When he saw them, he ran from the entrance of the tent to greet them; and bowing to
the ground,3he said: "Sir, if it please you, do not go on past your servant.4Let some water be brought, that you may bathe your feet, and then rest under the tree.5Now that
you have come to your servant, let me bring you a little food, that you may refresh
yourselves; and afterward you may go on your way." "Very well," they replied, "do as
you have said."
6Abraham hurried into the tent to Sarah and said, "Quick, three measures of bran flour!
Knead it and make bread."7He ran to the herd, picked out a tender, choice calf, and
gave it to a servant, who quickly prepared it.8Then he got some curds and milk, as well
as the calf that had been prepared, and set these before them, waiting on them under
the tree while they ate.
9"Where is your wife Sarah?" they asked him. "There in the tent," he replied.10One of
them said, "I will return to you about this time next year, and Sarah will then have a
son."

Colossians 1:24-28
24[Brothers and sisters,] now I rejoice in my sufferings for your sake, and in my flesh I
am filling up what is lacking in the afflictions of Christ on behalf of his body, which is
the church,25of which I am a minister in accordance with God's stewardship given to me
to bring to completion for you the word of God,26the mystery hidden from ages and
from generations past. But now it has been manifested to his holy ones,27to whom God
chose to make known the riches of the glory of this mystery among the Gentiles; it is
Christ in you, the hope for glory.28It is he whom we proclaim, admonishing everyone
and teaching everyone with all wisdom, that we may present everyone perfect in Christ.

Luke 10: 38-42
38 As they continued their journey he entered a village where a woman whose name was
Martha welcomed him.39 She had a sister named Mary [who] sat beside the Lord at his
feet listening to him speak.40Martha, burdened with much serving, came to him and
said, "Lord, do you not care that my sister has left me by myself to do the serving? Tell
her to help me."41The Lord said to her in reply, "Martha, Martha, you are anxious and
worried about many things.42 There is need of only one thing. Mary has chosen the better part and it will not be taken from her."

SEVENTEENTH SUNDAY IN ORDINARY TIME

Genesis 18:20-32; Colossians 2:12-14; Luke 11:1-13

O God, protector of those who hope in you, without whom nothing has firm foundation, nothing is holy, bestow an abundance of your mercy upon us and grant that with you as our ruler and guide we may use the good things that pass in such a way as to hold fast even now to those that endure; through our Lord Jesus Christ, your Son, who lives and reigns with you in the unity of the holy Spirit, one God for ever and ever. Amen.

One of the most fascinating things about the revelation we have of who God is, in the scriptures, is that when you look at the stories, it almost seems as if we're watching God change—almost like a parent who might start by raising children, and have one way of raising them and then somehow seeing that it doesn't work, and then changing it to something else, and eventually coming to a place where they have all the wisdom that they need, through the experiences they've had, to be truly a support, a source of wisdom for their children. But in the Old Testament, we see God often finding himself in a situation where he's decided to do something, and then the human beings who are on the receiving end, or at least one—a prophet—the one closest to God might *question* whether God's choice of what he's decided to do is the best choice. And if you think of it in a way, you know human beings know a little bit more about justice, a little bit more about love, so they have to train God! [chuckles] That's an exaggerated way of seeing it, because the stories are really there to reveal to us who God is. And the stories are loaded with wisdom and cannot literally be taken to mean what they seem to mean on the surface.

So in the story in the first reading, we know that God was upset with human beings. In the Old Testament, especially the book of Genesis, we see him oftentimes saying things like, "These people that I created—their hearts are just *filled* with wickedness, *filled* with wickedness." He said that about the people when he decided to destroy all human beings with the Flood. And the interesting thing about that story is that he did find a family, Noah's family, that seemed to be what he hoped people *could* be; and he saved them through the ark, and you know the story. But what's fascinating is that at the end of that, he says to Noah, "I'll never do this again. I will never, ever. I promise. I'll never destroy everyone again." It's like he had remorse, regrets. So the God who punishes—which is what people would expect a god to do when people didn't perform the way he expected them to perform—he begins to question whether punishment is the right thing to do.

So we have the same theme developed shortly later in the book of Genesis, when we see the story of Sodom and Gomorrah being cities notorious for all kinds of evil. Two angels came and visited Lot, and those angels were desired sexually by the people of the town, by the men of the town. All of this created a sense that there's something really evil here, and God decides to destroy Sodom and Gomorrah. Then Abraham argues the point saying, "Wait. I understand that people who do something wrong need to be punished, but it doesn't seem *just* if you also punish those who are *innocent*. Are you a god who punishes those who are innocent? That doesn't feel like a *just* god." And that's certainly the thing the Old Testament stressed. We have a God of *justice*! The New Testament, a God of *mercy*. But this God of justice questions whether this act of destroying Sodom and Gomorrah is really the right thing to do, so he seems interested in discovering whether there's anyone there who is *innocent*.

As the story unfolds we see that God says, "If there are a few innocent there, I will spare everyone because of the innocent." So we see a story of God's evolution in terms of his revealing who he is, that he is not vengeful or filled with anger and so upset that he'll destroy innocent people because of the guilty. No, he will *protect the innocent*. And then, Sodom and Gomorrah *are* destroyed, because there were only a very few, less than ten, and that was Lot and his wife and children; and they were asked to leave. So God *did* protect the innocent.

What do we *learn* from a story like this? What are we supposed to understand? It seems to me that the thing that's very essential is that we recognize that the God who reveals himself through the Old Testament and then the New Testament is a God who slowly reveals someone who is almost too good to be true. By the time we get to the New Testament, we recognize that we not only have a God that is just, we have a God who is so amazingly filled with forgiveness—that the whole notion of punishment seems not to be any part of who he is in the New Testament. Instead of *punishment*, he wants *transformation*. He wants *conversion*. And the way he convinces people that they have within them the potential to change is that he meets their imperfection not with "justice" but with *mercy*. And what does that do to the hearts of those in the Old Testament that God describes as "filled with evil"? It creates in them *a new heart.* Jesus said, What I'm going to do in the New Testament is going to take people's hearts that are stony and hard—let's say those that are filled with a lack of mercy, and let's just call it "evil"—I'm going to take hearts that are evil, and I'm going to heal that part, and then I'm going to give them hearts of flesh, hearts like mine so that they can have within them the potential to be the creatures that I've always intended them to be, creatures who reflect me, the master, the creator; and I've revealed myself finally, ultimately, to everyone so that they see me as a God not of justice only, but a God of mercy. So my intention always, always is to love the sinner—to be more engaged with those who are off track, just as a parent might be more concerned and more intensely involved in the life of a child who has some limitation, some addiction, some problem, than with the child who is doing fine.

So in that second reading, that beautiful second reading, we see what God is doing in Jesus. He's taking all of our faults and all of our sins and somehow taking them on in the cross, nailing them to the cross, and we're freed of everything we've ever done. The moment we do it we're freed in the sense of the way God looks at us. He doesn't hold anything against us and wants nothing more than for you and for me to *know* that we're forgiven. When we know that we're forgiven, it has something to do with awakening the heart that he's created through redemption. Amazing! We have the potential to be the most loving, forgiving people because first and foremost we've been remade, redeemed, and we are constantly given this gift.

In the gospel, when the disciples ask Jesus to teach them to pray, as John the Baptist taught *his* disciples to pray, he tells them something very simple. He says, *When you pray, I want you to acknowledge*—this is the way Jesus imagines prayer—*acknowledge that you know that the God who created you is holy. That means, his reason for being here is to make you whole, complete, full. Never to hold anything against you, but only to want you to move, transform, and change.* And he says also, *I want you to recognize that you are able to receive, on a daily basis, every single thing that you need. And you want to realize that when I give you these things, the reason I'm giving them to you is so that you can create the kingdom.* And the kingdom is nothing more than the place where people are truly who God made them to be. The kingdom is a place of awareness, truth, reality. It's not so much about *perfection,* in the sense that nobody's making mistakes, because mistakes will be made over and over again. But mistakes that are made that are *not* held against someone, mistakes that are made that are constantly forgiven, are often seen by those who fail to reach what they were struggling to reach—the forgiveness somehow is like a lubricant that enables the whole thing to keep moving into a direction that's positive.

So prayer is the belief that God is holy, that this kingdom is real, and that we're given everything we need to create it.

Now, do you believe that? That's the issue. He goes on to tell a story that's all about persistence and prayer. *When you think about persistence and prayer, I want you to think about it this way:* He's not saying pray over and over for it. Many times, he describes the Pharisees as just repeating prayers over and over again. It didn't do them any good. Persistence is another way of describing absolute conviction that what you pray for will be given. So *ask* and know that you are going to receive. If you ask, and know that you are going to receive, how do you *know* that you received it? Well, the next part is really interesting: *Seek, and you shall find. Knock, and the door will be opened.* I don't think that's saying the same thing three times. He's saying stage one, stage two, stage three: Ask, seek, knock.

I pray for something. I believe it will come to me. People come to me and they say, "I prayed for it and it happened." And they are so excited. So it's important, when you pray for something, know that it happens, so you have to *seek* to see the response to your prayer. Many times people pray for something, and then (I love this), "I prayed for it and it all turned out, so you know, I didn't really need to pray. It all worked out!" [chuckles] You pray and then you have to *look and find* the way in which the prayer was answered. Just give praise to God. "Thank you for working it out that way."

Then often when it's worked out, there's something new, something you're more aware of, so when you see a new opportunity to be someone you couldn't be before, or you see someone else finding something they couldn't see before, and you want to encourage them, or you want to *be* the one that *knocks* and opens and moves into that new place. So we pray with conviction, asking God to give us the thing that we need—I don't think we're doing that by cajoling God into doing what he promised to do. You don't pray to God to say, "Please love me. Please pay attention to me. Please have an interest in this horrible thing that's going on. Please *do* something for me." That's not a way to understand prayer, that we're talking God into being a good God.

So our prayer is an acknowledgment to God that he can do what we're going to ask him to do. It's a way of recognizing God's presence in our life, and giving him the credit that he deserves for what he's able to accomplish within us. And we believe in him, and we trust him, to know that he's there for you. And all you have to do is look around and watch and see the beauty of the way he works things out. Sometimes it takes a long time. Sometimes it's an instant response. But *seek* and you'll *find* the answer to your prayer. You'll see it. And then, whatever that answer is, it's usually an opportunity for growth; it's usually a new place to enter into, so "the knock" is, "I want to come in. Open up for me." And that's what we do. We knock and say, "God, I want to be in this new place; I want to be this person that you're calling me to be. That's all I want." That's the kingdom; that's awareness; that's consciousness; that's the place that the kingdom is all about. God is the holy God, the God who can do everything, to make everything whole, everything complete.

So it's a very, very powerful message today, to just think about how we pray, *why* we pray, and what is our response to the promise that he will always, always answer our prayer.

Father, your mercy, your unmerited love, is what awakens within us the hearts that you've created. Bless us with a great awareness of your goodness to each of us so that in turn we might find ourselves drawn to that same kind of goodness in our brothers and sisters, to love them and forgive them when they do not merit it, to somehow know that we are giving them the greatest, the greatest of gifts. And we ask this in Jesus' name. Amen.

Genesis 18: 20-32

So the LORD said: The outcry against Sodom and Gomorrah is so great, and their sin so grave, that I must go down to see whether or not their actions are as bad as the cry against them that comes to me. I mean to find out.

As the men turned and walked on toward Sodom, Abraham remained standing before the LORD.

Then Abraham drew near and said: "Will you really sweep away the righteous with the wicked?

Suppose there were fifty righteous people in the city; would you really sweep away and not spare the place for the sake of the fifty righteous people within it?

Far be it from you to do such a thing, to kill the righteous with the wicked, so that the righteous and the wicked are treated alike! Far be it from you! Should not the judge of all the world do what is just?"

The LORD replied: If I find fifty righteous people in the city of Sodom, I will spare the whole place for their sake.

Abraham spoke up again: "See how I am presuming to speak to my Lord, though I am only dust and ashes!

What if there are five less than fifty righteous people? Will you destroy the whole city because of those five?" I will not destroy it, he answered, if I find forty-five there.

But Abraham persisted, saying, "What if only forty are found there?" He replied: I will refrain from doing it for the sake of the forty.

Then he said, "Do not let my Lord be angry if I go on. What if only thirty are found there?" He replied: I will refrain from doing it if I can find thirty there.

Abraham went on, "Since I have thus presumed to speak to my Lord, what if there are no more than twenty?" I will not destroy it, he answered, for the sake of the twenty.

But he persisted: "Please, do not let my Lord be angry if I speak up this last time. What if ten are found there?" For the sake of the ten, he replied, I will not destroy it.

Colossians 2: 12-14

Brothers and sisters, you were buried with him in baptism, in which you were also raised with him through faith in the power of God, who raised him from the dead. And even when you were dead [in] transgressions and the uncircumcision of your flesh, he brought you to life along with him, having forgiven us all our transgressions; obliterating the bond against us, with its legal claims, which was opposed to us, he also removed it from our midst, nailing it to the cross;

Luke 11: 1-13

Jesus was praying in a certain place, and when he had finished, one of his disciples said to him, "Lord, teach us to pray just as John taught his disciples."
He said to them, "When you pray, say:
Father, hallowed be your name,
your kingdom come.
Give us each day our daily bread*
and forgive us our sins
for we ourselves forgive everyone in debt to us,
and do not subject us to the final test."

And he said to them, "Suppose one of you has a friend to whom he goes at midnight and says, 'Friend, lend me three loaves of bread,
for a friend of mine has arrived at my house from a journey and I have nothing to offer him,'
and he says in reply from within, 'Do not bother me; the door has already been locked and my children and I are already in bed. I cannot get up to give you anything.'
I tell you, if he does not get up to give the visitor the loaves because of their friendship, he will get up to give him whatever he needs because of his persistence.

"And I tell you, ask and you will receive; seek and you will find; knock and the door will be opened to you.
For everyone who asks, receives; and the one who seeks, finds; and to the one who knocks, the door will be opened.
What father among you would hand his son a snake when he asks for a fish?
Or hand him a scorpion when he asks for an egg?
If you then, who are wicked, know how to give good gifts to your children, how much more will the Father in heaven give the holy Spirit to those who ask him?"

EIGHTEENTH SUNDAY IN ORDINARY TIME

Ecclesiastes 1:2, 2:21-23; Colossians 3:1-5, 9-11; Luke 12:13-21

Draw near to your servants, O Lord, and answer their prayers with unceasing kindness, that for those who glory in you as their creator and guide, you may restore what you have created and keep safe what you have restored, through our Lord Jesus Christ, your Son, who lives and reigns with you in the unity of the holy Spirit, one God for ever and ever. Amen.

The Liturgy of the Word today starts with the phrase that everyone has heard many, many times: *Vanity of vanities; all is vanity*. So I want to start with an understanding of that word. What does it mean to be vain? Somehow, vanity has something to do with an excessive desire, and it tends to lead into a disposition called *greed*. But it's a desire for something to effect or bring about something in your life, but it doesn't. It can't. That's vanity. I used to think *vanity* was another word for *narcissistic*, and that isn't really what it means. It isn't about being selfish as much as it's about being *foolish*. Because when you look to something and you say, "This will make me valuable; this will bring me peace; this will make me happy," and there's nothing in it that can do that in the way in which we imagine it can do, then we're caught in this thing called *vanity*.

And the amazing thing, if you're with a lot of people who are caught up in vanity, it's very hard to see through it. It's very hard to see that it doesn't work. Now one of the things that's clear is that certain things that we can have, that we can own, make us happy: a good meal, a beautiful house (or just a house that's *comfortable*), to have a car that gets you around, that you enjoy driving; to be with friends that you enjoy—all those things create a certain amount of happiness and joy. But the lie of vanity is this: If a little of those things makes me happy, then a whole *lot* of those things is going to make me even happier. And that's the essence of greed, that the more you have, the better off you are, the happier you're going to be. And I've been thinking a lot about these images because I work on the readings pretty much the whole week before Friday, and I've been so uncomfortable with them, and I'm not quite sure why, because it seems like the more I dig in to them, the more I feel anxiety. And it's because I am caught, like so many of us, in *vanity*! And I'm caught in the lie.

Taking care of someone's needs, if somebody needs me, and I go in there and take care of them, I spend time with them, and they feel better—that makes me feel valuable, makes me feel happy. So maybe I should answer every single need that's out there. Maybe I should be doing this 24/7; maybe I should never stop, because I want to be happy, and then I find myself over-extended, burning out, anxious, upset, feeling abused by *something* [chuckles]. You know, it's *interesting*! The lie is out there and it just seems to be perpetuated in some way where it's really hard to see through it. How do we learn to be *balanced* in a sense, both in the things we are called to do and the things that we're called to become?

Qoheleth, "the Speaker," is trying in his whole book, called *Ecclesiastes*, to give us a very interesting direction to work for. He said, The essence of life, the essence of what God wants—and remember Qoheleth did not believe in an afterlife—so that means that he felt that what we're here for is to be at peace and to enjoy life; to enjoy it. Now one might say, if you're after enjoyment in life, then you're a narcissistic person. All you want to do is be happy. There's *nothing* wrong with wanting to be happy! It's all about *how* you become happy. So one of the things that seems so clear Qoheleth is trying to awaken in us in this book is, "Don't get caught up in anything that's excessive; so if you feel like having possessions will give you a sense of well-being, then stop running after possessions in a way that just keeps you awake at night. You're anxious, you're nervous; you're upset. If *friends* make you happy, don't try to have every friend in the world intimate and try to be everything for them. He's just saying that all that stuff is *vanity!* All that doesn't *work*. Try to get to what works, and when you get to what works, you're going to find that you are enjoying life. I love the image. *Enjoying* might sound kind of superficial, but think about a joy that is the kind of joy that knows that everything is as it should be, everything is fine. You know, that moment that you have sometimes? *That's* the joy that I'm talking about, that you're at peace inside. Not anxious, not worried. I say over and over again to people in my work that I want so much for them to realize that God is not so much interested in you and me becoming perfect and never making mistakes. He's not asking us to discipline ourselves and create this perfect figure that never is out of sync with God's will. That's *impossible*! And if we do that and try to do that, we'll never learn who we are. But here's what he really *wants*. He wants us to be free of excessive anxiety, anxiety that I'm not enough, the anxiety that things are not *working* right, the anxiety that I'm not going to make it. And if you really do have vanity as a major lie going on in your life, you *will* be looking for something that is going to frustrate you from the beginning because you're going to use things in a way that they really can't produce what you want them to produce. More of anything does not necessarily make you more happy!

Now St. Paul, in the second reading, it's interesting. He's saying something while he's speaking to the Colossians, but the group he's talking to are Gentile converts, so his language is pretty tough. When he tells them to get rid of everything that's earthly, that makes me a *little* nervous because there's something so positive about being connected to the earth, where *humility* comes from a connection to the earth. But he's using "the earth" in a way that is more like, "Don't be someone who is less than who you really are. Don't settle for something fake and phony. You've got a real self that God has given you that you need to discover. So work on that." But the two things that I love that he says: Stop lying; and stop being anxious. The *lie* is what I want to talk about—the lie. How we perpetuate it.

So let's look at the story in the gospel, because it's kind of interesting. It's one of those things I love about scripture. It's really a record of what was going on, and it gives you the context. It's not just a list of wise sayings. It's an experience of a man filled with wisdom—so much wisdom that we would say he is God, that he is so in touch with who he really is, but he is *fully* human, so he's not working out of some kind of celestial power only. He's a human being filled with divinity, just like you and I potentially are—and then what he's doing is somebody asks him kind of a silly question, and you know at the time that Jesus walked the earth, inheritance—whatever the father had developed, his land, his cattle, his house, whatever—a double share of it always went to the oldest son. So it's a younger brother who comes to Jesus and saying, *My older brother just got the inheritance and doesn't want to give me my share. Because that inheritance is going to make him happy, and I see my happiness slipping through my fingers while he holds on to my share.* That's the lie. And Jesus has a great answer. He just looks at him and says, *Why would you come to me? I'm a spiritual teacher. I'm a rabbi. I'm walking around talking about God. And you're asking me to settle some dispute that has to do with inheritance?* But it intrigues Jesus. It triggers something in him. And he tells a parable. And the most important thing about this parable is—because I used to read it always and hear it always as if it's saying, "Don't count on your savings to make you happy. Spend your money. Don't have anything in the bank." [chuckles] But the most important line in this thing is—the story, you know, is about a man who has a great crop and he decides what he can do with this great crop is to store it and build new silos so he can store it all. And he says, "Now I can eat, drink, relax, and be merry. My happiness depends on what I own." So Jesus says, *That's a lie! What I want you to do: I want you to be rich.* I love that line, and I wish someone had helped me understand it sooner. *I want you to be rich. I want you to have everything you imagine that riches can bring to you, talent can bring to you, prestige can bring to you, a position of great authority—all those things that say they give us value or a sense of importance—you can have all of that without having those things in particular. Those things may not be your true self.* And so he's saying, *I want you to grow rich in what matters. I want you to be in touch with the things that feed you, like you think money or position or authority will feed you. So I want you to be in touch with those things so that you can feel rich.* In a way, then, God is saying I want everyone that I've created to eat, drink, relax, and be merry! [chuckles] That's our destiny. And yet there's a lot of pain in life and we have to deal with that when it comes, but I'm using that as a kind of metaphor. It's not eating great dinners, drinking great drinks; it's whatever those things *imply*. To be well fed, to be relaxed, to feel safe. That's what he wants; that's what he wants us to have.

So I want to give you an image that came to me as I worked on this reading, because when I do a reading like this, I always try to look up words and find their true meaning, so I was thinking, What is it that the inheritance question triggered in Jesus? Why did this question about inheritance, why did it move him to a parable? Well, I think it's because he knew, and he said this often, that he has come into the world so that we can receive the inheritance from God, and the inheritance that God wants us to have is this kingdom—he calls it—a *kingdom*. He wants us to be in a place, a kingdom, a way of being, a way of seeing the world. *That's* our inheritance. That he has the capacity, if we're open, to help us see the lie, to help us understand whenever we're participating in it. And grace is that quality that comes into our life that is somehow beautifully able, beautifully able to lift us out of the lie.

That's one of the things that God wants so much for us to be aware of. This kingdom is *ours*. It's not something you create; it's not something you go looking for. It's not "over there." It just is; it's in you; it's all around you. And then he says something about possessions. They don't guarantee you life. I want to make a distinction between owning things and possessing things. I looked up the word to "own" and the word to "possess." And the most interesting thing is that the word "own" means it's mine, I earned it, or it was given to me. I have ownership over it, control over it; it's *mine, mine*! But there's something in that image that's somewhat impersonal. It's like you *have* these things, and you stack them up somewhere and you don't necessarily enjoy the fruits of them. You kind of put them aside and you know that they're there. It's like you hoard them. But then there's the word "possess." The word is really interesting, because the word "possess" means this: The actual, first definition of possess is "to abide in." Linda Poston Smith's first song is "Abide in me." *To possess* is to live *in* something. Well, that's the way we talk about the devil and someone who is possessed. That person is *possessed* by the devil. That doesn't mean that the devil *owns* him. It means that the devil is inside of him and motivating everything they're doing.

Well, what if the key to getting out of the lie is to recognize when we have something in this life that God gives us and we don't possess it, we don't enter into it, we don't abide in it. We try to abide in something else, or we don't really engage ourselves in it. Then I could see where vanity would start, greed would start raging, because we're not satisfied. And I'm trying to think of all the things that God gives to each of us that we're unaware of, that we sometimes evaluate them by what the culture around us says or what the family says, but just imagine that every single thing that would make us rich and therefore content and happy basically in this life—they're there, but we have to *possess* them. Not own them; *possess* them. It means we have to enter into them, be a part of them, be fed by them, be nurtured by them. What an incredibly beautiful experience to be in this world and to somehow know that God has given us the very perfectly designed situation, people—everything—he's designed it so that it is there for us and all we really need to do is possess it. That means that you possess the things that we sometimes overlook. There's an interesting diagnosis out there called NDD—nature deprivation disorder. It affects young people who have no connection with the earth. Think of it. We have this earth, we have nature. We have individuals; we have beauty all around us. We may own it, but we don't possess it. We don't enter into it, we don't *feel* it, and we don't resonate with it. *That's* the challenge! To enter in, to feel the goodness of the things around us, to know that every single one of us is rich. Not to buy into the things the culture might tell us will make us *feel* rich, but to listen attentively to the inheritance, to know what it is, and to believe as Jesus longs for *all* of us to believe—that we have *everything* we need.

Father, the joy that is our inheritance is your gift to us. Bless us with the eyes to see, the will to enter in to the places where you long to feed us. And as we experience the joy that is from you, let us resonate that joy to the world and to those that we love, and we ask this through Christ our Lord. Amen.

Ecclesiastes 1: 2, 2: 21-23

Vanity of vanities, says Qoheleth,
vanity of vanities! All things are vanity!

For here is one who has toiled with wisdom and knowledge and skill, and that one's legacy must be left to another who has not toiled for it. This also is vanity and a great evil.

For what profit comes to mortals from all the toil and anxiety of heart with which they toil under the sun?
Every day sorrow and grief are their occupation; even at night their hearts are not at rest. This also is vanity.

Colossians 3: 1-5, 9-11
[Brothers and sisters,] if then you were raised with Christ, seek what is above, where Christ is seated at the right hand of God.
Think of what is above, not of what is on earth.
For you have died, and your life is hidden with Christ in God.
When Christ your life appears, then you too will appear with him in glory.
Put to death, then, the parts of you that are earthly: immorality, impurity, passion, evil desire, and the greed that is idolatry.

Stop lying to one another, since you have taken off the old self with its practices
and have put on the new self, which is being renewed, for knowledge, in the image of its creator.
Here there is not Greek and Jew, circumcision and uncircumcision, barbarian, Scythian, slave, free; but Christ is all and in all.

Luke 12: 13-21
Someone in the crowd said to Jesus, "Teacher, tell my brother to share the inheritance with me."
He replied to him, "Friend, who appointed me as your judge and arbitrator?"
Then he said to the crowd, "Take care to guard against all greed, for though one may be rich, one's life does not consist of possessions."

Then he told them a parable. "There was a rich man whose land produced a bountiful harvest.
He asked himself, 'What shall I do, for I do not have space to store my harvest?
And he said, 'This is what I shall do: I shall tear down my barns and build larger ones.
There I shall store all my grain and other goods
and I shall say to myself, "Now as for you, you have so many good things stored up for many years, rest, eat, drink, be merry!"'
But God said to him, 'You fool, this night your life will be demanded of you; and the things you have prepared, to whom will they belong?'
Thus will it be for the one who stores up treasure for himself but is not rich in what matters to God."

NINETEENTH SUNDAY IN ORDINARY TIME

Wisdom 18:6-9; Hebrews 11:1-2, 8-19; Luke 12:35-40

Almighty, ever-living God, whom taught by the holy Spirit we dare to call our Father, bring we pray to perfection in our hearts the spirit of adoption as your sons and daughters, that we may merit to enter into the inheritance which you have promised, through our Lord Jesus Christ, your Son, who lives and reigns with you in the unity of the holy Spirit, one God for ever and ever. Amen.

For a very long time, I have sat here in this studio and closed my eyes and asked God to speak through me. And it's interesting that as I continue this work, it's fascinating to me that every time I go back to the same stories, there's more in them, there's a meaning I didn't see before. And I'm hoping I can engage you in this amazing discovery of the mystery of how God works in our life. I say "mystery" because it defies logic, and it doesn't always make sense, and especially when we try to understand God, why he does certain things the way he does them—he does things we expect him to do and then he does things we *never* expect him to do—and the mind kicks in and says, "I want to have a clear idea of who this God is, I want to *know* him." And somehow to know him is to understand everything he does. But that's *not* the way we know God. We don't necessarily understand everything he does.

The only way to *know* God is to allow him into us, allow his work to take root in us, to manifest itself in us. And when we feel it and sense it, it's irresistible, I think, in terms of what it effects in us, and we fall in love with him. Faith is really a matter of *relationship*. It's not so much about doctrine and things we are told to believe. In the Catholic tradition, it's very obvious that when—let's say someone who's already been baptized asks to become Roman Catholic, and I ask if they believe and accept everything the Church teaches, that God revealed in Jesus. And there's a list of things we say that Jesus fundamentally taught, and they're key issues that we need to believe in, such as he was born of the Virgin, that he rose from the dead, that he's coming back, that we're going to have our bodies back. All those things. And sometimes faith just seems to depend upon whether we can assent to those things. So many people have a hard time understanding how these things can be, so we often find people stepping away from God because they say, "My mind can't grasp this, and I'm looking for verification with my logic, and if I can't verify these mysteries of God, then I can't accept them."

And it misses such an exciting and amazing process, and the exciting, amazing process is, well, what if it's about not so much focusing only on the doctrine that has been taught to us through Jesus by God himself? What about imagining that through Jesus' death and resurrection, something radically changed? We're able to somehow engage in a more intimate way with God, that he now lives inside of us, we live inside of *him*; and in this intimacy we find something that can only be understood with the *heart*. The mind gets in the way at certain points. But the heart *has* to be engaged. We *have* to have a relationship with God that is based on the mystery that the heart is able to hold onto without any hesitation. The way to describe it perhaps is when you love someone and you believe in them and you *know* that you believe in them, and maybe you see them doing things that make no sense as far as what you think they potentially *are*, but you still *believe* in them. That kind of faith in someone is the faith I believe the Gospel continually calls us to. It's not so much belief in doctrine as it is a belief in the living presence of a God who is there for us. A God that is there inside of us, *for* us.

Now if you look at the overarching images throughout Scripture of what God always seems to be engaged in doing since we left the Garden, it's always somehow getting us *back* to that place called the Garden, and the images we have so often—*beautiful* images in the Old Testament; and to be honest, I don't see how you can understand the New Testament unless you really are grounded in the Old Testament. The Jewish faith is the rock upon which Catholicism sits. And so we see, in the beginning, and we see it in the story of Abraham, a man considered to be the man of faith, we see a promise being made to him that he will have posterity. So something about the way God works with us is to engage us in an understanding that we are important, valuable, and that our influence continues, continues, continues.

Abraham may not have believed in an afterlife the way we do, and he knew that the way a man's presence in the world continues is through his sons, and the sons of his sons, and on and on and on; and he was childless. When he was *really* old—way past even the time this promise of God was made, saying, "I will give you what you need, I will be there for you, I will answer your needs, I will supply you with what is essential." And somehow it seems essential to us to have this sense that our life continues. So when he was well past the age of even *hoping* for this, he must have still had that longing inside of him. And then it's so interesting to me that what God does in his relationship with Abraham is he takes him and lifts him out of the place where he is comfortable—like being lifted out of the preconceived notions of the way you think life is—and he must have thought, at 90, "I'm certainly not going to have any children now. My wife is sterile; she's in her 90s too, and we're not going to have any children."

But he was taken out of that which was familiar. God called him. "Come, Abraham, with me." "Where are we going?" Abraham asks. "I'm not going to tell you. Just come." And it's that image of *going*, when you don't know *where* you're going, that must be based on the trust you have in the one who calls you to go. So he's willing to *move*, to change his perspective, to see things anew. And out of that disposition of wanting to see things new, trusting the person who's guiding you—a new birth happens. A child is born—Isaac—the fulfillment of the promise. And then to make it even more dramatic, Abraham, who is the father of faith, so the emphasis in the life of Abraham is on how much could he trust in God without having proof, he's even asked to sacrifice Isaac. And in this particular passage in the second reading—it's so interesting because it seems that the Letter to the Hebrews is attempting to answer the age-old question: How could Abraham kill his son? And it's not in the story in the Old Testament, but it's in this reflection in the New Testament, in Hebrews, where Paul says, *He must have thought, if he was going to do this, somehow there would be a resurrection; Isaac would come back. And he was given back, as a symbol.* So it's like, when you doubt, when you're experiencing something that makes no sense—"Why would he give me this gift and then ask me to give it up?" (That's part of the lack of logic in the way God works. [chuckles]) That experience was something that became an amazing example of the kind of trust that God is asking from each of us. *If you really have faith in me, I can ask you to do anything, and no matter how crazy, insane, or how much of a loss it may seem to create for you, you'll do it. And that's what I want from you.*

Let's look at one other part of the Old Testament. Abraham is the one who leaves what is familiar and is given a promise that doesn't make any sense—logically. And then as it moves on in that story, we have the call of the Israelite people from slavery into freedom. And I love that image, that this is the work of the God who's asking us to trust him. Why do we trust him? Because he has a task he has to engage us in; he *longs* to engage us in. It has something to do with going through a process that's going to bring us from slavery to freedom. You've heard me say this over and over again. I think so often the "slavery" we get caught in is excessive anger, excessive fear, excessive shame. These things rob us of a sense of well-being, a sense that life is good. So what he's doing is calling us constantly out of that.

In the gospel, there's this *beautiful* story that is so essential if you and I want to be a people of faith, real faith in Jesus. He tells the story to his disciples, and he's really talking about the fact that he looks around and sees so many people in charge of religion not really being there to nurture the people that need to be nurtured. They tend to be self-centered. They're not self-giving. They're not life-giving. They're not loving the people they are caring for. They're functioning for a God they feel then will reward them for what they're doing for God. And they probably don't like doing it, so they just figure, "Alright, the more I struggle, the harder I push myself, the bigger the reward, the better the place at the banquet, whatever. [chuckles]

So we look at this gospel passage and it's talking about how much God wishes the people—and Jesus is speaking for God—how much God wishes the people to be more of who he longs for them to be. And the only way they can be that is through a relationship with him, an *intimate* relationship with him, and they have no clue that that's what it's all about.

Listen to the story. It's beautiful. He says, Be like men and women who are working constantly in their house to be a good servant, and one of the jobs of the servant is to be there to open for the master. When the master comes, he knocks—there weren't keys, there wasn't an easy way to get in unless there was somebody inside who could lift the bar that went across the door and let you in. So the only way in was somebody inside had to *let* you in. That just says *everything* to me about the relationship we have with God. There's no way that God is going to force himself on us—ever. He just says, "Can I come in?" And we have to say, "Yes, come in."

And it makes sense to me to say yes only when you realize what his "coming in" involves. It involves a transformation, a leaving where you're familiar with, going through something difficult, a sense of losing something you perhaps don't necessarily want, but it's familiar; it sort of works, but you know there must be more than that; you're not really that content, but maybe it seems more painful to go through a change than to stay where you are; and so we don't answer the door. And I find it *fascinating* that the example he gives about paying attention for when the master comes home is the anxiety one has about something going wrong. You know how sensitive we are when we're in danger or you think a thief might be coming. You'll be really attentive and listen to everything—Is he at the door? Is he at the window? That kind of attentiveness is what God is asking us to have. We know what it means to be attentive when we're afraid and we think we're going to be harmed. What about being attentive when we think we're going to be saved, we're going to be helped? Interesting! To be every day expecting, wondering, longing for some experience of God that affirms his love for us. And the love that he has, the effect of it is almost always going to be in transformation, building us up, strengthening us so that we can go through the pain of transformation.

So the story is beautiful because when the master enters in there is this surprise that must have shocked everybody who heard the story. The master comes in, and all of a sudden, instead of saying, "Thank you very much for opening the door. You're a good servant. I'll go upstairs now and go to bed." No, he sits the servants down, goes into the kitchen, prepares a wonderful meal, and brings it in and serves them. The master comes home, and being so pleased—in a way, you might say—that the servant opens for him. Then the master's *intention* is not that this servant so much serve him as much as he allows God (the master) to feed *him* so that he in turn can then serve the others—serve the others. That's what he wants! He wants to enter into your life and into my life to do something that encourages us, supports us, enables us to be the loving, compassionate vehicles of his grace to the world that we're intended to be. That's what faith is. Faith is an absolute, rock-solid, not so much *conviction* as much as a rock-solid *experience* of a loving God operating in your life, enabling you to become everything you need to be. He's on your side; he's a servant God; he longs for you to become all that you're intended to be.

I know in my own life, I haven't always lived that way, and I know that one of the things I've said often is, how wonderful it is to have God loving you, and then to experience yourself as you are and to be yourself. I hope I haven't said it too glibly because that is one of the most difficult, painful processes—to let go of illusions, to face the fullness of who you are, and then to accept it. And I don't know how you can do that without a deep knowledge that that core of who you are is so *beautiful* in the eyes of another that their love gives you the power to do it.

Lord, our faith is our "ticket." It is the thing that enables us to be taken to a place that's beyond our imagining. Bless us with courage, the courage to know, first and foremost, how ***much*** *we are loved, and then to follow the Lover, you, who calls us through difficult, dark places in order to bring us to the light. And we ask this through Christ our Lord. Amen.*

I'd like to say that the program today was dedicated by one of my very, very wonderful listeners, and he would like to dedicate this program to the musicians that I use most often. He enjoys their gifts. I enjoy them also, and that's Jubilant Sykes—whom we just heard—Lynda Poston Smith, whom we hear so often; and then also John Michael Talbot.

Wisdom 18: 6-9

The night of the passover was known beforehand to our fathers,
that, with sure knowledge of the oaths in which they put their faith,

they might have courage.
Your people awaited the salvation of the just
and the destruction of their foes.
For when you punished our adversaries,
in this you glorified us whom you had summoned.
For in secret the holy children of the good were offering sacrifice
and putting into effect with one accord the divine institution.

Hebrews 11: 1-2, 8-19
Brothers and sisters:
Faith is the realization of what is hoped for
and evidence of things not seen.
Because of it the ancients were well attested.

By faith Abraham obeyed when he was called to go out to a place
that he was to receive as an inheritance;
he went out, not knowing where he was to go.
By faith he sojourned in the promised land as in a foreign country,
dwelling in tents with Isaac and Jacob, heirs of the same promise;
for he was looking forward to the city with foundations,
whose architect and maker is God.
By faith he received power to generate,
even though he was past the normal age
—and Sarah herself was sterile—
for he thought that the one who had made the promise was trustworthy.
So it was that there came forth from one man,
himself as good as dead,
descendants as numerous as the stars in the sky
and as countless as the sands on the seashore.

All these died in faith.
They did not receive what had been promised
but saw it and greeted it from afar
and acknowledged themselves to be strangers and aliens on earth,
for those who speak thus show that they are seeking a homeland.
If they had been thinking of the land from which they had come,
they would have had opportunity to return.
But now they desire a better homeland, a heavenly one.

Therefore, God is not ashamed to be called their God,
for he has prepared a city for them.

By faith Abraham, when put to the test, offered up Isaac,
and he who had received the promises was ready to offer his only son,
of whom it was said,
"Through Isaac descendants shall bear your name."
He reasoned that God was able to raise even from the dead,
and he received Isaac back as a symbol.

Luke 12: 35-40
Jesus said to his disciples:
"Gird your loins and light your lamps
and be like servants who await their master's return from a wedding,
ready to open immediately when he comes and knocks.
Blessed are those servants
whom the master finds vigilant on his arrival.
Amen, I say to you, he will gird himself,
have the servants recline at table, and proceed to wait on them.
And should he come in the second or third watch
and find them prepared in this way,
blessed are those servants.
Be sure of this:
if the master of the house had known the hour
when the thief was coming,
he would not have let his house be broken into.
You also must be prepared, for at an hour you do not expect,
the Son of Man will come."

TWENTIETH SUNDAY IN ORDINARY TIME

Jeremiah 38:4-6, 8-10; Hebrews 12:1-4; Luke 12:49-53

O God who have prepared for those who love you good things which no eye can see, fill our hearts, we pray, with the warmth of your love, so that loving you in all things and above all things, we attain your promises, which surpass every human desire. Through our Lord Jesus Christ, your Son, who lives and reigns with you in the unity of the holy Spirit, one God for ever and ever. Amen.

Last Sunday the readings were challenging us to be more vigilant, more open, more receptive to the ways in which the God who created us longs to enter into us, to dwell there, to work within us, with us, to transform the world—to open the world to all the goodness and the beauty that is within it, placed there by the one who created it. And this Sunday, we have a kind of companion-piece to being vigilant, and that's to *persevere*.

It seems to me the reason perseverance is such an important thing is because one of the ways in which the Spirit of our God is able to enter into us is that we make room for that Spirit. We make *room* for God in us. And one might say, "All I have to do is say "yes" to God, and he wants to come in, and he comes in." The problem is that the place where God longs to dwell within us, our heart, the core of who we are, is often filled with things contrary to the Work that God longs to enable us to do *from* our hearts. So the *resistance* is sometimes something we're not even aware that we have because we're clinging to something that is not really compatible with the way in which, when God is dwelling in us, the way in which we live, the way he *invites* us to live.

The first reading is from one of my favorite prophets, the prophet Jeremiah. I think I like him because he seems so human. He was asked by God to be his prophet when he was very young, a teenager, and his complaint was, "I can't *talk* in front of people. I just can't do that." And I have to identify with that because when I was in my teenage years, the thought of getting up and talking in front of someone, the thought was almost paralyzing. I couldn't *imagine* standing in front of people, talking. And yet I've made my whole career nothing but talking in front of people! So somehow, God entered into a weakness that I had and overcame it and I was able to do the work that he calls me to do because somehow whatever that was—that fear that was deep inside of me of standing up in front of people—I know it was the fear of performance, meaning I would feel so vulnerable if I was performing because my performance was equal to my *value,* so obviously I couldn't take the risk of looking foolish if looking foolish meant that in the eyes of another I truly was valueless. That had to be weeded out of me, had to be taken out of me. I had to make room for the presence of God's working through me in a way that used my voice and all that. I had to make *room* for that, and so what I had to do was let go of that image of my value being connected to my performance. I would like to say that all I had to say was, "Oh. My value is *not* in my performance." And then go on. No, it doesn't work that way. [chuckles] It had to be sort of *dug* out of me over years and years.

And what I sense in Jeremiah, as he went into his work, he was told by God he would be the one who, if he opened his mouth and spoke as God called him to, he would be the one who would tear down and build anew. He would rip things out of people and put new things in them. And he *loved* that idea as a young man with idealism. He thought, "Yeah! I want to help; I want to help!" But what Jeremiah didn't realize is how difficult it was to reach people who were closed, who were filled with dispositions radically opposite of what God wanted them to be; how difficult it would be to reach them. So Jeremiah was one of those prophets that constantly was complaining to God, "You *duped* me! You fooled me. You said I could do this, and it's not working." Well, the fact that it wasn't working wasn't a problem with Jeremiah's performance. It was that the people were just so stiff-necked and so hardhearted. So it was a symbol of his struggle and a symbol of the depression that could come over someone like that, we find him in a cistern, placed there by the leaders who didn't like what he was saying. Think of the leaders as the ego of everyone who refuses to change when it knows it should change. Usually if the ego's attacked by some concept that changes the way it thinks, it feels like it should attack back. And so here we see Jeremiah sitting in a dark cistern, which is like a large room underground that is usually filled with water. In this case, the water's gone but the mud's still there. And Jeremiah is sinking down into it in the darkness. That's called *depression* [chuckles]—at least in *my* mind it is! So he's depressed, he's discouraged. The experience he's going through, is it all negative? Like digging out something inside of him. I remember when I went through a long period in my life when I was very discouraged and depressed—I felt like there was something in my stomach that was digging into it and ripping things out of it. And what I realized is that our sufferings, our difficulties that we have in accomplishing the things that we do, which is often a blow to the ego and to our pride, that when we go through that and endure that, something changes. It's like a process that is necessary in order for something to come into us, something to come into us.

And as we listen to the gospel, it's clear that what God, in Jesus, has wanted to do is to accomplish this powerful transformation in us, and the only way he can describe it is, "I'm trying to start a fire in people! I want them to be on fire, and I want that fire to be so strong that when other people are close to it, *they* burst into flame!" A *beautiful* image of what it means to live in this world, carrying in your heart the burning love that God has for the world as it is and wants to enter into it.

Now in the second reading, we see Paul—well, it's the Letter to the Hebrews. We don't really know who wrote that. I remember once I was giving a talk and my bishop was there and it was many, many years ago; and I announced very confidently and clearly: "A reading from St. Paul to the Hebrews." The bishop got up and said, "St. Paul did not write the Letter to the Hebrews." [chuckles] (Most scholars agree that someone other than Paul wrote the letter, but it's still a masterpiece.) Anyway, what I sense in that reading from Hebrews is a description of the process that Jesus went through, much like Jeremiah's, where he had to go through something that felt like enormous failure. It felt like, as far as his human nature goes and his pride and his desire to accomplish something, he looked like a fool. He was treated as if he was a fool, as if he was evil, as if he was valueless. And I love the line—I don't remember seeing it before—but it says that Jesus went to the cross despising its shame. There isn't anything more debilitating than shame; there is isn't anything that robs us more of value and goodness than shame. There *had* to be some experience of shame for Jesus as he saw his work fall apart; he wasn't able to reach the religious leaders; his disciples were not a band that was there *with* him—There was John; Jesus's mother, Mary; Mary Magdalene; a few people there, but as a human being, he had to feel that this work that he had, that he hoped would be so well-received, to have people open to this *fire* that he wanted to place in their hearts—there he is, laughed at, mocked at, spit upon, naked, hanging on a cross. How much more shame could anyone endure, and yet he endured it, and when he endured that, there was an explosion, a fire into the earth, into the world. Somehow he was completely emptied of anything that was in a sense resistant to a power greater than himself. And to miss that in the cross is almost to miss everything, because that's what we're taught we have to go through day after day in terms of the setbacks that happen to us, and we need to learn that when those setbacks come and when we're feeling in our humanity that somehow we're not succeeding or it's all falling apart or nothing is working or all the things we leaned on to make us feel good don't make us feel good any more . . .When we're feeling that, *that's the work*. Then it's like the fire. Your heart is being prepared to *ignite!* [chuckles] To be *filled* with fire, you know? It's a *powerful* image.

So I'm thinking, What is this? What *is* the fire that Jesus wanted to create? When you begin to have it, you're going to have all kinds of resistance. You're going to have people working against you and not understanding you. That image of son against father, father against son, mother against daughter—when the culture changes—look at the 60s—when there's a major shift in consciousness, people begin to see something different, and some get it and some don't. Those who get it and those who don't—don't get along! And that tension is what Jesus is wanting his disciples and you and me to understand. That's the work of holding on to this thing we know is real, that is coming inside of us, that changes the way we are. And that fire in the heart, and what I love about the fire in the heart is that there is a beautiful, beautiful tradition in the Catholic Church of the image of the sacred heart. It was Jesus revealing himself to someone with this open chest and this heart on fire. He was trying to say how much he wanted this to happen to everyone, and he wanted people to feel that there is this capacity that the heart has if it's been emptied of ego and emptied of all of its desire to be in charge of things—something radically changes and it becomes this place of fiery light resonance that goes out into the world and it *connects* with the world in a way that's beautiful and powerful. The way it connects is that it sees the beauty in things; it sees past the accidental and goes to the essential and looks deeply into things to the point where it doesn't just look at them but it enters into them, and something changes in what it looks into—if that makes sense [chuckles]. It's like *this fire* is something that bypasses all the normal things that might be resistances to us becoming a part of something because the person who has a heart that is *alive* with fire is a person who has the capacity to *connect* with things—to be *inside* of things. And when we're inside of something, we do what God is doing in Christ. Christ comes into the world with God inside of him so much that he *is* God. He walks this earth and longs to bypass all the things that keep us from entering in. So no judgment, no categories of who's more valuable than somebody else. It goes right into something and feels the goodness inside of it, and when it feels and senses that goodness, it awakens it. So when you look at someone and you love them deeply—even though they don't deserve it, they don't merit it—when you *do* that, something *changes* in them. Something is *awakened* in them. And that's "the work" of being a follower of Christ. Not to sit back and just worship him and honor him—that's a very big part of it—but it's a dynamic way of being in the world that is like going around trying to ignite fires wherever we can and recognizing that this is a *privilege*, this is something that is a gift to us as we become closer and closer and a part of things around us. What an amazing way for me—as I'm saying it, I'm feeling it—what an amazing way of seeing this thing that often leads us to a disposition where we're still sitting stuck in the mud. Think of Jeremiah as an image of what can happen to a person when they feel that they themselves are not the source of power and that it's not working and that therefore they're not valuable. Compare that with the image of Christ in the gospel saying, "Look. I'm here to do something, and I want you to do it with me, but the only way you can do it with me is to go through what *I* went through. There has to be some kind of baptism, some kind of dying and rising." And the dying and rising is the thing I think basically stops us from really entering into it. In other words, I don't necessarily *want* to face my limitations. It sounds so prideful, but I don't want to see that I'm *not capable*. But life has a way of presenting to us over and over again a sense that there is something that we're called to do that we can't do ourselves and that we are invited to hold that thought, let that feeling of emptiness stay with us for a while (crucifixion) and then once having experienced that and allowing that to be, then to feel this *fire* starting inside of us. We're emptied in order to be full; we're kind of stuck in the mud before we can become a blazing fire—and that's the challenge, to enter into that amazing process of death and resurrection and to become something, someone that is fully alive and capable of the most amazing, amazing things.

Father, your longing, your deepest longing is to enter into us and to create within us the presence of your love that takes the form of fire that ignites both our imaginations and our wills so that we become vessels of that light to the world around us. Bless us with perseverance in this task. Open us to the process of being emptied so that we can be filled more and more with your Spirit, and we ask this through Christ our Lord. Amen.

Jeremiah 38: 4-6, 8-10

In those days, the princes said to the king:
"Jeremiah ought to be put to death;
he is demoralizing the soldiers who are left in this city,
and all the people, by speaking such things to them;
he is not interested in the welfare of our people,
but in their ruin."
King Zedekiah answered: "He is in your power";
for the king could do nothing with them.

And so they took Jeremiah
and threw him into the cistern of Prince Malchiah,
which was in the quarters of the guard,
letting him down with ropes.
There was no water in the cistern, only mud,
and Jeremiah sank into the mud.

Ebed-melech, a court official,
went there from the palace and said to him:
"My lord king,
these men have been at fault
in all they have done to the prophet Jeremiah,
casting him into the cistern.
He will die of famine on the spot,
for there is no more food in the city."
Then the king ordered Ebed-melech the Cushite
to take three men along with him,
and draw the prophet Jeremiah out of the cistern before
he should die.

Hebrews 12: 1-4
Brothers and sisters:
Since we are surrounded by so great a cloud of witnesses,
let us rid ourselves of every burden and sin that clings to us
and persevere in running the race that lies before us
while keeping our eyes fixed on Jesus,
the leader and perfecter of faith.
For the sake of the joy that lay before him
he endured the cross, despising its shame,
and has taken his seat at the right of the throne of God.
Consider how he endured such opposition from sinners,
in order that you may not grow weary and lose heart.
In your struggle against sin
you have not yet resisted to the point of shedding blood.

Luke 12: 49-53
Jesus said to his disciples:
"I have come to set the earth on fire,
and how I wish it were already blazing!
There is a baptism with which I must be baptized,

and how great is my anguish until it is accomplished!
Do you think that I have come to establish peace on the earth?
No, I tell you, but rather division.
From now on a household of five will be divided,
three against two and two against three;
a father will be divided against his son
and a son against his father,
a mother against her daughter
and a daughter against her mother,
a mother-in-law against her daughter-in-law
and a daughter-in-law against her mother-in-law."

TWENTY-FIRST SUNDAY IN ORDINARY TIME

Isaiah 66:18-21; Hebrews 12:5-7, 11-13; Luke 13:22-30

O God who caused the minds of the faithful to unite in a single purpose, grant your people to love what you command and desire what you promise, and amid the uncertainties of this world, our hearts may be fixed on that place where true gladness is found. Through our Lord Jesus Christ, your Son, who lives and reigns with you in the unity of the holy Spirit, one God for ever and ever. Amen.

The liturgy, in the Roman Catholic tradition, is a kind of work in progress. At least during my lifetime, I've seen many changes in liturgy, moving from the Latin language to English. And now, recently, not so much from one language to another, but what happened in the last few years is we've had this presentation given to us in the countries that speak English. It came to us late because those who were assigned the translations for the prayers that we have at the liturgy were trying to find a way of speaking English that fits so many different cultures: New Zealand, Australia, United Kingdom, United States, Canada. The thing that changed the liturgy is that we've changed the *words* of the prayers in the direction of being more authentic to the original prayers that are *ancient* prayers. So we refined the translations, and they seem to me so rich, so beautiful, so powerful. There have also been changes in the actual ritual, which have been less easy to adjust to [chuckles] because when you have remembered so much the way the liturgy is, you tend to fall back into the way you *always* have said it, rather than the new way. But nevertheless we find in these opening prayers such beautiful theology, and what I love about the opening prayer we just listened to is it's a very clear statement that we have got to do what you ask us to do, we have to do what you command. And when we *do* that, we are setting ourselves up so we receive a promise, and we have to trust and believe in that promise. And that promise is the place of joy, the place of gladness, the place of peace.

So how do we get to the place of peace? The Alleluia verse today was Jesus' "the way, the truth, the life." He says that "everyone who wants to come to the Father must come through me." It doesn't mean you have to be a Christian to connect with God. It means that Jesus is the way, if we focus on his life and his teaching, he's the way that we're invited to live our life in this world so that we can become part of his family, part of his kingdom, which is the place of great peace and wholeness.

So let's look at the readings, because the opening prayer sets us up to find in the readings the essence of why they're there and what they're there to teach us. The first reading is the last part of the famous book in the Old Testament, the Book of Isaiah. And it ends with a very interesting image. It ends with God calling all people to come to the holy mountain, to Jerusalem, and to be there and to *see* the glory of God. And everyone comes as a kind of offering, which is an interesting image. I think the reason we use that image of the offering is because if you understand what it is that religion is always calling us to, you'll recognize that the thing that it's calling us to is a work that can be described best by saying, "I want to experience the glory of God, the *glory* of God." What *is* the glory of God? The most awesome, powerful thing about our God that makes him *so* glorious is his ability to invite you and me into a relationship with him. But it's never damaged or in any way injured because of our faults and our sins; and in and through that relationship with him, we're called to discover who we are, who we are.

The work of all good, healthy religion is the work of *discovery*, discovering who God is, discovering what creation is all about, and discovering who we truly are. One of the greatest complaints Jesus had of the religious leaders of his time, who should have been the models of what religion can do for people, he called *hypocrites*, phonies. They were acting in a way that wasn't really who they were. So let's just focus on the glory of God as his ability to enable you and me to discover who he is, how he's revealed himself and his Son. All of that is going to lead to discovery of who we are.

And that's the greatest challenge—to be who God has made us to be. And one of the things that Isaiah is saying at the end of this reading, it's interesting, it says that this God who is calling us to self-discovery warns us that one of the ways that we *tend* to think about our journey on this earth is that it's a journey that involves eradicating evil. "We've got to get rid of evil." And the glory of God is *not* that he is going to eradicate evil in the sense that it no longer exists. The glory of God is that in this process of growing into self-discovery, the evil that is in us, the evil that's all around us—instead of it being the thing that robs us of life—has something to do with disciplining us into being more authentic. Self-discovery leads to authenticity.

So the second reading speaks about the notion of a good parent as someone who wants their children to become all that they were intended to be. And one of the ways they help the child is to discipline them, which is often seen as a negative. So you tell a two-year-old that they can't do something that might harm them, and they're angry. They don't *like* discipline. But when all discipline is designed for the single purpose of bringing us into greater self-discovery, if you tell a child, a two-year-old, that they can't play with something that's sharp, what you're really trying to say to them is, "This is dangerous, and you have to be *careful* with it. And I don't want you to do something because of your lack of awareness and consciousness—I don't want you to do something with this sharp object that might harm you." So I'm going to say "No sharp objects, OK?" A good parent disciplines their child. It makes total sense. And many believe that God is a *punishing* God, a God who doesn't like those who are not doing what they are supposed to do. The Old Testament is filled with images of this, because the Old Testament is based in Law, and the Law demands justice, and justice is the objective observation of the way things are supposed to be, and when they're not, someone needs to pay. I remember the first time I did jury duty as a priest, I was shocked when they said, "Your job here is not to determine whether this person is good or evil. You're not even to go into what his intention was when he did what he did. We're going to show you the law, you'll understand the law, and then we'll show you what he did, and you tell us, 'Did that break the law?' And if it did, he's guilty." And my first instincts were, "Well, what were the circumstances? Where was he? What was going through his mind? How healthy was he? Did he *realize* what he was doing?" Doesn't matter! He *did* it! That's the world of justice. And that world of justice in the Old Testament became so strong that what was taught to the people who followed the God of Israel was that if there was somebody who was in pain or suffering, sick or somehow outcast, they were considered to be those that God is punishing because they didn't keep the Law, and you were not to have anything to do with them. You don't go *near* those people because they're evil, and if you do you'll become impure.

So the issue is, how do you walk through this earth, how do you go on this path, and somehow avoid evil and try to eradicate it from your life? That's where so many people still are when it comes to religion! They really believe that the way that God is calling us to live our lives is to get rid of evil, to discipline ourselves to the point where we no longer are able to engage in anything that touches upon something that might be considered evil. So we go through life in this rigid formula where the last thing we're going to do is touch into anything that's imperfect, so perfection becomes a goal. When perfection becomes the goal, then we become tight and rigid, and we begin to *hate* people [chuckles] because, Guess what? We're not *intended* to be perfect. Competition, envy—all of that enters the world when someone sees religion as the call to eradicate the evil in their life and to be perfectly like what God wants you to be:

a perfect person. But the horrible, horrible side-effect of all that is that you end up like the people that Jesus criticized in the Old Testament who were religious leaders. You end up being "actors." How many people have said something like this: "I *hate* myself. I hate myself for that." Who's the "I" and who's the "self"? It seems like the "I" is a superego that says, "I am not supposed to have any kind of major problems, and when I do, I don't like myself because God doesn't like me when I'm that way. Nobody that loves me is going to love me if they see me in this way. I *hate* this part of me."

So you go to the gospel, and what I want so much for you to understand is that that's what Jesus is concerned about when he talks about the wide and narrow gate. I was reading a lot of commentaries this week on the wide and narrow gate and was kind of shocked to see how often people describe the *wide* gate as the gate of somehow "indulgence, easy life, don't care what I do as far as its ramifications, I just do what pleases me." That's the *wide* gate. And the other is the *narrow* gate, which is tough and hard and difficult and painful—because there is a statement in there that says the wide gate is where everyone is going; the narrow gate is—people aren't strong enough to go in it; you need *strength* to go in the narrow gate. Let's just take "wide" and "narrow" as the conventional way of thinking, the way the mind thinks; the "narrow" is the less aware way, because the narrow way is the one that's hidden from most people's imaginations because a) they're not taught that way; b) they're not wired together that way. So what the narrow gate engages in is self-discovery, and the wide gate is in self-discipline. Most people go into religion believing that the obligation they have is to be *better*, to be their best all the time. There's *some* truth to that. But being the best that we can be and being better than we are means somehow not facing what's really going on inside of us, not peeling layer after layer back and finding deeper and deeper wounds, deeper and deeper negative thoughts. You can't *do* that work of getting closer and closer to the core of what has been damaged inside of us if the whole notion is "I have got to be the perfect one, the one that's acceptable, the one that everyone loves, the one that God loves, the one that's rewarded." And the way of *self-discovery* is this amazing journey that Jesus went on. And the only way to get to the Father is to go that way. And what did he say about evil that shocked his disciples? "I have to give in to it. I have to give in to evil, and I'll save the world." What was the evil that Jesus was talking about giving in to? Well, it seems to me the evil he was worried about is the worry we all have about evil, and even the word *Satan* means *the judge*. The evil he had to give in to was the fact that he would be perceived by so many people as evil. So he had to, in a way, endure the shame of looking to everyone around him as if he was a fool, a blasphemer, stripped naked, hanging on a cross, embarrassed. Just imagine that the crucifixion is about anything we have to face in life that is the will of God that we face it, but it carries so much shame. If you can *do* that, you are one strong dude [chuckles]. You are *strong*. And not many people go through life thinking that "my major issue is to deal with who I really am, face all that, give in to all of that, and say, Yes. That's me." And then what happens is this incredible gift, only found in the "narrow way," breaks through. It's called *mercy*. Unmerited love. And when you feel the darkest, most unpleasant part of you is not a block to being loved by God, when you find God loving you in that kind of mess that you're in, then you're beginning to see and understand the *narrow way*. Once you've experienced that mercy, the fear of being who you really are diminishes, and the competition and the envy and the anger that you have in the *wide* way just dissipates. We're no longer competing; we're no longer hiding; we're no longer doing violence to our nature by saying, "I feel these feelings but I refuse to acknowledge them because they might have some kind of connection with evil, so I repress, I repress, I repress." This is the wide gate. The narrow gate: "I am open, I am open, I am open. I want to see me *as I am*, and I want to love me as I am because I want to be like Jesus in my life, I want to be with myself without any judgment, without any condemnation, without any desire to punish, but only to heal and transform and to bring life."

The image that's so powerful is when the man who took the wide way appears before God, God looks at him and says, "I don't recognize you. Who are you? You don't look like the person I created." But the person who stands humbly before God, who goes through the narrow gate, looks *exactly* like who they are because they've accepted every single thing about themselves, and they are welcomed into that incredible place of peace.

Father, our journey with you is something that is so important, and we need to understand it as fully as we can. Bless us with wisdom—not just the wisdom of the mind, but the wisdom of the heart so that the narrow way, the way of the heart, will be the way that we choose and the way that brings us to the promised peace of your kingdom, and we ask this through Christ our Lord. Amen.

Isaiah 66: 18-21

Thus says the LORD:
I know their works and their thoughts,
and I come to gather nations of every language;
they shall come and see my glory.
I will set a sign among them;
from them I will send fugitives to the nations:

to Tarshish, Put and Lud, Mosoch, Tubal and Javan,
to the distant coastlands
that have never heard of my fame, or seen my glory;
and they shall proclaim my glory among the nations.
They shall bring all your brothers and sisters from all the nations
as an offering to the LORD,
on horses and in chariots, in carts, upon mules and dromedaries,
to Jerusalem, my holy mountain, says the LORD,
just as the Israelites bring their offering
to the house of the LORD in clean vessels.
Some of these I will take as priests and Levites, says the LORD.

Hebrews 12: 5-7, 11-13
Brothers and sisters,
You have forgotten the exhortation addressed to you as children:
"My son, do not disdain the discipline of the Lord
or lose heart when reproved by him;
for whom the Lord loves, he disciplines;
he scourges every son he acknowledges."
Endure your trials as "discipline";
God treats you as sons.
For what "son" is there whom his father does not discipline?
At the time,
all discipline seems a cause not for joy but for pain,
yet later it brings the peaceful fruit of righteousness
to those who are trained by it.

So strengthen your drooping hands and your weak knees.
Make straight paths for your feet,
that what is lame may not be disjointed but healed.

Luke 13: 22-30
Jesus passed through towns and villages,
teaching as he went and making his way to Jerusalem.
Someone asked him,
"Lord, will only a few people be saved?"
He answered them,

"Strive to enter through the narrow gate,
for many, I tell you, will attempt to enter
but will not be strong enough.
After the master of the house has arisen and locked the door,
then will you stand outside knocking and saying,
'Lord, open the door for us.'
He will say to you in reply,
'I do not know where you are from.
And you will say,
'We ate and drank in your company and you taught in our streets.'
Then he will say to you,
'I do not know where you are from.
Depart from me, all you evildoers!'
And there will be wailing and grinding of teeth
when you see Abraham, Isaac, and Jacob
and all the prophets in the kingdom of God
and you yourselves cast out.
And people will come from the east and the west
and from the north and the south
and will recline at table in the kingdom of God.
For behold, some are last who will be first,
and some are first who will be last."

TWENTY-SECOND SUNDAY IN ORDINARY TIME

Sirach 3:17-18, 20, 28-29; Hebrews 12:18-19, 22-24a; Luke 14:1, 7-14

God of might, giver of every good gift, put into our hearts the love of your name so that by deepening our sense of reverence, you may nurture in us what is good and by your watchful care keep safe what you have nurtured. Through our Lord Jesus Christ, your Son, who lives and reigns with you in the unity of the holy Spirit, one God for ever and ever. Amen.

The piece of music we just listened to is translated, "This is the day for rejoicing. This is a great celebration." And I want to begin my thoughts with the second reading, from Hebrews, because it seems to me that this author is trying to put us in touch with one of the great mysteries of what it means to be a spiritual person, a person engaged in religion, whose goal—as all religions have the same goal of putting us in touch with God, which is the truth, to be connected to the truth of who God is, who we are. And then to celebrate that union has been described over and over again in scripture as not an examination, a final exam, or a test, but rather a *celebration*—a wedding celebration: people gathered together excited, enthusiastic about the union of two people.

The union that God is *calling* us into is the union with God, with ourselves, with each other. *Connection* is a major, major part of everything that religion is trying to help us to accomplish. So in this reading from Hebrews, we see a contrast. The author is saying, "You're *not* being called by your faith into a place where there's this incredible, high goal of perfection, this blazing fire of goodness, or a place where you're shown that there's this dark, dark, deep abyss that you can fall into. You're not called to a place where somebody's yelling at you all the time, and the more you hear the voice, the more you just wish it would shut up." That's not what we're called to! That's not religion. And then there's the description: We're called to a *celebration*, a *festival*. And the image in this particular passage is so fascinating to me because when it's listing who's there, *we* are there. But it's not we alone, just us here on this earth, but we're gathered together in any kind of experience of the spiritual world in company with this great group of people who are higher, I should maybe say, in terms of their capacity to be in touch with the truth and reality. But it's festive angels—all the angels, all those beings that God has created. We're *surrounded* by them, every moment of every day. And then there are those who are being transformed in the place of continued growth after death. So we have those people who are struggling to grow and become. They are part of us, and they're watching us in our struggles, and they're there to support us. And then we have just this great *sense* that we're part of a group of people that have *made* it, that are on the other side. So it's like—[chuckles] if you can imagine it—it's like you're not just with a group of people who are struggling and frightened of whether they're going to make it or not—this kind of deep, dark, serious place. Or is it a place where we're surrounded by those who have succeeded and they're cheering us on, you know?

It's a *great* image of what it means to be engaged in a spiritual world that cannot be touched—meaning it can't be seen in the way we see the material world, but it's no less real. So we're living in an environment of a whole bunch of beings that are excited, celebrating, saying, "Come on, come on, come on. I'm going to teach you, I'm going to help you. You're on the journey. Come on, come on." I *love* that image!

One of the things that the first reading and the gospel—they're always designed to work together—are focused on today is the whole image of *humility*. And humility is a very interesting image, because it implies that we should think less of ourselves than we tend to. So it's sort of the opposite of pride. The *misconception* is that a humble person is a person who does not ever think that they're that valuable, OK? (That's the over-simplified version.) Because a prideful person just thinks they're the best thing that ever came along. The point is that neither extreme is right.

There's a lot said today about binary thinking, which is the kind of thinking that most of us grew up with in the church and religion, where everything is either/or. It's good; it's bad. It's healthy or it's unhealthy. And we want to categorize things and judge things; and yet so often I think people sometimes think that wisdom is the capacity to judge everything by putting everything in nice, neat categories. Yet that whole notion of "Thou shalt not judge," we tend to think it's just about not thinking something bad about your neighbor; but really, "no judgment" means stop trying to figure everything out. And stop *labeling* everything.

In the first reading, it's trying to say to all of us that anyone who's trying to build themselves up—you have to be really careful of that because the more you do it, the more you're going to be cast down. And those who are cast down . . . You have to be careful. If you cast *yourself* down, you'll be lifted up. It can be pretty tricky! And that's also the message, the theme, of the gospel.

So how are we going to understand all of this? Well, I go back and forth. I don't know if you're like me, but I can be thinking about myself and something can go wrong and somebody can be upset with me and they can say some things to me that are painful, and I can go into what I call *shame*. There's nothing more debilitating than shame. It's the darkest, gloomiest place because there's something in shame that implies not only did I not do the right thing, but there's something intrinsically evil, wrong about *me*. And I've somehow missed the point and failed, and it's really dark. It's the lowest form of consciousness, to be caught in shame. It almost seems that when you have an oversimplified understanding of humility, you think, what God wants us to do is to shame ourselves, to tell ourselves that we're no good; but whenever we happen to start acting in a way that is not real or true, then we may think ourselves *better* than we are.

How do you or how do I make this balance happen? It just seems like it's a constant, fluid kind of thing that's going on. And that gets me to what I am really trying to get across to you and to my heart today. What is it that we're really up to when we're striving to become who God wants us to be? How do we do this? I know people who say, "Well, I know how to do it. I'll think of myself as valueless and no good, and I'm just a no-good person. I'm a sinner, and I just hope for God's mercy. I'll wallow in my broken humanness." [chuckles] And other people are thinking, "No, God just wants me to get myself together, and I have a strong will and a strong mind, and I'm going to put everything in order—not only my life and the drawers in my house. I'm going to live this beautiful kind of pure life, where everything has order and everything is beautiful.

Well, *neither one* of those works, so what are we left with? Let's look at the wisdom of this incredible, fascinating figure, Jesus. He's walking into a party, and he's watching the Pharisees, who certainly were the ones he was most focused on, trying to heal, trying to transform. And I love the way this story starts. Everybody's watching him, and the truth is, no, he's really watching *them*, paying really close attention. I love this part of Jesus as a fully developed human being, that he pays attention to what's really going on. Do you know how few people, or how often we *don't* really pay attention to what's going on? We're living in a way of seeing things, where we see what we *want* to see, hear what we want to hear. We won't look at things that aren't attractive in ourselves or someone we love. It's like really a gift to be able to pay attention, to be *awake*, alert, *conscious*! What a gift, what a gift!

So Jesus is very conscious of what's going on. He's watching these people, and he sees them. He's not filled with judgment against them because they all would *like* to be in the place of honor. One of the shadows of being in any position of authority is that what slips in is the thing we might call *greed*, and if it feels good to be in a position of authority and be over people, then maybe it feels even better to be *the best* of those who are over people. So greed gets in. We fall into that trap of, if one thing makes us happy, then more of that same thing will make us happier.

So these guys are all looking for the moment to get the best, the highest seat in the room. Now you might think that Jesus would say, "Alright. You guys are a bunch of hypocrites. Stop doing this. Everybody should go and sit in the back, and nobody should ever, ever want to sit in the place of honor. It's wrong." He doesn't say that! With a kind of loving, amazing capacity to be sympathetic and understanding, he looks at them. He says, "I know what you're doing. You're trying to get the place of honor so people will see you and think you're really terrific!" And Jesus says, "There's nothing really wrong with you wanting other people to see you as good and valuable. That's *healthy*! Here's my suggestion"—And I think it's so interesting—"you want to look good, right? So here's the plan: Don't take the place of honor that may not quite fit you. Maybe you're needing to be a little below that. Let's say that anytime you're a little inflated about your importance, be careful, because if you're acting in an inflated way, someone, something, is going to come along and expose you, and then you look like a kind of jerk. So here's the deal: Pick the lower place, and then your host comes in and sees you in the lower place, and the room is full. 'Hey,' he says, 'come over here. You belong with me at the main table.' And everybody's going to be impressed, and you'll impress people." [chuckles] It's almost like he's saying, "You want to be important. I'll show you *how* to be important. You're not important because you *choose* to be there; you're important because of who you are. And everyone has a right to the place that is *for* them—their *place*. And that's determined not by you but someone else, by objectivity, by truth. So it's like, you *have* a place of honor. *Everyone* has a place of honor; everyone has a role in this incredible thing called our life. And the important thing is not so much to go around saying, 'I have no role; I have no importance.' No, it's to be in the place where you were meant to be, and to feel the importance of it, but not to be in competition or want to be better or more important than someone else."

And the second part is even *more* interesting to me. Jesus kind of shifts it, and he says, "You know, this is a great dinner party and it's honoring all these people, and everybody that's here is probably looking forward to this event. And then they may feel obligated that they have to do something in return. They feel that now they're at this party, this is going to be a way to increase their awareness; and more people are going to be paying attention to them. They're doing it not just to be at a party where they have their own place, but they're in it for what they're going to get out of it." So Jesus is saying—and I love parables. Remember, these are not advice; they're parables, which means they're mysterious sayings that you have to ponder and wonder about. Now for

Jesus in a parable to say something that makes no logical sense and goes counter to almost everything that's instinctual in us is not unusual at all. He's saying, When you have a party—let's say next Thanksgiving or Christmas—don't invite your family; don't invite your children. They've always come, but don't invite 'em. Go to some other part of town where there are people who are *really* alone. They don't really see much. They don't really understand much. They're blind, they're lame, they're crippled, they're deaf. They're people that are really in need. Go and invite *them*, because then you *will* get a reward. Notice again: "Don't do it for a reward." And then Jesus says, "But I will tell you *how* you can do it for a reward; and the reward you will get in this is that somehow you will know that you are doing the right thing, and there is a great gift in that. And somehow you are engaged in the real work." And what *is* the "real work"? You take your position of authority, you take the role that God has given you. Could be friend, brother, sister, teacher, whatever you're doing. Think about that as the place where you then do the work that is the most gratifying, and that is, in your position you try to be a source of life, hope, wisdom, guidance to those who don't really see, those who don't yet really hear, those who don't really have the capacity to get around, those who can get around a little bit but not very well—the lame—this is what it's all about, finding the place where you belong, feeling good about that place, but in that place you're there not to be served, not to be looked up to as someone important. But it's the place from which you feed, you *feed*.

I know I've been to a lot of dinner parties, a lot of celebrations. And there are two things that I've noticed about them. One is, if I'm the host and I'm putting it together in my house and I love the people who are there and I've cooked the food for them and I'm watching them enjoy it and I'm watching them enjoy each other—there's a kind of special, special joy in that kind of experience of knowing that somehow in this event, there's something really positive flowing around the table, radiating, from the chests, the hearts, of the people there; people are getting something that they long for; you're helping make that happen. It's not happening because you're *doing* it—you're sort of creating the context. Awesome feeling. Awesome! Satisfying. I *go* to parties, and it's also wonderful to be there and have that same experience. But I think we're often in both places, we're often in the place where we're receiving, often in the place when we're feeding and giving. And that's the two places. Both places need to feel comfortable: We know our place, and because we know our work, and those are the things I believe Jesus was so concerned about in the life of the Pharisees, so concerned about it in our lives. "I want you to be proud of who you are, I want you to be satisfied and fed by what you do. And just stay in the party, stay in the festival gathering. Stay with all these incredible figures around you, and then begin to delight in the most amazing, amazing process, and it's just called being fully alive."

Father, help us to understand the way in which you long for us to be engaged in this world that you have invited us into. Help us to feel the celebratory dimension of what it's like to be on this journey of self-discovery, discovering who you are; and be engaged more and more in a process of being a source of life. And we ask this through Christ our Lord. Amen.

Sirach 3: 17-18, 20, 28-29
My child, conduct your affairs with humility,
and you will be loved more than a giver of gifts.
Humble yourself the more, the greater you are,
and you will find favor with God.
What is too sublime for you, seek not,
into things beyond your strength search not.
The mind of a sage appreciates proverbs,
and an attentive ear is the joy of the wise.
Water quenches a flaming fire,
and alms atone for sins.

Hebrews 12: 18-19, 22-24a
Brothers and sisters:
You have not approached that which could be touched
and a blazing fire and gloomy darkness
and storm and a trumpet blast
and a voice speaking words such that those who heard
begged that no message be further addressed to them.
No, you have approached Mount Zion
and the city of the living God, the heavenly Jerusalem,
and countless angels in festal gathering,
and the assembly of the firstborn enrolled in heaven,
and God the judge of all,
and the spirits of the just made perfect,
and Jesus, the mediator of a new covenant,
and the sprinkled blood that speaks more eloquently than that of Abel.

Luke 14:1, 7-14
On a sabbath Jesus went to dine
at the home of one of the leading Pharisees,
and the people there were observing him carefully.

He told a parable to those who had been invited,
noticing how they were choosing the places of honor at the table.
"When you are invited by someone to a wedding banquet,
do not recline at table in the place of honor.
A more distinguished guest than you may have been invited by him,
and the host who invited both of you may approach you and say,
'Give your place to this man,'
and then you would proceed with embarrassment
to take the lowest place.
Rather, when you are invited,
go and take the lowest place
so that when the host comes to you he may say,
'My friend, move up to a higher position.'
Then you will enjoy the esteem of your companions at the table.
For every one who exalts himself will be humbled,
but the one who humbles himself will be exalted."
Then he said to the host who invited him,
"When you hold a lunch or a dinner,
do not invite your friends or your brothers
or your relatives or your wealthy neighbors,
in case they may invite you back and you have repayment.
Rather, when you hold a banquet,
invite the poor, the crippled, the lame, the blind;
blessed indeed will you be because of their inability to repay you.
For you will be repaid at the resurrection of the righteous."

TWENTY-THIRD SUNDAY IN ORDINARY TIME

Wisdom 9:13-18b; Philemon 9:10, 12-17; Luke 14:25-33

O God, by whom we are redeemed and receive adoption, look graciously upon your beloved sons and daughters, that those who believe in Christ may receive true freedom, an everlasting inheritance, through our Lord Jesus Christ, your Son, who lives with you in the unity of the holy Spirit, one God, for ever and ever. Amen.

That piece of music, *Create in me a clean heart,* is something that always touches me deeply because I feel so strongly in my work of wanting to awaken in you this mysterious thing that pumps blood in the center of our bodies, this heart. It is more than an organ that simply moves fluid through our bodies. It is somehow the spiritual center for each of us. And over and over again in scripture, in poetry in so many ways, in music, we hear the heart spoken of as the *core* of who we are. And that core is what a healthy spirituality is always trying to put us in touch with. Who *are* we? What is the core of our being? What do we long for the most? What are we made for?

The opening prayer of this liturgy invited you and me to put ourselves in the hands of God and allow him to give us a gift, and the gift we asked for is *true freedom*. Freedom. I think about my own struggles, my own life, and I think about the things that I long to accomplish. And I often think that the motivation behind the things that I'm called to do, to want to complete them, get them out of the way, get them off the list, whatever, is because I feel that if I just got everything taken care of, then I would be *free*. And yet I'm listening to a prayer in the first reading, and the prayer is a prayer of Solomon. He's just been given a role that is awesome to him. He realizes that he's going to be asked to be the king, and he's going to need wisdom. He's going to need to take care of one thing after another that comes up. He needs to be healthy and strong. And he's realizing something that pleases God so intensely that he says, "This prayer of Solomon is one of the most pleasing prayers I've ever heard. This man understands something. This man knows something that so few understand." And what he *knows* is that somehow he is not called upon to perform at his highest level, as if that would be enough. He somehow knows that there's something beyond *his* capacity to do the work. I believe he sets for me a way of seeing what most of us depend upon. In order to accomplish things, I need to be in a good, clear, healthy state. My body needs to be in a good place. I can't tell you how often when I'm sick—which thank God is not too often—but I know when my body's aching and responding to things I probably don't even realize I'm inflicting on it, and it cries out for relief, I don't have much energy to get the things done that I need to do. And so the body seems to burden me, to hold me back. And then there's the responsibility of taking care of everything I'm supposed to do, and I have to *think* about all the things that I need to do. And so I'm trying to use my brain to take care of everything, to make sure that everything on the list is there, and everything on the list is taken care of. And somehow my mind just gets so filled with one thing after another that my mind just sort of shuts down and I feel such a *burden*. So trying to get things done, trying to be in a good place all the time—this is a tremendous amount of energy we put forth.

And somehow Solomon knows that he's limited by his body, the limitations of his mind, the limitations of time. So then he goes on to say, "I know that you, God, are asking me to be engaged with you in a work of caring for people, and what I need is not just my own physical strength and my own capacity to think things through and figure things out and get them done, but what *you* are asking me to do is to surrender to something that is beyond me." It is called this mysterious thing: *wisdom*. And Solomon is so conscious that only God has the wisdom, the knowledge, to guide a human being through all the things that they're asked to do. Our decisions, as he says, are timid and not sure. Do I do this? Do I not do this? Should I make this decision? Should I not make this decision? And he's saying the only way to do that is not rely upon your body and your mind, but somehow to rely upon a gift. The gift is *Spirit, Wisdom*. And *she*, as he goes on to say, has been engaged in the work from the beginning. And the prayer continues with Solomon talking over and over again about all the times in which the Israelite community was looking like it was about to fail, and it comes back. Every time there was a great disaster, somehow Wisdom is there to use that disaster to bring about greater understanding. And so all of a sudden, Solomon realizes, "O God, don't just make me strong physically. Don't just give me a brain that can figure things out. No, give me wisdom because if I'm going to do this job, and if it's true that we are destined for something much more than this place—that this place we live in, this world we live in, is not everything. It's just a place where we go and stay, to work out all this struggle that we have between dependence on ourselves or dependence on you—boy, I want to be dependent on *you*. I want, Solomon says, to be gifted with this feminine, mysterious, wonderful thing called *wisdom*. It changes us, and it opens in us an awareness that there's something bigger than getting everything done. There's something bigger than having a healthy body or a young body. It's always fascinating to me that God has decided that the best way he can help us through this life is at the end of it is not to make our bodies their strongest and their most beautiful, but to let the body somehow wear out. It's a way of saying to us, this is about not achieving perfection or not getting everything done, because as we get older, we have to deal with imperfection, our bodies aren't able to do as much; we have to realize we can't get as much done. So there's this image at the end of our life where we're continually asked to let go of the work, and for some that's so depressing and dark—because there's nothing else—but what he's asking us to go to then is this mysterious thing called *wisdom.* If there's *anything* that old age is supposed to enable in us, it's the ability to be able to enter into the world of wisdom and to speak it to those who are still struggling, struggling with simply using and relying on their own talent, their own abilities.

So what we need is what old age brings us, what time sometimes brings us—an ability to let go of our dependence on things around us. So when Jesus, as he does in the gospel, shocks everyone with the statement—and I love the way Jesus does this. Parables are always stories that are told that have a secret, so they usually don't make much sense when you read them. And one of the most common mistakes that we make is we take something from them that's literal and we think, "Well, Jesus meant that literally" and very seldom when Jesus speaks does he mean it as literally as we might read someone else's words. Jesus is always inviting us not so much to be taught by him in the *words* that he uses, but to be taught by the Spirit that we need to *interpret* the words that he's given. So we're always needing to go to something that is more than we are, to get in touch with the things that are most essential, the things that when we're in touch with them, when we're *in* them, when we're living according to these mysterious pieces of wisdom, we are going to find the most amazing peace, the most amazing core center of calm.

So Jesus, in this gospel, has a line that is often spoken by Jesus in different contexts, and it's this: Unless you let go of all your possessions, you can't be my disciple. Now remember a disciple means "student, learner, those who listen." You can't really listen to me, you can't really hear me unless you're willing to let go of everything else. Now that does not mean that Jesus is asking you not to have a house, not to have a car, not to have a flat-screen TV. Those things *aren't* what he's talking about. He's talking about the things that we go to, our core possessions that we go to to find value, to find worth, to find a sense of accomplishment. And so he goes to the thing we would need to let go of—and he certainly doesn't mean I'm to let go of my family and my children—I mean those are things I'm responsible for. I have to take care of them. My parents—honor my parents. That's what he told us in the Commandments—honor your parents, take care of them. You can't leave your wife. Your *children*! You can't walk away from an infant, and just not feed them or anything. So he couldn't mean what he's really saying, that you have to *hate* all these people.

It just shakes everybody up. How can I *hate* my parents, my wife, my partner, the people you've given me to love and to be a source of life to them, and they're a source of life to me. What are you *doing* when you say that?

What he's doing is, he's trying to give us a sense that there is a way in which we cannot rely upon our own resources, we can't rely upon our own judgment. Look at the two images he gives you. Let's just say that God, in giving us human nature, gives us our foundation. That's what we're here to accept and to deal with. And unless you're in touch with who you really are as a human being, you're not going to get very far in this spiritual life. You have to *embrace* your humanity. Not the way we'd like it to be; we sometimes think it's a burden and it's awful and it's dirty and it's shameful. Or we think it's perfect and we pretend it's perfect. We can go in either extreme, but the point is, we are human. We have gifts, we have things that we can do, but we're not enough. We're not enough. So he says, "I'll give you that foundation. If you want to build your tower—which is an interesting image—if you're going to become who I want you to be, to stand tall; you want to be seen and be appreciated in a good sense; you want to be loved. If you want to do that, make sure that you understand what it's going to take to do that, because if you're relying upon your own resources—and that's what we tend to do—you're not going to have enough to finish the project. Nobody can make themselves into someone that is *whole*. No one. No practice, no discipline, no diet. Nothing is going to make us whole. We've got to rely upon something that's beyond us, outside of us, this thing called *Spirit*, that makes straight our path—which is another way of saying, "keeps us doing, going, without the deep valleys that are dark, and high mountains that we can't get over." And then he says, "If you're in a battle and you look at the battle and you say, 'Can I handle this with my strength? Is my strength enough?'" Or, "How are you going to deal with this? 'Can I conquer a king who has 20,000 troops if I have 10,000?'" Probably not.

So it's about discernment. You have to be able to see that you're not really enough, and if you're going to have this battle of always trying to get everything in right order and make all the right decisions, if that's your battle, and if you're saying my life would be better if I'd made that decision back then, if I hadn't done this, my life would be better, you know we can go through that war with my humanity, my frail humanity, and this image of perfection, you're *never* going to win it. Make *peace* with everything, make peace with what's real, and your limitations, the fact that you don't fit the nice, neat patterns that you would like to be fit in, or that the world tries to put you in.

So the readings today are so enormously essential for us understanding the work we have here on this earth. It's an amazing work, it's an amazing task to be engaged in this life fully. It's going to bring us more peace than we ever could imagine, but our greatest problem is our possessions, hanging on to things, hanging on to the things we think are going to be the support that we need to be enough, and they're never enough. We're going to use our own wisdom, we're going to read a book and decide how to make a decision—*instead* of this mysterious and most amazing relationship we're asked to make with this feminine dimension that's often called *intuition* when we're experiencing it. This openness and quiet that we need to have in order to be in touch with the most amazing, amazing peace, of marvelous, marvelous wisdom. A strength, an insight, a way of seeing that will enable us to be a *tower*, a man of peace, a woman of peace. Those are the two things that the example seems to point out: to stand tall and to surrender to everything as it is and to allow this mysterious, beautiful, feminine figure to enter into us and hold us and nurture us.

And then we have to *carry* something—the cross—and the cross it seems to me is to carry it when we know that she's there and yet she hasn't manifested herself—to be given the wisdom she's given us—which doesn't make sense to our minds, and have to wait and struggle through it and trust that we're going to make it. Unless we *carry* that, we're not going to be able to get to the place of transformation, new birth, new life, a new heart.

Father, your greatest gift is your longing, your deep desire to share with us the wisdom that only you know—that's beyond our ability to grasp, to figure out on our own, so we ask you to bless us most especially with the ability to be still, to let go of the things that we rely upon, that give us the illusion that we will make it—and listen, listen with our heart to your wisdom, which brings us the peace that is beyond all imagining, and we ask this in Jesus' name. Amen.

Wisdom 9:13-18B

Who can know God's counsel,
or who can conceive what the LORD intends?
For the deliberations of mortals are timid,
and unsure are our plans.
For the corruptible body burdens the soul
and the earthen shelter weighs down the mind that has many concerns.
And scarce do we guess the things on earth,
and what is within our grasp we find with difficulty;
but when things are in heaven, who can search them out?

Or who ever knew your counsel, except you had given wisdom
and sent your holy spirit from on high?
And thus were the paths of those on earth made straight.

Philemon 9: 10, 12-17
I, Paul, an old man,
and now also a prisoner for Christ Jesus,
urge you on behalf of my child Onesimus,
whose father I have become in my imprisonment;
I am sending him, that is, my own heart, back to you.
I should have liked to retain him for myself,
so that he might serve me on your behalf
in my imprisonment for the gospel,
but I did not want to do anything without your consent,
so that the good you do might not be forced but voluntary.
Perhaps this is why he was away from you for a while,
that you might have him back forever,
no longer as a slave
but more than a slave, a brother,
beloved especially to me, but even more so to you,
as a man and in the Lord.
So if you regard me as a partner, welcome him as you would me.

Luke 14: 25-33
Great crowds were traveling with Jesus,
and he turned and addressed them,
"If anyone comes to me without hating his father and mother,
wife and children, brothers and sisters,
and even his own life,
he cannot be my disciple.
Whoever does not carry his own cross and come after me
cannot be my disciple.
Which of you wishing to construct a tower
does not first sit down and calculate the cost
to see if there is enough for its completion?
Otherwise, after laying the foundation
and finding himself unable to finish the work
the onlookers should laugh at him and say,

'This one began to build but did not have the resources to finish.'
Or what king marching into battle would not first sit down
and decide whether with ten thousand troops
he can successfully oppose another king
advancing upon him with twenty thousand troops?
But if not, while he is still far away,
he will send a delegation to ask for peace terms.
In the same way,
anyone of you who does not renounce all his possessions
cannot be my disciple."

TWENTY-FOURTH SUNDAY IN ORDINARY TIME

Exodus 32:7-11, 13-14; 1Timothy 1:12-17; Luke 15:1-32

Look upon us, O God, creator and ruler of all things; and that we may feel the working of your mercy, grant that we may serve you with all our heart, through our Lord Jesus Christ, your Son, who lives and reigns with you in the unity of the holy Spirit, one God for ever and ever. Amen.

I can't tell you how many times people have asked me a question. Perhaps you've asked it yourself. But when they listen to the Old Testament and the New Testament, they often ask, Why is the Old Testament God always so angry and so mean, when the God in the New Testament is so nice? [chuckles] So *forgiving*, so *understanding*! Well, when you sit down and try to figure it out logically, it doesn't work very well. It seems sort of inconsistent. But here's the way I'd like you to imagine an answer.

Look at the beginning of your own spiritual life. Look at those first days when your parents are teaching you right from wrong, and what they are saying to you about when you do something wrong. About the only way they feel they can get your attention and train you is to use some kind of punishment, and even to express some kind of anger or disappointment. That's the way we begin to learn what is right and wrong in terms of following someone who has an insight that *we* don't have. "What's *wrong* with playing in the street? It's *nice*!" You don't see the *danger* of playing in the street, so if you go there, you're going to be punished. You'll understand *that*. You may not understand why it's dangerous, but you'll know that I don't want you to be there, and I need, as a parent who loves you, to express my disapproval, my anger, my desire to get your attention through some kind of limitation, of punishment.

That's the way God began working with us, and when I look back on my own experience of growing up in the Catholic

Church in the 40s and 50s, I know, certainly in the 40s, I was told story after story about this God who had a very strong opinion on one thing, and it was *sin*, and he hated it, and unfortunately I somehow got the message that he also hated the sinner. And they didn't have to *say* that he hated the sinner. What they'd tell me was, If you do the wrong thing, and you felt you *wanted* to do it—you knew it was wrong but you did it anyway—well, there was a punishment that was due to you, and it came from this "loving" God. The punishment was to burn in hell forever! So how could I imagine that that was coming from someone who *cared* about me—because if you were going to inflict that kind of punishment on somebody, the danger is that you would think that that person is filled with *hatred* for me.

So in our own spiritual journey, it seems, we move from a God of punishment and judgment to a God of understanding and compassion. And there is something about that as the *normal* process, and that's why I think we have the process when we look at the Old and New Testament—it's one continuous story about God revealing himself to human beings, and it's *our* journey, so most of us begin with a God who we're afraid of. The tragedy is that some people never get *past* that God, they never get past the God of punishment or judgment. And I think of all the times in my life as a young man when I was thinking—especially as a seminarian and someone who was called to some kind of higher level of spiritual truth—I was probably harder on myself than I would have been had I chosen another profession. But what I found was that when I was really hard on myself, what I was somehow doing was constantly putting myself down and feeling the fact that I was still sinning was somehow *wrong*. It was a mistake that I should have gotten past, I shouldn't be still *caught* in this. [chuckles] I love hearing the confession of people in their 80s saying, "I'm saying the same things. I have the same temptations I had when I was 18." And somehow, I always found that *encouraging*—Oh, good! That means that this business of getting your act together and finding a way to grow out of all your sinfulness is not the goal! But something else is the goal.

And I think the scriptures today give us a great insight, and I want to go to one statement that Paul makes in the second reading, and I love the introduction to the statement. He says, "What I'm going to tell you is really true; it's trustworthy. It's really important that you hear me say this." Now here's a man who spent his life persecuting sinners. Now *sinners* were considered those who didn't *believe* in God, and when Paul says, "I was a blasphemer," a *blasphemer* is one who uses the power of God to do something that God would never *want* to do. So if you ask God to damn someone or to condemn someone, that's a blasphemy. God is not interested in condemning or destroying *anyone*. But we can imagine a God like that when we look at the Old Testament, we can feel justified doing it, and we end up somehow hating ourselves and hating those who fail; so we're all a little bit like St. Paul.

Then something happened to him. He was changed. When he says, "I've been blessed with this change," look at the change! It wasn't something that he woke up one morning and said, "Oh, this is wrong, and I have a loving God. Oh, I see. No more of that. Today, rather than yesterday when I was such a blasphemer and such a bad guy, I'll just be a much better guy now. And that's all fixed." Now look at the story. He's in his job, he's working hard at going around destroying those who wouldn't follow the ways of God. He was arrogant because he had the power to destroy people—that's not good for anybody's ego, especially if you can justify it. So what he's basically saying is, "I went through something that was *really tough*!" He was going along and all of a sudden he's blinded. He can't see at all. It's like a great light; no one knows exactly why he was blinded, but the image is that he was on a journey, so probably he was on a horse or something, falls to the ground—at least that's the way artists depict it. Just imagine the image. He's doing the work that he's always done, and all of a sudden he realizes he didn't understand what he was doing any longer. He's blinded, and then he goes to a place where he's carried and doesn't know where he is because he can't see. Somehow, someone comes to him and begins to help him see, and then he spends three years rethinking his entire life, and *then* he comes out. Now that is what I would call *conversion, transformation*. It's not a nice, neat, easy thing.

So when you look back at the first reading, you see God, who is looking at the Israelite people. And let's take the side of the people for a minute, because the people basically are out there in the desert, and they don't know where they're going. They don't know how they're going to get there. They know they're not in slavery any more, and that's good, but they're not comfortable. So Moses has to go to God and spend time on Mount Sinai. Forty days he's gone. They're waiting to find out, "Where are we going and how are we going to get there?" So they go back to their old ways. Even Aaron, who was second in command, kind of encourages the people. "Well, you know, this *is* tough. Why don't you go back and pray to the gods that you're used to?"

And then God is so furious, so furious, because that is the biggest mistake we can make on this spiritual journey: to go back to the things that didn't really work, but we *thought* they did. And that really alarms God, so he wants our attention. "Don't play on Central Expressway when you're two years old. I'm not neutral on that. I'm not going to be gently saying, 'Don't do it.' I'm going to scream and say, 'You can't do that!'" So you see that they went through a transformation because of the anger of God, and then the story ends with finally God being convinced by Moses that he shouldn't do this. Moses plays on "Don't break your promises; you don't want to look bad," so God relents. But every time he relents, he comes back with a kind of change in him—which is so fascinating!—he almost always, when he gets mad and decides to destroy, he comes back and says, "You know, I'll never do that again."

So there's something about this dynamic of our failures, his disappointment, then somehow a process that we go through with him. Because of his anger and disappointment with us, it takes us to a new place—it's like the beginning of a new level of the relationship. That's the key. That's why the Gospel is filled with this image, over and over, of what Paul is saying, "We're here. God is with us to *change* us."

And the change is finding something that was hidden. The woman who loses the coin, the man who loses the sheep, the beautiful story of the prodigal son. They're all stories about, first, we lose something, we realize that we have somehow missed the mark so intensely—that means we're sinning. So once we see the emptiness or the foolishness of that, or the futility of it, and then we turn to a source that's at first perhaps irritated but then says, "No, I'll work with you in this," and *that's* the work of being a spiritual person. That's the spiritual path: constantly going through that cycle over and over again, until the *anger* of God becomes something quite different—it's his concern, it's his intense interest in the way you are living your life.

He's not neutral on your choices. He delights, in an *amazing* way, when you see something that you didn't see before, when you find that which was lost. That's what it's all about. And then that beautiful image, that everybody in heaven starts cheering every time someone goes through a process of finding an insight.

It means that all those people: angels, all the dead who have gone before us—they're all pulling for us, and that's what we're here for. Not to get it together and then live this perfect life, but to be constantly, over and over again, going through transformation, conversion, new life. He came to save sinners. He came to save the blind, give them sight, give them understanding, and give them wisdom. What a gift and what an incredible, important process to surrender to. *That's* our challenge, surrender to constantly being in that process of transformation, and then we've got it. It's not that it's depressing because you have to keep doing it. It's *exciting*! It's wonderful! It's what God has called us to.

Father, your desire, your intense longing, is to reveal yourself to us, and in that revelation to call us to authenticity, to see things as they are, to know what our choices truly are so that we can be drawn more and more into this place we call the kingdom, a place of freedom, a place of great inner peace. Bless us on this journey, and most especially never let us be discouraged by our faults but know that every time we face one, we have the opportunity to be freed of the illusion that has kept us there. And we ask this in Jesus' name. Amen.

Exodus 32:7-11, 13-14
The LORD said to Moses,
"Go down at once to your people,
whom you brought out of the land of Egypt,
for they have become depraved.
They have soon turned aside from the way I pointed out to them,
making for themselves a molten calf and worshiping it,
sacrificing to it and crying out,
'This is your God, O Israel,
who brought you out of the land of Egypt!'
"I see how stiff-necked this people is," continued the LORD to Moses.
"Let me alone, then,
that my wrath may blaze up against them to consume them.
Then I will make of you a great nation."

But Moses implored the LORD, his God, saying,
"Why, O LORD, should your wrath blaze up against your own people,
whom you brought out of the land of Egypt
with such great power and with so strong a hand?
Remember your servants Abraham, Isaac, and Israel,
and how you swore to them by your own self, saying,
'I will make your descendants as numerous as the stars in the sky;
and all this land that I promised,
I will give your descendants as their perpetual heritage.'"
So the LORD relented in the punishment
he had threatened to inflict on his people.

1Timothy 1: 12-17
Beloved:
I am grateful to him who has strengthened me, Christ Jesus our Lord,
because he considered me trustworthy
in appointing me to the ministry.
I was once a blasphemer and a persecutor and arrogant,
but I have been mercifully treated
because I acted out of ignorance in my unbelief.
Indeed, the grace of our Lord has been abundant,
along with the faith and love that are in Christ Jesus.
This saying is trustworthy and deserves full acceptance:
Christ Jesus came into the world to save sinners.

Of these I am the foremost.
But for that reason I was mercifully treated,
so that in me, as the foremost,
Christ Jesus might display all his patience as an example
for those who would come to believe in him for everlasting life.
To the king of ages, incorruptible, invisible, the only God,
honor and glory forever and ever. Amen.

Luke 15:1-32
Tax collectors and sinners were all drawing near to listen to Jesus,
but the Pharisees and scribes began to complain, saying,
"This man welcomes sinners and eats with them."
So to them he addressed this parable.
"What man among you having a hundred sheep and losing one of them
would not leave the ninety-nine in the desert
and go after the lost one until he finds it?
And when he does find it,
he sets it on his shoulders with great joy
and, upon his arrival home,
he calls together his friends and neighbors and says to them,
'Rejoice with me because I have found my lost sheep.'
I tell you, in just the same way
there will be more joy in heaven over one sinner who repents
than over ninety-nine righteous people
who have no need of repentance.

"Or what woman having ten coins and losing one
would not light a lamp and sweep the house,
searching carefully until she finds it?
And when she does find it,
she calls together her friends and neighbors
and says to them,
'Rejoice with me because I have found the coin that I lost.'
In just the same way, I tell you,
there will be rejoicing among the angels of God
over one sinner who repents."

Then he said,
"A man had two sons, and the younger son said to his father,

'Father give me the share of your estate that should come to me.'
So the father divided the property between them.
After a few days, the younger son collected all his belongings
and set off to a distant country
where he squandered his inheritance on a life of dissipation.
When he had freely spent everything,
a severe famine struck that country,
and he found himself in dire need.
So he hired himself out to one of the local citizens
who sent him to his farm to tend the swine.
And he longed to eat his fill of the pods on which the swine fed,
but nobody gave him any.
Coming to his senses he thought,
'How many of my father's hired workers
have more than enough food to eat,
but here am I, dying from hunger.
I shall get up and go to my father and I shall say to him,
"Father, I have sinned against heaven and against you.
I no longer deserve to be called your son;
treat me as you would treat one of your hired workers."'
So he got up and went back to his father.
While he was still a long way off,
his father caught sight of him,
and was filled with compassion.
He ran to his son, embraced him and kissed him.
His son said to him,
'Father, I have sinned against heaven and against you;
I no longer deserve to be called your son.'
But his father ordered his servants,
'Quickly bring the finest robe and put it on him;
put a ring on his finger and sandals on his feet.
Take the fattened calf and slaughter it.
Then let us celebrate with a feast,
because this son of mine was dead, and has come to life again;
he was lost, and has been found.'
Then the celebration began.
Now the older son had been out in the field
and, on his way back, as he neared the house,
he heard the sound of music and dancing.
He called one of the servants and asked what this might mean.

The servant said to him,
'Your brother has returned
and your father has slaughtered the fattened calf
because he has him back safe and sound.'
He became angry,
and when he refused to enter the house,
his father came out and pleaded with him.
He said to his father in reply,
'Look, all these years I served you
and not once did I disobey your orders;
yet you never gave me even a young goat to feast on with my friends. But when your son returns,
who swallowed up your property with prostitutes,
for him you slaughter the fattened calf.'
He said to him,
'My son, you are here with me always;
everything I have is yours.
But now we must celebrate and rejoice,
because your brother was dead and has come to life again;
he was lost and has been found.'"

TWENTY-FIFTH SUNDAY IN ORDINARY TIME

Amos 8:4-7; 1Timothy 2:1-8; Luke 16:1-13

O God, who founded all the commands of your sacred law upon love of you and of our neighbor, grant that by keeping your precepts we merit to attain eternal life, through our Lord Jesus Christ, your Son, who lives and reigns with you in the unity of the holy Spirit, one God for ever and ever. Amen.

St. Paul, in the second reading, is giving advice, and the advice is very, very basic. He's asking us all to pray, but it's interesting that he asks especially that we pray for people in roles of leadership: kings, those who take over the responsibility of guiding large groups of people. He says it's really good to pray for them because Paul realized something that all of us realize, that the person who's in charge of a place, the person who's overseeing a place, can have a great influence on the way that place *functions*.

And it's so clear to me that when you look at Christianity, the heart of it is that we're to treat each other in a way that is *life-giving*. It's *all* about relationships. And one way that Paul describes what we should be doing for each other is that we should somehow be saving each other—which is another word for *freeing* each other, from those things that would rob us of life, things I go back to all the time, just a way of, for me, explaining that the thing we are so likely to get caught up in is ways of being, ways of thinking, that create in us an excessive amount of fear, or shame, or anger. And we become, in a sense, in *bondage*, in slavery, when we're caught in those activities that keep creating these negative feelings. So to be saved is to be *freed* from that, be released from that.

And also he goes on to say, "Not only to be saved, but somehow also to live in the truth, to *know* the truth." And the truth is so very, very simple when it comes to what religion longs to place in our hearts that is true, and it's this: It's a distinction we get when we understand the truth, between the *clarity* that we understand: the difference between giving life and taking life. And we're always, always challenged to be in this world with the role of being one who bears witness to the reality of the love that God has for each of us as we are, and when we don't have some kind of core sense of the dignity of another person, and we don't understand the joy of giving them something that makes their life better, if that isn't somehow at the core of who we are, all *kinds* of problems arise [chuckles].

When we pray, when God asks us to pray, it is true that he asks us to ask him for things, but when we're asking for the *right* things, what prayer really is, it's a kind of exercise that aligns our will with his, and in a way *reveals* our will, our intention. And whatever we believe, whatever the core truth in us is, I'll guarantee you that whatever that truth is, you're going to see it manifested in our actions. That's the wisdom that Jesus is using as he teaches his disciples when he says, "If you're responsible in little things, you'll be responsible in big things. If you're irresponsible in little things, you'll be irresponsible for big things."

The point is that where our heart is is where you're going to see the source, coming from your heart, of everything that you're doing. And if you're in the world to take as much as you can, you're going to end up so empty. And if your basic intention, if you're paying attention to the rules, the laws of the heart, your attention draws you into a place of awareness. That awareness leads to an *integrity* in your intention. And you're there for others, with the amazing, amazing reality that the more we serve others, the more we're there for others, the richer our life becomes, and the *fuller* our life becomes.

So let's go to the first reading. The reading is a description in the book of Amos of the way in which many people do business. And I'll just use business in the broadest sense, as the way we operate. And sometimes we operate from a business principle that you might say is, How much can we get out of this, and how little do we put in? If we can fix something like the scales or work it out so that we're cheating just a little bit—not too much, just a little bit—then we make even more. And if making more is the goal, if *having* more is the goal, then taking advantage of the poor, those who are not in charge, those who are not able to evaluate what we're doing or judge us for what we're doing, then we end up being more "profitable." [chuckles] *Profit*. What an interesting image! We're in it "for profit." There is a way in which business can be seen as good when it gets as much profit out of what it does as possible. That could be a goal; it could be seen as good business practice. But when that intention of making money is the *highest* goal, getting as much as you can for the things that you offer, then you're in a very dangerous place when it comes to the work, the *business* of being a spiritual being in the world.

So we go to the gospel and we've heard some interesting parables addressed by Jesus in this section of Luke—the prodigal son the other day—and other things that draw us into a kind of *understanding* of the notion that God is forgiving. But what God wants more than anything else is for people to come to *him* and to recognize, accept their poverty and have an experience of God filling them, filling them, giving them things. There's something about that when you're in the experience of receiving so much abundance from God, it's very hard to be in the *business*, which in this gospel passage Jesus uses an interesting phrase to describe: He calls it some kind of wealth that is not healthy wealth. It's a kind of selfish wealth, unholy wealth. It's where we're taking, taking, taking. So what we're looking at is the challenge of the Gospel that Jesus longs to place in the hearts of the Pharisees.

And now he addresses his words to the hearts of his disciples. He's saying, "Look. There's a thing called dishonest wealth, and it's when people are taking too much. I want you to be very careful about this. So listen to this story I'm going to tell you." And he tells a story that doesn't make a lot of sense, because it seems that the story is condoning someone who is cheating someone. But listen to the major shift that's in this man. The man we're talking about is the man who works for his master. He's been cheating his master, getting as much profit from his job as he possibly can, using dishonest means to get more profit. The boss finds out about it and says, "Alright, you're being fired." And the man says to himself, "Now what am I going to do?" And he knows it himself: "I'm really not strong enough to dig ditches, and I really don't want to beg. I know what I'll do! I'll call in my master's customers, and instead of taking from them, like I just took from my master and lost my job, I'm going to *give* to them." So he makes this shift between taking, and now giving. So he's the giver, and he calls in the people who owe his master, and he gives them a 50% discount, a 20% discount, and they all say, "Wow, this guy is *giving* us something, giving us something. This is amazing. He is dear to us. We welcome him." So it's easy to see why Jesus would look at this and say, "It may be that the guy was doing the wrong thing. He was cheating his master in order to give to someone, but he made a major shift. He made a shift from seeing his life being taken care of by *taking* from others to seeing his life being taken care of by *giving* to others."

And that's what Jesus is trying to point out. This is smart. Make friends for yourselves with what you do and who you are. Friends. I haven't been cheated lately, that I know of, but you know when someone overcharges you or does something to you, you feel violated, you feel justified in being really angry. There's something basic in human nature that says human beings are not supposed to take advantage of other human beings. There's something just *basic* about it. And yet people think it's a way of *winning*. It's a way of getting what you want. And what they're perhaps not realizing, and what Jesus *wants* us all to realize is that, "Look. The only thing that's going to get you into the place of truth and the place of peace and free you from the shame and the anger and the fear that we get caught up in is good, solid relationships, living in community, living in a place where there's a flow of life between you and the people around you." That's what God, in the person of Jesus, is so interested in creating. He wants us to experience this thing called the *kingdom*. So often when Jesus will say a rich man cannot enter into the kingdom, he's not saying a rich man is going to go to hell. He's just saying a rich man—that's not necessarily that a rich man *has* money—that doesn't determine the category of "rich." It's really the person who's used dishonest means to get his riches, and is not interested at all in being a source of life as much as he or she is interested in taking life from others—taking, taking, taking.

So that's the image that Jesus is using. "If you're in that place of wanting and taking and you think that the things you're getting are going to bring you the gifts that we call the kingdom, a place of peace and happiness and fullness, you're just caught in an illusion that's never going to work." So it's so interesting, when you look at the teaching of a true religion, it's always giving you some kind of really practical way to live, where when you're living in the way religion asks you to live, you're binding yourself with others in a healthy relationship and there's a flow that happens between you that is so satisfying. That's the key of all religions. And it's so sad when you see the religion or an individual or a business, thinking "No, if I can just *take* from people." What's interesting about religion is if it becomes moralistic, and I think it's pretty easy to see that many churches become too moralistic, and in fact, the holy Father this week gave a beautiful interview where he shared his concern about a church that can become too moralistic, where the whole thrust and voice of the church ends up being moral dictates: Don't do this; do this; don't do this; do this—as if that's the litmus test for what a good, strong follower of the redeemer of the world looks like. He's one that is morally straight.

And yet we know, we have an understanding of human nature that when you are evaluated by your actions, you're being cheated. Something's being taken from you. What's being taken from you is the dignity that's there, the beauty that's there, the *person* who's there. That's what needs to be honored and recognized and *fed*, but it all filters *through* your actions, so if you're doing something that's wrong or have done something that's wrong, if that's an excuse not to be connected to that person, well, you can see how that becomes such a caricature of what Jesus is teaching—because Jesus says, "My biggest teaching is forgiveness." Forgiveness is seeing past our faults, overlooking them, not focusing on them, and always going to the heart of who we are. What an incredible place to be, in a community of people—whether it's two of you, ten of you, a hundred of you—where the core issue that keeps us connected is a deep recognition, acceptance, and awareness of the beauty of every human being—no matter what their actions are. Separating the essence from that which we sometimes *feel* is the essence, which is their *be-*

havior. Behavior is something that is very complex. And I'm not saying that someone can do horrible things and they're not a horrible person. Well, I *am* kind of saying that! So excuse me. They're *not* a horrible person. They're a person with dignity and beauty who's doing horrible things. And if you're saying the horrible things that you do are who you are, well then there's something really wrong with that.

So what Jesus is trying to do is create in his disciples—and that's who he's speaking to in this story—he wants them to have the same heart that Jesus himself has, that God has, this burning, loving heart that longs to do the work that is so core to who we are. The work of loving, the work of affirming, the work of acknowledging goodness and beauty.

And if a person has been abused and used in some way that violates their *person,* the damage is beyond anything that we can imagine. And isn't it sad that the church often comes across as someone who is violating another human being's dignity, by implying that it's not there, that it's somehow gone. So when they're judged, they're treated as if they're valueless. And when one is abused in some way, that is when the feeling is "I'm a piece of nothing. I'm not worth anything. The person who did this to me doesn't see any value in me, disregards my value, and maybe that's because I'm *not* valuable." And that's the *last* thing our savior wants anyone to feel. We *are* valuable, we are beautiful. We are all he created us to be. That's the *core* of who we are. And we need to work on what we do.

Father, you have made us all rich. We are all endowed with gifts that are your reflection in each of us. Bless us with a deep respect for who we are, who everyone else is around us so that we have a very, very real awe and reverence for everything you've created. And let us never take advantage of anyone and always be there to enhance and enrich that which you've created. And we ask this in Jesus' name. Amen.

I'd like to dedicate this program with a very special dedication. One of my loyal listeners asked me to dedicate this program to one who dedicated a program earlier this year. And what impressed him about this young woman, very young, when she made this dedication, she did it with an intention of it being a blessing to someone that she loved, someone that she honored, someone that she wanted God's grace to enter into. And so this loyal listener, who's dedicated this program to her, just wants to honor her faith, honor her trust in God, and to in a sense very much, I think, dedicate this program to all young people, our young listeners whose hearts are open to all that God longs to teach them.

Amos 8: 4-7
Hear this, you who trample upon the needy
and destroy the poor of the land!
"When will the new moon be over," you ask,
"that we may sell our grain,
and the sabbath, that we may display the wheat?
We will diminish the ephah,
add to the shekel,
and fix our scales for cheating!
We will buy the lowly for silver,
and the poor for a pair of sandals;
even the refuse of the wheat we will sell!"
The LORD has sworn by the pride of Jacob:
Never will I forget a thing they have done!

1 Timothy 2: 1-8
Beloved:
First of all, I ask that supplications, prayers,
petitions, and thanksgivings be offered for everyone,
for kings and for all in authority,
that we may lead a quiet and tranquil life
in all devotion and dignity.
This is good and pleasing to God our savior,
who wills everyone to be saved
and to come to knowledge of the truth.
For there is one God.
There is also one mediator between God and men,
the man Christ Jesus,
who gave himself as ransom for all.
This was the testimony at the proper time.
For this I was appointed preacher and apostle
— I am speaking the truth, I am not lying —,
teacher of the Gentiles in faith and truth.

It is my wish, then, that in every place the men should pray,
lifting up holy hands, without anger or argument.

Luke 16: 1-13
Jesus said to his disciples,
"A rich man had a steward

who was reported to him for squandering his property.
He summoned him and said,
'What is this I hear about you?
Prepare a full account of your stewardship,
because you can no longer be my steward.'
The steward said to himself, 'What shall I do,
now that my master is taking the position of steward away from me?
I am not strong enough to dig and I am ashamed to beg.
I know what I shall do so that,
when I am removed from the stewardship,
they may welcome me into their homes.'
He called in his master's debtors one by one.
To the first he said,
'How much do you owe my master?'
He replied, 'One hundred measures of olive oil.'
He said to him, 'Here is your promissory note.
Sit down and quickly write one for fifty.'
Then to another the steward said, 'And you, how much do you owe?'
He replied, 'One hundred kors of wheat.'
The steward said to him, 'Here is your promissory note;
write one for eighty.'
And the master commended that dishonest steward for acting prudently.
"For the children of this world
are more prudent in dealing with their own generation
than are the children of light.
I tell you, make friends for yourselves with dishonest wealth,
so that when it fails, you will be welcomed into eternal dwellings.
The person who is trustworthy in very small matters
is also trustworthy in great ones;
and the person who is dishonest in very small matters
is also dishonest in great ones.
If, therefore, you are not trustworthy with dishonest wealth,
who will trust you with true wealth?
If you are not trustworthy with what belongs to another,
who will give you what is yours?
No servant can serve two masters.
He will either hate one and love the other,
or be devoted to one and despise the other.
You cannot serve both God and mammon."

TWENTY-SIXTH SUNDAY IN ORDINARY TIME

Amos 6:1a, 4-7; 1Timothy 6:11-16; Luke 16:19-31

O God, who manifests your almighty power, above all, by pardoning and showing mercy, bestow, we pray, your grace abundantly upon us, and make those hastening to attain your promises, heirs to the treasures of heaven; and we ask this through our Lord Jesus, your Son, who lives and reigns with you in the unity of the holy Spirit, one God for ever and ever. Amen.

The stories that Jesus uses to teach are amazing. And they're designed to confuse the listeners and to ask *them* to see if they can figure out what it is that Jesus is trying to teach them. It's interesting because, in a way, there's a process going on where the answer that you come to, once you work through the problems of the story, somehow makes the answer that you find much more *yours* than if he just gave you the straight answer.

Now one of the things that we know about human nature is that the heart of our dilemma on this earth is our ego's need for autonomy and our separation from things that we might think that we need or are told that we need, and somehow becoming self-sufficient. And the ego *loves* that, and there's a part of all of us that enjoys that kind of strength of being able to handle things on our own. But the truth is, we've come into this world and the reason we're here is to engage with a power beyond ourselves, divine power, and when we're engaged with that divine power, we use our own creativity, our own uniqueness, and our own special gifts *connected* with this mysterious power called divinity dwelling in us, and together it's the perfect *companionship*; it's the perfect *partnership*. And when we look at the description that God gives us in Christianity of what that partnership involves, it involves something much more than just our relationship with God. It includes not only a relationship with God, but a relationship with each other, a relationship with the world, a relationship with *everything* that God has created. And the danger is that sometimes people will use their connection with God, and they will use that connection in a way that gives them a sense of autonomy from the world around them or from other people. There are stories of people who claim to love God with all their heart and all their mind and all their soul, and they can't *stand* human beings! [chuckles] And what St. John said, "If you do that, you're a liar. You can't love God and not love everyone around you, everything he's created."

So if we look at that as the core issue, autonomy versus union, then let's look at the religion at the time that Jesus walked the earth, and the Jewish religion—many of us think that the Jewish religion was one common, simple, universal acceptance of the truth—that there's no one religion that has that kind of uniformity in its believers. Yet there were three different sects, three different divisions, you might say, in Judaism, that were in a sense partly in different sects, but they represent three different ways that people fundamentally responded to God and to their human nature. When you look at denominations in our own present world, you'll find that each one somehow has something that the others don't have, that kind of reminds us of the broad teaching of our God, of different ways of interpreting it. And there's something *healthy* about multiple religions, in that sense; and traditions kept alive in each religion. But there still is the work of finding the *core* in *all* of them. And that's what Jesus was trying to do with the three sects that were there. There were the Pharisees, the Sadducees, and the Essenes. They were the three groups. I can describe them very simply. The Sadducees were the priestly class. They were the elite, they were the rich. They had strong political power. They're the ones that performed all the sacrifices in the temple. How about this? They were the priests that would appease God with your sacrifice, appease God's anger at your sins, but they were also the ones that collected your taxes. (How's that for a conflict of interest?)

Then the Pharisees were more like Judaism's blue-collar workers. They were the ordinary folks, the ones that basically didn't believe just in the letter of the Law. It was the Sadducees who were so very conservative. And the Pharisees were the ones that were probably the strongest and the most important in the long term. And then the Essenes were this strange kind of spiritual sect that was completely disgusted with both the Pharisees and the Sadducees—at least with their "shadow." And they went out in the desert and were mostly celibate, and they had their own kind of spiritual way of seeing things. They were sort of like the hippies, like "new-agers," that kind of people. And that's where John the Baptist was trained, and many people think Jesus went to the Essene communities.

One thing about these three different sects. One sect, the Sadducees, did not believe at all that there was any afterlife, there was no such thing as reward and punishment *after* life. And that's because it was never mentioned in the Torah. They were the very conservative, literal followers of the Torah. All right. So let's just say that there's a little of all of that in the audiences of Jesus, and the Pharisees were the most common ones, the most important ones. So a lot of times, he's addressing the Pharisees. (Sometimes he mentions Sadducees.) So let's just imagine his audience is filled with this particular aspect he wants to teach them in the story. There's a little bit of it in all of them, and it's this idea that there's no afterlife, and God is a God of justice, and the only way that you can understand justice is that the people who are bad have a really rotten time in this world, and the people who are good have a *great* time in this world. And that was kind of the way they thought.

And what it led to was the most debilitating disposition of separating yourself from those who were struggling, those who were in pain, those who were sick—seeing them as victims of their own stupid mistakes—you had no responsibility for them, and you stayed in a state of complete complacency. And that's what the first reading, from one of the earliest prophets, Amos, started screaming at the Israelite people. "You are so complacent. You don't *care* what's happening to anybody else. All you care about is yourself. You have no compassion, no empathy, no understanding of another person's pain." That's what this story is all about—*that* disposition.

So the rich man is not necessarily someone who has money. That's not the main thing. The "rich man" is the man who thinks that he's done everything right and he is completely self-satisfied. That's what it means to be complacent. "I'm just so happy with who I am and what I'm doing. I'm perfect." And then Lazarus represents the poor. But if you look at the two, what you're recognizing is, it seems to me, that Lazarus (it's an interesting name because that's the man Jesus was going to bring back to life), he's at the gate of the rich man, and he had no one to comfort him. And the rich man is the person, whether they're rich or poor in terms of money, who simply has no feeling or compassion for anyone else. What's interesting, I think, in the story—remember the story that Jesus used about the woman who said, "I need your help." And she was not a Jew. She was Gentile, and he said, "How can I throw what I'm here to give to my people, the Jews, just throwing it to you, it's like throwing it to the dogs." And her response was, "Even the dogs eat the scraps." "Dog" might be a very cutting thing to say of a human being, as it would be today, but notice that the only one who's compassionate to this figure Lazarus is the dog. Isn't that wonderful? A dog is coming and taking care of Lazarus while the rich man walks right by. What a great comparison!

So what Jesus is trying to say, to all of us, is we have to be careful to never imagine that Christianity has something to do with "just me." "Me and God, the two of us. I'm in love with him. He takes care of me. I do what he wants me to do." And if you're saying what he wants me to do is follow the rules, the laws, the moral rules and laws, do all the things that you're called to do as a Christian: Go to church, contribute, get involved in some kind of social ministry. But you still might miss the point that the real heart of Christianity is about growing a heart that is filled with compassion, empathy. I've said to you many times that *empathy* didn't exist as a word before 1912. *Compassion* has been around forever, and they mean something similar, but *empathy* is that capacity to actually experience and feel what someone is going through. And I don't know if you've ever noticed it, but some people can just look at someone in pain and suffering and they find it rather curious, maybe interesting, and "Gee, I wonder what that would be like"—with no sense of what the other person is *feeling,* what pain they're in. Women are much more compassionate than men by nature, but even in men and women there are different degrees of compassion. But it's so important to know that whenever you think about being a follower of the God of Israel, the God of Christianity, the God of every religion: When you see people abusing other people in the name of religion, you know there's something radically wrong, radically off center.

So here's this amazing story, and what I would love to do, and I think about this so often when I listen to Jesus tell a story like this—and you always have to check and see who he's talking to—here it's the Pharisees, not his disciples. So here he is, talking to them, and what he's really trying to point out to them is something that they probably are not conscious of, and that is this thing—I'll call it an infection, a kind of disease that takes over our heart, and it becomes weak, it doesn't feel, it doesn't intuit what another person is going through, and it doesn't have this wonderful capacity that God has created in us—and this is why we're here; this is why we're promised that God's divinity will breathe on us and come into us, and then we'll be this source of consolation and love and help to the people around us. And that's the only thing that really makes us happy. It's amazing how *core* that is in us, and when someone is not able to do that or has no desire to do it, nor even an awareness of what someone else is going through, you know there's something really, really out of balance.

So what I would say is that this story is primarily about awakening the heart, awakening the heart. Making it conscious. And you know sometimes we think of consciousness as being very attentive to everything. Like I'm conscious of what's going on, I'm planning for the future, I've thought it all through, I have a great awareness of everything I did in the past, so I'm very conscious. But consciousness doesn't really have to do with this kind of *compassionate* consciousness; it doesn't have much to do with the past or the future. It has everything to do with the capacity to be connected to what's in front of you, right here, right now, in this moment. It all happens in this present moment. So Jesus is saying to these people, "You all have fallen into the trap of giving yourself an excuse for not feeling compassion. You have been invited, by the way you imagine religion, to be *caught* in this thing." When I think about that, it's rather terrifying because it means actually people will create in religion a way that they can give in to what you might say is the lower part of human nature [chuckles], selfishness, self-centeredness, self-sufficiency. And they create a whole *theology* around it so that they're very *comfortable*.

So it means we *have* to be, in every religion, no matter what denomination, we have to be constantly working on the personal task of figuring out what it's really all about. Anyone who just looks to their religion to be this only source of what they are *receiving* from God makes a terrible mistake—because they're missing the thing that is at the heart of the ministry of Jesus. What I think Jesus did, more than anyone before him, or after him, is he kept pushing this one continuous theme: "You can't do this work alone. You have to do it connected to my Father. My Father's in me; I'm in my Father; and you can be in me, and we can be in the Father. The Father and I can be in you; the Spirit will radiate out of you." All that language—so essential, so powerful in its effectiveness of getting us into the place not simply where we're *supposed* to be, but the place where our very nature is *designed* to be.

When I say that my work is trying to free you from excessive fear, excessive anger, excessive shame, I *mean* that in the sense that if you see these truths that I find in the story, if you understand the core of what we're about, and you can *allow* that to happen to you—not *make* it happen, but *allow* it to happen to you—something radically changes. And you walk in a room and you are different, and people begin to *feel* it. And if they didn't know you before and they see you, they just say, "You know, there's something about that person I really enjoy being with." What a *gift*, to be able to be a source of life, a source of comfort. Not having to figure out what the problem is. You're just in a disposition where you are open, and desiring, to heal, strengthen, to support anyone in pain.

Father, your invitation always carries with it the promise of union, communion, connection. Bless us with hearts that are open to be transformed, to be awakened, to be engaged in your Spirit's work of healing and caring for and loving the world that you so deeply love. And we ask this through Christ our Lord. Amen.

Amos 6: 1a, 4-7
Thus says the LORD the God of hosts:
Woe to the complacent in Zion!
Lying upon beds of ivory,
stretched comfortably on their couches,
they eat lambs taken from the flock,
and calves from the stall!
Improvising to the music of the harp,

like David, they devise their own accompaniment.
They drink wine from bowls
and anoint themselves with the best oils;
yet they are not made ill by the collapse of Joseph!
Therefore, now they shall be the first to go into exile,
and their wanton revelry shall be done away with.

1 Timothy 6: 11-16
But you, man of God, pursue righteousness,
devotion, faith, love, patience, and gentleness.
Compete well for the faith.
Lay hold of eternal life, to which you were called
when you made the noble confession in the presence of many witnesses.
I charge you before God, who gives life to all things,
and before Christ Jesus,
who gave testimony under Pontius Pilate for the noble confession,
to keep the commandment without stain or reproach
until the appearance of our Lord Jesus Christ
that the blessed and only ruler
will make manifest at the proper time,
the King of kings and Lord of lords,
who alone has immortality, who dwells in unapproachable light,
and whom no human being has seen or can see.
To him be honor and eternal power. Amen.

Luke 16: 19-31
Jesus said to the Pharisees:
"There was a rich man who dressed in purple garments and fine linen
and dined sumptuously each day.
And lying at his door was a poor man named Lazarus, covered with sores,
who would gladly have eaten his fill of the scraps
that fell from the rich man's table.
Dogs even used to come and lick his sores.
When the poor man died,
he was carried away by angels to the bosom of Abraham.
The rich man also died and was buried,
and from the netherworld, where he was in torment,
he raised his eyes and saw Abraham far off

and Lazarus at his side.
And he cried out, 'Father Abraham, have pity on me.
Send Lazarus to dip the tip of his finger in water and cool my tongue,
for I am suffering torment in these flames.'
Abraham replied,
'My child, remember that you received
what was good during your lifetime
while Lazarus likewise received what was bad;
but now he is comforted here, whereas you are tormented.
Moreover, between us and you a great chasm is established
to prevent anyone from crossing who might wish to go
from our side to yours or from your side to ours.'
He said, 'Then I beg you, father,
send him to my father's house, for I have five brothers,
so that he may warn them,
lest they too come to this place of torment.'
But Abraham replied, 'They have Moses and the prophets.
Let them listen to them.'
He said, 'Oh no, father Abraham,
but if someone from the dead goes to them, they will repent.'
Then Abraham said, 'If they will not listen to Moses and the prophets,
neither will they be persuaded if someone should rise from the dead.'"

TWENTY-SEVENTH SUNDAY IN ORDINARY TIME

Habakkuk 1:2-3, 2:2-4; 2Timothy 1:6-8, 13-14; Luke 17:5-10

Almighty, ever-living God, who in the abundance of your kindness surpass the merits and the desires of those who entreat you, pour out your mercy upon us, to pardon what conscience dreads and to give what prayer does not dare to ask, through our Lord Jesus Christ, your Son, who lives and reigns with you in the unity of the holy Spirit, one God for ever and ever. Amen.

God is big! [chuckles] God is great. God is so strong, so powerful he can do *anything*. And what strikes me is that there is a paradox in all of that, because when you look at the way the world is, if he is so great and so powerful, why does he allow things to happen that are happening? Why is there so much strife? Why is there so much discord? Why can't things be settled and solved? Why is there so much pain? That's the very question that is posed to God in the Old Testament, in our first reading. What's interesting is the *answer*! And I want to try to explain, as best I can, what this set of readings is trying to lay out for us because it seems that it's so crucial. It's one of those teachings that really does go to the heart of how we see our God and how we see the world in relationship to this God.

He basically is saying that what you have to do is put up with all this stuff, and the way you put up with it—things not being the way you want (the violence, the discord, the pain, the suffering)—you put up with it with the recognition that there is something hidden in everything, something there that is all about holding on to the vision. What is "holding on to the vision"? Well, it seems that it's about something that God has promised from the very beginning. When he called the Israelite people, he said something so clear, so precise. He said, "Look, I love you. You are mine. You are my people. I will be there for you forever. I am your partner, I am your savior. I am the one who will take care of you forever."

Now if we believe, have faith in God, that means we believe what he says and most especially what he promises. So in that vision, we have a God who says, "I am taking care of you, and nothing can harm you." There's a very famous statement when Jesus is talking to his disciples and he's telling them that they will experience these very things that this first reading points out: suffering, persecution. And he uses rather strong language. He says, "They can do all *kinds* of things to you. They can boil you in oil; they can do all kinds of horrible, painful things to you. But let me tell you something: No one can harm you." "No one can harm you." Hello! Sounds like harm to me!

There's something in the way God imagines the world and the way he invites us to imagine it that there is something going on that is constantly there for us, constantly being there to take care of us and bring us into a place of great peace in the midst of everything that isn't as it should be. Well, *that's* hopeful! And that's *helpful*.

But there's one more stage I think you have to go through to understand fully what God is trying to teach us today; and that is, he's not only saying, "I will somehow allow all these things, though they are difficult and painful, not to harm *you*," meaning the core of you that he's created, the *you* that's eternal. But he's also going to *use* those things to somehow strengthen the *you* that he's created, the *you* that you are, the *you* that's eternal. So that *everything*—the promises, the vision—not only are we not going to be, the core of us, harmed; we're going to be strengthened, developed, and *deepened* by these experiences of pain and suffering. It's the great *mystery* of pain and suffering—that it actually has value. And yet when you're going through it, to see it as a value, to see it in a way, not to say there's no pain—that doesn't work, because if it's not painful, then it's not going to be very effective.

So when you or I are in a situation where we're really feeling stressed and pushed and like, "Where are you, God? And what's going on?" Those are times you should realize that there's something going on that frightens you, that causes you some stress—and that's stress and fear. A certain amount of it is alright. But what you realize somehow, deep inside of you, holding the vision, core inside, is a thing called your *faith*, your *belief*.

And there it is in the gospel, the most interesting statement about faith. Jesus is worried about his disciples. He's worried about whether they're going to be able to do what he's called them to do. He wants them so much to be ready for the persecutions and the difficulties, and at the same time he wants them so much to feel the peace that he longs for them to have in their heart, and he says, "The key is, you have to have faith." So the natural answer that all of us might have when we feel the pain and suffering, and we feel the doubt, we just say, "Make my faith stronger. Give me greater faith." And the answer is so interesting: "You don't need *more* faith. It's not a case of more or less faith. You simply have to have faith." So what *is* this thing that Jesus is talking about when he says, "If you *have* it, even the tiniest, tiniest piece of it, you have *all* of it." And what it is is this amazing capacity that you have to be an instrument, with God's help, to be in God and God in you in some way, and you're going through these situations and the impossible is possible. *The impossible is possible*—that's what faith is. It's not simply a belief that God exists; it's not even a belief, in a way, that God's promises are real. Those are things that faith includes, but the heart of it is to absolutely believe that when you see something that looks one way, when you experience it in one way, when your brain tells you it's something in one way, it can be just the opposite. It can be totally different. That's what it means to have faith.

So listen to the image. It's kind of weird: If you have the faith the size of a mustard seed, you can say to a tree, which has no power to move itself, you say, "OK, tree, I want you to do this. I want you to move out of the ground, get all your roots out of there, and I want you to go into the ocean and plant yourself in the bottom of the sea. And the thing at the bottom of the ocean that's going to keep you alive is really not there, but *grow* there!" [chuckles] A tree can't move and a tree can't live in the bottom of the ocean. Now how can you believe that? It seems so ridiculous to believe that a tree can do that, or if I really sat down and said, "I want to move this mountain; I want to move this chair; I want to move this situation, you know?" I don't experience my faith in that kind of way, but I *do* experience my faith when my mind tells me "No," and my heart tells me "Yes." When my mind says, that's not possible, that this situation that I'm in is really *for* me when everything about it seems to be everything that I don't want, I *know* that my faith has the capacity to give me the ability to go to that place of absolute, mysterious surrender, submission, and the word I love so much: *allowing.* I can allow all this to happen. I can allow the impossible to happen.

Now look at this as the task that we have in the world, the task that we have. There's a wonderful story that I always love using because it's a story really about how joyous God is when we *allow* him to come into us, when we answer his call that says, "Come and dwell with me. Let me dwell in you." The story, you remember, it's a man who comes and knocks on a door and the door is locked from the inside; and the person inside, who serves the master, opens the door, and you come in. So he's doing a servant's work, doing a servant's work. Then what happens is when the master comes in and the servant has opened the door and lets the master in, the master is so thrilled and so happy that what he does is, he sits the servant down and he creates a meal for him. The master puts on an apron and does everything a servant would do. So that's the image of God as the one who *longs* to serve us. We have a God who is a servant God. But at the *same* time, we have a responsibility to serve *him*. And the serving of him has something to do with the ability that we have to engage ourselves in the work that he's asked us to do—without resistance, without resentment, without doubt, without excessive fear or anger or shame. We need to *give in* to what we're called to do, and that's our work. Anyone who says, "I'm doing something really extraordinary. Wow! I'm so amazing, and it's hard work to do this, and I'm doing it for my God." Don't expect some kind of reward, because that's the job, that's the work. Simply allow the things to be as God has allowed *them* to be, knowing that somehow his promise, the vision he's given us is that in that action of his working the world out the way it is being worked out and our acceptance of that—*that's* the connection; that's the beauty of the relationship.

Now I want to add one more thing, that's a little bit tricky, but one might say, "Does that mean that God created all these situations, bad situations, particularly so that it helps each of us?" No, he doesn't will that these things exist, but here's his problem: God is the God of allowing. Richard Rohr talks about that. God is the God of allowing. And that means that we have been given free will, and when a person decides to do something that causes pain in someone else, God will not step in and take the freedom he *gave* to that person, to choose to do right or wrong, to choose to be with him or against him, he will not take that away. Now think about that. What does God do when he is watching human beings abuse and destroy each other. How do you imagine that God is sitting back and saying, "Well, that is just the way it is; I gave them free will." And I know this might be hard, but if you listen attentively to the Old Testament, you see so many ways in which God is depicted with the same kind of emotions that *we* have. Now what does a parent feel when their child chooses to do things that harm them or harm other people? There's a deep pain in those parents; there's a deep longing for some kind of change. I love images that people have given me. When God sees someone doing violence to another, God weeps! Or when he sees violence that is so awful, you could say that maybe he screams out. And I don't know if that fits your image of God, but it's fitting the image that I have of God now—it's not the same image I had when I began my work fifty years ago, but it's an image of a lover who is struggling with relationships, and the relationships—he does not have power over them. That's just the most amazing thing that God has done. He has created human beings and given them the power to say no. What an incredible thing! That he actually did that, and then in the midst of doing that and thinking that—actually, the God of the Old Testament shows over and over again that there are ways in which God gets so angry at human beings for failing to do what they're supposed to do that he, you know, seems to want to destroy them. You remember that the Old Testament is based on justice, and so many people in the Old Testament did not believe in an afterlife, so if there was justice to be meted out, it had to be meted out in *this* world. That was the God of justice; that was the system of justice in the Old Testament, but God never punishes, God never intends to harm anybody. If he allows anything to get worse in their life, it's because he wants that experience of the pain that they're in to be the source of getting them out of where they are that's *causing* the pain.

So we have this God who has this extraordinary capacity for love. He wants to enter into us. He wants to be a part of us. And his power, when we allow it to be in us is so amazing and so awesome that you really need to believe, you need to believe that this power can do *anything*, anything! And you don't have to know how, you don't even have to see it to know that it's happening. That's what I like about this image of faith. It is a core of our being. You know, I use this image often about faith. There's something about believing that something is going to happen, or we're waiting for something to happen, waiting for something to happen. But you're not sure that it *is* going to happen. And there's something about waiting for something that you know it *will* happen. Very, very different. One takes patience. The other one takes and needs *faith*, but without faith, it leads one to waiting with the expectation at times that this is useless, and it's not going to work, and why am I even doing this? That's the thing that we *cannot* have in our relationship with the power of God that he's promised to share with you and me. If we limit that power of God in any way, then probably it won't happen, or maybe it can't happen. But that "it can't" is the mistake. Maybe God chooses not to use the power the way *you* want him to use it. All right. That's different. But when you are in a situation of stress and difficulty, and you say to yourself, "I *know*, I know that I cannot be harmed; I know that if there's something that needs to be done for the good of myself and everyone around me because we're all connected and it's never about just ourselves; it's about all of us. If I can believe that this God will not let anything negative or harmful happen to *any* of us, without protecting us with something that is amazing, amazing power that comes into us— *that's* what faith is about. It's really an amazing, unique disposition in the world. And people who have it *look* different, they seem different, they seem younger, they seem more alive because they have this core, beautiful center piece that no one can take away from them. And they *know* they're right; they *know* that they're cared for. They absolutely know that they're loved. That's the key.

Father, you tell us that faith is a gift. Our life is a gift. Everything that you do is intended by your heart to be something that is <u>*for*</u> *us. Bless us with that confidence, that faith, that trust that you have everything in your hands; and that all that is unfolding is somehow part of a picture that will bring us all to a place of peace, oneness, unity, and joy; and we ask through Christ our Lord. Amen.*

Twenty-seventh Sunday in Ordinary Time

Habakkuk 1:2-3, 2:2-4
How long, O LORD? I cry for help
but you do not listen!
I cry out to you, "Violence!"
but you do not intervene.
Why do you let me see ruin;
why must I look at misery?
Destruction and violence are before me;
there is strife, and clamorous discord.
Then the LORD answered me and said:
Write down the vision clearly upon the tablets,
so that one can read it readily.
For the vision still has its time,
presses on to fulfillment, and will not disappoint;
if it delays, wait for it,
it will surely come, it will not be late.
The rash one has no integrity;
but the just one, because of his faith, shall live.

2 Timothy 1: 6-8, 13-14
Beloved:
I remind you, to stir into flame
the gift of God that you have through the imposition of my hands.
For God did not give us a spirit of cowardice
but rather of power and love and self-control.
So do not be ashamed of your testimony to our Lord,
nor of me, a prisoner for his sake;
but bear your share of hardship for the gospel
with the strength that comes from God.

Take as your norm the sound words that you heard from me,
in the faith and love that are in Christ Jesus.
Guard this rich trust with the help of the Holy Spirit
that dwells within us.

Luke 17: 5-10
The apostles said to the Lord, "Increase our faith."
The Lord replied,
"If you have faith the size of a mustard seed,

you would say to this mulberry tree,
'Be uprooted and planted in the sea,' and it would obey you.

"Who among you would say to your servant
who has just come in from plowing or tending sheep in the field,
'Come here immediately and take your place at table'?
Would he not rather say to him,
'Prepare something for me to eat.
Put on your apron and wait on me while I eat and drink.
You may eat and drink when I am finished'?
Is he grateful to that servant because he did what was commanded?
So should it be with you.
When you have done all you have been commanded,
say, 'We are unprofitable servants;
we have done what we were obliged to do.'"

TWENTY-EIGHTH SUNDAY IN ORDINARY TIME

2Kings 5:14-17; 2Timothy 2:8-13; Luke 17:11-19

May your grace, O Lord, we pray, at all times go before us and follow after; and make us always determined to carry out good works, through our Lord Jesus Christ, your Son, who lives and reigns with you in the unity of the holy Spirit, one God for ever and ever. Amen.

This is a fascinating story, the story of ten lepers being healed by Jesus, and only one seeming to recognize what had happened to him. And what I take from the story is that when God is working in your life and in mine, when he is doing everything that his love for us encourages him to do, then we have this problem of actually recognizing the effects of God's love in our life in a daily way. So it strikes me that in this particular story, he does something very dramatic. There are ten men that are caught in this disease called *leprosy*. You know that leprosy is a symbol in the Old Testament of sin, and the reason it works so well I think as a symbol for sin is the effects of leprosy are that we lose the definition of our features. It's almost like people who have leprosy, if you saw them, you wouldn't recognize them. So think of it as a disease that somehow hides our true identity. And sin has that effect on us. When we get caught up in it, when we're believing it works for us on some strange level, when we decide this is the best we can do with life—to take instead of give, something like that—we end up somehow being someone that we're really not.

And this amazing, loving God of ours is trying constantly to draw us into the place that we were intended to be, by him. He wants us to be truly ourselves, and he wants us to experience an inner peace and inner joy that can only come from knowing that you are living out the life that the *core* of who you are, your heart, loves, knows that it's right. It feels so good to be authentic, to be true to yourself.

So in this miracle, Jesus doesn't go through any kind of gestures, he doesn't put his hands on the lepers and say some special prayers. He sees them and they say, "Please help me" and he says (to himself of course, I will *do* that). "So go show yourselves to the priest." Well, to show yourself to a priest (they practically ran everything, so imagine him as a kind of social service), the priest would check out people who claimed to be healed of leprosy, since it was so contagious (and sin is contagious); they would check to make sure that the disease was gone. So to check with the priest was to check to see if you had your identity back. (I'm playing with that image of *identity.*) And the point is, all were healed! Everyone somehow was freed from this burden that they were under, yet only one, only one comes back to thank God. And it's interesting who he is. He's a Samaritan, a Samaritan. Now who's a Samaritan? A Samaritan is somebody outside of the Jewish community and someone who basically has not really known God in terms of the teachings that were so clearly found in the Israelite community. The Old Testament scriptures were very much a part of how they had formed their image of God.

So you might say the Samaritan is a person who doesn't really know God, but what he's experienced is the *effects* of God's *love* for them. It's an interesting image! That image, in that particular story, shows that the effect on a person when they realize that they have been gifted—for no reason; they didn't earn it, they didn't deserve it; it just happened!—they're so overwhelmed that this God of Israel would reach out to them and free them from something they were under the influence of, that kept them from being themselves, that there was only one natural reaction: "Thank you! Thank you! Thank you! This is incredible!"

So what happened to the other 90% of the people that God shows his love to every day? I don't know. It would be interesting if you could interview all the other nine and say, "Excuse me. You just had this experience. What happened?" Well I could think of a lot of things. "Well, I was taking this herb, and it finally kicked in, it worked, and I'm healed." Or, "You know, I've been suffering a lot, and I decided that all of that suffering was due to my sins, so I figured this was punishment; so I guess the punishment's over, so now I'm freed. So I sort of earned this healing by my suffering." All *kinds* of things that people come up with that make it seem like it wasn't really a generous, awesome act of love as much as it was a sort of *justice* issue. "I deserved it. I worked for it. I earned it."

So let's take *that* image and go to the first reading, because the first reading is *also* about the healing of leprosy. Naaman is a Samaritan, by the way, a non-Jew, and he is very, very well-loved by his king and he was very successful in battle, so his king calls on the ruler of Israel and says, "I'm sending Naaman to you because one of your people is a servant in my house, and she said that your God does all kinds of wonderful things for people, so I'm sending Naaman to you to heal him, and he's brought tons of clothes and gold and silver, and he's going to pay for this. So would you please heal him?" And of course the king of Israel just rends his garments. "I'm set up to fail. This is horrible." Interesting. The king of Israel doesn't believe that God can do this, or *would* do it for a Samaritan.

So when Elisha the prophet hears about it, he said, "Well, send him to me." And the interesting thing about the story is, Elisha doesn't do anything for him. Naaman comes with his retinue, and he's standing outside of Elisha's house and, it's funny, because Elisha doesn't even come out of the house to see him. His servant comes in and says, "Naaman's here," and Elisha just tells him to go into the River Jordan and go under the water seven times. And that doesn't sound like anything special.

So Naaman, like a lot of us say, "If I'm expecting a miracle, I want something: major words spoken, hands placed on me, thunder clapping, lightning—I don't know, I want some manifestation if this is really God—this is so ordinary, to go wash in the River Jordan. Come on!" But then the servant—and it's always interesting: Servants are the ones who are telling the people who have power how they should really *see* life—and so the servant of Naaman says, "You know, if he asked you to do something really extraordinary, you'd probably do it, so why not go try this?" And he does, and he comes out on the seventh dip. I love the image: His skin is like that of a newborn baby.

So Naaman races back and he wants to *pay* for this, and the prophet won't take any payment. It's like, "This isn't something you buy or that you deserve because you've *done* something. This is because the God of Israel is so loving and so connected to your struggle that he longs to free you from everything that would bind you and hold you back. He wants you to be free to be yourself. He wants you to know how much he *loves* you. That's the point." So what are we supposed to take from this story?

Well, the second reading gives us an indication also of what we should hold onto to figure out what this teaching is. The second reading ends with something that's kind of strange. It says, if you deny God—that means if you write him off as not there, not existing. If you deny something, you say, "That never was, that never happened." Well, if you deny him, then he denies you. What that says is that if you choose to separate yourself from the gifts of God, he'll back off. He is not going to force himself on anybody. But if you're really unfaithful to him, if you fail and you don't do things right, he will never, ever be unfaithful to you. He will always be there for you, because he can't deny himself! Meaning he can't negate who he is. He is a lover. He is the God who wants, more than anything else, to come into your life and to do something for you. And here's the key: He's doing it every single day, all day long. And we miss it. We don't pay attention to it.

I think there's a *reason* why we don't do that. It's because there are *two* ways people tend to come into knowledge of God. One is using the intellect; the other is using the heart. St. Thomas Aquinas and St. Bonaventure lived at the same time. They were both professors at the University of Paris. In the Middle Ages, they were the ones who were called to be the most influential in terms of their own interior searching for an understanding of a relationship with God. And Thomas began his connection with God, and he taught people to do this—and I grew up in the 40s and 50s, as a young boy, and I was very much influenced by Thomas Aquinas (at least the *teachers* were, that taught me), and he always started with the *mind*. "The task, the way you get to know God is, you figure out who he is, you study him, and you get to know him." I don't know if any of you are old enough to remember the Baltimore Catechism, but that's what I was trained in, and I remember the second question, after "Who made you?" (God), then "Why did he make you?" to *know* him. And *then* to love him. Then to *serve* him.

Well, if knowledge is the way you begin your understanding of God, then what's *crucial* is that whoever's teaching you gives you the right image of who God is. If I'm counting on somebody else to describe God for me, well, they *better do a good job!* Because not only do we hear things like words that tell us who God is, but when you're a child, you look at every authority figure around you and figure that that's something like who God is. So your parents are sort of like what God is, and if they're loving and giving to you, that might increase your capacity to understand God as a lover, but if they're really strong disciplinarians and they "ride" you a lot, and they keep implying to you that you're only valuable if you are doing the right thing, I think your knowledge of God is going to be limited.

So there's a little bit of a danger in the Thomas Aquinas way, even though it's certainly authentic and approved by the Church, that you start your relationship with God by *knowing* him, and then you fall *in love* with him. But then St. Bonaventure lived at the same time and he was strongly, strongly influenced by St. Francis of Assisi. He was Franciscan, and Francis' direction was very different from Thomas Aquinas' because for Bonaventure, the *first* thing you do is fall in love with God. You're in love with him before you know him. I don't know if I can describe this very well, but I know that I fall in love with people that I meet and I feel that I love them after meeting them for ten minutes or so. I just *feel* something, and what I feel feels so good, it feels so comforting that I want to get to know them because what I'm feeling when I feel that I love someone is I feel a *connection*, because basically if you *look* at love, love is a very, very interesting thing. We tend to think of it as emotion, but think of it primarily as *union*. Love is *union*. If you have an experience of God in you, God with you, God all around you—if you have that sense, that's what it means to *love* God, you know there's a oneness there, and that's different from getting to know him by figuring out who he is. Once you figure out, in Thomas Aquinas' way, who he is, then you understand logically what he's asking you to do: develop virtues, and when we get the virtues down, you receive the reward. That's all pretty much of a brain kind of approach.

But Francis, you know, you recognize his love in some situation, whether it's someone else loving you or whether it's the beauty of nature or whether it's some awesome experience of the wonder of the universe. I know people who found God looking through a telescope or standing on a mountain in Colorado. These experiences of saying, "I know something, there's something of this creator in this whole thing that is so satisfying to me, and when I feel that resonance of his love coming through all creation and it fills me, then I'm in love with this God."

And that's what Francis did, you know? He gave up everything. He loved poverty, but his poverty wasn't about not having things. It was about letting go of things that were not *nearly* as satisfying: money, power, all that. Letting go of that so you could experience something that is so much more satisfying—like the awesome beauty of creation that is a reflection of the love that God has for you and for me.

So I think the story of the ten lepers then is really an interesting one. It seems to say so clearly to us that, you know, the difference that one out of ten realized something: All he experienced from this God that he was encountering through Jesus, all he knew about him was his power to heal and his power to love without this Samaritan doing anything to deserve it or to pay for it! I can just feel that as I'm saying those words. That's an experience so different from a struggle to understand someone, figure out what they're asking me to do, doing what he asked me to do, and then receiving a reward. It's in a whole different category. The category of the heart versus the category of the mind. So our *challenge*. What is our challenge? Our challenge from this story, it seems to me, is to start recognizing something intellectually—we start with that, and we say, "Here is what I need to realize. I need to realize that the God who created me has made a promise to me that he is going to take care of me, and he will do this 24/7, and everything that's happening to me is happening in a sense *for* me, and all the things around me are *for* me, and there's this awesome sense of being loved and cared for 24/7. That's what it means to recognize how much he is in love with us. Once you have a sense of that God as love, then the natural response in you is to love in return. And this has *nothing* to do with merit. It's not saying that God now *deserves* my love. It's just that I can't *not* love someone who is so good to me, so powerfully effective in helping me to come to my fullness. *That's* the key: fullness and life in relationship with a loving, an incredibly loving God.

Father, we ask you to open our eyes and our hearts so that we have a sense of who you really are, all that you're doing for us. Make us conscious, make us aware of it so that the most natural response in all of us will be to fall in love with you. In relationships of union that love celebrates, we then find the peace that is our inheritance, and we ask this through Christ our Lord. Amen.

2 Kings 5: 14-17
Naaman went down and plunged into the Jordan seven times
at the word of Elisha, the man of God.
His flesh became again like the flesh of a little child,
and he was clean of his leprosy.

Naaman returned with his whole retinue to the man of God.
On his arrival he stood before Elisha and said,
"Now I know that there is no God in all the earth,
except in Israel.
Please accept a gift from your servant."

Elisha replied, "As the LORD lives whom I serve, I will not take it;"
and despite Naaman's urging, he still refused.
Naaman said: "If you will not accept,
please let me, your servant, have two mule-loads of earth,
for I will no longer offer holocaust or sacrifice
to any other god except to the LORD.

2 Timothy 2: 8-13
Beloved:
Remember Jesus Christ, raised from the dead, a descendant of David:
such is my gospel, for which I am suffering,
even to the point of chains, like a criminal.
But the word of God is not chained.
Therefore, I bear with everything for the sake of those who are chosen,
so that they too may obtain the salvation that is in Christ Jesus,
together with eternal glory.
This saying is trustworthy:
If we have died with him
we shall also live with him;
if we persevere
we shall also reign with him.
But if we deny him
he will deny us.
If we are unfaithful
he remains faithful,
for he cannot deny himself.

Luke 17: 11-19
As Jesus continued his journey to Jerusalem,
he traveled through Samaria and Galilee.
As he was entering a village, ten lepers met him.
They stood at a distance from him and raised their voices, saying,
"Jesus, Master! Have pity on us!"
And when he saw them, he said,
"Go show yourselves to the priests."
As they were going they were cleansed.
And one of them, realizing he had been healed,
returned, glorifying God in a loud voice;
and he fell at the feet of Jesus and thanked him.
He was a Samaritan.
Jesus said in reply,
"Ten were cleansed, were they not?
Where are the other nine?
Has none but this foreigner returned to give thanks to God?"
Then he said to him, "Stand up and go;
your faith has saved you."

TWENTY-NINTH SUNDAY IN ORDINARY TIME

Exodus 17:8-13; 2Timothy 3:14 – 4:2; Luke 18:1-8

Almighty, ever-living God, grant that we may always conform our wills to yours and serve your majesty in sincerity of heart, through our Lord Jesus Christ, your Son, who lives and reigns with you in the unity of the holy Spirit, one God for ever and ever. Amen.

Prayer. It's always seemed mysterious to me that you and I are asked to pray to God that his will be done, that what he longs for will happen. But at the same time, I know there's nothing more in his heart than that he wants those things to happen, and his *intention* is that they *will* happen. So why do we have to ask? Why doesn't he just take care of us without our participating in the process in the form of saying, "Please do this; please do that."

It goes to the very heart of this thing we call our life here on this earth. Why are we here? What are we *doing*? Probably the oversimplification is that we're living in a world that is guided by a God who wants us to do certain things. He gives us the law; he tells us what to do; we ask for his support so we'll be *able* to do it; and we *do* it. And if we do it well, we're rewarded. If we don't do it well, we're punished. How very superficial, but so often a very *common* way that people imagine their relationship with God. He's the one who tells us what to do, and our job is to do it.

But it's much more than that. It's all about *relationship*; it's all about a God who wants to *partner* with us, a God who wants to enter into us; a God who wants us to be a part of the process of bringing life to the strange creatures that he made that have *free will*. We are rare in all of his creation. We are these strange characters that have the freedom to say no to everything that God wants us to say yes to. And nothing else that he created has that power. So we're different from the rest of creation. And what are we supposed to *do* with this freedom? It's clear that we should surrender to whatever God wants. But is it just that, or is there something more to it? It is more like, what he wants is someone free, like himself, who will join with him in living out the role that we have so that it's not just him manipulating the world to act in a certain way, but it's God with me, me with God, being able to accomplish the things that need to happen. It's *almost* like he's saying, "Alright, I've given you this gift of free will. I didn't give it to you just so you'd have a choice, a chance to say no. No, I gave it to you so in your chance to say yes, we would work together in a way that we can sit back when it's all over and say, 'We, we, we did this. God in me, me in God.'" So it seems so important that we have this connection between ourselves, our work, our words, our gestures, our actions, and the intention of God. The two need to be in sync.

I want to call that somehow being *aligned,* aligned with the will of God. Let's imagine that *prayer* is an expression to God that we are open and willing to align ourselves with him, and once we do—I don't know how to describe this, because it's about the mystery of the spiritual world (which is actually the only real world in some ways [chuckles]), but it's often considered that there's the real world and there's the spiritual world. Imagine that the *spiritual* world is really what it's all about, and so this world that we're called into, the spiritual world, has rules and laws we need to submit to, and one of the things about this rule of the spiritual life that I want to get to is that for the grace of God to flow from him into the world, he needs us. And for the spirit of human beings to flow into God, we need each other. We call this community; we call it church; we call it this mysterious thing where we are in a process where the union between ourselves and God, our union between ourselves and each other, these are the key roles that need to be undertaken in order for the work of God to be accomplished. What's the work of God? The glory of God? The glory of God is you and I fully alive, fully all that we're called to be, and the *kingdom* being established. And the kingdom is a way of life—not necessarily in the next world, but a way of life here.

So let's look at the "Our Father" for a minute. It's such a powerful prayer because it carries with it so much wisdom about prayer. It starts by simply acknowledging that we have a Father, a God who has created everything. He is awesome, great. And he is in the universe. He is everywhere, he is in heaven, and he is so holy! And *holy* means not just that he is perfect but that his role is to make the world whole. He is a God who calls us to wholeness. And his kingdom is what we want, so we're asking, you know, "God, when we pray, what we're saying is, I want to align my will with yours. Your will be done. And I want the kingdom to come! I want people to live the way they're called to live. I want this place that you have promised us, called *the Promised Land,* where there is unity and oneness and forgiveness and understanding. I want to help create that.

"So what I want you to do, God," and this is at the heart of the *Our Father,* "Give me whatever I need, give me my daily bread." I know there's such a deep connection between daily bread in that prayer and the Eucharist Christ gave us. And when we say, "Give me today my daily bread," we're saying "Give me you, let me take you in. I want to eat of your body, that gives me strength." And the Eucharist includes wine, which is forgiveness, so then "Feed me, strengthen me with your body, then fill me with forgiveness, which is your blood. So when I feel that forgiveness, when I see you as you see me, when I understand that you are filled with forgiveness, I *will* be able to forgive my brothers and sisters so easily. Just guide us and keep us from all those things that would rob us of life. Keep us free from temptation, deliver us from evil." So simple a prayer, but so powerful! It sets the tone for the whole thing.

So let's look at the readings we have today because I want you to go back to the image I was using about prayer as aligning yourself with God's will. And there's something *powerful* in that. It's not just you talking God into *doing* something. He already knows what he needs to do. You're saying, "I'm *with* you in this. I will be whatever you need me to be to enable this to happen."

So when there's a battle that Moses recognizes is important, and they go to battle with Amalek, what he's doing by extending his hands is making it clear that whenever his hands are extended, they're winning the battle; whenever his hands drop, they're losing. Just imagine this situation that you're in a battle with, something that you want to see happen, something you're struggling for. Well, prayer is your aligning yourself with whatever it is that needs to happen so that this prayer will be answered. So to pray isn't just asking for something; it includes an offering, a willingness to be used by God for whatever he needs you to do or be in the situation.

So if you can feel this connection with, "I'm here. I want this to happen. I'm connected to your intention," there's *power* in that. And it's a beautiful image of Moses, and I love the image—it's so literal—he gets tired, they give him a stone to sit on. And his arms—have you ever tried to hold your arms out for a long time by yourself, all day?—so he has two people holding his arms up. It's such a beautiful thing because it's so clear that human beings are engaged in some mysterious way in God's will being accomplished on this earth. And it's not just asking for it; it's somehow being a part of what the answer to the prayer will be.

Now many times God has compared *his* goodness to ours, and he's always—and Jesus would do this; he does it in the gospel—he'll say, "If you, with all your sin and all your selfishness, if you know how to give your children what is good, why do you think that God would give you something bad when you ask for something good?" And furthermore, in this gospel, "If a judge who doesn't respect anybody, doesn't fear God or believe in God, you pester him and pester him and pester him and ask him to do something; and he finally does it, that's an indication that persistence with someone usually works. So why do you give up on your God when you pray once or twice and nothing happens? Am I ever going to find faith on this earth? Am I ever going to find anyone who believes in who I really am?" It's so interesting. All of us probably that are listening to me believe that God exists. That's kind of a given, or you wouldn't be listening to a program like this. But not all of us believe in who he actually is. We believe there *is* a God. He is strong; he's powerful. But this image of a God who is so *dependent* on us? That doesn't always fit what we've been taught about God. A God who *needs* me to accomplish what *he* needs to do? He needs *our* support?

And that doesn't always fit, but if you really look at it, what was it that saved the world? Who *is* the Messiah? It's a human being! Yes, filled with divinity, and we know the mystery is that he truly was God, but to focus too much on Jesus' divinity robs us somewhat of the mystery of what it means to be human and how our humanity is our greatest asset in the sense of accepting it, its weaknesses and forgiving it—but also accepting its strength, its power. So when you look at the story of our redemption, it's about a human being who is cooperating with divinity within him, going through life saying certain things, believing something, surrendering over and over again to something that he didn't really want to do. So the idea of the human being, Christ, in the agony of the garden saying, "Alright. If this can't pass away from me, then let your will be done." That's the surrendering of a human being to the will of God, but knowing that he also had to *do* something. Jesus didn't just say, "I'll let whatever you want to have happen, happen, but it doesn't affect me." No, it *really* affected him! "I'll be what you need me to be, I'll go where you need me to go, I'll let happen to me what needs to happen to me." *That's* the disposition that true prayer creates within us, so that we really are partners with this strange, mysterious unfolding of things.

How do you *know* that you're spontaneously open and receptive to this role? I'd say one thing is you let go of the kind of way in which most of us pray, and that is, I pray and I want an answer and usually it's time-related: I want this to happen now. That's usually what we pray for: *now*. And we pray and nothing seems to happen right away, so we tend to say, "Well, either God's too busy or I'm not worthy or this whole thing really doesn't work." And so we drift back into the anxiety and the worry and the fear that we often live with because we're not sure that things are going to work out.

That's the lack of faith that Jesus is so worried about when he's talking about this whole notion of turning to God and asking him to do something for you; and our loss of trust in those moments of waiting, or those moments of having to adjust to what the real answer is going to be. It takes great unselfishness to be able to be a part of something that you know you're being used, you know that your intention is going to be, if you pray in the name of Jesus, that means you pray with *his* desires in mind, the same desires Christ has, which is the desire of a human being fully alive, fully awake, fully aware of God inside of him; so that means God's will and Jesus' will and God's intention and Jesus' intention were one. So if we can believe that when we're praying for the right thing, it *will* happen. It will *always* happen.

It happens, but we have to be ready to be the part that we're supposed to be in it happening. Maybe it's just trust. Maybe it's being open to an intuition that you need to say something, go somewhere. I *love* all those images of a person who's truly spiritual—there's an instinct to go do something. Pick up the phone and call someone. What you're following when you're doing that is promptings of the Spirit. And there's something about that kind of docility that is needed every time you pray for something, especially if it's something that you know needs to happen in a more immediate circle. That would probably make it more valuable to being more open and ready. I know that when I get ready to go see someone who's in a lot of pain, and I'm worried about what am I gonna say? How am I gonna say it? I certainly don't write it out and then go and read it to them. But when I get there, I try to be open and receptive and say, "I know you'll give me the thing to say and I'll say it." Takes some practice to be that docile, that open, that ready to follow things. And God uses different motives—we don't always say, "I want to say what you want me to say." Maybe you say, "I want to say what works." Or even, "I don't want to say something that sounds stupid." But it always boils down to the same thing: God is going to give us what we need, our daily bread. He's going to give us what we need to enable the kingdom to come. When our will is in sync with his, we should have the most confident petition to him connected to a willingness to be used by him. And then, and then the kingdom is now.

Father, as I pray this prayer for an opening of hearts and minds to all that you are, I recognize that I'm also asking you to empower me, empower all of us to be instruments of enabling this to happen. So bless us with the faith that you call us to in this gospel passage, bless us with the conviction that your will, when we surrender and submit to it, will always, always accomplish what you long to see happen. And we ask this in Jesus' name. Amen.

Exodus 17:8-13

In those days, Amalek came and waged war against Israel.
Moses, therefore, said to Joshua,
"Pick out certain men,
and tomorrow go out and engage Amalek in battle.
I will be standing on top of the hill

with the staff of God in my hand."
So Joshua did as Moses told him:
he engaged Amalek in battle
after Moses had climbed to the top of the hill with Aaron and Hur.
As long as Moses kept his hands raised up,
Israel had the better of the fight,
but when he let his hands rest,
Amalek had the better of the fight.
Moses' hands, however, grew tired;
so they put a rock in place for him to sit on.
Meanwhile Aaron and Hur supported his hands,
one on one side and one on the other,
so that his hands remained steady till sunset.
And Joshua mowed down Amalek and his people
with the edge of the sword.

2 Timothy 3:14 – 4:2
Beloved:
Remain faithful to what you have learned and believed,
because you know from whom you learned it,
and that from infancy you have known the sacred Scriptures,
which are capable of giving you wisdom for salvation
through faith in Christ Jesus.
All Scripture is inspired by God
and is useful for teaching, for refutation, for correction,
and for training in righteousness,
so that one who belongs to God may be competent,
equipped for every good work.

I charge you in the presence of God and of Christ Jesus,
who will judge the living and the dead,
and by his appearing and his kingly power:
proclaim the word;
be persistent whether it is convenient or inconvenient;
convince, reprimand, encourage through all patience and teaching.

Luke 18: 1-8
Jesus told his disciples a parable
about the necessity for them to pray always without becoming weary.
He said, "There was a judge in a certain town

who neither feared God nor respected any human being.
And a widow in that town used to come to him and say,
'Render a just decision for me against my adversary.'
For a long time the judge was unwilling, but eventually he thought,
'While it is true that I neither fear God nor respect any human being,
because this widow keeps bothering me
I shall deliver a just decision for her
lest she finally come and strike me.'"
The Lord said, "Pay attention to what the dishonest judge says.
Will not God then secure the rights of his chosen ones
who call out to him day and night?
Will he be slow to answer them?
I tell you, he will see to it that justice is done for them speedily.
But when the Son of Man comes, will he find faith on earth?"

THIRTIETH SUNDAY IN ORDINARY TIME

Sirach 35:12-14, 16-18; 2Timothy 4:6-8, 16-18; Luke 18:9-14

Almighty, ever-living God, increase our faith, hope, and charity; and make us love what you command so we may merit what you promise, through our Lord Jesus Christ, your Son, who lives and reigns with you in the unity of the holy Spirit, one God for ever and ever. Amen.

The theme of the liturgy today is a very curious thing to work with. It's the image of somehow knowing that when we are called to respond to God's love and we struggle to become all that he wants us to be, we have to be so careful with that energy that can be created inside of a human spirit that is fundamentally about the ego that really wants to do well—we *really* want to do well. And in my experience growing up when I was around adults and teachers and parents, I always wanted to perform at a high level because I wanted their approval.

So there's something basic in human nature that realizes that if one pleases another, one is often in their favor. But in the world of religion, in the world of Christianity, and the world of so many religions, what's very crucial is this image of *humility*. And humility isn't putting yourself down and saying that you're not any good. Humility has something to do with radical honesty, radical honesty. "This is the situation; this is what is."

So what *is* our relationship with God if it isn't supposed to be that we perform at a high level so that we receive our reward? What *is* it all about? Well, the image in the gospel is so powerful that you almost need none of the other readings to really get what I want to say. Let's not ignore the other readings, but let's start with this gospel image that here are two men praying. And the theme that Luke is working with here is righteousness, and *righteousness* is a word that, for me, as a Roman Catholic, in my tradition, we didn't use the word very much. But I know that it means that we are in a right relationship with God, where whatever is going on between us is healthy and life-giving and what he wills. As these two men are kneeling there, one of the things that is so radically different about them is that one is there very, very much aware of the work that he's done. And let's just say that work is really good. He's done his job; he's paid his taxes; he does his prayers. Let's not imagine that he's doing anything literally wrong. He is doing everything right. But he has one major flaw, one major flaw, and that is that he despises everyone else! What an interesting word for Luke to use: He *despises* everyone else. "Thank God, I'm not like the rest of the trash that I see around me!"

That's the tip-off that something is radically out of balance in the Pharisee. So he puts all his effort into creating a world he lives in that makes him feel like he is absolutely in favor with God, and yet he is anything *but*, because he's missed the most essential thing. He has no compassion, no empathy. And here's the other man kneeling there. He's just beating his breast, saying, "I am really one of those people that just can't do it without you, God. Help me. Help me. Have mercy on me. I'm a sinner."

One of the things I've always enjoyed about the Roman Catholic liturgy—it's not unique to Roman Catholicism, but our liturgy always begins with a greeting from the celebrant to the people, and no sooner have we greeted each other, and wanted the Lord to be in each of us, then we go right into the Penitential Rite, where we sit there and say to each other, and to God, "Have mercy on me, a sinner. I really can't do what you're asking me to do, and please help me," because all of us here in this room, and this is the way I would love for it to work—and I think it does work this way often—everyone in the room has the feeling that none of us are there because we've done something wonderful. We're there because we *need* something that's wonderful. We *need* something that's wonderful.

And I suppose that's one of the major issues in this story: When we are in relationship with God, what is that relationship about? Is it about our performance? Or is it about God's performance? If it's about *our* performance, then we better work our tails off trying to get everything in order. We really have to do everything to get it right. If it's about *God's* activity, God's work, it's about *receiving*, about being in a disposition where whatever it is that we need, we can rely upon God to give it to us so that there's a kind of inner core peace when we're dealing with everything around us that is demanding something of us.

Well, there are two ways we can look at our life. You can be in control of the things that you do to please God. I'll do this exercise; I'll do this activity; I'll go to this service; I'll get involved in that project. The way that seems to me to be working inside of the human being is that we have a clear idea of something that I know how to do: It begins, it ends; I'm in control of it. But there's a whole other aspect of life, which is the interactions of human beings with each other, the spontaneity of the ways events flow. And you know, 90% of what I think God wants from us is going to be acted out in those situations where we're not beginning something and ending something. It's when we're in relationship on a daily basis with everything going on around us, and our reactions to that are the key to knowing whether or not we're in the kingdom, whether or not we're righteous. How do we react to the things that are going on around us? *Naturally* how do we react? Not when we think about it, "What should I do here? Well, I guess I better do this."

But the goal is to be in a disposition, with the help of grace, with the help of God inside of us, that our responses to the things around us are both protecting us from the excessive fear and shame and anger that we often get caught up in. At the same time, that grace inside of us is enabling us to be a vehicle that helps others not to get caught up in shame, fear, and anger; where we're absolutely not there to judge them, to evaluate them, tell them where they're wrong. Those are the things that we often do to each other instinctively when we're caught up somewhat in this disposition that the Pharisee represents. I don't know how *you* hear the story, but there's a way in which I can identify with *both* figures. There are times when I really do feel that I'm honestly looking at myself and saying, "You know, I can't do this. I can't make this without you. Without God's support, I can't do it." But there are a lot times when I'm doing things and it seems like I'm doing alright and I seem to be effective and I get full of myself and then I sit back and I sort of say to myself, "You're in great shape because God has really been pleased with you. You've done *such* a great job." And then, without my realizing it, what I've lost, it seems to me, is some kind of empathy, compassion for my brothers and sisters around me who aren't doing so well. In fact—this is frightening—it's almost like when I'm in that disposition of the Pharisee, when I'm focusing on my performance, there's something almost *sweet* about the fact that somebody else fails, because it makes me look *so* good! [chuckles] How's *that* for being sick? But that's the way it works.

This thing that Luke is pointing out is something that is only known by evaluating where we are in our relationship with others, particularly in the area of compassion. Do you really *feel* what other people are going through? Do you really sense their struggle? Do you realize that everything that you're able to do that's good is somehow part of the effect of God's creation—he's created us as good—but also there's something that he designed in this whole thing that we call our life here on this planet. He's designed it so that we're supposed to not be able to do the things we're called to do—on our own. Anybody who says, "This is all in my court. I can handle anything that comes to me. I don't need anything or anyone outside of myself." That's not really something that people go around saying, but if you hypnotize them and get them into a state of complete honesty, they might say, "Yeah, I'm responsible for myself, totally. *I'm* the one that gets everything done. And I resent sometimes all the work that's on my plate. I've got a lot to do, and I see other people who are lazy, that aren't really performing, that aren't really responsible. They *irritate* me! They *really* irritate me." Because somehow I am seeing something that doesn't make sense: I really think that what people do, when you're working out of your own stuff and you're pushing yourself and you're pushing yourself, there's something about the whole thing that seems unfair—"it's just too hard; there's just too much on my plate." Or, "Why does God create *this* problem for me? Why do I have *that* problem?" When you're in that disposition, it seems to me that that's another good indication that you're not really connected to the God who says, "I'm there for you every single moment, and there's nothing that I expect you to do on your own. All I want you to do is invite me into your life, into your very being, and let me *partner* with you in everything that we're doing." That means you've got to ask for assistance all the time. How many of us are really comfortable in asking for assistance? I *never* ask anyone, when I walk into a store, where something is [chuckles] unless it's Home Depot or Lowe's or whatever. Most places, I'll go find it. I can find it myself.

All of that is so intertwined in a disposition that is so dangerous for us as Christians. It's like, Why do we do that? Why is it that we have such an intense sense that we're supposed to handle it on our own? I think it's partly because that's the culture we live in. We honor people who succeed. We give them great credit, as if they have done all this work themselves. And then we have another way of putting people down who somehow *aren't* working at a high, high level, and we see them as "there's something wrong. They're lazy. They're not putting forth the effort." So it seems like we reward people who are able to handle things, and we seem to criticize people who *can't* handle everything.

So there's something in a balance here that's necessary. Something needs to balance us as we go through this life together. And I don't know how I can say it because it's still unclear to me, but there's something necessary that enables us to see the way life is, so that we have this seeming contradiction: We all realize that we all should work as hard as we can to accomplish things. At the same time, we have to realize that what's really essential, we can't do. That means that whenever we *are* successful, there's a sense that we've been *helped* to do that; we've been *guided* to do that; we've been *empowered* to do that. And that's a blessing, and we should be filled with thanksgiving for it. And when somebody else *doesn't* perform, it's not that we're judging them, as saying, "Well, you don't turn enough to God," but there's something about compassion and empathy that lead us to a place where we're not so quick to condemn, not so quick to judge, not so quick to put somebody down because they're struggling. Sometimes the people publicly in great need of something are simply being seen as true humans [chuckles]; and we look at other people who are so successful and we think, "Oh, *that's* what a true human is. They're successful; they pull it all together; they do everything right. "

We need *balance*. We need a God who loves us, who's going to give us everything we need, and we need to be humble enough to say, "Please, please help me." And then we need to stop judging each other, stop putting pressure on each other. The pressure we put on people is important as long as it's understood that it's done with great compassion for the human condition. Not everybody can achieve what we think they should achieve, at the time *we* think they should achieve it, and they can't necessarily achieve it to the level *we* think they should. That's judgment. And it's frightening to think that that would be a kind of person we would despise, or be angry at, that we'd be hateful toward. Yet that's the attitude of the Pharisee, and *our* attitude has to be that of the one kneeling next to him.

Father, your heart is open to our human struggles. You understand us beyond anything we could imagine, so bless us with the recognition that as we honestly face ourselves we know that we're seeing what you see, and yet we know when you see it, you're filled with compassion and love. So fill us with that same compassion and love for our weaknesses and the weaknesses of our brothers and sisters, and we ask this through Christ our Lord. Amen.

Sirach 35: 12-14, 16-18
The LORD is a God of justice,
who knows no favorites.
Though not unduly partial toward the weak,
yet he hears the cry of the oppressed.
The Lord is not deaf to the wail of the orphan,
nor to the widow when she pours out her complaint.
The one who serves God willingly is heard;
his petition reaches the heavens.
The prayer of the lowly pierces the clouds;
it does not rest till it reaches its goal,
nor will it withdraw till the Most High responds,
judges justly and affirms the right,
and the Lord will not delay.

2 Timothy 4: 6-8,16-18
Beloved:
I am already being poured out like a libation,
and the time of my departure is at hand.

I have competed well; I have finished the race;
I have kept the faith.
From now on the crown of righteousness awaits me,
which the Lord, the just judge,
will award to me on that day, and not only to me,
but to all who have longed for his appearance.

At my first defense no one appeared on my behalf,
but everyone deserted me.
May it not be held against them!
But the Lord stood by me and gave me strength,
so that through me the proclamation might be completed
and all the Gentiles might hear it.
And I was rescued from the lion's mouth.
The Lord will rescue me from every evil threat
and will bring me safe to his heavenly kingdom.
To him be glory forever and ever. Amen.

Luke 18: 9-14
Jesus addressed this parable
to those who were convinced of their own righteousness
and despised everyone else.
"Two people went up to the temple area to pray;
one was a Pharisee and the other was a tax collector.
The Pharisee took up his position and spoke this prayer to himself,
'O God, I thank you that I am not like the rest of humanity --
greedy, dishonest, adulterous -- or even like this tax collector.
I fast twice a week, and I pay tithes on my whole income.'
But the tax collector stood off at a distance
and would not even raise his eyes to heaven
but beat his breast and prayed,
'O God, be merciful to me a sinner.'
I tell you, the latter went home justified, not the former;
for whoever exalts himself will be humbled,
and the one who humbles himself will be exalted."

THIRTY-FIRST SUNDAY IN ORDINARY TIME

Wisdom 11:22 – 12:2; 2Thessalonians 1:11 – 2:2; Luke 19:1-10

Almighty and merciful God, by whose gifts your faithful may offer you right and praiseworthy service, grant, we pray, that we may hasten without stumbling to receive the things you have promised, through our Lord Jesus Christ, your Son, who lives and reigns with you in the unity of the holy Spirit, one God for ever and ever. Amen.

The first reading is interesting because it invites you and me to think about the way in which God has created the world. For some reason, he wanted us to have the ability to make mistakes, and we *do* make them [chuckles]. We make a *lot* of them. Some of us make them more than others; some of the mistakes we make are more serious than others. But that whole notion that God has created us with free will and that we are able to fail is an essential part of the relationship that we have with God. And the most important thing he wants us to understand is that his reaction to our failures is not anything like what we *tend* to think—that he's angry, that he wants to punish us. But since he created our human nature, he created us as we are, he created us with this potential to do things that are wrong; he didn't give that to any other creature that he created.

So somehow we have to look carefully at the first reading and realize that what this particular passage is saying is so important: This is the way he intended it, and his response is that the reason I'm in the world, the thing that we're going to do together is we're going to move from the dark into the light; we're going to move you from being lost to being saved, from being "off track" to being right on target. And that's the work. That's what God wants to partner with us to do in this world, to help us to grow and to change. So he does this with enthusiasm and excitement, and he doesn't do it with anger and resentment. And yet I know at the heart of every human being I've ever met, there's a kind of gnawing little place where we hold on to a fear that our mistakes are somehow something that makes God angry. And even below the surface of some of the most, I think the holiest people, if you dig deep enough, you'll find there's a little bit of fear and anxiety of being judged by God.

Now it seems to me that if you listen attentively to the *core* of the scriptures, you'll find that there is nothing in the core of the teaching, particularly in the New Testament, that would give you the sense that God is absolutely disgusted by what we do, and that he's so frustrated that nothing seems more natural than that he would condemn us, punish us. If you look at the whole notion of redemption, it's interesting—if you look at the history of the Christian Church in terms of how it understood redemption, if you go to the early Church Fathers, one of the things you'll see as a way of people understanding this mystery of our weakness and God's strength, our need for his forgiveness and the need that someone had to come to free us from this negative thing that's in us—we had to be saved from it by an act of God, called our *redemption,* and one of the first images of redemption was somehow paying back the devil for this offense—meaning that he was the one who felt that this whole thing that God had intended to do, saving his people, all that, giving them free will, the story is that the great angel Lucifer was *totally* opposed to that and said it's never going to work. So it seems that the anger inside of this figure Lucifer was so intense that some people thought, "Well, God is going to come down and appease the anger of Lucifer, and the way he's going to do that is by suffering and dying. So it's like it was a ransom. And somehow we needed to pay off Lucifer [chuckles]. That's something that doesn't make a lot of sense today.

Another one is that *God* is so angry over human beings, and *he's* needing justice and wants so much to punish, and so instead of punishing each of us individually, Jesus comes along and *he* dies for all of us. So God doesn't *have to* punish us all because Jesus took on the debt, paid off the vengeance of God, and ransomed us.

Both of those seem to be pretty negative. But what if redemption was the intention that St. Bonaventure says, that the intention of God from the beginning is that he wanted to become a part of us. He *always* wanted to enter into the world and be one with us. And what if that wasn't really about trying to make up for something in the past, making up for our sins, but rather it was just God's love that wants to be in us, and he wants us to be in him, and that's always there. And one of the benefits of that is that we were saved from sin, but the saving from sin wasn't about paying off somebody, but it's just being empowered so we're not as susceptible and as vulnerable to sin. Interesting!

At the heart of what I'm trying to get to is, you have to understand that the God who created us, the God who has walked this earth with us in the person of Jesus, the God inside of you, inside of me, has nothing in him that implies that he's angry or upset or wants to punish or condemn.

The second reading is a message that Paul gave in the beginning because people were scared to death about the Second Coming and they thought if it was coming, they would be terrified and afraid that they were going to be judged, and so he said, "Be careful. Don't listen to people who are going around, supposedly representing us, saying, 'The end is coming. You're all going to die and be thrown into hell.'" I just think it's so fascinating that still that's preached in some subtle form. Fear is one of the great motivators, so people end up thinking, Alright, if you tell people that God is going to be really angry, you won't fail. If God is going to cut you down if you do something bad, you won't do something bad. Wrong motivation! Now what you need to see and what you need to know is the compassion, the understanding, the love that is in the heart of your God for you, and when you *see* that and *feel* that, and you fall in love with him, then your faith really begins.

So the story of Zacchaeus is perfect. Here's a man who is an Israelite, but he was considered by his fellow Israelites as lower than the lowest—because he was doing a couple of things. First of all, he was working for the oppressor, Rome. He was collecting all the taxes from the people there, so that those taxes could go to pay the wages of those who were oppressing them. So it's not really something people would want to do. But here's the other thing. Rome said, "If you want to charge people more than what the taxes require, we give you authority to do that, and that's all yours." So they would grow very, very wealthy by feeding off of the oppression of their brothers and sisters, their neighbors. So they were anything but respected. And here's the key. It's one of those characters basically hated by the Israelites, and of course the Israelites would have believed that God, too, hated Zacchaeus.

So Zacchaeus wants to *see* Jesus. He's curious. He listens to a prompting from God, *I want to see him*, so he goes and he can't see because he's short, so he gets up in a tree. If you were walking in a parade and people were all on either side of you, you would say, "Well, there are a lot of faces out there. I can't focus on one or the other." But if somebody was hanging on some telephone pole, you might pay attention to that one. What the story is about is the Messiah *seeing* you. Zacchaeus says, "I want to see Jesus." But the *real* story is about Zacchaeus seeing Jesus *see* him! And what he feels and sees in return and what he hears is so unexpected and so generous and so loving and so warm and hospitable to Zacchaeus, who expected the opposite. His heart just melts, because there's Jesus, seeing this despicable character and saying, "Ah, Zacchaeus, I want to stay with you today, stay inside your house; I want to eat with you." That's a statement saying, "I like you, and I want to befriend you, and I want you to be my friend." So shocking to everybody around him.

And notice that the stories, the parables, are always filled with some shock value if you really get to the heart of them. Such is the story about somebody standing in a tree. It's about Jesus seeing you and all of the things that you do that are not what you feel that you *should* be doing, and somehow deep down inside of you, you know they're wrong. And then you say, "What does Jesus see when he sees that part of me?" Shame, the most debilitating emotion, so often kicks in. And when we think about God, Jesus, seeing the parts of us that we want to hide from him—anytime you feel you want to hide something from him, there's something wrong there because it's like saying you're going to a doctor, and you have this problem or this pain. And he asks, "How are you doing?" And you say, "Everything is fine." And even though you have this chronic, horrible pain in your knees, say, you don't mention it, because you're embarrassed that your knees are not as strong as they should be. That's the way we so often deal with God, out of the fear that we don't want to even imagine what his feeling toward us is about the things that we're not proud of. And we're afraid.

And then we go back to this beautiful story, this very simple, beautiful story. It's simply saying, When God looks at you and God looks at me, and he sees the things that we're involved in, there's not condemnation. But here's the key word: *compassion.* He *feels* for us. He *created* this weakness in you and me. He's not shocked that it's there. The only thing he gets shocked at and upset with are the people who *pretend* it's not there, and they put on a show and they act as if they're something and they refuse to look at who they really are. *That* irritates him. That's the thing that really worries him.

But he wants so much for you and for me to feel comfortable in our weaknesses—not that the weaknesses aren't negative, not that they don't have destructive aspects to them, but they are not things that this beautiful, divine physician, they're not things that he can't take care of, they're not things that disgust him, they're not things where he goes, "Oh, my God, I can't handle this." Any more than you would expect a doctor to open your chest and try to fix something in there and see the mess and just close it up and say, "I'm disgusted. Send this person away. It's just a mess in there. I don't want to have anything to do with them." Isn't it *funny* we think that way about God!

So the challenge is to recognize that this God of compassion, this God of understanding sees us as we are and then is filled with nothing but empathy and compassion. And all of a sudden we feel *good* about ourselves and then we get in touch with the core of our goodness and there's a thing called *conversion* and you see it in the story, happening instantly. Once Zacchaeus understands that he's loved by this Messiah as intensely as he feels it in this invitation that Jesus places before Zacchaeus saying, "I want to come, I want to be your friend, I want to be in your house"—it just stirs something inside of him that awakens him to the generosity that is a core of who we all are; and so he's immediately moved to a radical change of heart, and he wants to pay back *everyone* that he has taken money from. So if he took 25 shekels from somebody, he's going to pay them back 100. And then he's going to give half of all his wealth to the poor. It's just a beautiful image of complete, radical change: from taking and hoarding, he's going to become generous and free. What a wonderful image of conversion, and isn't it interesting that the simplest thing that we're told, that triggered all of that radical change inside of him was Zacchaeus seeing God, in Jesus, seeing him. And when he saw in the eyes and the face of this Messiah love, compassion, understanding, "I want to be with you, I want to be your friend," it just worked so well in terms of changing him.

But yet, when we deal with, when the church, when religion deals with people, they're prone *not* to tell them that. They're prone to tell them they're in trouble, they're going to go to hell, they're going to be punished—because that seems to be more effective, it seems to work faster. And it *does* work faster only insofar as it leaves out the core ingredient. You don't have to fall in love with God in order to be afraid of him. And since we are already prone to believing that we're in trouble, then it's easier to believe that we are going to be punished or judged or condemned. Unfortunately, for most of us living in systems, you know, when we fail, there isn't this reaching out from those who are calling us to be more, to enter into us and tell us how good we are, who want to build us up and give us all that we need to continue to grow, let go of our past, let go of our mistakes. No, that's not the experience we have in the world, and so it makes sense that this core sort of anxiety that we're going to be judged and condemned is not just coming from the image of God but it's coming from our image of those around us who are in the same role in our lives as God is: our boss, our parents, the persons that are *over* us. So we need to trust, we need to understand who God really is, and we need to feel and see his gaze, which is so beautiful, so loving, so compassionate, and so capable of changing our heart.

Father, our sins are such a great source of pain and disappointment in who we are. We carry this burden but need to remember how much you long to free us of this burden, so we pray that you'll open us, open our eyes so that we see you as you see us, and we would see the look in your eye to us that is filled with compassion, understanding, and love and a desire to change us. So bless us with the peace that comes from this awareness, and we ask this in Jesus' name. Amen.

Wisdom 11: 22 – 12:2

Before the LORD the whole universe is as a grain from a balance
or a drop of morning dew come down upon the earth.
But you have mercy on all, because you can do all things;
and you overlook people's sins that they may repent.
For you love all things that are
and loathe nothing that you have made;

for what you hated, you would not have fashioned.
And how could a thing remain, unless you willed it;
or be preserved, had it not been called forth by you?
But you spare all things, because they are yours,
O LORD and lover of souls,
for your imperishable spirit is in all things!
Therefore you rebuke offenders little by little,
warn them and remind them of the sins they are committing,
that they may abandon their wickedness and believe in you, O LORD!

2 Thessalonians 1: 11 – 2:2
Brothers and sisters:
We always pray for you,
that our God may make you worthy of his calling
and powerfully bring to fulfillment every good purpose
and every effort of faith,
that the name of our Lord Jesus may be glorified in you,
and you in him,
in accord with the grace of our God and Lord Jesus Christ.

We ask you, brothers and sisters,
with regard to the coming of our Lord Jesus Christ
and our assembling with him,
not to be shaken out of your minds suddenly, or to be alarmed
either by a "spirit," or by an oral statement,
or by a letter allegedly from us
to the effect that the day of the Lord is at hand.

Luke 19: 1-10
At that time, Jesus came to Jericho and intended to pass through the town.
Now a man there named Zacchaeus,
who was a chief tax collector and also a wealthy man,
was seeking to see who Jesus was;
but he could not see him because of the crowd,
for he was short in stature.
So he ran ahead and climbed a sycamore tree in order to see Jesus,
who was about to pass that way.
When he reached the place, Jesus looked up and said,

"Zacchaeus, come down quickly,
for today I must stay at your house."
And he came down quickly and received him with joy.
When they all saw this, they began to grumble, saying,
"He has gone to stay at the house of a sinner."
But Zacchaeus stood there and said to the Lord,
"Behold, half of my possessions, Lord, I shall give to the poor,
and if I have extorted anything from anyone
I shall repay it four times over."
And Jesus said to him,
"Today salvation has come to this house
because this man too is a descendant of Abraham.
For the Son of Man has come to seek
and to save what was lost."

THIRTY-SECOND SUNDAY IN ORDINARY TIME

2Maccabees 7:1-2, 9-14; 2Thessalonians 2:16 – 3:5; Luke 20:27-38

God of power and mercy, protect us from all harm, give us freedom of spirit and health of mind and body to do your work on earth. We ask this through our Lord Jesus Christ, your Son, who lives and reigns with you in the unity of the holy Spirit, one God for ever and ever. Amen.

The theme of this liturgy may seem at first to be pretty gruesome—at least the first reading is really a tough one to listen to, and the Church often takes out certain parts of the scripture because they don't really add to the point that the scripture is trying to make. In this case, I think a *lot* was left out because it's so hard to listen to!

And I remember when I first heard this story, I was so struck by the fact that all this torturing and all this pain that was inflicted upon these seven sons and then their mother—all of them tortured and limbs cut off and skin ripped off and boiled in oil—all these things. And they just had to watch each other die, and all over an issue of pork? And yet I realize, as I grow and mature in my faith, that this is not simply about pork. It's about an understanding of what it means to believe and trust in something that's real, and to be willing to do anything, *anything,* to stand up for that very thing that we believe in. And what's interesting in this story is what these young men and this woman, the mother, are so strongly stating to all those over the centuries who have listened to this story, that it's not about so much keeping the law but how suffering and those who are in this world who decide they can somehow make us do something out of our fear that they might destroy us—that those people and that suffering have absolutely no power whatsoever over a person who trusts and believes that nothing, nothing can separate them from the life that God has called them into.

Probably the most dramatic statement is when one of the young brothers is being tortured and killed and these parts of his body are being taken away from him, and he is just so clear and convinced that he can say, "Go ahead. Take them away. I'll get them right back. Go ahead and kill me. I'll be alive in *no time,* and I will be in a place of fullness and richness and completeness." And when you think about it, it's an amazing thing, because once someone takes away the core fear that keeps us from doing things—once someone can take *away* that fear, we are invincible! We can *endure* anything!

So let's take this first story, then, as an indication that there is a way to enter into a place of peace, a way to enter into a place of conviction that our God is a God who takes care of us in *all* situations, that everything that is happening is somehow *for* us, that no matter what we go through, it's somehow going to bring about growth and change if we surrender to it, submit to it, and we *allow* it to be what it is. But we have to do all that with the absolute conviction that somehow all of this is *for life.* For *life*! And that the life that God has given us cannot *ever* be destroyed. I'm always struck by the reading where Jesus is talking to his disciples and says, "People will drag you in front of synagogues and they'll beat you and they'll torture you and they'll kill you, but no one will ever harm you." [chuckles] I always have to laugh when it says, "they'll kill you but they won't harm you." What he's talking about is there's two different "you's" there. Yeah, they can destroy your body. They can't destroy *you.* Nothing can destroy *you.*

So let's look at this promise of resurrection, this promise of life. And you know, there are people in the Old Testament called the *Sadducees.* The Sadducees were interesting. They were aristocratic, they were wealthy, they were scholars; and they didn't believe in anything but the first five books of the Bible, the Torah. So they were focused primarily on those works. One of the things that isn't specifically mentioned—at least they didn't think it was mentioned in those five books—is anything about the resurrection after death, that we would rise, that we would live forever. So the Sadducees, across the board, did not believe in life after death. And it's a kind of humorous story, in a way—I don't think it's *meant* to be humorous, but it always strikes me as kind of humorous—this tradition, it was actually a religious law, and this law was always to make sure that if a man died, and he had brothers who were unmarried, his wife should be married to one of the brothers so that there could be the continuation of the family line. And the story is humorous to me because there are seven brothers, and none of them are married. The woman marries the oldest brother, who dies, and then the second and then the third through the seventh, always trying to have a child. The brothers all die, and then *she* dies (and I always heard she dies because she heard there was an *eighth* brother [chuckles]; just kidding). Anyway, there was, obviously, in this story great exaggeration, because the Sadducees using the story wanted to say to Jesus, "Look, this would be impossible. If everybody lives after death, and everybody is married forever, then how is this going to work when you have seven husbands appearing with you after you die? Which one are you married to?"

Jesus first takes on the issue on a kind of superficial level in a sense, because the real issue, you know, is that they don't believe in resurrection, but he just says, "After we die, when this new life comes, we shed our bodies, we take on a new form, it's a spiritual form, and the things that we did on earth are not necessarily the same things we're going to do in heaven, and one of them is, it's not going to be necessary to be married." And when you think about that, in a way, marriage has two roles. One is certainly the possibility of creating new life, children; and the other is the mutual fulfillment of the couple. And it would seem that after death, you know, when we enter into this new life, there may well be—and I think there is, in our Catholic teaching of Purgatory—the chance to continue to grow and change after we die. But we're not going to be in need of the same kinds of things that we were in need of on earth, like challenging companions and someone to work out our stuff with, you know? So Jesus says, it's going to be different when you die.

But *then* he nails them with scripture, because they were scholars, scripture scholars, and they were sophisticated and they thought they had pretty well figured it all out. And Jesus quotes something from scripture that makes it clear. There's a statement there that God is the God of Jacob, the God of Abraham, the God of Moses. He's the God of all these people. So when it says that he is Abraham's God, it implies very clearly that Abraham is still alive. So he's saying, well, it's clear from this that God is the God only of the *living*. You wouldn't say he's the God of the dead. So *everything* is alive, and *everyone* is alive. I *love* that statement because it's so all-inclusive. It simply says, "What you have to believe in is this force, this thing that I've created in you, and it is never, ever going to be destroyed."

Now how do we interpret this, and how does it work in us? I pray you and I will not ever be tortured like these young men and their mother in the first story. I pray that will never happen to us, but there is a kind of torture that goes on in life. I'm always hard-pressed to talk about it in a way that's broad enough that it doesn't narrow it to one particular problem, but it just seems like there are so many challenges in our life that are calling us to move toward *fuller life*. And just imagine it as a movement toward resurrection, towards the fullness that God has created for us. In that process there are difficult, difficult things that we have to deal with. In many ways, they—some of them—are torturous. The fact that we have to face our fears, to face the fact that we failed, to face the fact that we're "not enough" to do the work that we think we need to do, and we have to admit our *dependence* on a source, a power outside of ourselves. All of these things for us are difficult, you know?

And what is it that would enable us to keep going, to keep moving, to keep changing, to not give in to the inertia that so often is there when we say, "I just can't move forward." It would have to be some kind of deep conviction that there is this force in me that is never, ever going to stop. It's always going to be moving forward. It has a life of its own, a real life of its own. I *love* that image, because it means there is a power in you that strives for life and let's say that it's stronger, *I* believe it's stronger, than anything in you that wants to *resist* life. And maybe that's an intellectual decision that we have to make, that that's really true. Sometimes our inertia, sometimes our statements, you know, seem so powerful and so strong: "I just can't possibly get past this." But just imagine if you have this conviction that this life force in you is stronger than anything else, and all you want to do is build it up. If it's like a spark, you want to fan it into gigantic flame; you want to ignite something in you that is absolutely certain that there is this powerful force in me that longs to connect, wants to connect with a powerful source outside of itself and wants to continue to move in a direction, a really powerful direction of life and fullness.

So the work, then, is *trust*, confidence, surrender—all the things I talk about over and over again. But one last thought that I want to focus on is this whole notion of what it's like to look forward to a life after death. I see so much resistance, even though people believe "I won't die," there's always the fear, because we do know that there's the possibility of separation from God. We're free beings, so we can say no to him; so, yes, we could literally choose to be without him forever. If we couldn't choose that, we really couldn't be free. I find it very difficult to imagine anyone actually choosing that consciously, knowing what they're choosing, but it's possible. When we think about life after death, if we think about it as something very, very vague, something that doesn't make any sense, isn't attractive other than we're told there will be no pain and no suffering (*that's* certainly attractive), but I challenge you to imagine what this thing is like, what *life* is like after we die.

My sense is that there's so much more to it than we perhaps realize, and if you dig into Scripture, so often you'll see statements like, when you die, you become like angels. [chuckles] What are angels? Intercessory beings that work between God and man, and they help people on earth, and they are messengers to people on earth, and they can take human form on earth; they're engaged in the lives of those they're guarding and taking care of. It's just a very exciting thing to me to think about death as not something where I go into this vague euphoric fog and never have any more feelings that are discomforting. But I would rather be engaged in something that's exciting and challenging and life-giving to me and definitely life-giving to someone else. So try to imagine that this life that God has created for you is a continuation of *this* life's work; where the core of this life's work is to become whole as best we can—not perfect, just more whole than we were; to grow, to change, to become more conscious, and then to use whatever the wisdom, whatever gifts that brings to us, to be nurturing spirits to one another.

And I believe that's the thing that brings us the greatest joy, to love and to be loved that way. So why *wouldn't* it be that after we die that we would be engaged in this kind of work of loving—loving the God that's created us, loving the people we're with in heaven who've helped us to *be* there. And then being an agent where we are able to help those people who are not *yet* there, the people that we loved here on this earth, that we want to draw into a union with us, and to do that with great joy and great confidence. It would be just a wonderful way of imagining this force in you, which we're calling *life*, but I can call it also *love*. It never can be quenched; it never can be put out; it's always going to be there drawing, drawing people into its grace and into its power and into its potential to awaken us and change us. So we look then at this set of readings with an eye toward the *Promise*, the wonderful promise that there is this life that God has created for us, and nothing, nothing can take it from us.

Father, we ask you to awaken us to a greater awareness of all that you have planned for us, and most especially that we understand more fully the grace that you have placed within us that longs for fulfillment, longs to be connected to you, and we ask this in Jesus' name. Amen.

2 Maccabees 7: 1-2, 9-14

It happened that seven brothers with their mother were arrested
and tortured with whips and scourges by the king,
to force them to eat pork in violation of God's law.
One of the brothers, speaking for the others, said:
"What do you expect to achieve by questioning us?
We are ready to die rather than transgress the laws of our ancestors."

At the point of death he said:
"You accursed fiend, you are depriving us of this present life,
but the King of the world will raise us up to live again forever.
It is for his laws that we are dying."

After him the third suffered their cruel sport.
He put out his tongue at once when told to do so,
and bravely held out his hands, as he spoke these noble words:
"It was from Heaven that I received these;
for the sake of his laws I disdain them;
from him I hope to receive them again."

Even the king and his attendants marveled at the young man's courage,
because he regarded his sufferings as nothing.

After he had died,
they tortured and maltreated the fourth brother in the same way.
When he was near death, he said,
"It is my choice to die at the hands of men
with the hope God gives of being raised up by him;
but for you, there will be no resurrection to life."

2 Thessalonians 2:16 – 3:5
Brothers and sisters:
May our Lord Jesus Christ himself and God our Father,
who has loved us and given us everlasting encouragement
and good hope through his grace,
encourage your hearts and strengthen them in every good deed
and word.

Finally, brothers and sisters, pray for us,
so that the word of the Lord may speed forward and be glorified,
as it did among you,
and that we may be delivered from perverse and wicked people,
for not all have faith.
But the Lord is faithful;
he will strengthen you and guard you from the evil one.
We are confident of you in the Lord that what we instruct you,
you are doing and will continue to do.
May the Lord direct your hearts to the love of God
and to the endurance of Christ.

Luke 20: 27-38
Some Sadducees, those who deny that there is a resurrection,
came forward and put this question to Jesus, saying,
"Teacher, Moses wrote for us,
If someone's brother dies leaving a wife but no child,
his brother must take the wife
and raise up descendants for his brother.
Now there were seven brothers;

the first married a woman but died childless.
Then the second and the third married her,
and likewise all the seven died childless.
Finally the woman also died.
Now at the resurrection whose wife will that woman be?
For all seven had been married to her."
Jesus said to them,
"The children of this age marry and remarry;
but those who are deemed worthy to attain to the coming age
and to the resurrection of the dead
neither marry nor are given in marriage.
They can no longer die,
for they are like angels;
and they are the children of God
because they are the ones who will rise.
That the dead will rise
even Moses made known in the passage about the bush,
when he called out 'Lord, '
the God of Abraham, the God of Isaac, and the God of Jacob;
and he is not God of the dead, but of the living,
for to him all are alive."

THIRTY-THIRD SUNDAY IN ORDINARY TIME

Malachi 3:19-20; 2 Thessalonians 3:7-12; Luke 21:5-19

Father of all that is good, keep us faithful in serving you, for to serve you is our lasting joy. We ask this through our Lord, Jesus Christ, your Son, who lives and reigns with you in the holy Spirit, one God for ever and ever. Amen.

This thirty-third Sunday in ordinary time is the last of the ordinary Sundays of our liturgical year. And always it's a puzzle and a kind of strange thing that at the end of this period of time that we've reflected, particularly this year, on the words of St. Luke's gospel, that we would end it with such a seemingly negative feeling that horrible, terrible things are going to happen, that the end of the world is going to come—it's frightening, terrible stuff.

So how do we understand this teaching and how do we understand why it's placed where it is, at the very end? Think of it this way. This is the last part of the teaching of this liturgical year. What I think it's doing is reminding us of what we would call *the work.* In the second reading, Paul talks about how he's worked hard and done a good job. And that's one of the things that Paul talked about at the end of his life. I think it's something that I pray I'll be able to say, and I pray you, too, will be able to say at the end of your life, "I've done the work, I've done the work."

But it's so subtle in terms of understanding what the work *is* because we work out of our minds more than our hearts. And the mind is the place where we are in charge, where we determine pretty much what is. And we decide things and then we engage the will so that we get things done and make ourselves into who we are supposed to be for God. When the will works with the mind, it seems that it works out of a kind of *force.* I will *make* myself, *make* myself into something.

What are we supposed to be? We are supposed to be like God, like Christ. What keeps us from being like him? It's sin. What is sin? Sin is that decision that *we* are the ones who determine what is good and what is bad. We are independent beings making the world into what it's supposed to be, making ourselves into what we are supposed to be, and trying to make everybody around us into who *we* think they should be. That would be what I would call the core original weakness.

And we have usually some very interesting images of the way the world is supposed to be. And I would say that generally they are not quite the same as God's. So *pride* is another way to say that this original sin lurks in us, hangs around us, and continually strives to seduce us.

The first reading, from the book of Malachi, is saying, *The day is coming, blazing like an oven, when all the pride and all the evil is going to be burned and purified.* Now it sounds like he could be saying that all those proud people are going to be destroyed and all the evil people will be destroyed. But I think that's too simple. I think it's about you and me and what's *in* us.

What this prophet is saying is, *There is a time when we are called to go through a process,* and that's what this whole liturgical year has been preparing us for and helping us to do. We need to do the work of *allowing* this process of crucifixion of pride, crucifixion of our ego, whatever you want to call it. It's a death to what *we* think needs to be and a birth into what God *longs* for us to be and for the world in which we live to be. So let's take this first reading as an indication that we are on this planet, in this world, to do some work. And the work is to *allow* something.

Let's talk about the heart for a moment and not the mind. The heart is a very interesting organ. We think of it as a pump, but there have been some fascinating things discovered about the heart. And if you look at the ancient writings of the early Church Fathers, they spoke of the heart all the time. How do we live out of our hearts? God dwells in our hearts. Modern science has realized that over half of the cells in our hearts are actually brain cells; that the heart is connected to the endocrine system, which affects our hormones and the way we feel. So just imagine if you can, without making this too literal, that there could be two centers within us: the mind, which is more in our control and the heart, which is more reflective of who we really are. Real transformation takes place in the heart, and so we become more and more like Christ. But imagine that this heart is *already* like Christ, and what we are invited to do is to *awaken* the heart, *awaken* it.

When it's awakened, something has to be allowed, and what has to be allowed is the ego moving to second place. Pride has to take a second place. Eventually, the pride has to be burned out of us—root and branch, but that doesn't mean we don't need a healthy mind and a healthy ego. Yes, I'm talking about pride. I'm talking about independence. I'm talking about somebody who believes they are the source of everything, without saying it. (No one says that literally, but they *live* that way.) The belief that it's up to *me* to make my life the way it's supposed to be.

Then we look at this reading from Paul, and it's interesting. He's talking about eating and working. I'd like you to imagine this in a more metaphorical way, because listen to what he's really saying. He's saying that people who are engaged in this extraordinary experience of trying to embrace and live as fully as we can in this world, who want to be instruments of life and goodness to other people—if we really want that, we better do our homework. We better do our work. And when we do the work, we're fed. And nobody can quite feed us like the heart, like the *wisdom* that's in the heart, like the wisdom that's in us that's grace. That is what feeds us. The mind tends to put us in the wrong direction when it comes to the spiritual world. The mind is fabulous at getting things done in the world. We couldn't live without it. It gets tasks done. I *love* to finish a task. I love to have a project. I love enjoying figuring out *how* to do the project. And when it's over, I can look back and say, "I did that." But when it comes to me as a human being who longs to be who I really am, I need to be able to surrender to what that is because it's going to be given to me as *wisdom*. I need to surrender to it no matter what it is—no matter how different I am from what the culture expects me to be, how different I am from what my parents thought I should be, how different I am from what the world expects of me. It's real work to embrace yourself as you are, and it is so nourishing. You really are fed. You really do receive a lot: strength, peace, the capacity to love.

So look at the gospel. The gospel is again about the end times. And what they say about this gospel, and it seems so true, is that it's talking about two things at the same time. It's talking about what *we* go through in this process that I'm just describing: this process of transformation, dying to self, rising to Christ. The action of baptism sets that up at the very beginning of our life. Why do we have the experience of entering into this kingdom through baptism as an experience of dying and then rising? Something has to die and the thing that has to die is this overactive mind that wants to control everything.

So let's look at the gospel because it's interesting. The words of Jesus are triggered by looking at the temple. And the temple is a beautiful, beautiful expression of perfection. Here's the best that human beings can do to create this beautiful edifice. I can't imagine what it really looked like literally, but it must have been absolutely awe-inspiring and awesome. I'm sure they looked at it and said, "We did this. We built this. We created this." What an incredible, incredible accomplishment. We can say that about a lot of things in the world that have been built by human beings. My God, they're just incredible! We can put people on other planets. We can figure things out. We have learned so much about the body and how it needs to be healed, all this stuff. We can look at ourselves and say, "We really are amazing."

But Jesus is saying in this story—if you can imagine the image of the temple is perfection and what human beings have accomplished—and he's saying, "All this has to be torn down." Literally, that happened to the temple. But what had to be destroyed was this image I think he is addressing and saying, *What you need to understand is, you have got to surrender. You have got to allow those things that you hold so dear, that give you a sense of your self-worth and your value are not rooted in me but rooted in your performance; you've got to let all of that go. And it's going to feel terrible. It's going to be the end of your mind running your life.*

So he describes all these things that are going to happen. And he talks about the world, saying there's going to be earthquakes and famines. When people hear this, they ask, "How does this happen? When is this going to happen?" I've asked myself that question. How much longer do I have to deal with my egocentricity? How much longer do I have to deal with this fact I get so bummed out of shape when somebody criticizes me? How much longer do I have to deal with the fact that I'm always trying to make people do what I want them to do? When is that going to be over? Well, it's going to take a long time. It's going to take your whole life to work through this. It's what life is about.

So when there are these earthquakes and famines and wars and insurrections, think of those as the conflicts that are inside of us. All the tensions and conflicts, all those things are going to happen.

And then listen to this: When there are earthquakes and famines and plagues, think of that symbolically. Earthquakes. Have you ever had the feeling where everything in your world that you created feels unsteady? It's like the ground beneath you is falling. It's not there anymore. There is no support. Or that you're not being fed by anything? Everything you worked for, everything you thought was going to make you happy, doesn't produce that and you're starving. Or there's some kind of plague that seems to be infecting you over and over again and you can't be cured.

These are feelings we have in our journey of faith as we open ourselves to the transforming grace of God—which takes its own time. So what is the challenge in this set of readings? Perseverance. Trust. Waiting. It's not easy. Then he goes on to say, and listen to this, he says, *You are going to be basically on your own. You are going to have to finally stand there with no support whatsoever. And when you can do that, you have reached the point where I wanted you to be in this life. And then you can come and be with me.*

I'm seventy-three, and I'm feeling what it's like to be seventy-three! [chuckles] I love my life, don't get me wrong. I love my life. I still have health and I still have energy and I'm very, very happy to be alive. But I know that aging is a slow process of letting go of how you look and what you can do and the strength that you used to have. Even your mind begins to slip. Your sight becomes a little fuzzy. You can't quite hear as well. Why is aging that way? Why did God choose to put us through a process where we have to let go of everything that gives us a sense of being independent and strong in the world? For those of us who get the chance to live a long life (and not everybody does, because that's not what *they* need), but for those of us who need it, we have to look at it as a gift, as a kind of process that is so essential and important to us. In surrender and perseverance and trust, waiting—that's the key. That is the amazing key.

So as we end a long liturgical year, we are going to have one more Sunday and that's Christ the King. That's a kind of wonderful tradition of honoring the king who is ruling the world. The spiritual world is his world, and he wants us to flourish in it. I don't know if you remember that the first lines of Advent liturgy always are the same: *Wake up. Wake up. Pay attention. Look around you. See, see, and see what's going on. See this process that you have to get into.*

So it makes sense that we end the year on that same theme of needing to be aware of what it is that we are here to do. There's a time in life to make all things happen. There's a time to create new relationships. There's a time to create a family. There's a time to make your mark. There's a time to do all that and those are good things. There's nothing negative in achieving in this world and using your will and your ego and your strength to get it done. That's great. But if that's *all* that's happening, if we're not doing the *other* work, if we're not feeding the other parts of us—the soul, the heart—if we're not doing that, we are going to find ourselves in some very, very frightening places. I remember when my father died, I was in the room with him, not at the moment that he died, but I was watching him struggle. Whatever was going on in him at the time, I swear when we watched him it was like he was seeing things and shaking his head, not wanting whatever was going to happen. And I thought to myself, What is it like, the last few moments of consciousness on this earth? What would God want to show you? What would he want to say to you? I think he would want to show you so much. And maybe part of it would be, *You didn't need to do what you did like you did. I was always here. I was always showing you. I was always there to take care of you.* Sometimes I see people so at peace and their countenance becomes like light. And it seems like they see it all, you know? They see it all.

So let's pray that those opening words of Advent have taken root in us over this past year and that we *do* see, that we are willing and open to *allowing* this mystery of transformation, this death that has to happen to parts of us so that a new, wonderful being emerges—full of life, light, and eternity.

Father, your voice resonates with radiance and life that lift us up from the temptation of independence from you and to embrace you as our partner in this life. Let us trust in your way and your will, accept all that you send to us. And we ask this in Jesus' name. Amen.

Malachi 3:19-20 (4:1-2 in the NRSV Bible)
1See, the day is coming, burning like an oven, when all the arrogant and all evildoers
will be stubble; the day that comes shall burn them up, says the LORD of hosts, so that
it will leave them neither root nor branch.
2But for you who revere my name the sun of righteousness shall rise, with healing in its
wings.

2 Thessalonians 3: 7-12;
7For you yourselves know how you ought to imitate us; we were not idle when we were
with you,
8and we did not eat anyone's bread without paying for it; but with toil and labor we
worked night and day, so that we might not burden any of you.
9This was not because we do not have that right, but in order to give you an example to
imitate.
10For even when we were with you, we gave you this command: Anyone unwilling to
work should not eat.
11For we hear that some of you are living in idleness, mere busybodies, not doing any
work.
12Now such persons we command and exhort in the Lord Jesus Christ to do their work
quietly and to earn their own living.

Luke 21: 5-19
5When some were speaking about the temple, how it was adorned with beautiful stones
and gifts dedicated to God, he said,
6"As for these things that you see, the days will come when not one stone will be left
upon another; all will be thrown down."
7They asked him, "Teacher, when will this be, and what will be the sign that this is
about to take place?"
8And he said, "Beware that you are not led astray; for many will come in my name and
say, 'I am he!' and, 'The time is near!' Do not go after them.
9"When you hear of wars and insurrections, do not be terrified; for these things must
take place first, but the end will not follow immediately."
10Then he said to them, "Nation will rise against nation, and kingdom against kingdom;
11there will be great earthquakes, and in various places famines and plagues; and there
will be dreadful portents and great signs from heaven.
12"But before all this occurs, they will arrest you and persecute you; they will hand you
over to synagogues and prisons, and you will be brought before kings and governors

because of my name.
13This will give you an opportunity to testify.
14So make up your minds not to prepare your defense in advance;
15for I will give you words and a wisdom that none of your opponents will be able to
withstand or contradict.
16You will be betrayed even by parents and brothers, by relatives and friends; and they
will put some of you to death.
17You will be hated by all because of my name.
18But not a hair of your head will perish.
19By your endurance you will gain your souls.

FEAST OF CHRIST THE KING

2Samuel 5:1-3; Colossians 1:12-20; Luke 23:35-43

Almighty, ever-living God, whose will is to restore all things in your beloved Son, the king of the universe, grant, we pray, that the whole creation, set free from slavery, may render you majestic service and ceaselessly proclaim your praise, through our Lord Jesus Christ, your Son, who lives and reigns with you in the unity of the holy Spirit, one God for ever and ever. Amen.

For 52 weeks, I have been speaking to you about the mysteries of God, revealed for us in the person named Jesus, who became the perfect model of who we are to be—a human being filled with divinity. We remembered his birth, we remembered his public life, his sufferings, his passion, his resurrection, and the effect of that resurrection on a community, called the early Christian community. And now we come to the end of a church year, and our focus is on what I would like to have you imagine—it's "What did Christ do? What is so great about what he did for us?" Let us focus for a moment on his *kingship*.

Now Jesus, when he lived on this earth, didn't take on anything that made him look like a literal king. But if you look at the first reading and you listen to David accepting the role of being the king, and if you look at what he was honored for, and why they thought he'd be a good king, it's he was such a successful warrior. He would always fight against the enemies of the Israelite people, and he would win. So it's interesting that people choose a king who they believe will take care of their enemies, protect them from their enemies.

It strikes me that what Jesus did, the genius of his ministry, is he taught us a way that we had never suspected to *be* the way—he taught us the way to overcome our enemies. And it's not by going to war with them, conquering them in the sense of destroying them. But the greatest mystery is that Jesus comes into the world to teach us how to surrender and submit to our enemy. And in doing so, to somehow completely confound them and to somehow overcome every negative thing that the enemy longs to do to us.

In the second reading, from Paul to the Colossians, we have the same image of being saved from that which is an enemy, and we call the enemy in this reading *darkness*. The Christ who is, for you and for me, the model of who we are to become, when Paul goes into this beautiful exhortation saying that everything is created in him, for him, with him, it's like saying that everything that God has been doing since the beginning has been directed toward revealing to us his enormous passion, his longing to be inside of us, to be *with* us. That's what he longs for most. And the *benefit* of that, if we understand what his indwelling presence is about, what it enables us to do, will save us from all darkness, all things that could destroy us, and bring us into this mysterious kingdom, the kingdom of light, the kingdom of peace, which is within us. Interesting image—it's within us. *What* is within us? *Divinity* is within us. Where does it dwell? In our hearts. Is it real? Yes. Does it change everything? Yes. If it is believed, and then if we allow it to enter into us, allow it to enter in.

So we look at the image that the church feels is the crowning moment of our king, the moment that he conquers death, conquers destruction, conquers darkness. And it's in this great mystery of a man, naked, stripped, humiliated, spit upon, laughed at, surrendering to a will that is not his own, that in a sense flies in the face of every lie that the world has ever come up with to seduce us into being great, into being successful, into being powerful—particularly, the world loves autonomously powerful people, it rewards them over and over and over again. There's something the world loves about a person being independently powerful. And when we don't understand that, when we seek to be powerful, and I think it's true that all of us on some level do that because in a sense, when we are under stress, when we're under a lot of pressure, when there's a lot of *fear* that we're not going to make it, *shame* that we're not enough, just all those things, *anger* that things aren't going the way they're supposed to go, we tend to revert to a more basic element in our human nature, and that's our oldest brain, the reptilian brain. We get into that place and we know that when that brain is operating, it's so instinctual, it's so immediate—it never has to process or think. It just knows that what I have to do is either fight or I need to flee. I need to fight this enemy or I need to hide.

When I see people taking on the Christian message, and realizing their weaknesses and the struggles that they have, to live the life that God is calling us to, and they see it as a battle, and they seek to overcome this enemy that seems to rob them of their freedom to choose the things that they somehow deeply know are right, and they go into a battle, they're in a disposition that is radically different from Jesus on the cross, and they're in this *dangerous* place of fighting. And they do it with one fundamental, basic instinct: *I've got to survive.* And the only way you can do that is to be completely disconnected from everything else around you other than *you.* "I must survive." And then the battle begins. For those who flee, for those who can't deal with the enemy, who don't feel that they're strong enough, they will go into a place of hiding, which I would simply call becoming *unconscious*. And they busy themselves in the world with all the normal, ordinary duties of life, and they try to be good. And there's really nothing wrong with that. They do the best they can, but when they go to this basic part of their life and they see the battle is before them and they're overwhelmed and fearful, perhaps angry, and they go into a place of not participating in this amazing adventure of allowing a God to enter into you in order for you and for me to be able to achieve the goal of surrendering to our enemy. Surrendering.

When we're in this selfish place, when we're in this place of taking, taking, taking so that we can have what we feel we need in order to survive, we are like thieves in the world, and remember Jesus said at the Temple: "You know, you all here, you are creating not a house for God or a house of openness to the mystery of God's power in the world, but you are basically somehow creating a den of thieves, a den of thieves."

So isn't it interesting, that here is Jesus hanging on the cross, and on either side are two thieves, two thieves. And that makes sense to me, that these represent human nature. And the most interesting thing is that one gets it and the other doesn't. I think it's easy to see that in this world are people who see the heart of Christianity and they understand it and they live it, and there are many who are religious—some not religious—and they simply don't grasp at all what this whole thing is basically about—about entering into a relationship with God that is so intimate, so profound, so much a part of his longing, so it's only up to us not to earn it, not to merit it, but to somehow *allow* it.

And when that happens, everything changes; *everything* changes. So a typical thing that an aggressive person might do, who is working on survival and he looks at the power of God and says, "OK, God, I can't deal with this problem in my life. I can't deal with my marriage, with my teenage son. I can't deal with my teenage daughter. Whatever is in me right now, this disease, the sickness of someone I love, I can't deal with this. I don't know how. I don't have anything in me to deal with it. It terrifies me, it frightens me, it makes me angry. I'm filled with fear." And all I know is that what God is trying to say at that moment is, "No, I'm not here to take away the difficulties that are in your life. I'm here to enter into you, to empower you to go through them in a way that is beyond anything you could imagine."

So we have a selfish thief on one side saying, "Look, if you're God, if you're so great, what are you doing hanging on a cross, because isn't God the one who's here to save us?" And so we should be saved by getting out of or conquering or getting rid of all of our problems. Then we'll be saved and we'll have this euphoric life with no tension, no pressure, no problems. And the other thief, that beautiful man on the other side, looks at this whole situation and sees something that he doesn't fully comprehend. And I don't know that it's necessary that we fully comprehend the plan of God, but we need to know what it is. He's looking at a man who's doing something *so different,* that he somehow knows, "that man has something that none of us have, and I want it." It's the ability to let things happen as they are, to be working as hard as we can with divinity inside of us to change us. Not that we're passive and don't *care* what's happening. We care *deeply.* But there's never that gnawing, anxious, angry, bitter side of us saying, "None of this is fair, and where the heck are you, God? Why aren't you taking care of these situations for me?" No, he sees someone surrendering with an amazing amount of peace, and somehow knowing in surrendering to this humiliating, almost impossible to imagine, end of the life of one of the greatest ministers that ever, ever walked the earth. So he had more power to save and transform, but here he is not accepted in this world, rejected in this world, which is so clearly the way human nature is when it comes to understanding the value of this figure, this incarnated God, what he's really trying to say just somehow goes against one very basic part of our nature, the most primitive side, the primitive side that says, "I am going to conquer or I am going to hide."

And so he sees this, and he says the most beautiful thing. He says, "All I want, all I want is what you have. I see this man next to you angry and bitter. I see you calm and relaxed. *He* deserves it; *you* don't even deserve it. You're still in the most amazing disposition of not being angry, bitter, so somehow you must know something that *we* don't know, that somehow all of this is the way it's written, all of this is the way it has to happen." What a gift, to be able to sit in any moment in your life—I don't care how beautiful or how painful or dark—and say, "This is the way it has to be." And from there, to then feel this indwelling strength, this indwelling power from God entering into you, enabling you then to be an instrument, not just surviving, but here's the mystery, transforming, transforming. We're transforming the world when we live in that disposition, that incredible disposition that Christ has taught us, that we are able to deal with all things because we have within us a capacity and a power to love.

Now love might seem like, well, you're supposed to like everybody, to always be approving of everybody. No, it's much more complicated. I want you to think about love that is the result of the indwelling presence of divinity in us, that then enables us to be lovers. Think about this love not so much as telling the other person that they're so good, wonderful, beautiful, and valuable because many times they're just the opposite. But it's offering something that you believe in your heart, you *know* in your heart, that this love that you have for this person is wanting so much for them to be able to become what they are *called* to be but they can't do it on their own, so *you're* going to be the ingredient, you're going to be the catalyst, you're going to be the bridge to bringing them the divinity they're *not* in touch with, that keeps them from fully developing and fully becoming who they are. So your love is more like offering them this gift, believing that when a person offers it to another, it works. It transforms, it changes.

People are transformed more by love, the spirit of divinity, flowing from your heart to the person who is in need much more than criticism, much more than sarcasm, much more than anything that smacks of being judged. How often does Jesus say it? "Don't judge, don't condemn." But at the same time, he condemns behavior. He told us the biggest problem with human nature is both its desire to fight or to flee instead of connecting with me who will help them, hold them, care for them. And also at the same time, he's saying, "I want you to understand the main thing: that you are invited to be with me as a vehicle of grace to your brothers and sisters," and the world can be changed in no way that I know of other than this one-on-one work. One person to another. One person believing in this incredible gift that is inside of them and generously offering to everyone, *everyone* they come in contact with. It's a *decision* that you make. "I can *do* this. I have this *in* me." And you'll begin to feel and know the peace that this gift gives and brings. And when people see it in you, it is *so attractive*! It reminds me that mostly Christianity, any good, solid religion that draws a person into this divinity inside of them, I guarantee you, the evangelization of it, the teaching of it, is mostly by example, not by words. And certainly not by rules and laws.

And I pray, I pray so much for *all* religions, that they somehow see the mistake that so often seems to be made. I know the mistake is there, because when I listen to people talk about religion, over and over again they feel it is something that is not able to reach their need, and they don't *need* to be criticized, they don't need to be told what to do and then be told if they don't do it, they're not going to make it. They need to be *loved.* They need to be *inspired.* They need to be transformed. And to know that you have that power, to know that you can do this in the world? What an amazing gift to bring to the world. How can you feel that you are not very valuable when you have this incredible gift to carry around? It's not *me* that is able to do this, but I have this power, this gift inside of me I can give, and I feel like the richest man in the room. That's the kingdom. That's the peace of the kingdom. That's the *light* of the kingdom. And it's ours, if we believe.

Father, your gift of opening us to the awareness that we need to have of the gift of God dwelling in us, enabling us to be an instrument of such peace, such grace, such transformation for others. We give you praise for this gift on this feast of Christ the King. You truly are the one who has come to conquer the darkness, and we delight, we delight in your love and the light that that love creates in us. And we ask this in Jesus' name. Amen.

2 Samuel 5:1-3
In those days, all the tribes of Israel came to David in Hebron and said:
"Here we are, your bone and your flesh.
In days past, when Saul was our king,
it was you who led the Israelites out and brought them back.
And the LORD said to you,
'You shall shepherd my people Israel
and shall be commander of Israel.'"
When all the elders of Israel came to David in Hebron,
King David made an agreement with them there before the LORD,
and they anointed him king of Israel.

Colossians 1: 12-20
Brothers and sisters:
Let us give thanks to the Father,
who has made you fit to share
in the inheritance of the holy ones in light.
He delivered us from the power of darkness
and transferred us to the kingdom of his beloved Son,
in whom we have redemption, the forgiveness of sins.

He is the image of the invisible God,
the firstborn of all creation.
For in him were created all things in heaven and on earth,
the visible and the invisible,
whether thrones or dominions or principalities or powers;
all things were created through him and for him.
He is before all things,
and in him all things hold together.
He is the head of the body, the church.
He is the beginning, the firstborn from the dead,
that in all things he himself might be preeminent.
For in him all the fullness was pleased to dwell,
and through him to reconcile all things for him,
making peace by the blood of his cross
through him, whether those on earth or those in heaven.

Luke 23: 35-43
The rulers sneered at Jesus and said,
"He saved others, let him save himself
if he is the chosen one, the Christ of God."
Even the soldiers jeered at him.
As they approached to offer him wine they called out,
"If you are King of the Jews, save yourself."
Above him there was an inscription that read,
"This is the King of the Jews."
Now one of the criminals hanging there reviled Jesus, saying,
"Are you not the Christ?
Save yourself and us."
The other, however, rebuking him, said in reply,
"Have you no fear of God,
for you are subject to the same condemnation?
And indeed, we have been condemned justly,
for the sentence we received corresponds to our crimes,
but this man has done nothing criminal."
Then he said,
"Jesus, remember me when you come into your kingdom."
He replied to him,
"Amen, I say to you,
today you will be with me in Paradise."

About the Author

Don L. Fischer, a Catholic priest in the Diocese of Dallas, is the host of Pastoral Reflections, a weekly radio program broadcast Sunday mornings on WRR-FM (101.1). Focusing on the Sunday liturgy of the word, his listening audience spans the Dallas-Fort Worth area. The homilies in this book are based on the church year, 2012 – 2013. With his unique ability to break open the Word, he touches the hearts of his many listeners' deepest concerns as they relate to a life of faith.

A common theme resonates throughout the book—growth in our awareness of who we are called to be and who God is, and of what God is really doing in the world. The tone is never judgmental or critical, but always uplifting and deeply appreciative of the work of Christ in our world.

Don attended the University of Dallas, St. Bernard College in Cullman, Alabama, and St. John's Seminary in Little Rock, Arkansas. In the Dallas area, he has served as associate pastor of St. Thomas Aquinas and St. Monica Catholic churches, as chaplain at the University of Dallas, as pastor of St. Bernard of Clairvaux and then as pastor of St. Joseph Catholic church in Richardson, Texas.